# PHP Web Development with MySQL

## A Hands On Approach to Application Programming

by Kenneth E. Marks

a php[architect] guide

# PHP Web Development with MySQL
# A Hands On Approach to Application Programming

php[architect] edition published: July 2021

| | |
|---|---|
| Print ISBN: | 978-1-940111-95-7 |
| PDF ISBN: | 978-1-940111-96-4 |
| ePub ISBN: | 978-1-940111-97-1 |
| Mobi ISBN | 978-1-940111-98-8 |

Produced & Printed in the United States

---

**Written by**
Kenneth E. Marks

**Managing Editor**
Oscar Merida

**Editor**
Kara Ferguson

**Layout**
Oscar Merida

**Published by**
musketeers.me, LLC.
4627 University Dr
Fairfax, VA 22030 USA

240-348-5PHP (240-348-5747)
info@phparch.com
www.phparch.com

# Table of Contents

# Dedications

**To my wife, Debbie,** *who always encourages me to strive for what's good and to "do the next right thing." I never would have finished this project without your love, support, and gentle prodding.*

**To my students,** *who made me realize I am not here to teach you, but rather to enable your learning.*

# Acknowledgements

I never set out to write a book. In fact, when a couple of my colleagues shared their experience of writing a book, I thought I was sufficiently scared off from the process. So when I first met my editor (before he even told me he was an editor), he suggested I consider writing a book after I said I was a PHP web development instructor at our local community college. I immediately informed him that it would be a bad idea because I would have to write something that some editor would want just to sell books. Then I asked him what his vocation was 😄.

**To my editor, Oscar,** who not only encouraged me to write a book on PHP web development but also to make it my own. Thank you for making this such a collaborative and enjoyable process!

**To my friend Beth Tucker Long,** who not only encouraged me to engage the local and broader community of PHP web developers but has been a mentor to me in modeling how to better engage this wonderful community of people. Thank you for your passionate devotion to equity in the development community, challenging me, and showing me what it looks like to be others-centered.

# Foreword

Almost a decade ago, I was running our local PHP user group, and Ken heard about and attended one of our events. He instantly became an ever-enthusiastic member of our community. Ken is always ready to say hi to everyone and make sure they feel welcome. On top of that, he is also always happy to give a talk, which is a surefire way to endear yourself to a user group leader. When we needed a new space to hold our meetings, Ken once again stepped up and volunteered his classroom space at the local tech college where he was teaching. It was a perfect fit with plenty of space, easy transportation access, a projector, and great Wi-Fi—a user group's dream come true! Eventually, Ken made the mistake of mentioning that he wouldn't mind helping more if we needed anything. He had barely finished saying that before I made him a co-organizer of the group.

Throughout the years, Ken has been invaluable in building our amazing local PHP community. He has an infectious enthusiasm that draws people in, and his love of teaching is second to none. He doesn't just teach the material, but he truly cares about helping his students succeed. Not only that, but you can always rely on him. When he started toying with the idea of writing a book, Ken wasn't sure he would be able to finish the book, but I never doubted he would. I knew that once he agreed to do it, he would persevere and get it done. That's just the kind of person Ken is.

Ken's teaching style focuses on real-world skills and hands-on practice. This book is no exception. When you are done with this book, you will have working examples of code talking with databases and interacting with users. You will have a good understanding of what happens during these interactions, which will help you immensely during your future debugging sessions and give you a solid foundation to stand on as you learn about more advanced programming techniques, frameworks, and libraries.

So even though Ken and I agree to disagree on specifically which framework you should learn next, I am so grateful for his love of PHP and his love of sharing knowledge with others. Our community is far better for having Ken around, and I'm so excited for you to get to know him a bit through this book.

Welcome to the PHP community. We are glad you are here!

– Beth Tucker Long, July 2021

# About the Author

Ken Marks has been working in his dream job as a Programming Instructor at Madison College in Madison, Wisconsin, teaching PHP web development using MySQL since 2012. Prior to teaching, Ken worked as a software engineer for more than 20 years, mainly developing medical device software.

Ken earned his Bachelors of Science in Computer Science from California State University at Fullerton and earned his Masters of Science in Adult Education from the University of Wisconsin at Platteville.

Ken is actively involved in the PHP community, speaking and teaching at conferences.

In his spare time, he's a man of many hobbies such as 3D printing, board game development, Ham radio, Fly fishing, and of course, Coffee Roasting :-)

Ken has two grown daughters and lives in the Madison area with his wife and their cat Ophelia who thinks she's a dog.

# Introduction

*The best way to predict the future is to invent it.*

*–Alan Kay*

## Who Should Use This Book?

Do you want to learn how to create dynamic database-driven web applications? This book guides you through building a typical CRUD (Create-Read-Update-Delete) application with PHP and MySQL.

### Introductory Programming Knowledge

If you have an introductory understanding of programming concepts, this book is for you. You should be familiar with the following concepts:

- How to create variables
- The following kinds of logic:
  - sequential
  - conditional
  - looping
- Modularization using functions and object methods
- Arrays

You should be familiar with all of the above concepts using any modern programming language you are familiar with.

### Basic HTML/CSS Knowledge

You should have a basic understanding of how to create simple static web pages using HTML and CSS. A good place to brush up on these skills is https://www.w3schools.com.

### Introductory Knowledge of Databases and SQL

Although not required, it is helpful to understand how relational databases work and have some introductory knowledge of the Standard Query Language (SQL).

## Why PHP and MySQL?

Both PHP and MySQL are open source which means you can freely download them and modify the source code if you so desire. Moreover, PHP and MySQL are commonly used together.

Both PHP and MySQL have a low barrier to entry. All you need to develop dynamic web applications with databases is access to a computer. All the applications necessary to develop using PHP and MySQL are freely available at no cost.

## Who This Book is NOT For?

If you are unfamiliar with any of these concepts, you would be best served by first getting a hold of an introductory programming book. While we introduce how PHP implements common programming concepts like loops and arrays, we expect you to know how and when to use them. Likewise, if you are not comfortable with basic HTML/CSS, you should spend some time brushing up on these skills as well.

## PHP Versions, MySQL, and This Book

PHP version 7.0 provides a significant upgrade over version 5.6 in both performance and security. Therefore, all PHP code and concepts presented in this book will be based on version 7.0.

There are many database management systems (DBMS). However, this book uses a DBMS based on the Standard Query Language (SQL). We use the MySQL DBMS because it is frequently used with PHP, free to download and use, and it is the most popular DBMS in the world.

## How Code Samples are Presented

Code samples are used throughout the book to illustrate each topic. Longer code listings are numbered and include line numbers for ease of reference. Syntax highlight similar to what you find in a modern text editor or integrated development environment (IDE) is used to make the code more readable by making variables, strings, and keywords stand out. Finally, you can also download the code samples from the phparch.com website.

Bear in mind that the code samples in the book have been formatted to fit in the narrower widths afforded by the screens for PDF and electronic readers as well as the printed page. None of the changes made to accommodate this limitation affect the functionality of the code. As such, the code archive for this book also includes the unaltered versions of the application code found here.

## How to Use This Book

This book is split into two major parts. Part one is a basic reference to the PHP language. While not an exhaustive reference, it explains all the features needed for the web applications presented in this book. As more web applications are presented, you will be applying more of the PHP language concepts. Part two shows how to apply the PHP language through the presentation of various web applications. It is intended to give the web developer a complete understanding of how to apply PHP and MySQL for many of the most common web development challenges. To illustrate the process, it works through the development of a full-featured application implementing the typical CRUD (Create-Read-Update-Delete) operations found in one.

## A Brief History of PHP

PHP was created in 1994[1] by Rasmus Lerdorf and was originally designed to be a simple set of Common Gateway Interface (CGI) binaries written using the C-programming language for interacting with HTML forms. Rasmus called this suite of scripts "Personal Home Page Tools." Rasmus continued to add more functionality to his toolset, including database interaction and a framework for developing dynamic web applications. In early June of 1995, Rasmus released PHP Tools to the public through the comp.infosystems.www.authoring. CGI newsgroup. In October of that year, Rasmus released a new version that consisted of an advanced scripting interface that resembled C and Perl. In April of the next year, Rasmus added database support for several DBMSs, and in June of 1996, version 2 of PHP was released. In May of 1998, 1% (approximately 60000) web servers had PHP/FI installed.

In 1997, Andi Gutmans and Zeev Suraski collaborated with Rasmus to rewrite the PHP Parser. When they released version 3 (in June of 1998), the programming language was renamed "PHP," which is a recursive acronym meaning "PHP: Hypertext Preprocessor." PHP 3 allowed for easy extensibility, with many developers contributing useful modules. PHP 3 also included Object-Oriented Programming (OOP) extensions to the language. PHP 3, at one point, was installed on 10% of the web servers on the internet.

During the winter of 1998, Andi Gutmans and Zeev Suraski started working on performance and modularity improvements to the PHP interpreter. This rewrite of the core of PHP came to be known as the 'Zend Engine' (named for Zeev and Andi's first names) and

---

[1] *PHP was created in 1994: http://php.net/en/history.php*

was released in the middle of 1999. The official release of PHP 4 occurred in May of 2000 and added support for more web servers and session management.

In July of 2004, PHP 5 was released was powered by the "Zend Engine 2.0." This release included improvements for OOP, PHP Data Objects (PDO - which defines connections and interactions with databases), and other features.

In December of 2015, the PHP development team released version 7.0 of PHP[2]. This release improved the performance of PHP applications up to twice as fast as version 5.6. It also included a number of security enhancements and improved Exception handling.

PHP 8.0[3] was released in November of 2020. It further enhances the language's type hinting system and adds named arguments while making the language more consistent and performant. Like previous releases, the core contributors have worked to minimize the impact of backward-incompatible changes such that upgrading from PHP 7 is not a monumental undertaking for most code bases.

## An Even Briefer History of PHP

- June 8, 1995 PHP 1.0 is posted to the usenet group comp.infosystems.www.authoring.cgi
- It was created by Rasmus Lerdorf[4] as PHP Tools
- Then Rasmus set to work integrating his tools with the Apache web server, and less than a year later, PHP 2.0 was posted to the same Usenet group
- PHP originally stood for "Personal Home Pages."
- PHP now stands for "PHP Hypertext Preprocessor" (a recursive acronym)
- It is most likely the fastest and simplest tool available for creating database-enabled websites
- It will work with any UNIX-based web server on every UNIX flavor out there. The package is completely free of charge for all uses, including commercial

Here is how Rasmus described PHP at the time:

> *PHP/FI is a server-side HTML embedded scripting language. It has built-in access logging and access restriction features and also support for embedded SQL queries to mSQL and/or Postgres95 backend databases.*

---

[2]  *7.0 of PHP: http://php.net/releases/7_0_0.php*
[3]  *PHP 8.0: https://www.php.net/releases/8.0/en.php*
[4]  *Rasmus Lerdorf: https://en.wikipedia.org/wiki/Rasmus_Lerdorf*

# Chapter

# 1

# The Life and Times of a PHP Script

*Most good programmers do programming not because they expect to get paid or get adulation by the public, but because it is fun to program.*

*– Linus Torvalds*

## Static Vs. Dynamic Websites

HTML alone only allows you to create static web pages. This approach is fine if you just want to display images of your cat. However, if you want a web application with the ability to interact with a database and for your web pages to update based on content that can change, you need a dynamic website. This is where PHP comes in. The PHP interpreter runs in the webserver. PHP will deliver HTML to the webserver, and since PHP is also a programming language, it allows you to build the HTML dynamically.

## The Browser and the Server

HyperText Transfer Protocol (**HTTP**) is the protocol used to communicate between a web server (which I will call the server) and the web browser (which I will call the client).

### HTTP Requests and Responses

When you open up a web browser on your computer and type in a Uniform Resource Locator (URL) in the address bar (let's say flibbertigiblets.com)…

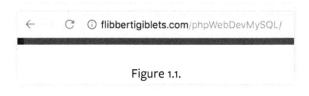

Figure 1.1.

As soon as you press the Return key on your computer, your browser sends an *HTTP Request* to the web server at flibbertigiblets.com. That request might look something like Listing 1.1.

### Listing 1.1.

```
 1. GET /phpWebDevMySQL/ HTTP/1.1
 2. Host: flibbertigiblets.com
 3. Connection: keep-alive
 4. Cache-Control: max-age=0
 5. Authorization: Basic ZmFsbDIwMTd0waHA6dXNlIHRoZSBmb3JjZQ==
 6. Upgrade-Insecure-Requests: 1
 7. User-Agent: Mozilla/5.0 (Macintosh; Intel Mac OS X 10_12_6)
 8.  AppleWebKit/537.36 (KHTML, like Gecko) Chrome/62.0.3202.94 Safari/537.36
 9. Accept: text/html,application/xhtml+xml,application/xml;q=0.9,image/webp,
10.  image/apng,*/*;q=0.8
11. Accept-Encoding: gzip, deflate
12. Accept-Language: en-US,en;q=0.9
13. If-Modified-Since: Mon, 13 Nov 2017 21:51:51 GMT
```

The server can send various responses back to your browser (the client). However, the most common is a 200 OK response that looks like:

```
HTTP/1.1 200 OK
Server: nginx/1.12.2
Date: Fri, 17 Nov 2017 00:31:35 GMT
Content-Type: text/html
Transfer-Encoding: chunked
Connection: keep-alive
Last-Modified: Mon, 13 Nov 2017 21:51:51 GMT
Content-Encoding: gzip
```

Assuming everything is OK with the header, the server sends HTML to the browser, so you should see the web page shown in Figure 1.2.

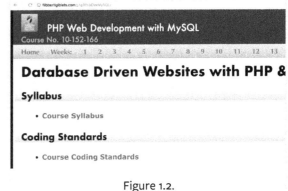

Figure 1.2.

## The Server and PHP

As previously mentioned, PHP runs with the web server and is responsible for interpreting PHP code.

### What the PHP Interpreter Does

When the web server encounters PHP code, it hands the code to the PHP interpreter. The interpreter executes the code according to the rules of the PHP language. Within the code, text will frequently need to be echoed or printed out to the web page. This text will be sent from the PHP interpreter back to the web server to be rendered as HTML back to the browser.

Let's take a look at a simple web page with HTML and PHP integrated together that outputs today's date:

```
<html>
  <head>
    <title>My Awesome Page</title>
  </head>
  <body>
    <h1>Today is <?php echo date("m-d-Y"); ?></h1>
  </body>
</html>
```

When the web browser encounters the `<?php` tag, everything from the opening `<?php` to the closing `?>` tag is handed off to the PHP interpreter for processing. When the PHP script is done processing, any resulting HTML is sent back to the web server for output to the client.

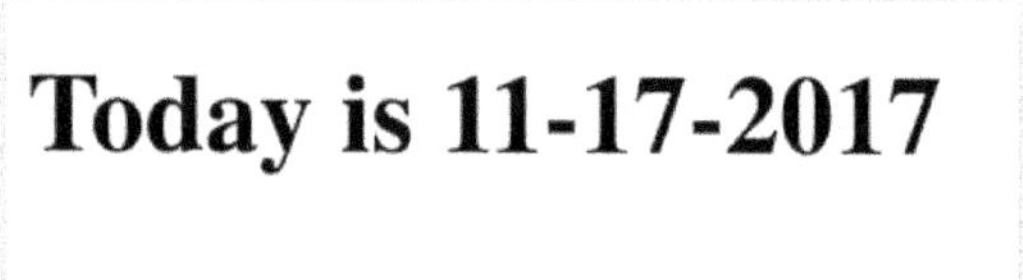

## Today is 11-17-2017

Figure 1.3.

The output of the above script is shown in Figure 1.3.

### The php.ini File and Important Settings

The `php.ini` file is where we set and change directives to configure PHP. This file is read every time the web server is started or restarted, and it is how PHP is initialized. This file is well documented with comments regarding the various directives. Visit the PHP manual[1] for a detailed explanation of the `php.ini` directives. Many directives can affect the security and behavior of your application, so change them with care.

To find the `php.ini` file used by the PHP interpreter, you can inspect the output of `phpinfo()` in a browser or look at the output of `php -i` at the command line.

### Error Reporting Settings

When working through this book, you should tell PHP to show any errors it encounters in your browser. You'll get feedback about parse errors, uninitialized variables, and more. Otherwise, when you run your code, you may get the dreaded White Screen of Death (WSOD) when PHP encounters a syntax error like a missing semi-colon. In your `php.ini` file, check to verify that `display_errors` is enabled:

```
display_errors = On;
```

In a production environment, this setting should be `off` to prevent disclosing sensitive information.

[1] PHP manual: http://php.net/ini

# Chapter

# 2

# Writing Your First PHP Script

*I have always wished for my computer to be as easy to use as my telephone; my wish has come true because I can no longer figure out how to use my telephone.*

– Bjarne Stroustrup

## Setting Up a Development Environment

To write PHP, all you need is a text editor. However, since PHP runs with a web server, you need access to a PHP development environment. I will show you how to install and configure a Unix-based development environment for writing and debugging your PHP web applications.

### Downloading a Unix Operating System (OS)

Since most PHP web applications run on a Linux distribution of the Unix OS, it makes sense to develop on one. I find Ubuntu Desktop one of the easiest operating systems to develop in. As of this writing, the current version is Ubuntu 20.04.1 LTS.

> *LTS stands for long-term support. Canonical, the organization that maintains Ubuntu, guarantees free security and maintenance updates for five years on LTS releases.*

The first thing we need to do is head over to https://www.ubuntu.com/download/desktop and download the latest 64-bit version of Ubuntu Desktop and press the **Download** button as in Figure 2.1.

Figure 2.1.

It takes you to the page shown in Figure 2.2, and the `.iso` image should begin down-loading.

## Installing the Unix OS

Once your download is complete, you will need to locate the `.iso` image file. It should be named `ubuntu-20.04.1-desktop-amd64.iso`. You will need to mount it to be installed on the computer you want to use. You can either install it as a standalone OS, on a partition if your computer is configured for multi-boot partitioning or in a Virtual Machine (VM) environment. If you install it in a VM, I recommend you set the memory utilization to 4 GB.

Start the installation (Figure 2.3).

When the installation completes, enter your password and press **Enter** to log in (Figure 2.4).

Next, select *Activities*, type in `terminal` in the search box, and run the `terminal` program. You'll see output like Figure 2.5 (following page).

In the `terminal` window, update the `apt` installation package manager by running the following command as super-user. When apt runs, you'll see something similar to Figure 2.6.

```
sudo apt update
```

Figure 2.2.

Figure 2.3.

Figure 2.4.

## 2. WRITING YOUR FIRST PHP SCRIPT

Next, in the terminal window, upgrade all the applications with the apt installation package manager by running the following command as superuser:

```
sudo apt upgrade
```

You will need to type Y or press Enter to accept the changes. This update can take several minutes since the package manager will be upgrading all of the program packages that have been updated since the release of Ubuntu 20.04.31 LTS (Figures 2.7, 2.8, and 2.9).

Figure 2.5.

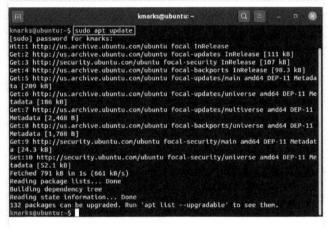

Figure 2.6

```
kmarks@ubuntu:~$
kmarks@ubuntu:~$ sudo apt upgrade
Reading package lists... Done
Building dependency tree
Reading state information... Done
Calculating upgrade... Done
The following package was automatically installed and is no longer required:
  libfprint-2-tod1
Use 'sudo apt autoremove' to remove it.
The following packages will be upgraded:
  alsa-ucm-conf apport apport-gtk base-files bind9-dnsutils bind9-host
  bind9-libs command-not-found evolution-data-server
  evolution-data-server-common firefox fonts-noto-mono fonts-opensymbol
  ghostscript ghostscript-x gir1.2-javascriptcoregtk-4.0 gir1.2-mutter-6
  gir1.2-webkit2-4.0 gnome-shell gnome-shell-common
  gnome-shell-extension-desktop-icons im-config language-selector-common
  language-selector-gnome libasound2 libasound2-data libatopology2
```

Figure 2.7.

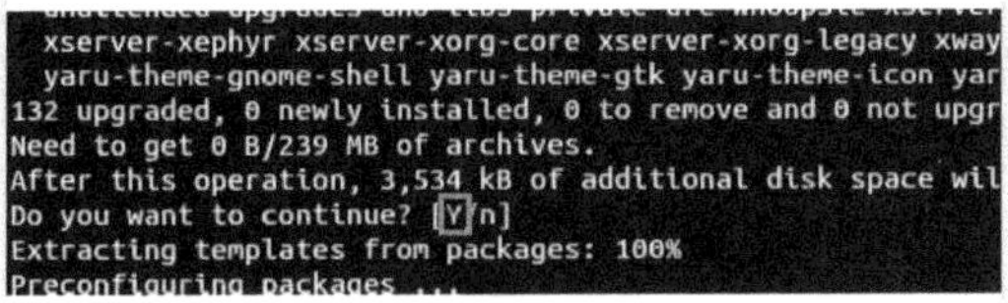

Figure 2.8.

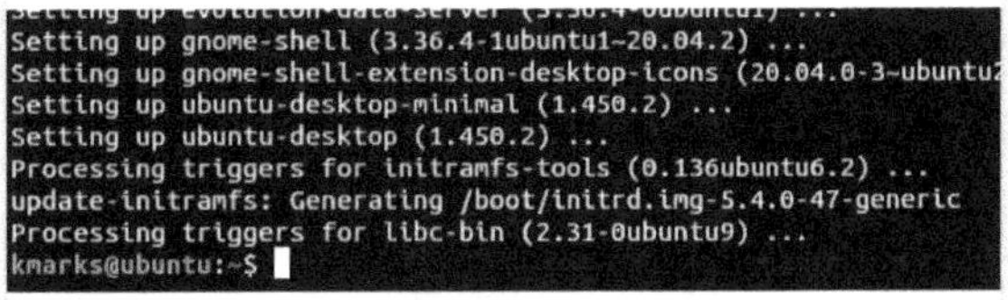

Figure 2.9.

## Installing and Testing Apache

In the terminal window, install Apache using the apt installation package manager by running the following command as super-user:

```
sudo apt install apache2
```

You will need to type Y or press Enter to accept the changes (Figure 2.10).

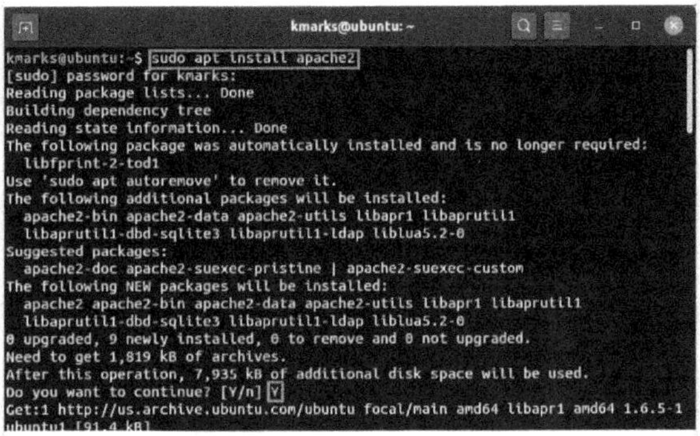

To ensure Apache is running, run the following command in the terminal window as superuser. You should see output as shown in Figure 2.11.

```
sudo systemctl status apache2
```

Type the q key to exit the systemctl status command.

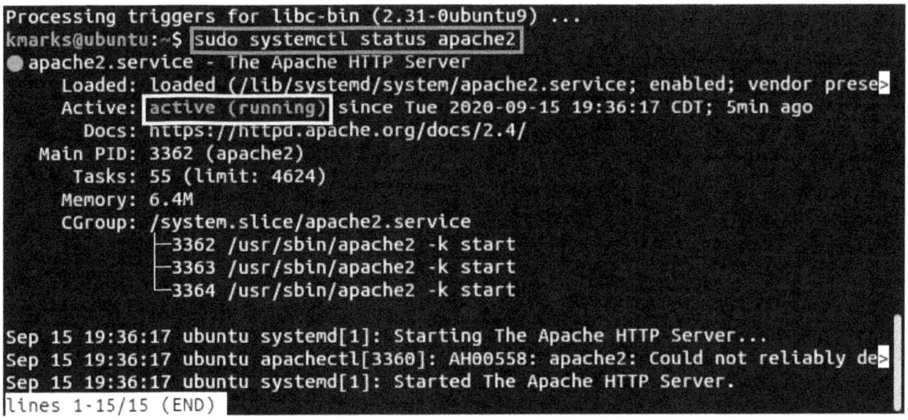

Figure 2.10.

Figure 2.11.

The best way to make sure Apache is running is to bring up a web browser and navigate to localhost. If you see the webpage in Figure 2.12, you can be sure your installation of Apache is running.

Figure 2.12.

## Installing and Testing MySQL

In the terminal window, install the MySQL server and client using the apt installation package manager by running the following command as superuser.

```
sudo apt install mysql-server mysql-client
```

You will need to type Y or press Enter to accept the changes (Figure 2.13).

To ensure MySQL is running, run the following command in the terminal window as superuser.

```
sudo systemctl status mysql
```

The startup output looks like Figure 2.14.

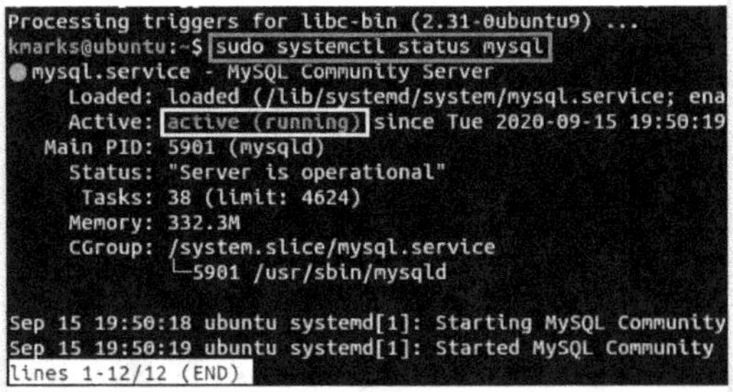

Type the q key to exit the systemctl status command.

Figure 2.13.

## Installing, Configuring, and Testing PHP

As of this writing, the stock version of PHP for Ubuntu 20.04.1 LTS is 7.4. All the code in this book should work well with a PHP version of 7.2 or greater.

In the terminal window, install PHP and supported modules using the apt installation package manager by running the following command as superuser:

```
sudo apt install php php-mysql php-curl php-json php-cgi libapache2-mod-php
```

Figure 2.14.

You will need to type Y or press Enter to accept the changes (Figure 2.15).

Verify PHP is installed by running the following command in the terminal window:

```
php -v
```

You should see the output in Figure 2.16.

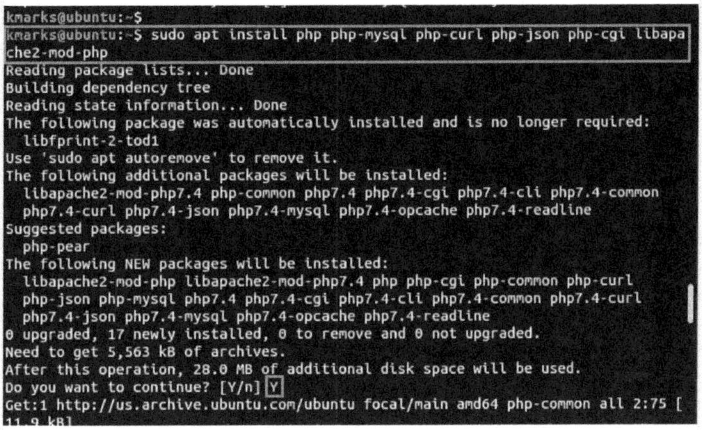

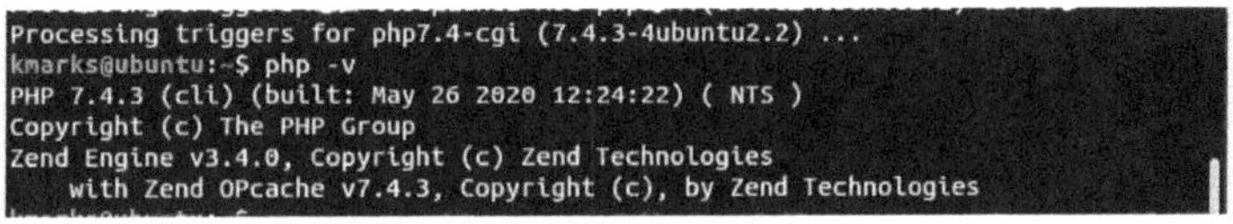

Out of the box, PHP installs with error reporting turned off. This default is a good thing since we don't want to advertise to potential hackers where our files or bugs are for our deployed websites. Since we are creating a development environment, we will want to know

Figure 2.15.

Figure 2.16.

when we have PHP errors. Most of our PHP configuration settings are found in the php.ini file. We will use the installed nano editor that comes installed with Ubuntu to modify this file for displaying our errors.

In the terminal window, type the following command to edit the php.ini file:

```
sudo nano /etc/php/7.4/apache2/php.ini
```

You need to search for the second occurrence of display_errors using the ^W "Where Is" command (ctl+W) in nano and change it from Off to On (Figures 2.17).

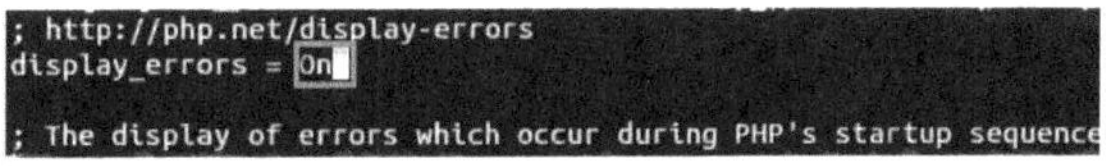

Figure 2.17.

Then write out the changes using the ^O (control plus capital letter O) "Write Out" command (ctl+O). Next, press the return key to confirm the name of the file to write out.

Figure 2.18.

Finally, exit nano using the ^X Exit command (ctl+X). See Figure 2.18

In the terminal window, type the following command to restart Apache for these changes to stick:

```
sudo systemctl restart apache2
```

## Installing the Database Management Tool Adminer

Next, we're going to install a web-based database management tool. There are a few out there, the most popular being phpMy-Admin[1]. However, I like to use one called Adminer because it is contained in a single PHP file, runs faster, and has a reputation for having greater security.

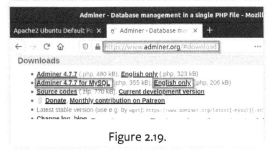

Figure 2.19.

Open up a browser and navigate to the Adminer Download Page[2]. From there, select the latest version of Adminer for MySQL as in Figure 2.19.

Doing so downloads the Adminer PHP file to your Downloads folder.

Next, we need to rename this file index.php and copy it somewhere into our html/ folder where Apache serves up our web pages. The root of our html/ folder is located in the directory /var/www/html. The best way to do this is by using the terminal window.

In the terminal window cd to the /var/www/html directory by typing:

```
cd /var/www/html
```

The output of the command is shown in Figure 2.20.

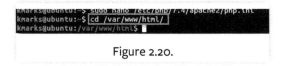

Figure 2.20.

---

[1]  phpMyAdmin: _https://www.phpmyadmin.net/_
[2]  Adminer Download Page: _https://www.adminer.org/#download_

Since the root user owns the html/ directory, we need to move the Adminer PHP file using superuser privileges here. Let's first create a new folder called adminer and change to it by typing the following commands in the terminal window (Output is in Figure 2.21):

Figure 2.21.

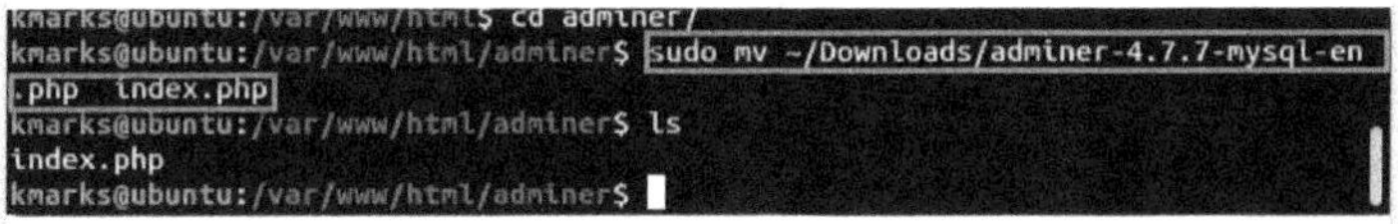

Figure 2.22.

```
sudo mkdir adminer
cd adminer
```

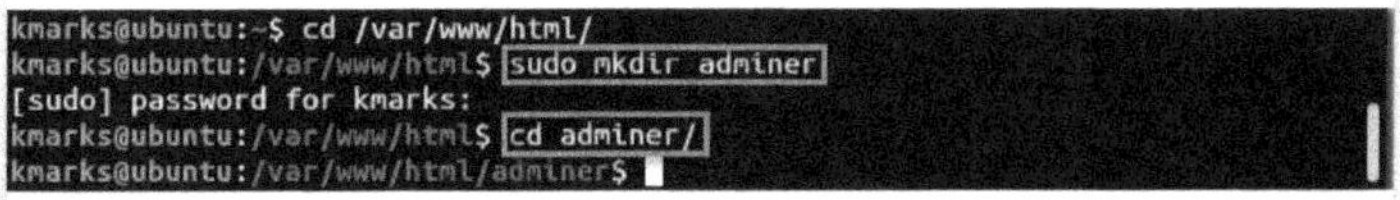

Now let's move the downloaded PHP file from our Downloads directory to the adminer directory and rename it index.php by typing the following command as superuser (Figure 2.22):

```
sudo mv ~/Downloads/adminer-4.7.7-mysql-en.php index.php
```

## Create a Test Database User and Database

By default, we cannot access MySQL databases using the root account. This default is a robust security constraint. For us to use Adminer—or PHP for that matter—to access our databases, we need to use the MySQL command-line interface (CLI) tool as root to create a database user account and grant access to that user to a database.

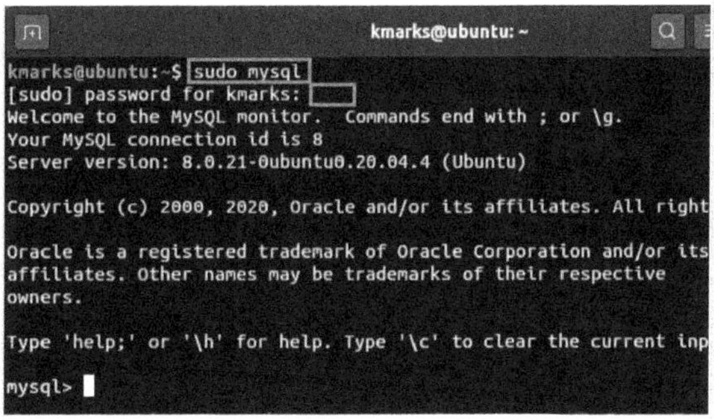

In a terminal window, enter the MySQL CLI by typing the following command:

Figure 2.23.

```
sudo mysql
```

Then enter your password when prompted as in Figure 2.23

## 2. WRITING YOUR FIRST PHP SCRIPT

Now let's create a test database called testdb by typing the following command in the MySQL CLI (Figure 2.24):

```
CREATE DATABASE testdb;
```

Figure 2.24.

Next, we need to create a user with a password for our database, so enter the following command:

```
CREATE USER 'testuser'@'localhost' IDENTIFIED BY 'testuser';
```

The command should look like Figure 2.25.

Finally, we need to grant all privileges to our testuser for our testdb database. Enter the following command (Figure 2.26):

```
GRANT ALL PRIVILEGES ON testdb.*
TO 'testuser'@'localhost';
```

It's also a good idea to flush the privileges for the database as a standard practice. See Figure 2.27.

```
FLUSH PRIVILEGES;
```

Exit the MySQL CLI by entering quit (Figure 2.28).

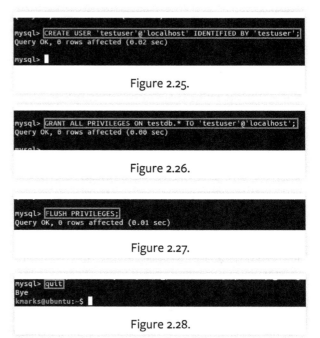

Figure 2.25.

Figure 2.26.

Figure 2.27.

Figure 2.28.

To make sure Adminer runs correctly, open up a browser and navigate to http://localhost/adminer/. Enter testuser for the username and the password you selected when you created the testuser account in the MySQL CLI (testuser), and login as shown in Figure 2.29.

If you see the webpage in Figure 2.30, Adminer is working correctly, and MySQL is also installed and running correctly.

Figure 2.29.

Figure 2.30.

# Hello World!

Now that we have our development environment installed and configured, we can write our first PHP program! First, since the root user is the owner of the /var/www/html directory, change the group privileges and access rights on it so that our user can create and modify files in it.

In the terminal window, navigate to the /var/www directory and change the group privileges and access rights on the html directory as a superuser by typing the following commands. Make sure you change the username to yours.

```
cd /var/www
sudo chgrp kmarks html/
sudo chmod 775 html/
```

When you perform a long listing (ls -al), you should see that your user has group and write access, and you can now create files in the html/ directory (Figure 2.31).

Figure 2.31.

Now let's use the Files application (Figure 2.32) to create a couple of directories.

Figure 2.32.

## 2. Writing Your First PHP Script

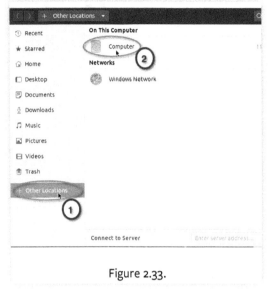

Figure 2.33.

Figure 2.34.

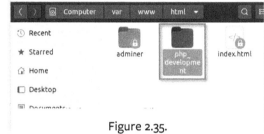

Figure 2.35.

In the **Files** application, select the **+ Other Locations** in the left pane, then **Computer** in the main pane (Figure 2.33).

Navigate to the /var/www/html folder, and create a new folder called "php_development" as in Figure 2.34 and 2.35.

To keep organized, we will create a new folder for each chapter in the book to hold that particular chapter's exercises under the php_development/ folder.

In the php_development/ folder, create another folder and call it "chapter1."

Figure 2.36. gedit

I will be using the gedit[3] editor that comes with Ubuntu (Figure 2.36) to write our code. It is a useful editor that provides line numbering, indentation, and syntax highlighting.

---

[3]   gedit: *https://wiki.gnome.org/Apps/Gedit*

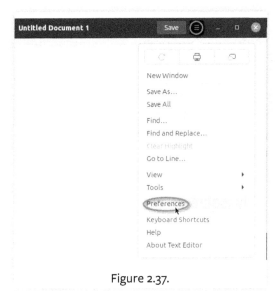

Figure 2.37.

When you start it up, you will see a blank document. Here are some preferences I like to set up for the gedit editor. In the hamburger menu for the Text Editor window, select the **Preferences** menu item as in Figure 2.37.

In the Preferences dialog under the View tab, select **Display line numbers** and **Highlight matching brackets** as shown in Figure 2.38.

Under the Editor tab, change the Tab width to 4, select **Insert spaces instead of tabs**, and **Enable automatic indentation**. See Figure 2.39.

Figure 2.38.

Figure 2.39.

## 2. Writing Your First PHP Script

Alright, finally we can write our first program! It is a tradition among programmers that the first program we write in a new language we are learning should be called *Hello World!* Let's stick with tradition and create a "Hello World!" PHP program.

In your gedit window, type the lines of code shown in Listing 2.1.

Listing 2.1.

```
1.  <html>
2.    <head>
3.      <title>PHP-Hello World!</title>
4.    </head>
5.    <body>
6.      <?php
7.        echo "<h1>Hello World!</h1><br/>";
8.        date_default_timezone_set("America/Chicago");
9.        echo "<h2>Today is: " . date('l jS \of F Y h:i:s A') . "</h2><br/>";
10.     ?>
11.   </body>
12. </html>
```

After keying this code in, save the file as hello_world.php in the chapter1/ folder (Figure 2.40).

Notice after you save this as a .php file that gedit syntax highlights the code as shown in Figure 2.41.

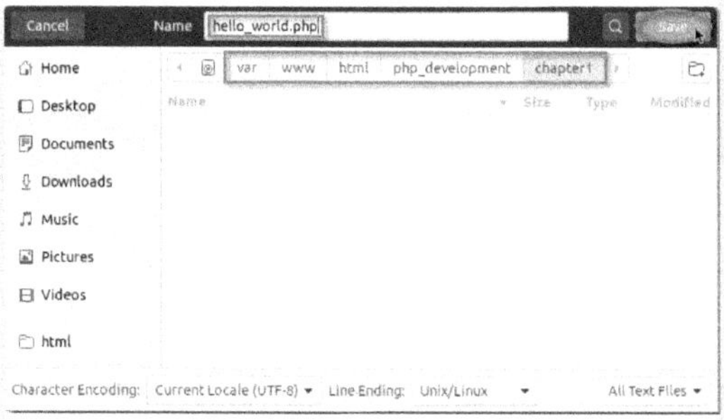

Figure 2.40.

```
1 <html>
2   <head>
3     <title>PHP-Hello World!</title>
4   </head>
5   <body>
6     <?php
7       echo "<h1>Hello World!</h1><br/>";
8       date_default_timezone_set("America/Chicago");
9       echo "<h2>Today is: " . date('l jS \of F Y h:i:s A') . "</h2><br/>";
10    ?>
11  </body>
12 </html>
```

Figure 2.41.

Open up your web browser and navigate to http://localhost/php_development/chapter1/.

You will see a listing of the files so far in the chapter1 directory. You should see a page like Figure 2.42.

Select hello_world.php. You should see the following web page (Figure 2.43) with today's date and time for the U.S. Central Timezone (unless you changed it for your timezone).

Awesome! You just wrote your first PHP program!

## Index of /php_development/chapter1

| Name | Last modified | Size | Description |
|------|---------------|------|-------------|
| Parent Directory | | - | |
| hello_world.php | 2020-09-23 15:02 | 280 | |

*Apache/2.4.41 (Ubuntu) Server at localhost Port 80*

Figure 2.42.

**Hello World!**

Today is: **Wednesday 23rd of September 2020 03:06:05 PM**

Figure 2.43.

### General PHP Format

There are a few general rules required by PHP.

1. PHP code is enclosed by the <?php and ?> tags

```
<?php
...
?>
```

2. Every PHP statement must end in a semicolon ;

```
echo 'Thanks for submitting the form.';
```

3. PHP variables must begin with a dollar sign $

```
$email = $_POST['email'];
```

- A variable name must be at least one character in length.
- The first character after the dollar sign $ can be a letter or an underscore _, and characters after that can be a letter, an underscore, or a number.
- Spaces and special characters other than $ at the beginning and _ are not allowed in any part of a variable name.

*If you forget the opening PHP tag, you'll see your raw code displayed in the browser. In the interest of space, many of the code examples in this book omit the opening and closing tags.*

## Comments

When we write code, we do it for a reason. Frequently we need to share why something works the way it does. Like many modern programming languages, PHP allows you to create single and multi-line comments, as shown in Listing 2.2.

### Listing 2.2.

```
1. <?php
2. //Single line comment
3.
4. # Also a single line comment
5.
6. phpinfo(); //comment after code
7.
8. /*
9. Multi line block, you can add as many
10. lines as you want, but don't write a book
11. */
```

When we comment our code, our comments should reflect why our code exists instead of how our code works. The how is most often explained by the actual code.

Here are a few examples of bad and good commenting.

*Bad Commenting Example*

In Listing 2.3, the comment repeats how the code works instead of explaining why it's done that way. If our regular expression changes, we must remember to update the comment—a step that's often overlooked. If comments don't match the code, future developers may get confused.

### Listing 2.3.

```
1. <?php
2. /*
3. We are formatting phone numbers by stripping all characters
4. then putting parens around the first 3 numbers adding a
5. space then grouping the next 3 numbers adding a dash
6. then the last 4 numbers
7. */
8. function formatPhoneNumber($phone_string)
9. {
```

```
10.    if (preg_match('/^\+\d(\d{3})(\d{3})(\d{4})$/', $data,  $matches))
11.    {
12.        $result = "($matches[1]) $matches[2]-$matches[3]";
13.        return $result;
14.    }
15. }
```

### Good Commenting Example

Now in Listing 2.4, the comment clearly describes the expected format for phone numbers and leaves the implementation details to the code.

### Listing 2.4.

```php
1. <?php
2. /*
3. The business has a requirement that all phone numbers be
4. formatted with the (123) 123-1234 format
5. */
6. function formatPhoneNumber($phone_string)
7. {
8.     if (preg_match('/^\+\d(\d{3})(\d{3})(\d{4})$/', $data, $matches))
9.     {
10.        $result = "($matches[1]) $matches[2]-$matches[3]";
11.        return $result;
12.    }
13. }
```

## Exercises

1.  Install the LAMP (Linux Apache MySQL & PHP) Stack.
2.  Create a hello_world.php script and verify it runs.

# Chapter

# 3

# Why Variables Matter

*"Always code as if the guy who ends up maintaining your code will be a violent psychopath who knows where you live."*

*– Martin Golding*

## Variables in PHP

PHP supports several kinds of variables. Predefined variables are defined already by the PHP language, while user-defined variables are defined by you, the developer, in your code. Then there are form variables defined by the name attributes in an HTML form and become keys in a predefined variable.

### Valid Variable Names

- PHP variable names must begin with a dollar sign ($).
- A variable name must be at least one character in length.
- The first character after the dollar sign $ can be a letter or an underscore _, and characters after that can be a letter, an underscore, or a number.
- Spaces and special characters other than _ and $ are not allowed in any part of a variable name.

Here are a few examples of valid variable names:

```
$name1
$price_tag
$_abc
$Abc_22
$A23
```

Here are a few examples of invalid variable names:

```
$10names
box.front
$name#last
A-23
$5
```

### Recommendations for Naming Your Variables

PHP does have a set of coding standards, which this book follows. You can find them on the PHP-FIG website at PSR-1: Basic Coding Standard[1] and PSR-2: Coding Style Guide[2]. However, the coding standards intentionally give little guidance on how to name your variables. The standards recommend using camelCase for naming your methods, StudlyCaps for class names, and ALL_CAPS separated by underscores for naming constants[3].

[1]  PSR-1: Basic Coding Standard: http://www.php-fig.org/psr/psr-1/
[2]  PSR-2: Coding Style Guide: http://www.php-fig.org/psr/psr-2/
[3]  naming constants: http://www.php-fig.org/psr/psr-1/#1-overview

I like to use the following conventions when creating variables, functions, methods, constants, and classes in PHP, which I will be using throughout this book:

| Property | Example |
|---|---|
| Variable Names | `$snake_case` |
| Function/Method Names | `function camelCase()` |
| Classes | `class StudlyCaps` |
| Constants | `const ALL_CAPS` |

Regarding naming your variables, a recommended practice is to choose good descriptive names for your variables (e.g., `$temperature_fahrenheit`). Also, most predefined PHP variables start with a `$_` (i.e. `$_POST[]`). I recommend that you do not create any variables starting with an underscore (_) as this might be confusing to other PHP developers that have to maintain your code.

## Types of Variables

All data is eventually represented to a computer using `1`s and `0`s. However, a programming language interpreter or compiler must know the data type representation before correctly converting the data into a format the computer can use. Like several other programming languages (e.g., JavaScript), PHP is a dynamically typed language (as opposed to a statically typed language like Java). A variable will dynamically change its type implicitly based on the data type of the value assigned to it or the context in which it's used.

### Scalar Data Types

PHP supports the following *scalar* data types:

- Boolean
- integer
- float
- string

## 3. Why Variables Matter

### Booleans

A Boolean data type contains a logical value that is either TRUE or FALSE. Boolean values are typically used in conditional logic statements:

```php
$passed_drivers_license_exam = TRUE;

if ($passed_drivers_license_exam == TRUE)
{
    echo "Award driver's license.<br/>";
}
```

The online PHP documentation has more information about Boolean data types[4].

### Integers

An integer data type contains a whole number that can be negative, zero, or positive. They are typically represented in the base-10 number system but can be represented using base 2, 8, 10, or 16.

For more information, see the PHP docs about integer data types[5].

### Floats

A floating-point data type contains real numbers which can be expressed either using decimals and/or scientific notation:

```php
// Pascal to Pound per square inch
$pa_to_psi = 0.000145037738;

// Pascal to Pound per square inch
$pa_to_psi = 145037738e-12;

// Pascal to Pound per square inch
$pa_to_psi = 1.45037738e-4;
```

See the PHP documentation for more information about floating point data types[6].

---

[4]   Boolean data types: http://php.net/language.types.boolean
[5]   integer data types: http://php.net/language.types.integer
[6]   floating point data types: http://php.net/language.types.float

## Strings

A string is a group of characters enclosed in either single (') or double (") quotes. The type of opening quote must match the closing quote:

```
echo "This is a string";
echo 'This is also a string';
echo "This is a string with 'singe-quotes' embedded";
echo 'This is a string with "double-quotes" embedded';
```

If you have a string surrounded by double-quotes (") you can contain a double-quote in your string by escaping it with the back-slash (\). Likewise, you can embed single-quotes by escaping them if they are inside of a string surrounded by single-quotes:

```
echo "This is a string surrounded by \"";
echo 'I don\'t like using contractions';
```

See the PHP manual for more information about string data types[7].

## Compound Data Types

PHP defines several "compound" data types which allow you to contain or aggregate multiple pieces of data of the same data type under a single entity. PHP supports the following compound data types:

- array
- object
- callable
- iterable

## Array

Arrays in PHP are ordered maps, which are a way to associate a key with its corresponding value. Therefore, arrays in PHP are known as "associative arrays."

An array is created using the array() language construct. Here's how to create an empty array:

```
$fahrenheit_temperatures = array();
```

---

[7]  string data types: http://php.net/language.types.string

> *PHP also supports short array syntax, which lets you define an array like this:*
> ```
> $temperatures = [];
> ```

To add (or push) values onto the end of an array, use the [] syntax immediately following the variable name. Without specifying a key when adding values to an array, the key will be the next integer value:

```
$fahrenheit_temperatures[] = 32;  // 32 is associated with key 0
$fahrenheit_temperatures[] = 100; // 100 is associated with key 1
```

Keys can be specified using either strings or integers. Associative arrays often use strings as keys to give meaning to the values they associate with in the array. To initialize an array with named keys, use the rocket (=>) operator:

```
$us_state_captials = array(
    "Wisconsin" => "Madison",
    "California" => "Sacramento"
);
```

To add a named key to the end of the array, specify it in between []s:

```
$us_state_captials["Florida"] = "Tallahassee";
```

Note that arrays in keys are unique, so if you specify a key that already exists, you will be replacing its value.

A useful function for viewing the contents of an array is print_r()[8]. Embed print() in a set of <pre> tags as shown in Listing 3.1.

## Listing 3.1.

```
1.  <pre>
2.  <?php
3.  $us_state_captials = array(
4.      "Wisconsin" => "Madison",
5.      "California" => "Sacramento"
6.  );
7.
8.  print_r($us_state_captials);
9.  ?>
10. </pre>
```

---

[8] print_r(): http://php.net/print_r

This function call produces the following output:

```
Array
(
        [Wisconsin] => Madison
        [California] => Sacramento
)
```

You can find more information on array data types[9] online.

## Object

PHP is an "Object-Oriented" programming language, and it allows you to create objects. Objects are created from "class" definitions. Class definitions are like complex types that allow you to group your program data (what your program knows) and your program functions (what your program does) in one place to represent modular components in software better. We will cover object-oriented programming in more detail later in the book.

To create an object, you "instantiate" it from a class definition using the new keyword as in Listing 3.2.

## Listing 3.2.

```
 1. <?php
 2.
 3. class Radio
 4. {
 5.     function turnOnRadio()
 6.     {
 7.         echo "Turning radio on";
 8.     }
 9. }
10.
11. $car_radio = new Radio();
12. $car_radio->turnOnRadio();
```

The PHP manual has more information on objects[10].

---

[9]  array data types: http://php.net/language.types.array
[10]  objects: http://php.net/language.types.object

### Callable

"Callables" can be created in PHP by naming a function to call as a string and invoking it with the `call_user_func()` function[11]. You can do this with simple functions, static class methods, and instantiated class methods. The following is a simple example of using a callback.

```php
function exampleCallbackFunction()
{
    echo "Hello world!";
}

call_user_func('exampleCallbackFunction');
```

For more information on callables[12], check the online manual.

### Iterable

An `iterable`[13] is a pseudo-type. It enforces arguments to functions or return values from functions are traversable like arrays. You may see this typehint when looking at the API for PHP functions. It mainly means that you can loop through the variable using a `foreach`.

## Special Data Types

PHP defines a couple of special data types as well. These are:

- resource
- NULL

### Resource

A "resource" is a special variable containing a reference to an external resource. Resources are typically used for working with files and databases:

```php
$db_connection = mysqli_connect(
    'localhost', 'db_user', 'db_password', 'db_to_use'
);

$file_handle = fopen('file.txt' 'r');
```

For more information on resources[14] and their usages, see the online documentation.

---

[11] `call_user_func()` function: http://php.net/call_user_func
[12] callables: http://php.net/language.types.callable
[13] `iterable`: http://php.net/language.types.iterable
[14] resources: http://php.net/language.types.resource

*NULL*

A "NULL" value[15] is a special variable that does not contain a value. A variable is NULL if:

- it is assigned the constant NULL,
- it has not been assigned any value,
- or it has been unset().

## Constants

Constants are values that do not change. Named constants are created in PHP using the define()[16] function:

```php
define("BOILING_TEMP_IN_CELCIUS", 100);
echo BOILING_TEMP_IN_CELCIUS; // outputs 100
```

## Exercises

Create a script variables.php and do the following:

1. Assign numbers to two variables and echo their values.
2. Create a variable to hold a name, echo the string "Hello NAME" where NAME is the value of your variable.
3. Define a constant that represents the acceleration due to gravity (9.81 m/s). Echo the value of this constant.

---

[15] "NULL" value: *http://php.net/language.types.null*
[16] define(): *http://php.net/function.define*

# Chapter

# 4

# Basic String Interpretation

*"The purpose of software engineering is to control complexity, not to create it."*

– *Pamela Zave*

## Concatenation

In PHP, strings can be joined together by concatenating them using the dot (.) operator:

```
$name = "Fred Flintstone";
echo "Hello " . $name . " !";
```

This outputs:

```
Hello Fred Flintstone!
```

You can also successively concatenate onto a string variable using the compound assignment operator .=:

```
$some_fruit = "apple";
$some_fruit .= ", orange";
$some_fruit .= ", banana";

echo "Here are some fruit: " . $some_fruit . ".";
```

This outputs:

```
Here are some fruit: apple, orange, banana.
```

## Interpolation

In PHP, when a variable is contained within a string using double-quotes ("), the variable's contents are interpolated, which outputs the value of the variable within the string. An example would be helpful:

```
$name = "Fred Flintstone";
echo "Hello $name, how are you today?";
```

This outputs:

```
Hello Fred Flintstone, how are you today?
```

However, variable interpolation does not work within a string defined by single-quotes ('). Whatever is contained in between the single-quotes is literally output to the web page:

```
$name = "Fred Flintstone";
echo 'Hello $name, how are you today?';
```

This outputs:

```
Hello $name, how are you today?
```

# Escaping

Strings can be contained in either double-quotes (") or single-quotes ('). To use a literal ' in a string with single-quotes, you must escape it using the backslash \ character:

```
echo 'You\'re an awesome programmer!';
```

This outputs:

```
You're an awesome programmer!
```

To use a literal " in a string with double-quotes, you have to escape it as well (using the \):

```
echo "A famous programmer, Olav Mjelde said, \"They don't make bugs like Bunny
anymore.\"";
```

This outputs:

```
A famous programmer, Olav Mjelde said, "They don't make bugs like Bunny anymore."
```

Note that strings contained in double-quotes can contain single-quotes without escaping them. Likewise, strings contained in single-quotes can contain double-quotes without escaping the latter:

```
echo 'Jane said, "Hi John!"<br/>';
echo "John said, 'Hi Jane!'";
```

This code outputs:

```
Jane said, "Hi John!"
John said, 'Hi Jane!'
```

See the online docs for more on single-quoted strings[1] and on double-quoted strings and string escape characters[2].

---

[1]   single-quoted strings: http://phpa.me/php-single-strings
[2]   string escape characters: http://php.net/language.types.string.php#language.types.string.syntax.double

## Heredoc

PHP defines a special way to delimit strings called heredoc which allows you to define an identifier after the the <<< sequence followed by a newline. EOT ("end of text") is a popular character sequence used as an identifier. Everything after this line up until the same identifier followed by a semicolon ; on its own line is delimited as a string. This syntax allows you to define large portions of text without the need for escaping single or double quotes:

```
echo <<<EOT
Cupcake ipsum dolor. Sit amet cake ice cream sweet pudding
tootsie roll marshmallow cake. "Lemon" drops apple pie fruitcake
caramels lollipop's sweet roll. Sesame snaps lemon drops topping.
EOT;
```

This outputs:

```
Cupcake ipsum dolor. Sit amet cake ice cream sweet pudding
tootsie roll marshmallow cake. "Lemon" drops apple pie fruitcake
caramels lollipop's sweet roll. Sesame snaps lemon drops topping.
```

The online documenation has more detail on Strings[3].

## Exercises

Create a script strings.php to do the following:

1. Assign a first and a last name to two separate variables. Then, use concatenation to echo the full name.
2. Again, with first and last name, use string interpolation to output the last name, a comma, and then the first name.
3. Set the last name to "O'Connor" and output the full name.

---

[3]   Strings: http://php.net/language.types.string

# Chapter

# 5

# Operators, Expressions, and Basic Arithmetic

*"Don't worry if it doesn't work right. If everything did, you'd be out of a job."*

*– Mosher's Law of Software Engineering*

## Operators and Expressions

### Operators

An operator is a symbol that produces a result based on some rules. Examples include:

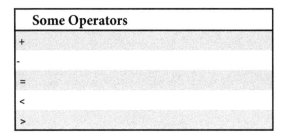

| Some Operators |
|---|
| + |
| - |
| = |
| < |
| > |

Operators can be surrounded by an operand on the left or the right.

### Operands

Operands are data objects that are manipulated by operators. Operands can be a string, number, Boolean, object, or combination of these.

### Expressions

An expression is a group of operators and operands that the PHP interpreter evaluates. Figure 5.1 shows a simple example of an expression.

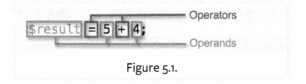

Figure 5.1.

### Assignments

Literal values and the contents of variables are assigned to variables using the assignment (=) operator. The variable on the left of the = is assigned the value or contents of a variable on the right of the =. Consult the manual for a complete explanation of how the assignment operator[1] works.

---

[1]   assignment operator: http://php.net/language.operators.assignment

Here is an example using the = operator:

```
$temperature_fahrenheit = 32;
$current_temperature = $temperature_fahrenheit;
```

## Compound Assignment operators

Like many modern programming languages, PHP has compound assignment operators. Here are a few examples using the arithmetic compound assignment operators:

| Compound Assignment | Shorthand for... | Meaning |
|---|---|---|
| $a += $b | $a = $a + $b | Addition |
| $a -= $b | $a = $a - $b | Subtraction |
| $a *= $b | $a = $a * $b | Multiplication |
| $a /= $b | $a = $a / $b | Division |
| $a %= $b | $ = $a % $b | Modulus |

## Operator Precedence

In PHP (as in many other programming languages), precedence determines the order in which operators are evaluated and their associativity. The following table lists the precedence and associativity of all the PHP operators:

| Operator | Description | Associativity |
|---|---|---|
| () | Parentheses | Left to right |
| new | Creates an object | Non-associative |
| [] | Array subscript | Right to left |
| ++ -- | Auto increment, decrement | Non-associative |
| ! ~ - | Logical not, bitwise not, negation | Non-associative |
| (int) (float) (string) (array) (object) | Cast | Right |
| instanceof | Determines if a variable is an instantiated object of some class | Left |
| ! | Not | Non-associative |
| () | Parentheses | Left to right |

| Operator | Description | Associativity |
|---|---|---|
| * / . | Arithmetic multiply, divide, string concatenation | Left |
| << >> | Bitwise shift left, right | Left |
| < <= > >= | Less than, less than or equal, greater than, greater than or equal comparison | Non-associative |
| & | Bitwise and | Left |
| ^ | Bitwise xor | Left |
| \| | Bitwise or | Left |
| && | Logical and | Left |
| \|\| | Logical or | Left |
| ?? | Null coalesce | Right |
| = += -= *= **= /= .= %= &= \|= ^= <<= >>= ??= | Assignment, compound assignment, compound modulus, compound bitwise logical, compound bitwise shift, compound null coalesce | Right |

See the online docs for more information on Operator Precedence[2].

## Basic Arithmetic

Like many programming languages PHP provides five basic arithmetic operators:

| Operator | Name | Example | Meaning |
|---|---|---|---|
| + | Addition | $a + $b | Sum |
| - | Subtraction | $a - $b | Difference |
| * | Multiplication | $a = $a * $b | Product |
| / | Division | $a / $b | Quotient |
| % | Modulus | $a % $b | Remainder |

---

[2]   Operator Precedence: http://php.net/language.operators.precedence

When performing division the / operator returns an integer if the divisor divides evenly into the dividend, otherwise a float is returned:

```
$whole_number = 12 / 4  // $whole_number will be an integer (3)
$float_value = 7 / 2    // $float_value will be a float (3.5)
```

The *modulus* (%) operator returns the remainder of a division operation. A typical use of the *modulus* operator is to find out if a number is even or odd:

```
if (($odd_or_even % 2) == 1)
{
    echo "$odd_or_even is an odd number.";
}
else if (($odd_or_even % 2) == 0)
{
    echo "$odd_or_even is an even number.";
}
```

This further boils down to:

```
if (($odd_or_even % 2) == 1)
{
    echo "$odd_or_even is an odd number.";
}
else
{
    echo "$odd_or_even is an even number.";
}
```

The PHP documentation has more information about the basic arithmetic operators[3].

# Math Functions

The PHP language provides a relatively standard set of math functions for you to use. Here are some examples of a few common math functions.

## abs()

The abs() function returns the absolute value of the argument given:

```
$value = -42;
$absolute_value = abs($value);
echo "The absolute value of $value is $absolute_value";
```

---

[3]  basic arithmetic operators: http://php.net/language.operators.arithmetic

Outputs:

```
The absolute value of -42 is 42
```

## pow()

The pow() function returns the first argument raised to the power of the second argument:

```
echo pow(10, 3) . '<br/>'; // 1000
echo pow(10, -1) . '<br/>'; // 0.1
```

This outputs:

```
1000
0.1
```

## round()

The round() function returns the rounded value of a given argument by a default or given precision in number of digits after the decimal point. If a precision is not specified, the default precision is 0:

```
echo round(4.4) . '<br/>'; // 4
echo round(4.5) . '<br/>'; // 5
```

Outputs:

```
4
5
```

See the online docs for more information on the Math Functions[4].

## Exercises

Create a script operators.php for the following:

1. Assign two numeric values to separate variables. Output the numbers and their sum, difference, product, and quotient on a new line.
2. Output the modulus of the two values above.
3. Use pow() to raise your first value to the second and third power. Output each result.
4. Multiply the second value by 1.15 and round it to the nearest whole number—bonus: round it to 2 decimal places. Output your results.

---

[4] *Math Functions: http://php.net/ref.math*

# Chapter

# 6

# Arrays

*"Python's a drop-in replacement for BASIC in the sense that Optimus Prime is a drop-in replacement for a truck."*

– Cory Dodt

# 6. ARRAYS

When we have data that logically relate to each other, we often want to group that data together into a single data structure to contain them. The most basic data structure for gathering a collection of related information is an `array`.

An `array` in PHP is an ordered map that associates values to keys. Arrays in PHP can be represented using either `integer` or `string` keys that match an associated value.

## Simple Arrays in PHP

A simple array uses `integers` as keys, typically starting from `0` and going to `n-1` (where `n` is the number of elements in an array). This implementation is similar to how arrays are accessed in other programming languages. These are called "numeric" or "indexed" arrays.

### Creating

Here is how you create a numeric array in PHP:

```
$us_states = array(); // Empty array

// Populated array
$us_states = array("California", "Florida", "Wisconsin");
```

#### Short Array Syntax

Prior to version 5.4 of PHP, programmers had to create arrays using the `array()` function. Version 5.4 introduced short array syntax, which allows you to create arrays using square brackets ([ & ]). Here is how to create the above arrays using the short array syntax:

```
$us_states = []; // Empty array (short array syntax)

// Populated array (short array syntax)
$us_states = ["California", "Florida", "Wisconsin"];
```

### Accessing Single Elements

Using `$us_states` as an example, we can access our array's individual values through the numeric keys. The indexed keys for our numeric array will start at zero (`0`), and we access the corresponding values by placing the key in between a set of square brackets ([ & ]) following the variable name of our array:

```
echo "Sacramento is the capital of $us_states[0].<br/>";
echo "Tallahassee is the capital of $us_states[1].<br/>";
echo "Madison is the capital of $us_states[2].";
```

# Associative Arrays

An associative array uses a string as a key connected with a value in an array.

## Enumerated Versus Associative

Associative arrays are great to use because they allow the developer to associate a meaningful word as a key to a value instead of relying on an arbitrary numeric value that typically has no significant association to the value it is mapped to.

## Creating

The syntax for creating an associative array in PHP is a little different because it requires that you specify both the key and it's associated value upon creation of the element pair. The key and it's value are separated by the => operator (sometimes called the "rocket" operator):

```php
$us_state_capitals = array(
    "California" => "Sacramento",
    "Florida" => "Tallahassee",
    "Wisconsin" => "Madison"
);
```

### Short Array Syntax

Here is how to create the above arrays using short array syntax:

```php
$us_state_capitals = [
    "California" => "Sacramento",
    "Florida" => "Tallahassee",
    "Wisconsin" => "Madison"
];
```

## Accessing Single Elements

Using $us_state_capitals as an example, we can access individual values of our array through the associated keys. Like the numeric array, values are accessed by specifying the key in between a set of square brackets ([ & ]) following the variable name of our array:

```php
echo "The capital of California is {$us_state_capitals['California']}.<br/>";
echo "The capital of Florida is {$us_state_capitals['Florida']}.<br/>";
echo "The capital of Wisconsin is {$us_state_capitals['Wisconsin']}.<br/>";
```

## Adding Values

Arrays in PHP are immutable. That is, they can change after they are initially created. This property allows us to add and delete items from an array.

There are two ways to add values to the end of arrays. The first is to use the array_push()[1] function:

```php
// Add value to end of numeric array
array_push($us_states, 'Wisconsin');

// Add value to end of associative array
array_push($us_state_capitals, 'California' => 'Sacramento');
```

The second is to use the following syntax:

```php
// Add value to end of numeric array
$us_states[] = 'Wisconsin';

// Add value with this key to end of associative array
$us_state_capitals['California'] = 'Sacramento';
```

## Explicit Versus Short Array Syntax

Short array syntax is generally preferred over using the array keyword because it's less verbose.

## Useful Array Functions

### count()

You will often need to know how many elements are in your array. The count()[2] function returns the number of items in an array:

```php
$us_states_i_lived_in = ["California", "Florida", "Wisconsin"];
$number_of_states = count($us_states_i_lived_in);

echo "I have lived in $number_of_states<br/>";
```

---

[1]  array_push(): http://php.net/array-push
[2]  count(): http://php.net/count

## array_pop()

If you need to get the last element and remove it from an array, you will want to use the function array_pop()[3]. Here is an example how to use it:

```
$us_states = ["California", "Florida", "Wisconsin"];
$last_state = array_pop($us_states);

echo "I currently live in $last_state<br/>"; // Wisconsin
// Count of $us_states is now 2
echo "There are now count($us_states) left in the us_states array";
```

## shift()

If you need to get the first element and remove it from an array, you will want to use the function array_shift()[4]. Here is an example how to use it:

```
$us_states = ["California", "Florida", "Wisconsin"];
$first_state = array_shift($us_states);

echo "I was born in $first_state<br/>"; // California
// Count of $us_states is now 2
echo "There are now count($us_states) left in the us_states array";
```

## array_merge()

The array_merge()[5] function appends one or more arrays to the end of the previous array:

```
$us_states = ["California", "Florida", "Wisconsin"];
$more_us_states = ["Virginia", "Maryland", "New York"];
$merged_us_states = array_merge($us_states, $more_us_states);

echo "<pre>";
print_r($merged_us_states);
echo "</pre>";
```

---

[3]  array_pop(): http://php.net/array_pop
[4]  array_shift(): https://php.net/array_shift
[5]  array_merge(): http://php.net/array_merge

Results in:

```
Array
(
    [0] => California
    [1] => Florida
    [2] => Wisconsin
    [3] => Virginia
    [4] => Maryland
    [5] => New York
)
```

## array_key_exists()

The array_key_exists()[6] is used to check if a given key exists in an array (Listing 6.1).

## Listing 6.1.

```
1.  <?php
2.  $us_state_capitals = [
3.      "California" => "Sacramento",
4.      "Florida" => "Tallahassee",
5.      "Wisconsin" => "Madison"
6.  ];
7.
8.  if (array_key_exists('California', $us_state_capitals))
9.  {
10.     echo "{$us_state_capitals['California']} is the captital of California<br/>";
11. }
12.
13. if (!array_key_exists('Montana', $us_state_capitals))
14. {
15.     echo "The key 'Montana' was not found in us_state_capitals<br/>";
16. }
```

Results in:

```
Sacramento is the capital of California.
The key 'Montana' was not found in us_state_capitals.
```

## array_keys()

In order to get all of the keys for an array, you can use the array_keys()[7] function as shown in Listing 6.2.

---

[6] array_key_exists(): *https://php.net/array_key_exists*
[7] array_keys(): *http://php.net/array_keys*

## Listing 6.2.

```
1. $us_state_capitals = [
2.    "California" => "Sacramento",
3.    "Florida" => "Tallahassee",
4.    "Wisconsin" => "Madison"
5. ];
6.
7. echo "<pre>";
8. print_r(array_keys($us_state_capitals));
9. echo "</pre>";
```

Results in:

```
Array
(
    [0] => California
    [1] => Florida
    [2] => Wisconsin
)
```

Here is an example if you are only looking for a key (or keys) mapped to a value (or values) contained in an array as in Listing 6.3.

## Listing 6.3.

```
1. $us_state_capitals = [
2.    "California" => "Sacramento",
3.    "Florida" => "Tallahassee",
4.    "Wisconsin" => "Madison"
5. ];
6.
7. echo "<pre>";
8. print_r(array_keys($us_state_capitals, "Madison"));
9. echo "</pre>";
```

Results in:

```
Array
(
    [0] => Wisconsin
)
```

### array_values()

In order to get all of the values for an array, you can use the `array_values()`[8] function as follows in Listing 6.4.

### Listing 6.4.

```
1. $us_state_capitals = [
2.     "California" => "Sacramento",
3.     "Florida" => "Tallahassee",
4.     "Wisconsin" => "Madison"
5. ];
6.
7. echo "<pre>";
8. print_r(array_values($us_state_capitals));
9. echo "</pre>";
```

Results in:

```
Array
(
    [0] => Sacramento
    [1] => Tallahassee
    [2] => Madison
)
```

### array_splice()

`array_splice()`[9] is a useful function that we can use to remove a range of elements from an array and replace that range with another range of elements or not at all. Listing 6.5 is an example that removes items from an array.

### Listing 6.5.

```
1. $us_states = [
2.     "California",
3.     "Arizona",
4.     "Florida",
5.     "Wisconsin"
6. ];
7. array_splice($us_states, 1, 2); // Removes 'Arizona' and 'Florida'
8.
9. echo "<pre>";
10. print_r($us_states);
11. echo "</pre>";
```

---

[8]  array_values(): *http://php.net/array_values*
[9]  array_splice(): *http://php.net/array_splice*

Results in:

```
Array
(
    [0] => California
    [1] => Wisconsin
)
```

Listing 6.6 is an example that replaces the removed section with all the elements in another array.

## Listing 6.6.

```
1. $us_states = [
2.     "California",
3.     "Arizona",
4.     "Florida",
5.     "Wisconsin"
6. ];
7.
8. $more_us_states = ["Virginia", "New York"];
9. // Removes 'Arizona' and 'Florida', and replaces
10. // them with 'Virginia' and 'New York'
11. array_splice($us_states, 1, 2, $more_us_states);
12.
13. echo "<pre>";
14. print_r($us_states);
15. echo "</pre>";
```

Results in:

```
Array
(
    [0] => California
    [1] => Virginia
    [2] => New York
    [3] => Wisconsin
)
```

### Sorting

After populating an array, you may need to work with it in sorted order. asort()[10] will reorder an array with the values in sorted order and preserve the key-value pairs. Listing 6.7 is an example where that resorts U.S. state capitals in alphabetic order.

### Listing 6.7.

```
1. $us_state_capitals = [
2.     "California" => "Sacramento",
3.     "Florida" => "Tallahassee",
4.     "Wisconsin" => "Madison"
5. ];
6.
7. asort($us_state_capitals);
8.
9. echo "<pre>";
10. print_r($us_state_capitals);
11. echo "</pre>";
```

Results in:

```
Array
(
    [Wisconsin] => Madison
    [California] => Sacramento
    [Florida] => Tallahassee
)
```

> *PHP provides many built-in functions for sorting arrays. For example, if you need to reverse sort an array, use* arsort()[11]. *For a complete list, see "Sorting Arrays"[12].*

## Multidimensional Arrays

The arrays we have dealt with so far are all single-dimensional arrays. However, like many other programming languages, PHP allows for the creation of multidimensional arrays. One way to visualize multidimensional arrays is to think of each dimension as an axis of numbers. For example, a single-dimensional array could be a single number line of values such as an X-axis. Using this metaphor, you can think of a two-dimensional array as the

---

[10] asort(): *http://php.net/asort*
[11] arsort(): *http://php.net/arsort*
[12] "Sorting Arrays": *https://php.net/array.sorting*

X- and Y-axis, which might represent points contained in an area. Taking this example one step further, a three-dimensional array could represent the X-, Y-, and Z-axis, representing points contained in a volume.

Multidimensional arrays work for both numeric and associative arrays. Listing 6.8 is an example of creating and accessing a two-dimensional numeric array holding a simple grid for a "Battleship" game.

## Listing 6.8.

```
1. $battleship_grid = [
2.    ["miss", "miss", "miss", "miss"],
3.    ["miss", "miss", "miss", "hit"],
4.    ["miss", "miss", "miss", "hit"],
5.    ["miss", "miss", "miss", "hit"],
6. ];
7.
8. // Coordinates to sink my battleship
9. echo "{$battleship_grid[1][3]},"
10.    . "{$battleship_grid[2][3]},"
11.    . "{$battleship_grid[3][3]}";
```

Results in:

```
hit,hit,hit
```

Listing 6.9 is an example of how to create and access a two-dimensional associative array holding some of the cities keyed by the state that Oscar and I have lived in.

## Listing 6.9.

```
1. $us_cities_we_lived_in = [
2.    "Ken" => [
3.        "California" => "San Diego",
4.        "Florida" => "Orlando",
5.        "Wisconsin" => "Madison"
6.    ],
7.    "Oscar" => [
8.        "New York" => "New York",
9.        "Maryland" => "Baltimore",
10.        "Virginia" => "Richmond"
11.    ]
12. ];
13.
14. echo "I live in {$us_cities_we_lived_in['Ken']['Wisconsin']},<br/>";
15. echo "and Oscar lives in {$us_cities_we_lived_in['Oscar']['Virginia']}.";
```

Results in:

```
I live in Madison,
and Oscar lives in Richmond.
```

See the online docs for more information about arrays[13].

## Exercises

Create a script arrays.php for the following:

1. Create an array to hold a list of at least five book titles. Echo the title of the third and fourth books.

2. Create an associative array to hold a list of at least three book titles and their authors. Use book titles as the keys. Output the title and author of each book on a new line.

3. Append another book and author to the list of books above. Use print_r() to see the array's structure.

4. Output how many books are in your list of books.

5. Use asort() to sort your books by title. Use print_r() to confirm the array is sorted correctly.

---

[13] arrays: http://php.net/language.types.array

# Chapter

# 7

# Truth, Comparisons, Conditions, and Compound Conditions

*"I had a nightmare once in which I had convinced a friend how wonderful C++ is. A while later he came back., and he was mad."*

*– Robin Rosenberg*

This chapter deals essentially with conditional logic. This is the part of your code where decisions are made. You typically find these decisions being made inside if/else statements. The path of execution the code takes is dependent upon the result of a comparison that is done within these if/else statements. Let's take a look at the different ways to create conditional logic statements.

## Comparison Operators

We first need to create an expression that produces a Boolean value of true or false. This can be done using comparison operators. The following table shows all the comparison operators available in PHP:

| Operator and Operands | Explanation |
|---|---|
| $x == $y | $x is equal to $y |
| $x != $y | $x is not equal to $y |
| $x > $y | $x is greater than $y |
| $x >= $y | $x is greater than or equal to $y |
| $x < $y | $x is less than $y |
| $x <= $y | $x is less than or equal to $y |
| $x === $y | $x is identical to $y in value and type |
| $x !== $y | $x is not identical to $y in value and/or type |

- The result of the comparison is either true or false.
- Numbers are compared as expected.
- Strings are compared letter by letter using ASCII values until an inequality is found.

Here is a simple if/else statement:

```
if ($age > 18)
{
    echo 'You can vote';
}
else
{
    echo 'You can not vote';
}
```

## What is Equality?

- == tests whether the value is equal
- === tests whether the value is equal and also if it's same data type

The == operator will do automatic type conversion for an equality test, see Listing 7.1.

## Listing 7.1.

```
1. $age_string = "18";
2.
3. if ($age == 18)
4. {
5.     echo 'You can vote';
6. }
7. else
8. {
9.     echo 'You can not vote';
10. }
```

Outputs the following:

```
You can vote
```

However, === requires that two values be of the same type and equal in order to be true as in Listing 7.2.

## Listing 7.2.

```
1. $age_string = "18";
2.
3. if ($age === 18)
4. {
5.     echo 'You can vote';
6. }
7. else
8. {
9.     echo 'You can not vote';
10. }
```

Which results in:

```
You can not vote
```

## Spaceship Operator (<=>)

The <=> is a new operator in PHP added to PHP 7.0. It is used for comparing two expressions and returns -1 if the left-hand expression is less than the right-hand expression, 0 if the two expressions are equal, and 1 if the left-hand expression is greater than the right-hand expression:

```
echo 1 <=> 2 . '<br/>';
echo 1 <=> 1 . '<br/>';
echo 2 <=> 1 . '<br/>';
```

Results in:

```
-1
0
1
```

A better example of how you might use the <=> looks like Listing 7.3.

## Listing 7.3.

```
 1. <?php
 2. $a_number = 1;
 3. $another_number = 2;
 4.
 5. $comparison_result = $a_number <=> $another_number;
 6.
 7. switch ($comparison_result) {
 8.     case -1;
 9.         echo "$a_number < $another_number";
10.         break;
11.     case 0;
12.         echo "$a_number == $another_number";
13.         break;
14.     case 1;
15.         echo "$a_number > $another_number";
16.         break;
17.     default:
18.         echo "Error!";
19.         break;
20. }
```

Results in:

```
1 < 2
```

# Conditional Logic

You have already seen how the simple if/else statement works. Let's take a look at other ways we can write conditional statements in PHP.

## if/else if/else

A typical block of if/else statments looks like Listing 7.4.

### Listing 7.4.

```
1. if ($age > 18)
2. {
3.     echo 'You can vote';
4. }
5. elseif ($age > 16)
6. {
7.     echo 'You can drive';
8. }
9. else
10. {
11.     echo 'Get back to school!';
12. }
```

You can also embed conditional logic directly into your HTML as follows:

```
<?php if ($age > 18) : ?>
  <h1>You can vote</h1>
<?php elseif ($age > 16) : ?>
  <h1>You can drive</h1>
<?php else : ?>
  <h1>Get back to school!</h1>
<?php endif; ?>
```

Note that in the above examples else if can also be substituted for elseif[1] when using curly braces ({}). However, when using a colon (:) to define if/elseif conditions, a parse error results if you separate elseif into two words (i.e. else if).

---

[1]  elseif: http://php.net/control-structures.elseif

# 7. Truth, Comparisons, Conditions, and Compound Conditions

## Ternary

Most modern programming languages have a ternary operator that works essentially like a shorthand if/else statement. Suppose you needed a piece of code that held a Boolean value indicating if someone was old enough to vote. Listing 7.5 shows how you might write it.

## Listing 7.5.

```
1. $able_to_vote = NULL;
2.
3. if ($age > 18)
4. {
5.     $able_to_vote = true;
6. }
7. else
8. {
9.     $able_to_vote = false;
10. }
```

A more compact way to write this code would be to use the ternary operator like so:

```
$able_to_vote = ($age > 18) ? true : false;
```

The ternary operator has a conditional statement in between two parentheses, followed by a question mark (?), then the value that will be assigned if the condition is true, followed by a colon (:), then a value that will be assigned if the condition is false. You typically create a variable and assign the results of the ternary operation to the variable. See the Ternary Operator[2] documentation for more information.

[2]   Ternary Operator: http://phpa.me/php-ternary

## Switch

Another useful way to write conditional statements are with a switch and several case statements. Programmers typically use a switch statement when they have more than four conditions they want to check for. Listing 7.6 is an example of how you might use a switch and case statements.

### Listing 7.6.

```
1.  $hungry_for = 'ice cream'
2.  switch ($hungry_for)
3.  {
4.      case 'burgers':
5.          echo 'The Nitty Gritty on Frances St. is great!';
6.          break;
7.      case 'ice cream':
8.          echo 'Get some Babcock Ice Cream at the Memorial Union at UW Madison!';
9.          break;
10.     case 'chocolate':
11.         echo 'Gail Ambrosius Chocolatier on Atwood Ave. is my favorite!';
12.         break;
13.     case 'laotian':
14.         echo 'Lao Laan Xang on Atwood Ave. is the best!';
15.         break;
16.     default:
17.         echo 'There are so many great places to eat in Madison!!';
18.         break;
19. }
```

The switch statement will contain several case statements with each *case* ending in a colon (:). The code statements following the colon (:) will be executed upon the case matching the variable specified in the parenthesis following the switch up until the first break statement is encountered. Therefore, it is very important (in most cases) to have a break statement separating your case statements. Note that it is a best practice to always have a default case, even if you do not expect your default case to be executed. It can be very helpful in debugging and error handling.

## Compound Conditional Logic Using Logical Operators

We can create quite complex conditions by combining them using various logical operators.

### Logical Operators

PHP defines several logical operators. Here is a table of them:

| Operator | Example | Meaning | Result |
|----------|---------|---------|--------|
| && | $a && $b | AND | TRUE if *both* $a AND $b are **TRUE** |
| \|\| | $a \|\| $b | OR | TRUE if *either* $a OR $b is **TRUE** |
| ! | !$a | NOT | TRUE if $a is **NOT TRUE** |
| xor | $a xor $b | XOR | TRUE if *either* $a OR $b is **TRUE**, but not *both*. (operates at different precedence) |
| and | $a and $b | AND | TRUE if *both* $a AND $b are **TRUE**. (operates at different precedence) |
| or | $a or $b | OR | TRUE if *either* $a OR $b is **TRUE**. (operates at different precedence) |

Note that the use of and, or, and xor use a lower order of operator precedence[3] than &&
and ||. I do not recommend using and & or, but prefer && and || for a couple of reasons. The
first is as mentioned, or & and operate at different precedences and would almost always
require the use parenthesis for correct use. Second, most every modern programming
language has standardized on the use of || for logical OR and && for logical AND. Regarding
xor, it would be nice if ^^ were used as a standardized symbol for logical XOR and it oper-
ated at the same precedence level as && and ||, however most programming languages do not
have a logical XOR symbol. A good solution to this problem that operates at the same level
of precedence would be: !$a != !$b

### Compound Conditional Statements

The combining of logical operators within conditional statements can be quite handy and
add to the readability of your code. Consider the problem of executing some code only if a
number is within a certain range. Suppose we want to assign a letter grade of "B" only if a

---

[3]   operator precedence: *http://php.net/language.operators.precedence*

student gets a score of between 80 and 90 (inclusive) on a test. We might solve this problem with the code in Listing 7.7.

## Listing 7.7.

```
1. $letter_grade = NULL;
2.
3. if ($score >= 80)
4. {
5.     if ($score <= 90)
6.     {
7.         $letter_grade = 'B';
8.     }
9. }
```

A better, and more readable solution, would be to use the logical operator && to eliminate the interior if:

```
$letter_grade = NULL;

if ($score >= 80 && $score <= 90)
{
    $letter_grade = 'B';
}
```

Using logical AND to create compound conditional statements is often used when matching inclusive range values. Conversely, the use of logical OR is used in a compound conditional statement when you want to exclude a certain range. Consider the problem of applying a ten percent discount for people that are either children or senior citizens. For this example let's arbitrarily say someone is a child if they are under 18 years old and a senior citizen if they are 55 years or older:

```
$child_or_senior_discount_applies = false;

if ($age < 18 || $age >= 55)
{
    $child_or_senior_discount_applies = true;
}
```

## Exercises

Create a script comparisons.php for the following:

1.  Use $x = random_int(1,10) to pick a number between 1 and 10. Output the value of $x. Then indicate if it is between 3 and 7 inclusive.

2.  Use $x = random_int(1,10) to pick a number between 1 and 10. Output the value of $x. Indicate if it's less than 3, between 3 and 7 inclusive, or greater than 7.

3.  Redo the previous exercise using compound conditional statements.

# Chapter

# 8

# Verifying Variables and Type Checking

*"A C program is like a fast dance on a newly waxed dance floor by people carrying razors."*

*– Waldi Ravens*

## Verifying Variables

PHP is most often used for developing web applications. As such, you need to get data from your form entries. For security reasons and standard practice, you want to verify the content of this input. Maybe you want to check if a user entered anything at all into a field. You could use == to check for empty strings, however it is better to use the built-in PHP functions isset()[1] and empty()[2]. isset() checks that a variable exists and is set. empty() checks that a variable has any contents. See Listing 8.1.

Listing 8.1.

```
1.  <?php
2.  $word1 = 'flibertigibbits'; // $word1 is set, but not empty
3.  $word2 = '';                // $word2 is set, but it is also empty
4.
5.  if (isset($word1))
6.  {
7.      echo '$word1 is set<br />';
8.  }
9.  else
10. {
11.     echo '$word1 is NOT set<br />';
12. }
13.
14. if (empty($word1))
15. {
16.     echo '$word1 is empty<br />';
17. }
18. else
19. {
20.     echo '$word1 is NOT empty<br />';
21. }
22.
23. if (isset($word2))
24. {
25.     echo '$word2 is set<br />';
26. }
27. else
28. {
29.     echo '$word2 is NOT set<br />';
30. }
31.
```

[1]  isset(): *https://php.net/isset*
[2]  empty(): *https://php.net/empty*

```
32. if (empty($word2))
33. {
34.     echo '$word2 is empty<br />';
35. }
36. else
37. {
38.     echo '$word2 is NOT empty<br />';
39. }
40.
41. if (isset($word3))
42. {
43.     echo '$word3 is set<br />';
44. }
45. else
46. {
47.     echo '$word3 is NOT set<br />'; // $word3 doesn't exist so it is not set
48. }
49.
50. if (empty($word3))
51. {
52.     echo '$word3 is empty<br />'; // $word3 is considered empty although it doesn't exist
53. }
54. else
55. {
56.     echo '$word3 is NOT empty<br />';
57. }
```

This outputs:

```
$word1 is set
$word1 is NOT empty
$word2 is set
$word2 is empty
$word3 is NOT set
$word3 is empty
```

## Verifying and Checking Variable Types

Since PHP is a dynamically typed language, you might also want to use some of the built-in functions[3] to verify the types of PHP variables:

| Function | Type Checked | Explanation |
|----------|--------------|-------------|
| is_bool() | boolean | returns true if parameter is a boolean |
| is_int() | integer | returns true if parameter is an integer |
| is_float() | float | returns true if parameter is a float |
| is_string() | string | returns true if parameter is a string |
| is_scalar() | scalar data types | returns true if parameter is a scalar type, any of the above |

Listing 8.2 shows how to check for types.

### Listing 8.2.

```
1.  <?php
2.  $bool_value = false;
3.  $int_value = 42;
4.  $float_value = 37.4;
5.  $string_value = "The answer to life, the universe, and everything";
6.
7.  if (is_bool($bool_value))
8.  {
9.      echo '$bool_value IS a boolean data type<br/>';
10. }
11.
12. if (is_int($int_value))
13. {
14.     echo '$int_value IS an integer data type<br/>';
15. }
16.
17. if (is_float($float_value))
18. {
19.     echo '$float_value IS a floating point data type<br/>';
20. }
21.
22. if (is_string($string_value))
23. {
24.     echo '$string_value IS a string data type<br/>';
25. }
```

---

[3]  built-in functions: https://php.net/book.var

This code outputs:

```
$bool_value IS a boolean data type
$int_value IS an integer data type
$float_value IS a floating point data type
$string_value IS a string data type
```

Listing 8.3 is an example of checking variables if they are scalar types.

## Listing 8.3.

```php
1.  <?php
2.
3.  $a_word = "serendipity";
4.  $some_words = array("some", "random", "words");
5.
6.  if (is_scalar($a_word))
7.  {
8.      echo '$a_word IS a scalar variable<br/>';
9.  }
10.
11. if (!is_scalar($some_words))
12. {
13.     echo '$some_words IS NOT a scalar variable<br/>';
14. }
```

This outputs:

```
$a_word IS a scalar variable
$some_words IS NOT a scalar variable
```

> *Note that Booleans, integers, floats, and strings are scalar types. Arrays, objects, callables, and resources are not.*

It is also sometimes handy to use gettype()[4] to determine the type of a variable. Consider the following code that outputs an HTML table of several PHP variable types, their values, and the gettype() response. See Listing 8.4.

---

[4] gettype(): *https://php.net/gettype*

## Listing 8.4.

```php
1.  <?php
2.
3.  class Car {}
4.
5.  $boolean = true;
6.  $integer = 123;
7.  $integer_negative = -13;
8.  $float_double = 12.35;
9.  $string = "Hello World";
10. $array = array('one', 'fish', 'two', 'fish', 'red', 'fish');
11. $object = new Car();
12. $null = NULL;
13. ?>
14.
15. <table border='1px solid;'>
16.   <tr>
17.     <th>Type</th>
18.     <th>Value</th>
19.     <th>gettype() response</th>
20.   </tr>
21.   <tr>
22.     <td>Boolean</td>
23.     <td><?= $boolean ?></td>
24.     <td><?= gettype($boolean); ?></td>
25.   </tr>
26.   <tr>
27.     <td>Integer</td>
28.     <td><?= $integer ?></td>
29.     <td><?= gettype($integer); ?></td>
30.   </tr>
31.   <tr>
32.     <td>Integer Negative</td>
33.     <td><?= $integer_negative ?></td>
34.     <td><?= gettype($integer_negative); ?></td>
35.   </tr>
36.   <tr>
37.     <td>Float</td>
38.     <td><?= $float_double ?></td>
39.     <td><?= gettype($float_double); ?></td>
40.   </tr>
41.   <tr>
42.     <td>String</td>
43.     <td><?= $string ?></td>
44.     <td><?= gettype($string); ?></td>
45.   </tr>
46.   <tr>
47.     <td>Array</td>
48.     <td><?= implode(',', $array); ?></td>
49.     <td><?= gettype($array); ?></td>
50.   </tr>
```

```
51.    <tr>
52.      <td>Object</td>
53.      <td><?php print_r($object); ?></td>
54.      <td><?= gettype($object); ?></td>
55.    </tr>
56.    <tr>
57.      <td>Null</td>
58.      <td><?php print_r($null); ?></td>
59.      <td><?= gettype($null); ?></td>
60.    </tr>
61. </table>
```

Figure 8.1 shows the output.

| Type | Value | gettype() response |
|---|---|---|
| Boolean | 1 | boolean |
| Integer | 123 | integer |
| Integer Negative | -13 | integer |
| Float | 12.35 | double |
| String | Hello World | string |
| Array | one,fish,two,fish,red,fish | array |
| Object | Car Object ( ) | object |
| Null | | NULL |

Figure 8.1.

# Exercises

Create a script types.php for the following:

1. Write and run the code in Listing 8.4 using gettype().
2. Change the values of the variables in Listing 8.4 and run it again to see if the output changes.

# Chapter

# 9

# Looping

*"They don't make bugs like Bunny anymore."*

*– Olav Mjelde*

Looping in PHP is used to run a block of code either a predetermined number of times or until a specific condition is reached. When looping a predetermined number of times, this is known as a counting loop. We don't know how many times a code block will repeat, but we know the condition for ending the repetition. This state is known as a sentinel loop.

There are four loop structures in PHP.

1. for
2. while
3. do/while
4. foreach

for and while loops are the most common looping structures in all programming languages.

## Counting Loops

for and foreach are considered counting loops. They repeat a block of code based on a counter variable or the number of items in a collection.

### for Loops

A for loop has three clauses separated by two semi-colons (;). We call the first clause the "initializer." It is executed only the first time upon encountering the loop. The second clause is called the "conditional" and is executed every time the compiler encounters the loop. The last clause is called the "incrementer" and is used to either increment or decrement a variable upon completing a loop iteration.

The syntax looks like this:

```
for (_initializer_; _conditional_; _incrementer_)
{
    _code to execute_
}
```

Listing 9.1 is a simple for loop that adds ten to a variable ten times.

## Listing 9.1.

```
1. $looping_value = 0;
2. $counter;
3.
4. for ($counter = 0; $counter < 10; $counter++)
5. {
6.    $looping_value += 10;
7. }
8.
9. echo "After $counter times through the loop, looping_value = $looping_value";
```

This outputs:

```
After 10 times through the loop, looping_value = 100
```

It is important to note when incrementing a variable in a loop, the variable to increment (in this case, $looping_value) must be initialized. Otherwise, you end up with a NULL value as your final result. This bug is common in looping. Also, note the incrementer (in this case, $counter) will be set to 10 because the last successful iteration of the loop increments the variable to the next value. This final value causes the loop to exit—the incrementer at this point no longer passes the conditional expression with a value of true.

## foreach Loops

The foreach loop is a convenient way to iterate through all values in an array without the need for indexing each array item. The foreach loop has two values separated by the word as. The first value is the actual array you will iterate over. The second value is an arbitrary variable name used for accessing each element of the array from the beginning to the end.

The syntax looks like this:

```
foreach (_array_ as _array_element_)
{
   _code to be executed_
}
```

Here is a simple foreach loop that outputs each value in an array:

```
$colors = array('red', 'green', 'blue', 'orange');

foreach ($colors  as $color)
{
   echo "The current color is $color<br/>";
}
```

This loop produces this output:

```
The current color is red
The current color is green
The current color is blue
The current color is orange
```

# Sentinel Loops

while and do/while are sentinel loops. They execute until some condition is false.

## while Loops

When new programmers learn about looping, they are first taught how to use the while loop because it only has one clause and is the simplest loop to create. In fact, it is typically shown as a counting loop:

```php
$looping_value = 0;
$counter = 0;

while ($counter < 10)
{
    $looping_value += 10;
    $counter++;
}
```

This example, however, is not the best use of a while loop because the programmer has to separately initialize the counter variable and then remember to increment the counter variable at the bottom of the loop. The for loop was designed to be used as a counting loop.

> *It's essential to ensure your loops terminate. If not, you create an infinite loop that only ends if PHP's max execution time is reached.*

The proper use of the while loop is to continue executing a block of code until a particular event occurs.

Let us assume we have a MySQL database that contains product information stored in a table. Let us say we want to output the product name and unit price for every row in the table, but we don't know how many rows it contains. We just want to output all of them.

PHP offers several functions for storing and retrieving data in MySQL databases. When querying a database, we get an associative array returned that contains the whole result set. This result set needs to be passed into a function (mysqli_fetch_array()) that returns the next row in the record set as an associative array that uses the field names as element references for the values contained for this row. Each subsequent call to mysqli_fetch_array() returns the next row until there are no more rows left in the record set. When there are no more rows in the record set, NULL is returned, which allows you to exit a loop. Listing 9.2 an example of a while loop.

## Listing 9.2.

```
1.  <html>
2.      <head>
3.          <title>Fetching Multiple Rows</title>
4.      </head>
5.      <body>
6.          <?php
7.              $dbc = mysqli_connect('localhost', 'testuser', 'testuser', 'northwind')
8.                  or trigger_error('Error connecting to MySQL server.', E_USER_ERROR);
9.
10.             $query = "SELECT ProductName, UnitPrice FROM Products";
11.
12.             $result = mysqli_query($dbc, $query)
13.                 or trigger_error('Error querying database.', E_USER_ERROR);
14.         ?>
15.         <table border='1px solid;'>
16.             <tr><th>Product Name</th>
17.                 <th>Unit Price</th></tr>
18.         <?php
19.             while($row = mysqli_fetch_array($result))
20.             {
21.                 echo '<tr><td>' . $row['ProductName'] . '</td><td>'
22.                     . $row['UnitPrice'] . '</td></tr>';
23.             }
24.             mysqli_close($dbc);
25.         ?>
26.         </table>
27.     </body>
28. </html>
```

Figure 9.1 shows the table of product information from the database using a `while` loop.

| Product Name | Unit Price |
|---|---|
| Northwind Traders Chai | 18.0000 |
| Northwind Traders Syrup | 10.0000 |
| Northwind Traders Cajun Seasoning | 22.0000 |
| Northwind Traders Olive Oil | 21.3500 |
| Northwind Traders Boysenberry Spread | 25.0000 |
| Northwind Traders Dried Pears | 30.0000 |
| Northwind Traders Curry Sauce | 40.0000 |

> We will look at *creating and using functions* and *working with databases* in upcoming chapters.

Figure 9.1.

`do/while`[1] loops are helpful if you can guarantee you will enter the loop at least once. In PHP, you can rarely guarantee this condition. Therefore it is seldom used.

## Exiting and Continuing a Loop

Occasionally, you will want to either exit a loop early or continue iterating through a loop but skip executing some code for the rest of the current iteration. PHP offers the `break` and `continue` commands for this.

### break

Use the `break` command in a loop if you want to exit a loop. Listing 9.3 is an example that exits a `foreach` loop if an element in an array equals `finished`.

### Listing 9.3.

```php
1. <?php
2. $random_words = ['happy', 'sad', 'finished', 'anxious', 'ecstatic'];
3.
4. foreach ($random_words as $word)
5. {
6.     if ($word == 'finished')
7.     {
8.         break;
9.     }
10.     echo "$word<br/>";
11. }
```

Here's the output:

```
happy
sad
```

[1] `do/while`: *http://php.net/control-structures.do.while*

## continue

Use the continue command in a loop if you want to skip the rest of the current iteration and continue to the next. See Listing 9.4 for an example that skips every third iteration of a loop.

### Listing 9.4.

```php
1. <?php
2. $random_words = ['one', 'two', 'three', 'anxious', 'ecstatic'];
3.
4. for ($i = 1; $i <= 9; i++ )
5. {
6.     if ($i % 3)
7.     {
8.         continue;
9.     }
10.
11.     echo "$i<br/>";
12. }
```

This loop produces the following output:

```
1
2
4
5
7
8
```

# Exercises

Create a script loops.php for the following:

1. Write a loop to count from one to ten and output each value in one column. In a second column, output the square of the number.

2. Use a foreach loop to output your list of book titles from arrays.php in Chapter 6.

# Chapter

# 10

## Functions

*"Walking on water and developing software from a specification are easy if both are frozen."*

*– Edward V. Berard*

It is very easy to write code and continue to add functionality to it. The problem is that our program code becomes too large and unwieldy. It is common to write code modularized into functions and limit that functionality to a specific task. Doing so allows us to reuse these modules throughout our program. Functions also give us the ability to pass in arguments and return results.

## Simple Function

The simplest function takes no arguments and does not return anything; it just performs some functionality. Let's say you want a function that will output the greeting, "Welcome to my Website!" you display for every page of your website. Here is what it might look like:

```
function outputGreetingToWebsite()
{
    echo "<h1>Welcome to my Website!</h1>";
}
```

When creating a function in PHP, you always start using the function keyword. Next, you want to give your function a good name. Since your function is invoked to do something, it is usually a good idea to start the name of your function with a verb. In this case, we want to output a greeting to the website. Naming your function as specifically as possible helps with the readability and maintainability of our code. Therefore outputGreetingToWebsite is a good name. Although not specified in the PHP Standards, I usually like to name my functions using something called "camel case." As you can see by the above example, we start the first word of the function using a lowercase letter, then with each subsequent word joined together in the function, we capitalize the first character of the joined word. Next, the function defines parameters that are passed into the function in between a set of parenthesis. In this case, we do not have any parameters to pass, so we will just use an empty set of parenthesis. Next, the code within the function is contained within two curly braces ({}). Additionally, each time a new opening curly brace is encountered, you will want to indent your code. I usually use four spaces for indentation levels and double indentation (eight spaces) for line continuations.

It is also a good idea to organize our functions. Later, when I talk about object-oriented programming, we will put functions (called methods) into something called a "class." For now, let's assume we have several functions used to output information to our website collected into a single PHP script called outputToWebsite.php.

When we want to invoke or call our function somewhere else in our code (like in another PHP script), we need to do a couple of things. First, we need to make sure we include the code where our function is defined. We do that using the require_once() statement and include the name of the script containing the function we want to use inside a set of quotes:

```php
<?php
require_once('outputToWebsite.php')
```

Next, we call our function. In the example below, let's call it twice:

```php
outputGreetingToWebsite();
outputGreetingToWebsite();
```

# Welcome to my Website!

# Welcome to my Website!

Figure 10.1.

The output of calling the function twice looks like Figure 10.1.

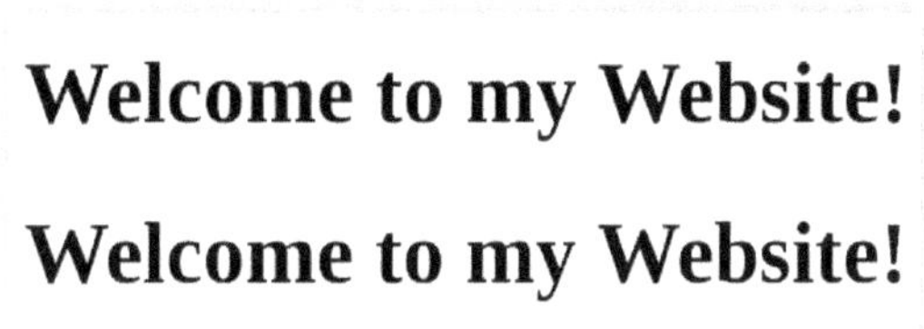

## Function Parameters/Arguments

Functions can also take parameters. Let's say we want to create a function that adds two numbers as arguments to the function. Let's call this function addTwoNumbers. We need two parameters in between the parenthesis separated by a comma. These variables are parameters to the function and are considered local variables scoped to the function. It is a good idea to be descriptive if you can with the name of these parameters as well:

```php
function addTwoNumbers($num1, $num2)
{
    $sum = $num1 + $num2;
    echo "$num1 + $num2 = $sum<br/>";
}
```

When we call this function, we need to pass in two arguments to this function in the same order they are defined in the function:

```php
addTwoNumbers(4, 5);
```

This results in the output:

```
4 + 5 = 9
```

This will also work when passing in variables:

```
$the_first_number = -2;
$the_second_number = 5;
addTwoNumbers($the_first_number, $the_second_number);
```

Resulting in the output:

```
-2 + 5 = 3
```

When calling the function, the values passed in are considered arguments to the function. However, from the function's perspective, the values are considered parameters. I don't think this bit of Computer Science will get you into any trouble if you happen to mix these two perspectives up. When you call the function, the values of the arguments (whether literal values or variable values) are copied to the function's parameter variables.

## Returning Values from a Function

Finally, we can write functions so that they return results to us. Expanding upon our adding two numbers example above, let's modify this function. Instead of echoing out the results of the function, we can return the result and allow the code that called the function to do whatever it wants with the result. First, let's change the name of this function to sum since this would be a more accurate name for what the function is doing. The only modification we need to make to the code is to replace the echo statement to return the variable $sum:

```
function sum($num1, $num2)
{
    $sum = $num1 + $num2;
    return $sum;
}
```

Now when we call this function we can create a variable that will hold the result of the call and set it equal to the call of the function:

```
$first_num = 5;
$second_num = 7;

$sum_of_two_numbers = sum($first_num, $second_num);
echo "The result of adding $first_num and $second_num is $sum_of_two_numbers<br/>";
```

This results in the following output:

```
The result of adding 5 and 7 is 12
```

> *If a function returns a result, and you fail to assign that result to a variable, the result is lost.*

# Further Advice On Writing Good Functions

As we close this chapter, I want to give advice regarding writing good functions. Writing functions is tricky, and it's more of an art than science, but it's also 90% common sense. Let's look at some advice for writing functions with high readability and maintainability.

## Global Variables are Evil!

I cannot overemphasize this point that global variables are evil. The problem with global variables is all of your code (at a minimum, the code within a single script) has access to it and could change its value. This practice makes debugging and maintenance difficult. Unfortunately, it is a lazy substitute for proper design.

In software design, it is a best practice to limit data exchanges between functions. In other words, we pass data into functions through arguments/parameters, and we get data out of functions through return values without affecting the rest of the program. You should not use the global keyword inside of a function or method in PHP.

### The Only Good Global is a Constant

This is not to say you cannot or should not have any global values. Constant values are a good use of global values because any code that needs them can access them. However, because it is constant, it cannot change. However, you want to be careful to limit the number of global constants to what is needed.

### Variable Scope

Variable scope is defined as what parts of your code can access which variables. Global scope is the outer- or top-most level.

### Scoping Operators ({})

In PHP (and most other programming languages), we limit the scope of variables using scoping operators ({}). For example, all function code is contained within a set of scoping operators:

```php
function sum($num1, $num2)
{
    $sum = $num1 + $num2;
    return $sum;
}
```

> *In the above example, the parameters $num1 and $num2 are defined outside the function scoping operators in the function signature. However, because we are defining a function, these parameters only have scope—that is, hold a value—within the function scoping operators. This is also true of variables defined within a for() loop.*

Therefore, variables created within a set of scoping operators can only be directly accessed by the code within these scoping variables. However, variables (and constants) defined outside of scoping operators are accessible by code within the scoping operators. Consider the example in Listing 10.1.

### Listing 10.1.

```php
1. <?php
2.
3. function doSomething()
4. {
5.     $value1 = 10;
6.
7.     if ($value1 >= 10)
8.     {
9.         $value2 = $value1;
10.    }
11.    else
12.    {
13.        $value3 = $value1;
14.    }
15.
16.    echo $value2; // This outputs an undefined value
17. }
```

In the code above on line 9, $value2 can access $value1 because $value1 is within $value2's scope. This is also true of $value3 on line 13. However, on line 16, we create a new variable called $value2 because the one created on line 9 went out of scope after encountering the closing scoping operator on line 10. The result of echoing out $value2 on line 16 is undefined.

*Scalers are Passed in by Value*

In PHP, arguments are passed to functions by value (i.e., a copy). Therefore you cannot modify the passed-in variable. The values of the arguments are copied to the parameters. Consider the following function and a call to it. See Listing 10.2.

## Listing 10.2.

```php
1.  <?php
2.  function incrementValueNotWorking($value)
3.  {
4.      $value++;
5.  }
6.
7.  $number = 42;
8.
9.  echo "Before function call: $number<br/>";
10.
11. incrementValueNotWorking($number);
12.
13. echo "After function call: $number";
```

Because scaler values are passed by value, the output of $number on lines 9 and 13 are the same, thus failing to increment $number. What happens if we re-write the code like Listing 10.3?

## Listing 10.3.

```php
1.  <?php
2.  function incrementValue($value)
3.  {
4.      $value++;
5.
6.      return $value;
7.  }
8.
9.  $number = 42;
10.
11. echo "Before function call: $number<br/>";
12.
13. $number = incrementValue($number);
14.
15. echo "After function call: $number";
```

Now the output of `$number` on line 15 will be one greater than on line 11.

### Functions Should Do One Thing and One Thing Only.

When designing your functions, make sure they do one thing. First, it lowers the complexity of your code, and second, it increases the reusability of your code.

### Name Your Functions Completely and Succinctly.

Back in the early days of programming, we did not have the luxury of adequately naming our functions because of the limited amount of memory available to program code. I can remember sitting on the floor with reams of code printed out, trying to decipher the meaning of functions called x and y as if I were using a secret decoder ring. Today, there is no excuse for poorly naming your functions.

You want to name your functions completely and succinctly because it makes your code self documenting. For example, if I needed to write a function for calculating the state income tax for an employee, a good name for this function might be: `calculateEmployeeStateIncomeTax()`. I know. It's long, but there is no ambiguity as to what this function is intended to do.

As mentioned earlier, a good template to follow is to name your function using a verb+noun with adjectives sprinkled in as needed. If your function returns a boolean `true` or `false` (your function answers a question), consider naming it something like `isX()` or `hasY()`. Look for other conventions like this in the projects your work in. For example, some projects use `fetchQ()` to indicate a method that works with the database or an external API.

## Exercises

Create a script `functions.php` for the following:

1. Create functions to add, subtract, divide, multiply two numbers that return the result. Echo the result of each operation and the two input values.
2. Create a function that accepts two arguments: a total and a sales tax rate expressed as a percent (so 5% sales tax is expressed as `0.05`). Return the sales tax owed on the total. Then echo the total, the tax rate, and the sales tax owed.

# Chapter

# 11

# Working with HTML Forms

*"Debugging is twice as hard as writing the code in the first place. There-*
*fore, if you write the code as cleverly as possible, you are, by definition, not*
*smart enough to debug it."*

*-Brian W. Kernighan.*

PHP was designed from the beginning to be a Web programming language. Working with data entered into HTML forms is an excellent example of how easy it is to develop Web applications with PHP. This chapter discusses how data gets from your HTML forms into your PHP code and how to work with it. We will create a simple form and output what the user enters into the form back to the web page as a greeting.

## A Simple Form

Let's start by creating a simple form. Figure 11.1 shows a simple form for entering the full name.

Listing 11.1 is the HTML markup for our form.

### Listing 11.1.

**Enter Full Name**

First name:

Last name:

Submit Name

Figure 11.1.

```
1.  <html>
2.    <head>
3.      <title>Form for Entering Full Name</title>
4.    </head>
5.    <body>
6.      <h2>Enter Full Name</h2>
7.      <form action="postfullname.php" method="POST">
8.        First name:<br/>
9.        <input name="first_name"/><br/>
10.       Last name:<br/>
11.       <input name="last_name"/><br/>
12.       <p>
13.       <input type="submit" value="Submit Name" />
14.     </form>
15.   </body>
16. </html>
```

Note the value of the name attributes for the input elements of the form. In our PHP code, we get access to data the user enters into the input field through the value of the name attribute. These are called form variables. We access them using these values, which are first_name for what the user enters into the input field for the first name and last_name for what the user enters for the last name.

Note that once the user selects the submit button, the form sends an HTTP POST message to the URL location identified by the action attribute. In this case, it is the PHP script postfull-name.php residing on the local server in the current directory. All the data from the form will be sent via the POST message and be available to this script.

# Processing Our Form and Outputting Back to the Web Page

Once the form is submitted, the browser sends the form data to our postfullname.php script. Here, we take the form data, process a greeting out of it, and then display it on the webpage.

Assuming I enter "Ken" for the first name and "Marks" for the last name, I would like the greeting to look like Figure 11.2. Our postfullname.php script is shown in Listing 11.2.

### Listing 11.2.

```
1.  <html>
2.  <head>
3.      <title>Full Name</title>
4.  </head>
5.  <body>
6.  <h2>Greetings!</h2>
7.  <?php
8.  $first_name = $_POST['first_name'];
9.  $last_name  = $_POST['last_name'];
10.
11. echo "Hello " . $first_name . " " . $last_name . ". Thanks for submitting the form!";
12. ?>
13. </body>
14. </html>
```

## Greetings!

Hello Ken Marks. Thanks for submitting the form!

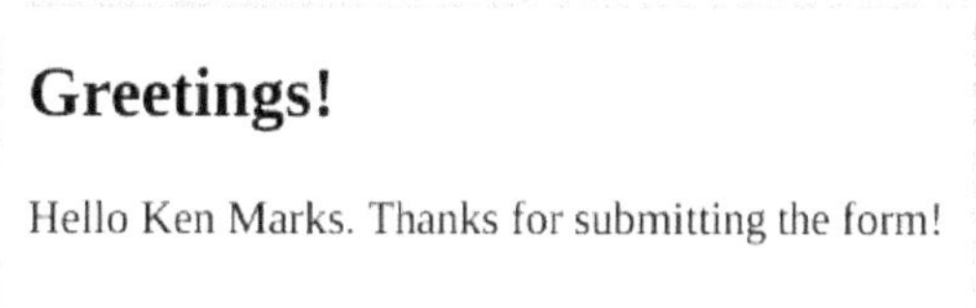

Figure 11.2.

There are several things I want you to notice. First, PHP was designed to be mixed with HTML. You can move in and out of PHP and HTML with ease. Second, if you have any PHP code in your script, you need to name the script using the .php extension.

### $_POST Superglobal Variable

$_POST is a special variable built into PHP that holds form data, and it is available throughout your entire set of scripts as a result of an HTTP POST. $_POST is an associative array. You access the form data by using the name attributes from the form as associated keys into the $_POST superglobal array.

Looking at the postfullname.php script, you can see that $_POST['first_name'] comes from the input element name attribute identified by first_name (<input name="first_name"/>) from postfullname.html. Likewise, $_POST['last_name'] comes from the input element name attribute identified by last_name (<input name="last_name"/>).

You will also notice that I assigned the $_POST['first_name'] and $_POST['last_name'] to local variables. Doing so is not necessary. However, it is often done to aid in the readability of the code. I want to point out that using echo to output HTML to a web page should be used sparingly as it can be cumbersome to create HTML output using echo. Listing 11.3 is a modified example of our postfullname.php script showing another method of moving in and out of HTML and PHP to output HTML.

## Listing 11.3.

```
1.  <html>
2.    <head>
3.      <title>Full Name</title>
4.    </head>
5.    <body>
6.      <h2>Greetings!</h2>
7.        Hello <?= $_POST['first_name'] . " " . $_POST['last_name'] ?>
8.        Thanks for submitting the form!
9.        <br/>
10.       <?php print_r($_POST) ?>
11.    </body>
12. </html>
```

Instead of using echo we use the PHP short tag `<?=`. This syntax is a shortcut for `<?php echo`, which is incredibly convenient since you will more than likely be using PHP to process data before turning it into HTML for output.

One other thing to notice about this simplified example is that I removed the local variables and directly access the appropriate elements using the $_POST superglobal.

One final note about using the $_POST superglobal or working with arrays in general. Often you need to inspect the contents of an array. For example, it might be nice to know if you got what you expected from your form. You can use the developer tools that come with your browser for this (most developers do this), but this only shows you what the client will send. It is handy to quickly output the contents of an array from your PHP script under development. You can easily do that by using the function print_r()[1].

If I add the following lines just before the closing </body> tag of the above script, I get the output shown in Figure 11.3.

```
    <br/>
    <?php print_r($_POST) ?>
  </body>
</html>
```

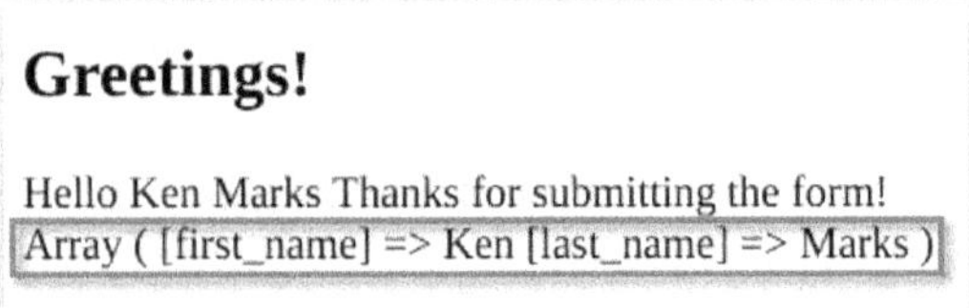

**Greetings!**

Hello Ken Marks Thanks for submitting the form!
Array ( [first_name] => Ken [last_name] => Marks )

Figure 11.3.

---

[1]  print_r(): https://php.net/print_r

# Cleaning It Up Using a Self Referencing Page

One thing to note when running this small web program is that we first navigate to a URL that contains our form. Then after submitting our form, we navigate to a second page containing our PHP code. We don't have to do this, and it would be better if we could somehow contain the entire form into a single script and call ourselves when the user is ready to submit the form.

We can accomplish this by creating what's known as a self-referencing page. To do this, we need to use another superglobal provided by PHP that references the current web page URL called $_SERVER['PHP_SELF'].

Let's use our above example of outputting a greeting to a user who enters their first and last name.

The script is made up of two sections: the form and the output of the greeting. For this program, we want to output the form first. Then when the user submits the form, we want to output the greeting without the form. Note that some designs will have you output the greeting along with the form again (after submitting), but for this example, we want to output the greeting without the form once the user submits it.

This behavior requires a little conditional logic (if/else), so I suggest making a simple decision tree or some pseudo-code:

```
IF user submitted form
    Output greeting with first and last name.
ELSE IF
    Output first and last name form
END IF
```

So how do we know if the user has submitted the form? We know this if $_POST['submit'] exists or not by passing it as an argument to the function isset(). If we get to this page without the user pressing the **Submit Name** button (i.e., this is the first time the page was rendered), then $_POST['submit'] is not set and is NULL. Let's take a look at the modified script that is now self-referencing. See Listing 11.4.

## Listing 11.4.

```
1.  <html>
2.    <head>
3.      <title>Form for Entering Full Name</title>
4.    </head>
5.    <body>
6.      <?php if (!isset($_POST['submit'])) { ?>
7.        <h2>Enter Full Name</h2>
8.        <form action="<?= $_SERVER['PHP_SELF'] ?>" method="POST">
9.          First name:<br/>
10.         <input name="first_name"/><br/>
11.         Last name:<br/>
12.         <input name="last_name"/><br/>
13.         <p>
14.         <input type="submit" name="submit" value="Submit Name" />
15.       </form>
16.     <?php } else { ?>
17.       <h2>Greetings!</h2>
18.         Hello <?= $_POST['first_name'] . " " . $_POST['last_name'] ?>
19.         Thanks for submitting the form!
20.     <?php } ?>
21.   </body>
23. </html>
```

The above code splits what to display in the body of the HTML document depending on whether the user has submitted the form. The first time this page is rendered, the user has not submitted the form, so $_POST['submit'] will not be set. As a result, all the HTML within the first if statement—which displays the form—is rendered to the page. None of the HTML from within the else statement will be rendered.

Once the user submits the form, the browser sends the HTTP POST to the very same script (as evidenced from the form's action attribute set to $_SERVER['PHP_SELF']). The script starts executing from the beginning. However, when the if statement is next encountered, it is false because the user did submit the form, and $_POST['submit'] is now set.

At this point, the code and HTML within the else statement will execute and render, respectively, which causes the greeting to be output to the web page (instead of the form).

Incidentally, $_SERVER[2] is another superglobal associative array provided by PHP. It contains information about the webserver and the execution environment. Be careful in using its contents because they depend on the server you use and how it's configured.

---

[2]  $_SERVER: *http://php.net/reserved.variables.server*

# Exercise: Badlibs, Part 1

1. Create the self-referencing `postfullname.php` script and ensure it works.
2. Create the "BadLibs" part 1 program.

This exercise is based on the popular game fill-in-the-blanks word game. Write a simple web application with a form that takes a: noun, verb, adjective, and adverb. Once the user submits the form, your application should join the noun, verb, adjective, and adverb into a funny sentence or short paragraph of your creation. For an extra challenge, consider making it a self-referencing form and making a more extensive story/paragraph by using more nouns, verbs, adjectives, and adverbs, etc.

Figure 11.4 is an example of what it might look like.

And Figure 11.5 is an example of the output.

Figure 11.4. Badlibs form

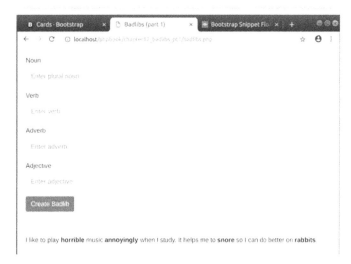

Figure 11.5. Badlibs output

# Chapter

# 12

# Inserting Data Into a MySQL Database

*"For a long time, it puzzled me how something so expensive, so leading edge could be so useless. And then it occurred to me that a computer is a stupid machine with the ability to do incredibly smart things, while computer programmers are smart people with the ability to do incredibly stupid things. They are, in short, a perfect match."*

*–Bill Bryson*

MySQL is the most popular Open-Source Standard Query Language[1] (SQL) database management system. A database provides a fast and reliable method for retrieving persistent information that can be stored and managed securely. PHP was designed to integrate seamlessly with databases, and PHP provides specific functions that simplify interacting with MySQL.

## Using the MySQL CLI

There are several tools available for interacting with your MySQL server. Some are easier to use than others and provide a web interface that makes interacting with your databases more intuitive. In the Writing your first PHP chapter, you saw how to install one of those visual tools called Adminer.

However, before getting too comfortable using Adminer, you should become familiar with the Command Line Interface (CLI) tool installed with every installation of the MySQL server. That is what we will use here.

First, you will want to open a Terminal window in your OS. Every time you bring up a new Terminal window, you start in your home directory (denoted by the ~) with the Bash shell running (indicated by the $ just before the cursor). The Bash shell is one common way we interact with our OS—commonly referred to as the command line.

To use the MySQL CLI_tool, type the following command in the Terminal:

```
sudo mysql
```

After entering your password, you should see Figure 12.1 displayed in your Terminal window.

You have left the Bash shell and are now in the MySQL CLI tool as denoted by the mysql> prompt preceding the cursor.

At this point, the tool is ready to respond to SQL commands. This book is not meant to be a complete resource for using MySQL, nor the topics around database design. For a complete

```
kmarks@ubuntu:~$ sudo mysql
[sudo] password for kmarks:
Welcome to the MySQL monitor.  Commands end with ; or \g.
Your MySQL connection id is 8
Server version: 8.0.21-0ubuntu0.20.04.4 (Ubuntu)

Copyright (c) 2000, 2020, Oracle and/or its affiliates. All rights reserved.

Oracle is a registered trademark of Oracle Corporation and/or its
affiliates. Other names may be trademarks of their respective
owners.

Type 'help;' or '\h' for help. Type '\c' to clear the current input statement.

mysql>
```

Figure 12.1.

---

[1]  Standard Query Language: https://en.wikipedia.org/wiki/SQL

reference guide on how to use SQL with MySQL, consult the MySQL documentation[2]—currently version 8.0 in the Ubuntu LTS release. More than likely, you will be interested in the SQL Statement Syntax[3].

You can quickly identify the version of your MySQL installation by typing the following command in the Bash shell (not the MySQL CLI). You should see output similar to Figure 12.2.

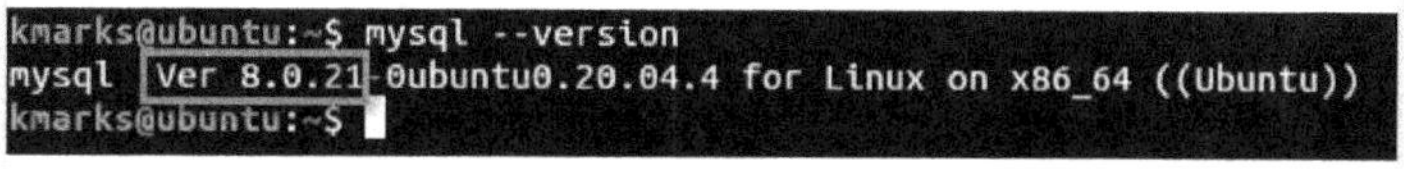

Figure 12.2.

```
mysql --version
```

## Creating the "Northwind" Database

To demonstrate some of the functionality of MySQL, let's download a famous sample database Microsoft created years ago for teaching people how to use the Access database application. Since then, it has been ported to support IIS and MySQL. The Northwind database holds sales, inventory, and employee data for the fictitious company called "Northwind Traders."

First, we need to create an empty database using SQL. We do that by typing the following command in the MySQL CLI tool (Figure 12.3).

Figure 12.3.

```
CREATE DATABASE northwind;
```

If you typed everything correctly, you should get a Query OK, 1 row affected message.

In chapter 2, we created a user called testuser. Let's grant privileges on the northwind database to testuser. Enter the following command (Figure 12.4).

```
GRANT ALL PRIVILEGES ON northwind.* TO 'testuser'@'localhost';
```

Exit the MySQL CLI tool by typing exit, and return to the Bash shell:

Figure 12.4.

---

[2] MySQL documentation: https://dev.mysql.com/doc/refman/8.0/en/
[3] SQL Statement Syntax: https://dev.mysql.com/doc/refman/8.0/en/sql-statements.html

## Loading Up the Northwind Database

Figure 12.5.

The Northwind database is contained in two SQL files; one containing the schema, the second containing the data. It is available to download from:

- https://raw.githubusercontent.com/jpwhite3/northwind-MySQL/master/northwind.sql
- https://raw.githubusercontent.com/jpwhite3/northwind-MySQL/master/northwind-data.sql

You can download them using wget in the Bash shell. I like to download files into a Downloads folder under my home folder. Once you have navigated to the folder where you want to download the Northwind SQL file, type the following commands:

```
wget https://raw.githubusercontent.com/jpwhite3/northwind-MySQL/master/northwind.sql
wget https://raw.githubusercontent.com/jpwhite3/northwind-MySQL/master/northwind-data.sql
```

You will see the output shown in Figure 12.6 after downloading the files and doing a directory listing (ls).

```
kmarks@ubuntu:~$ cd Downloads/
kmarks@ubuntu:~/Downloads$ wget https://raw.githubusercontent.com/jpwhite3/north
wind-MySQL/master/northwind.sql
--2021-02-03 13:31:44--  https://raw.githubusercontent.com/jpwhite3/northwind-My
SQL/master/northwind.sql
Resolving raw.githubusercontent.com (raw.githubusercontent.com)... 151.101.192.1
33, 151.101.128.133, 151.101.64.133, ...
Connecting to raw.githubusercontent.com (raw.githubusercontent.com)|151.101.192.
133|:443... connected.
HTTP request sent, awaiting response... 200 OK
Length: 19955 (19K) [text/plain]
Saving to: 'northwind.sql'

northwind.sql        100%[===================>]  19.49K  --.-KB/s    in 0.003s

2021-02-03 13:31:44 (7.26 MB/s) - 'northwind.sql' saved [19955/19955]

kmarks@ubuntu:~/Downloads$ wget https://raw.githubusercontent.com/jpwhite3/north
wind-MySQL/master/northwind-data.sql
--2021-02-03 13:31:53--  https://raw.githubusercontent.com/jpwhite3/northwind-My
SQL/master/northwind-data.sql
Resolving raw.githubusercontent.com (raw.githubusercontent.com)... 151.101.192.1
33, 151.101.128.133, 151.101.64.133, ...
Connecting to raw.githubusercontent.com (raw.githubusercontent.com)|151.101.192.
133|:443... connected.
HTTP request sent, awaiting response... 200 OK
Length: 149945 (146K) [text/plain]
Saving to: 'northwind-data.sql'

northwind-data.sql  100%[===================>] 146.43K  --.-KB/s    in 0.05s

2021-02-03 13:31:53 (2.97 MB/s) - 'northwind-data.sql' saved [149945/149945]

kmarks@ubuntu:~/Downloads$ ls
northwind-data.sql  northwind.sql
kmarks@ubuntu:~/Downloads$
```

Figure 12.6.

Now let's import the Northwind SQL schema and data files into the MySQL CLI tool by redirecting the Unix Standard Input from the keyboard to use the files we downloaded by typing the following commands in the Bash shell:

```
mysql -u testuser -p northwind < northwind.sql
mysql -u testuser -p northwind < northwind-data.sql
```

If everything works OK, in typical Unix fashion, we won't get any responses. See Figure 12.7.

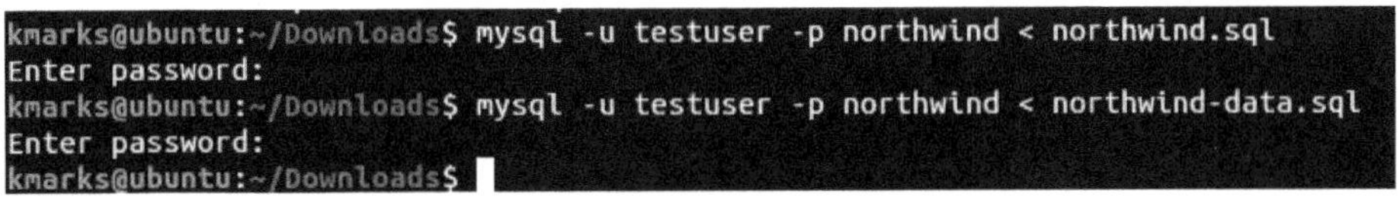

```
kmarks@ubuntu:~/Downloads$ mysql -u testuser -p northwind < northwind.sql
Enter password:
kmarks@ubuntu:~/Downloads$ mysql -u testuser -p northwind < northwind-data.sql
Enter password:
kmarks@ubuntu:~/Downloads$ 
```

Figure 12.7.

## Basic SQL Commands

The following sections will demonstrate some basic SQL commands we will use to work with databases and tables.

Let's log back into the MySQL CLI tool by typing in the Bash shell:

```
mysql -u testuser -p
```

### Show Databases

If we are interested in the names of the databases that are available to us, we can type the following SQL command:

```
SHOW DATABASES;
```

We should see the output in Figure 12.8.

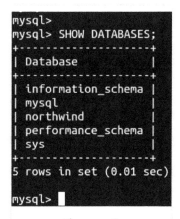

```
mysql>
mysql> SHOW DATABASES;
+--------------------+
| Database           |
+--------------------+
| information_schema |
| mysql              |
| northwind          |
| performance_schema |
| sys                |
+--------------------+
5 rows in set (0.01 sec)

mysql> 
```

Figure 12.8.

## 12. INSERTING DATA INTO A MySQL DATABASE

### Use a Databases

Let's verify we imported the Northwind database correctly. To work with a database, we need to issue an SQL command indicating we want to use it. At the mysql> prompt type:

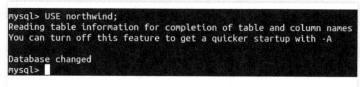

Figure 12.9.

```
USE northwind;
```

You should see something like Figure 12.9.

### Show Tables

We can show all the tables in the northwind database by issuing the following SQL command:

```
SHOW TABLES;
```

You should see output like Figure 12.10.

### Describe a Table

Let's say we are interested in finding out more information about the structure of the products table. We can describe all the fields (or columns) in a table by issuing the following SQL command:

```
DESCRIBE products;
```

Figure 12.11 shows the output.

DESCRIBEing a table shows the Field names in order, their data types, and other important information regarding the table.

Figure 12.10.

Figure 12.11.

## SELECTing from a Table

Selecting data from a table is incredibly powerful and allows us to retrieve rows and specific columns from a table based on criteria we specify in the SELECT statement.

If we are interested in retrieving ALL the rows and columns in the invoices table, we can issue the following command:

```
SELECT * FROM invoices;
```

And we will see a table with all our columns as in Figure 12.12.

```
mysql> SELECT * FROM invoices;
+----+----------+---------------------+----------+--------+----------+------------+
| id | order_id | invoice_date        | due_date | tax    | shipping | amount_due |
+----+----------+---------------------+----------+--------+----------+------------+
|  5 |       31 | 2006-03-22 16:08:59 | NULL     | 0.0000 |   0.0000 |     0.0000 |
|  6 |       32 | 2006-03-22 16:10:27 | NULL     | 0.0000 |   0.0000 |     0.0000 |
|  7 |       40 | 2006-03-24 10:41:41 | NULL     | 0.0000 |   0.0000 |     0.0000 |
|  8 |       39 | 2006-03-24 10:55:46 | NULL     | 0.0000 |   0.0000 |     0.0000 |
|  9 |       38 | 2006-03-24 10:56:57 | NULL     | 0.0000 |   0.0000 |     0.0000 |
| 10 |       37 | 2006-03-24 10:57:38 | NULL     | 0.0000 |   0.0000 |     0.0000 |
| 11 |       36 | 2006-03-24 10:58:40 | NULL     | 0.0000 |   0.0000 |     0.0000 |
| 12 |       35 | 2006-03-24 10:59:41 | NULL     | 0.0000 |   0.0000 |     0.0000 |
| 13 |       34 | 2006-03-24 11:00:55 | NULL     | 0.0000 |   0.0000 |     0.0000 |
| 14 |       33 | 2006-03-24 11:02:02 | NULL     | 0.0000 |   0.0000 |     0.0000 |
| 15 |       30 | 2006-03-24 11:03:00 | NULL     | 0.0000 |   0.0000 |     0.0000 |
| 16 |       56 | 2006-04-03 13:50:15 | NULL     | 0.0000 |   0.0000 |     0.0000 |
| 17 |       55 | 2006-04-04 11:05:04 | NULL     | 0.0000 |   0.0000 |     0.0000 |
| 18 |       51 | 2006-04-04 11:06:13 | NULL     | 0.0000 |   0.0000 |     0.0000 |
| 19 |       50 | 2006-04-04 11:06:56 | NULL     | 0.0000 |   0.0000 |     0.0000 |
| 20 |       48 | 2006-04-04 11:07:37 | NULL     | 0.0000 |   0.0000 |     0.0000 |
| 21 |       47 | 2006-04-04 11:08:14 | NULL     | 0.0000 |   0.0000 |     0.0000 |
| 22 |       46 | 2006-04-04 11:08:49 | NULL     | 0.0000 |   0.0000 |     0.0000 |
| 23 |       45 | 2006-04-04 11:09:24 | NULL     | 0.0000 |   0.0000 |     0.0000 |
| 24 |       79 | 2006-04-04 11:35:54 | NULL     | 0.0000 |   0.0000 |     0.0000 |
| 25 |       78 | 2006-04-04 11:36:21 | NULL     | 0.0000 |   0.0000 |     0.0000 |
| 26 |       77 | 2006-04-04 11:36:47 | NULL     | 0.0000 |   0.0000 |     0.0000 |
| 27 |       76 | 2006-04-04 11:37:09 | NULL     | 0.0000 |   0.0000 |     0.0000 |
| 28 |       75 | 2006-04-04 11:37:49 | NULL     | 0.0000 |   0.0000 |     0.0000 |
| 29 |       74 | 2006-04-04 11:38:11 | NULL     | 0.0000 |   0.0000 |     0.0000 |
| 30 |       73 | 2006-04-04 11:38:32 | NULL     | 0.0000 |   0.0000 |     0.0000 |
| 31 |       72 | 2006-04-04 11:38:53 | NULL     | 0.0000 |   0.0000 |     0.0000 |
| 32 |       71 | 2006-04-04 11:39:29 | NULL     | 0.0000 |   0.0000 |     0.0000 |
| 33 |       70 | 2006-04-04 11:39:53 | NULL     | 0.0000 |   0.0000 |     0.0000 |
| 34 |       69 | 2006-04-04 11:40:16 | NULL     | 0.0000 |   0.0000 |     0.0000 |
| 35 |       67 | 2006-04-04 11:40:38 | NULL     | 0.0000 |   0.0000 |     0.0000 |
| 36 |       42 | 2006-04-04 11:41:14 | NULL     | 0.0000 |   0.0000 |     0.0000 |
| 37 |       60 | 2006-04-04 11:41:45 | NULL     | 0.0000 |   0.0000 |     0.0000 |
| 38 |       63 | 2006-04-04 11:42:26 | NULL     | 0.0000 |   0.0000 |     0.0000 |
| 39 |       58 | 2006-04-04 11:43:08 | NULL     | 0.0000 |   0.0000 |     0.0000 |
+----+----------+---------------------+----------+--------+----------+------------+
35 rows in set (0.00 sec)

mysql>
```

Figure 12.12.

Let's say instead, we want to retrieve ALL the rows in the products table, but we only want data from the id, product_name, list_price, and reorder_level columns. We would issue the following command:

```
SELECT id, product_name, list_price, reorder_level FROM products;
```

You should see a potentially long list of rows as in Figure 12.13 and 12.14.

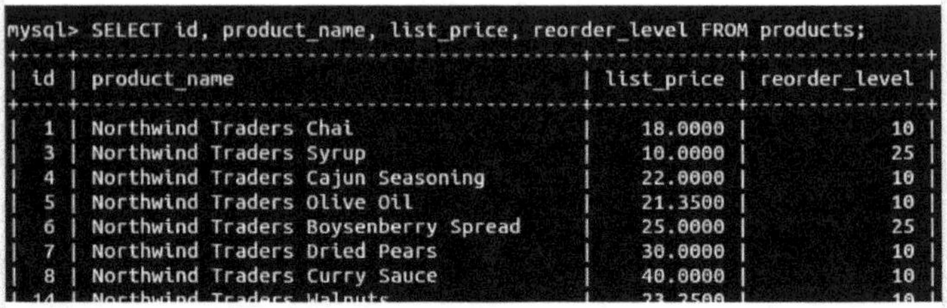

Or maybe we just want to retrieve the same information as above, but just products where the reorder level is greater than 25. We need to qualify the rows we are going to retrieve using a WHERE clause. Our query would look like this:

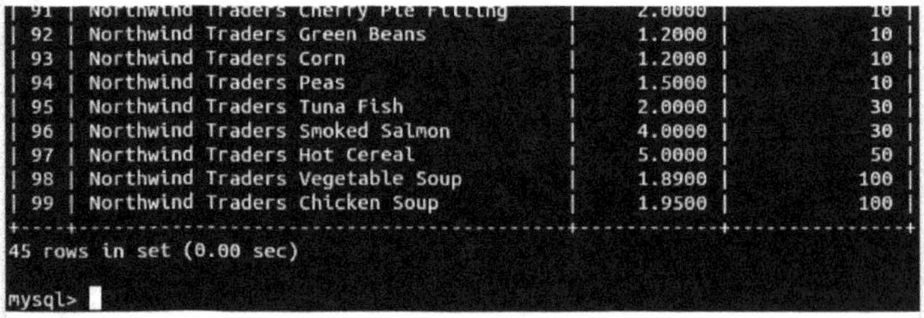

```
SELECT id, product_name,
list_price, reorder_level
FROM products
WHERE reorder_level > 25;
```

Figure 12.15 shows the matching rows.

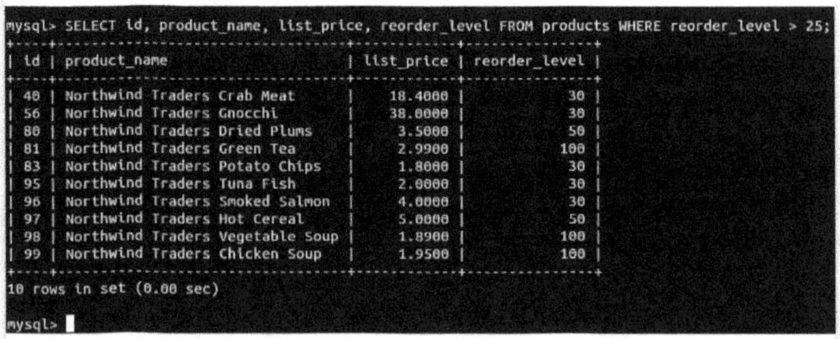

We can have multiple criteria in our WHERE clause as well by adding a boolean value. For example, we might be interested in only the products with a reorder_level greater than 20 AND less than 100. We would use a query like this:

```
SELECT id, product_name, list_
price, reorder_level
FROM products
WHERE reorder_level > 20 AND reorder_level < 100;
```

Figure 12.13.

Figure 12.14.

Figure 12.15.

And get the results shown in Figure 12.16.

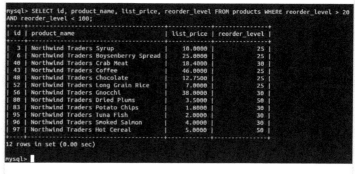

Figure 12.16.

There are far more examples of how to use SELECT[4]. If you want to dig in deeper, you should refer to the online documentation.

## Creating and Inserting Data

Creating tables using the MySQL CLI tool is pretty straightforward. As a simple example, let's create a database with one table for holding first and last names.

> *I use the following naming convention for naming databases, tables, and column or field names:*
>
> - *All names will be singular (not plural)*
> - *Database names will use StudlyCaps (e.g.* FullName*).*
> - *Table names will use camelCase (e.g.* fullName*).*
> - *Column/Field names will use snake_case (e.g.* first_name*).*

### Creating a Table

We want to create a table called fullName with fields for a first_name and a last_name. It is also a good idea to create a field for an id that gives each row a unique identifier. This id field will be created as a primary key. A field used as a primary key must be unique, cannot be repeated, must have a value (it cannot be NULL), and cannot be changed, and it should be efficient. Auto-incrementing integers make great primary keys.

First, let's exit the MySQL CLI tool as testuser, log back in to the MySQL CLI tool as sudo, and grant all privileges to this new database we'll call FullName to testuser. To create a new database and users, you generally have to log in as MySQL's root user.

```
exit
```

---

[4]  SELECT: *https://dev.mysql.com/doc/refman/8.0/en/select.html*

Then in Bash:

```
sudo mysql
```

Next, we create the user for our FullName database.

```
GRANT ALL PRIVILEGES ON FullName.* TO 'testuser'@'localhost';
FLUSH PRIVILEGES;
exit
```

Your MySQL command line should look similar to Figure 12.17.

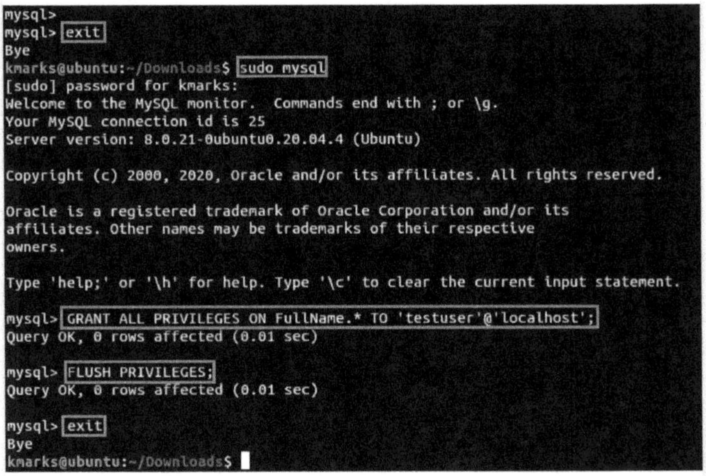

Now let's log back into the MySQL CLI tool as testuser:

```
mysql -u testuser -p
```

Next, let's create our database, which we need to call FullName. We'll do that with the following SQL command:

```
CREATE DATABASE FullName;
```

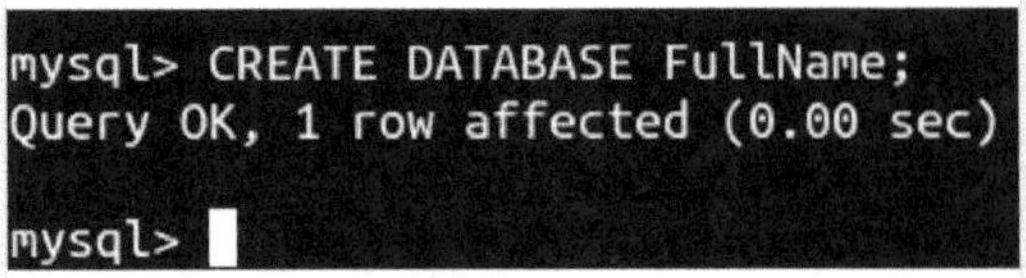

Figure 12.17.

Next, we need to USE our FullName database to work with it.

```
USE FullName;
```

Now let's create our fullName table using the following CREATE TABLE command for all the fields in our table using the following SQL command. You can type this all on one line. The CLI ignores returns and looks for a ; to terminate a command.

Figure 12.18.

Figure 12.19.

```
mysql> CREATE TABLE fullName ( id INT NOT NULL AUTO_INCREMENT, first_name varchar(20), last_name varchar(20), PRIMARY KEY (id) );
Query OK, 0 rows affected (0.05 sec)
```

Figure 12.20.

```
CREATE TABLE fullName (
    id INT NOT NULL AUTO_INCREMENT,
    first_name varchar(20),
    last_name varchar(20),
    PRIMARY KEY (id)
);
```

If we describe our fullName
table, we get Figure 12.21.

```
DESCRIBE fullName;
```

```
mysql> DESCRIBE fullName;
+------------+-------------+------+-----+---------+----------------+
| Field      | Type        | Null | Key | Default | Extra          |
+------------+-------------+------+-----+---------+----------------+
| id         | int(11)     | NO   | PRI | NULL    | auto_increment |
| first_name | varchar(20) | YES  |     | NULL    |                |
| last_name  | varchar(20) | YES  |     | NULL    |                |
+------------+-------------+------+-----+---------+----------------+
3 rows in set (0.00 sec)

mysql>
```

Figure 12.21.

*Inserting Data Into a Table*

Now we want to use our table
and insert a few names using the INSERT INTO SQL command:

```
INSERT INTO fullName (first_name, last_name) VALUES ('Ken', 'Marks');
INSERT INTO fullName (first_name, last_name) VALUES ('Oscar', 'Merida');
```

We can perform a SELECT on all the rows in the table to see what we inserted:

```
SELECT * FROM fullName;
```

And we see Figure 12.23.

```
mysql> INSERT INTO fullName (first_name, last_name) VALUES ('Ken', 'Marks');
Query OK, 1 row affected (0.01 sec)

mysql> INSERT INTO fullName (first_name, last_name) VALUES ('Oscar', 'Merida');
Query OK, 1 row affected (0.02 sec)

mysql>
```

Figure 12.22.

Figure 12.23.

## Create a PHP Application to Insert Data

What is cool about PHP is that it lets you easily insert data into your MySQL database. PHP provides several ways for accomplishing this. One way is using mysqli function calls, and another is PHP Data Objects (PDO). PDO is a more object-oriented way of interacting with your database. For this example, we'll use the mysqli[5] functions.

Let's take our self-referencing postfullname.php script from [chapter 11](#) and modify it to insert the first and last name into the fullName table of our FullName database. Listing 12.1 shows our initial form.

Listing 12.1.

```
1.  <html>
2.    <head>
3.      <title>Form for Entering Full Name</title>
4.    </head>
5.    <body>
6.      <?php if (!isset($_POST['submit'])) { ?>
7.        <h2>Enter Full Name</h2>
8.        <form action="<?= $_SERVER['PHP_SELF'] ?>" method="POST">
9.          First name:<br/>
10.         <input type="text" name="first_name"/><br/>
11.         Last name:<br/>
12.         <input type="text" name="last_name"/><br/>
13.         <p>
14.         <input type="submit" name="submit" value="Submit Name" />
15.       </form>
16.     <?php } else { ?>
17.       <h2>Greetings!</h2>
18.       <p>Hello <?= $_POST['first_name'] . " " . $_POST['last_name'] ?>
19.         Thanks for submitting the form!</p>
19.     <?php } ?>
20.   </body>
21. </html>
```

### Add Code to Insert the Data Into the Database

In this else block of code:

```
<?php } else { ?>
  <h2>Greetings!</h2>
    <p>Hello <?=$_POST['first_name'] . " " . $_POST['last_name'];?>
    Thanks for submitting the form!</p>
<?php } ?>
```

---

[5]  mysqli: *https://php.net/book.mysqli*

You want to do three things:

1. Connect to the database
2. Query the database
3. Close the connection to the database

Before we do these three things, lets create two variables for our first and last names:

```
$first_name = $_POST['first_name'];
$last_name = $_POST['last_name'];
```

### Opening the Database Connection

Right after the else { statement (but before the closing ?>) we connect to the database using the mysqli_connect()[6] function. This function takes four string parameters (by default): host, username, password, and database_name. Our mysqli_connect() statement should look like this:

```
$dbc = mysqli_connect('localhost', 'testuser', 'testuser', 'FullName')
       or trigger_error('Error connecting to MySQL server.', E_USER_ERROR);
```

> *It is not a good idea to have our password entered in clear text in our source code (especially if we accidentally post it up on some git repository). The better way to manage this is to use a configuration or environment variable.*

If the call to mysqli_connect() is successful, $dbc will contain a resource connection referring to our database. It is a good idea to use the or trigger_error() statement so that you can determine if you run into a problem connecting to your database. If there is a failure, you will see the error message displayed on the web page, and execution of your PHP script will halt.

> *Why not or die()? You're likely to run into legacy code or old tutorials online that use the die() statement to stop and display a message. Since it halts the execution of the PHP interpreter, your error messages are not logged to PHP's error logs and not passed to any custom error handlers. Furthermore, the only way to be notified that a user ran into an error is to wait for someone to report an outage. trigger_error() with the E_USER_ERROR severity have the same effect without the downsides.*

---

[6] mysqli_connect(): *http://php.net/function.mysqli-connect*

## 12. Inserting Data Into a MySQL Database

### Inserting the Full Name Into the Database

Next we want to build a SQL SELECT query and send it to our database using the `mysqli_query()` function[7]. This function takes two parameters: a database connection resource, and a query string. Our query string and `mysqli_query()` statement should look like this:

```
$query = "INSERT INTO fullName (first_name, last_name)"
       . " VALUES ('$first_name', '$last_name')";

$result = mysqli_query($dbc, $query);
```

If the call to `mysqli_query()` is successful, `$result` contains TRUE. Otherwise, if the query fails, FALSE is returned. You can also use an `or trigger_error()` statement as well.

### Closing the Database Connection

Finally, close the database connection using the function `mysqli_close()`. This function takes one parameter: the database connection. Our `mysqli_close()` statement should look like this:

```
mysqli_close($dbc);
```

*Whenever we want to query a database, one approach is to connect to the database, perform the query, and close the database connection. It is not a good idea to leave a database connection open. It takes up thread resources and can be a potential problem if you have a large-scale application where multiple connections can be open simultaneously. Suppose you're writing a large-scale application that may have many open connections to the database at one time. In that case, you should consider closing connections when you finish interacting with the database rather than waiting for the script to finish.*

*On the other hand, PHP will automatically close any open database connections when your script terminates. For small to medium-size applications, or if your queries are spread out across many functions, you can skip calling `mysqli_close()` explicitly.*

Putting it all together, our script now looks like Listing 12.2.

---

[7]  `mysqli_query()` *function:* http://php.net/mysqli_query

Listing 12.2.

```
1.  <html>
2.    <head>
3.      <title>Form for Entering Full Name</title>
4.    </head>
5.    <body>
6.      <?php if (!isset($_POST['submit'])) { ?>
7.        <h2>Enter Full Name</h2>
8.        <form action="<?= $_SERVER['PHP_SELF'] ?>" method="POST">
9.        First name:<br/>
10.       <input type="text" name="first_name"/><br/>
11.       Last name:<br/>
12.       <input type="text" name="last_name"/><br/>
13.       <p>
14.       <input type="submit" name="submit" value="Submit Name" />
15.       </form>
16.     <?php } else { ?>
17.       <h2>Greetings!</h2>
18.         <?php
19.           // Grab full name from form
20.           $first_name = $_POST['first_name'];
21.           $last_name = $_POST['last_name'];
22.
23.           // Insert full name into database
24.           $dbc = mysqli_connect('localhost', 'testuser', 'testuser', 'FullName')
25.                   or trigger_error('Error connecting to MySQL server.', E_USER_ERROR);
26.
27.           $query = "INSERT INTO fullName (first_name, last_name)"
28.                   . " VALUES ('$first_name', '$last_name')";
29.
30.           $result = mysqli_query($dbc, $query;
31.                   or trigger_error('Error querying database.', E_USER_WARNING);
32.
33.           if (!$result)
34.           {
35.               trigger_error("Query Error description: "
36.                           . mysqli_error($dbc), E_USER_WARNING);
37.           }
38.
39.           mysqli_close($dbc);
40.         ?>
41.
42.         <br/><br/>Hello <?= $first_name . " " . $last_name; ?>
43.               Thanks for submitting the form!
44.     <?php } ?>
45.   </body>
46. </html>
```

## Test and Verify

*Expected Results*

Let's run our application and verify we are inserting items in our database correctly.

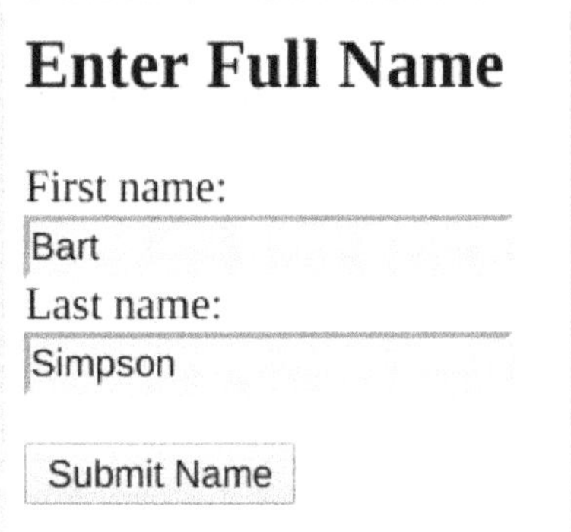
Enter Full Name
First name:
Bart
Last name:
Simpson
Submit Name

Figure 12.24.

If all goes well, we should get the expected output shown in Figure 12.25.

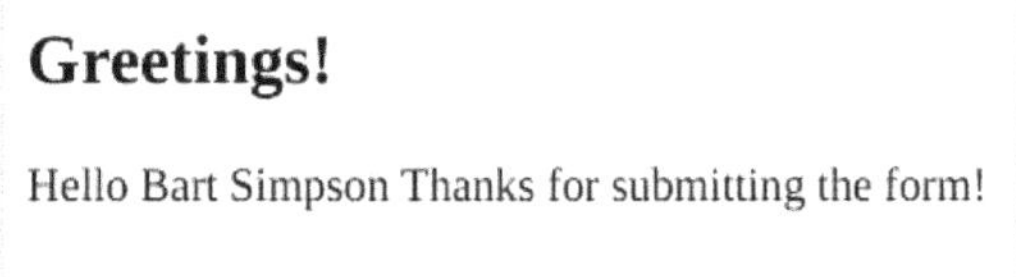
Greetings!
Hello Bart Simpson Thanks for submitting the form!

Figure 12.25.

Now let's check to see if our full name actually was inserted into our `fullName` table. In the MySQL CLI tool, select all fields and rows in the `fullName` table:

```
SELECT * FROM FullName;
```

Depending on your input, you should see a new row like the one in Figure 12.26.

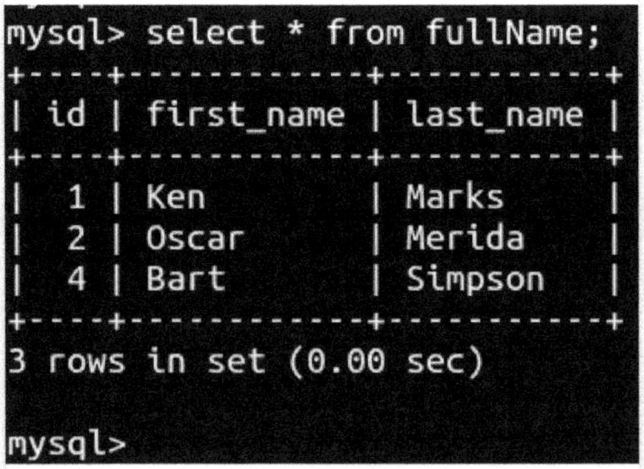

```
mysql> select * from fullName;
+----+------------+-----------+
| id | first_name | last_name |
+----+------------+-----------+
|  1 | Ken        | Marks     |
|  2 | Oscar      | Merida    |
|  4 | Bart       | Simpson   |
+----+------------+-----------+
3 rows in set (0.00 sec)

mysql>
```

Figure 12.26.

**SUCCESS!**

## Things That Can Go Wrong

A few common bugs may crop up now, and then that will prevent your application from running successfully. The most common tend to be those related to communicating with the database. Bugs due to PHP coding errors can be found with a standard debugger and using tools like Xdebug[8] and PHP Integrated Development Environments (IDE) like JetBrains' PhpStorm.

Regarding database communication bugs, it is helpful to use a database management tool like Adminer or (for our example) the MySQL CLI tool to verify your connection parameters work. Database communication bugs typically involve a failure to connect to the database or a malformed SQL query. Let's look at both of these.

[8] *Xdebug: http://xdebug.org*

## Failed Database Connection

Failing to connect to the database usually involves one or more incorrect parameters to the mysqli_connect() function, which could be incorrect credentials or a non-existent database name.

For example, you might see output like Figure 12.27.

**Warning**: mysqli_connect(): php_network_getaddresses: getaddrinfo failed: Name or service not known in **/var/www/html/phpbook/chapter13_insertingintomysqldatabase/postfullname.php** on line 24

**Warning**: mysqli_connect(): (HY000/2002): php_network_getaddresses: getaddrinfo failed: Name or service not known in **/var/www/html/phpbook/chapter13_insertingintomysqldatabase/postfullname.php** on line 24

**Notice**: Error connecting to MySQL server.', E_USER_ERROR in **/var/www/html/phpbook/chapter13_insertingintomysqldatabase/postfullname.php** on line 25

Figure 12.27.

Error output can be pretty tricky to decipher. However, we do know that our mysqli_connect() call failed. We can also see the reason given is:

```
php_network_getaddresses: getaddrinfo failed: Name or service not known in
```

The fact that we see a problem with the network address is a clue as to what's wrong. Looking up the mysqli_connect()[9] function definition in the PHP manual, we see that the first parameter expected is the hostname or IP address of the SQL server we are trying to connect to. Looking at line 24 of our code, we see Figure 12.28.

We quickly identify that we typed localhosed instead of localhost, which we can quickly fix.

```
23    // Insert full name into database
24    $dbc = mysqli_connect( localhost , 'testuser', 'testuser', 'fullname' )
25         or trigger_error("Error connecting to MySQL server.', E_USER_ERROR );
26
27
```

Figure 12.28.

Let's say we see the output in Figure 12.29 instead.

**Warning**: mysqli_connect(): (HY000/1045): Access denied for user 'testusers'@'localhost' (using password: YES) in **/var/www/html/phpbook/chapter13_insertingintomysqldatabase/postfullname.php** on line 24

**Notice**: Error connecting to MySQL server.', E_USER_ERROR in **/var/www/html/phpbook/chapter13_insertingintomysqldatabase/postfullname.php** on line 25

Figure 12.29.

The reason given is:
```
Access denied for user
'testusers'@'localhost'...
```
Because we see that access was denied, it tells us that either the username or password parameter to mysqli_connect() is incorrect. Looking at line 24 of our code, we see Figure 12.30.

```
23    // Insert full name into database
24    $dbc = mysqli_connect( localhost , testusers , 'testuser', 'fullname' )
25         or trigger_error("Error connecting to MySQL server.', E_USER_ERROR );
26
```

Figure 12.30.

Looking at the user name parameter, we can see it is misspelled and has an extra s on the end.

---

[9] mysqli_connect(): *https://php.net/mysqli_connect*

> **Warning**: mysqli_connect(): (HY000/1044): Access denied for user 'testuser'@'localhost' to database 'FullNames' in **/var/www/html/phpbook/chapter13_insertingintomysqldatabase/postfullname.php** on line **24**
>
> **Notice**: Error connecting to MySQL server.', E_USER_ERROR in **/var/www/html/phpbook /chapter13_insertingintomysqldatabase/postfullname.php** on line **25**

Figure 12.31.

One other connection error you might see is shown in Figure 12.31. Here the reason given is:

```
Access denied for user 'testuser'@'localhost' to database 'FullNames'
```

This error is more interesting because it is also giving you an access denied error. However, it is not denying the credentials for the user, just access to the specific

Figure 12.32.

database named FullNames. If you recall, the name of our database is not FullNames but FullName (singular). FullNames doesn't exist. If we look at line 4 of our code, we see Figure 12.32.

If we go into the MySQL CLI tool and GRANT PRIVILEGES to testuser on all tables in FullNames, we get a different error, shown in Figure 12.33.

Now, if we rerun postfullname.php we see the error in Figure 12.34.

Figure 12.33.

This error message tells us that the database FullNames we tried to connect to does not exist. There are subtle differences between this and the previous error. If a user has been granted privileges to all databases (a bad idea, by the way), then you would get this error if the database does not exist. In the previous error, no attempt is made to connect to a database that a user does not have access rights to regardless if it exists or not.

> **Warning**: mysqli_connect(): (HY000/1049): Unknown database 'FullNames' in **/var/www/html/phpbook/chapter13_insertingintomysqldatabase/postfullname.php** on line **24**
>
> **Notice**: Error connecting to MySQL server.', E_USER_ERROR in **/var/www/html/phpbook/chapter13_insertingintomysqldatabase/postfullname.php** on line **25**

Figure 12.34.

### *Malformed SQL Query*

**Notice**: Error querying database. in **/var/www/html/phpbook/chapter13_insertingintomysqldatabase/postfullname.php** on line **31**

Figure 12.35.

Another frequent error that occurs is due to malformed SQL queries. In our above example, if we have an error in our query string, we should see an error like the one shown in Figure 12.35

Not very useful other than we know we have a query error. It is possible to retrieve the error and display it. If we add the following code below our INSERT query:

```
if (!$result)
{
    trigger_error("Query Error description: " . mysqli_error($dbc), E_USER_WARNING);
}
```

> *Again, we use `trigger_error()` to display the warning. In this case, on a local site with `display_errors` set to `on`, you see the errors. The error would be logged on a production site and shouldn't display anything to the user because `display_errors` should be `off` in that environment.*

We see the output shown in Figure 12.36. It tells us specifically that there is no table named `fullNames` in the `FullName` database.

**Notice**: Error querying database. in **/var/www/html/phpbook/chapter13_insertingintomysqldatabase/postfullname.php** on line **31**
Query Error description: Table 'FullName.fullNames' doesn't exist

Figure 12.36.

### *SQL Injection*

I'll leave you hanging on this one and address it in the chapter on Security later on.

## Exercises

1. Create the code samples in this chapter in your development environment and ensure they work.

# Chapter

# 13

# Returning Data from a MySQL Database

*"Sometimes it pays to stay in bed on Monday, rather than spending the rest of the week debugging Monday's code."*

*–Christopher Thompson*

In the previous chapter, we created a database with a table for holding a first and last name. In this chapter, we'll query data from that table and display it on a webpage.

If you recall, when we were using the MYSQL CLI tool, I introduced the SQL SELECT command that shows all the rows in a table:

```
SELECT * FROM fullName;
```

This query gives us the output seen in Figure 13.1.

Within PHP, we can use the mysqli function calls to retrieve data from our database queries and write code that allows us to display our results to the webpage.

We already know how to use mysqli_connect() and mysqli_query() to connect to and query our database. With the function mysqli_fetch_assoc(), I'll show you how to iterate through the rows you get back from your queries.

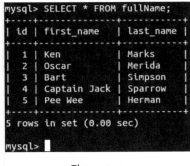

Figure 13.1.

## Returning Database Rows in a PHP Application

### Querying for Data from the fullName Table

We know that if we want to display the results for all the fields (first_name, and last_name) in the fullName table, we can use the SQL SELECT command with the *:

```
SELECT * FROM fullName;
```

However, let's assume we only want to display the results for the first_name field. We need to use this query:

```
SELECT first_name FROM fullName;
```

Testing this in the MYSQL CLI tool, we see Figure 13.2.

Our query string in our PHP code looks like this:

```
$query = "SELECT first_name FROM fullName";
```

Figure 13.2.

When we pass our query string to `mysqli_query()`, this function returns the results of our query so we need to assign it to a variable:

```
$result = mysqli_query($dbc, $query)
        or trigger_error('Error querying database.');
```

The `$result` variable contains the results of our query, which is all the rows in the `fullName` table for the `first_name` field.

## Looping Through the Row Set

Since the query results return the entire row set, we need a mechanism to operate on each row in the results. This scenario is where the function `mysqli_fetch_assoc()` comes into play.

The manual reference for `mysqli_fetch_assoc()`[1] says this function returns an associative array that corresponds to the fetched row or `NULL` if there are no more rows. The field names in the table you are querying are the keys of the associative array, whereas the values will contain the data in that row for the key/field.

For example, consider the snippet of PHP code in 13.1.

## Listing 13.1.

```php
1. <?php
2.
3. $dbc = mysqli_connect('localhost', 'testuser', 'testuser', 'FullName')
4.      or trigger_error('Error connecting to MySQL server.', E_USER_ERROR);
5.
6. $query = "SELECT first_name FROM fullName";
7.
8. $result = mysqli_query($dbc, $query)
9.      or trigger_error('Error querying database.', E_USER_ERROR);
10.
11. // show first row
12. $row = mysqli_fetch_array($result);
13.
14. echo "First Name: <strong>" . $row['first_name'] . "</strong>";
15.
16. // show second row
17. $row = mysqli_fetch_array($result);
18.
19. echo "<br/>First Name: <strong>" . $row['first_name'] . "</strong>";
```

---

[1] `mysqli_fetch_assoc()`: *http://php.net/mysqli-result.fetch-assoc*

This code produces the output shown in Figure 13.3.

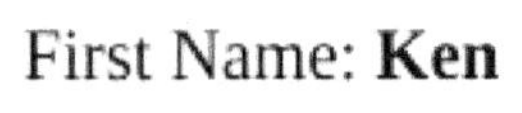

In the above code, the first call to mysqli_fetch_assoc() immediately following the call to mysqli_query() will return the first row in the table. The manual entry for mysqli_fetch_assoc() does not clarify that subsequent calls to mysqli_fetch_assoc() return the next row in the table unless there are no more rows.

First Name: **Ken**

Figure 13.3.

So, if we add the following code to the end of our example:

```
    $row = mysqli_fetch_assoc($result);

    echo "<br/>First Name: <strong>" . $row['first_name'] . "</strong>";
?>
```

First Name: **Ken**
First Name: **Oscar**

Figure 13.4.

We will see output like Figure 13.4.

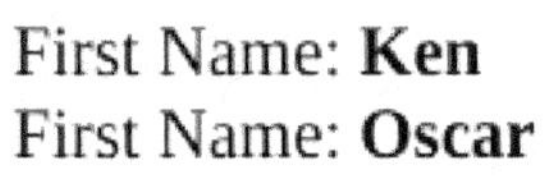

In the case there are no more rows in the table, NULL is returned. We can use this to our advantage by placing the mysqli_fetch_assoc() call in a while loop that checks for NULL.

First Name: **Ken**
First Name: **Oscar**
First Name: **Bart**
First Name: **Captain Jack**
First Name: **Pee Wee**

Figure 13.5.

So, if I want to output all the first names from the fullName table to the web page, I could use the code in Listing 13.2.

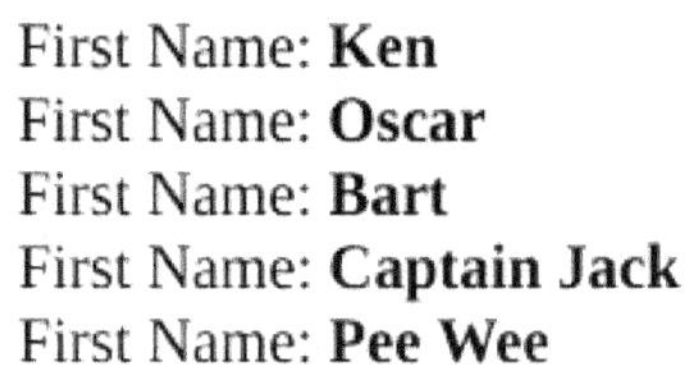

Listing 13.2.

```
1. <?php
2. $dbc = mysqli_connect('localhost', 'testuser', 'testuser', 'FullName')
3.      or trigger_error('Error connecting to MySQL server.', E_USER_ERROR);
4.
5. $query = "SELECT first_name FROM fullName";
6.
7. $result = mysqli_query($dbc, $query)
8.      or trigger_error('Error querying database.', E_USER_ERROR);
9.
10. while ($row = mysqli_fetch_array($result))
11. {
12.   echo "<br/>First Name: <strong>" . $row['first_name'] . "</strong>";
13. }
```

Figue 13.5 shows the output produced.

# Exercise: Badlibs, Part 2

Let's take our Badlibs application we wrote for the exercise in chapter 12 and add the following features:

1. Create a database called `Badlibs` with a table called `badlibs`.
2. Create the following fields in your `badlibs` table:
   - A primary key called `id`,
   - `varchar` fields for your noun, verb, adjective, and adverb,
   - and a sufficiently long enough `varchar` field called `story` to hold your completed story.
3. When a user submits a `Badlib`, insert the noun, verb, adjective, adverb, and constructed story into the database.
4. Below the form, display all the stories from newest to oldest.

Figure 13.6 is an example of what the output might look like after our modifications.

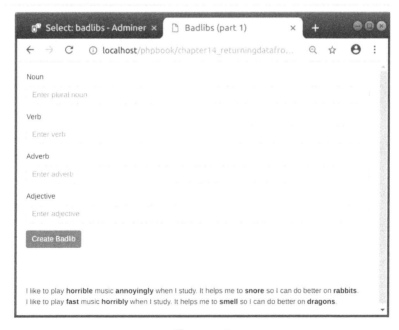

Figure 13.6.

# Chapter

# 14

# Validating Form Data and Creating Sticky Fields

*"C is quirky, flawed, and an enormous success."*

*–Dennis M. Ritchie*

When creating a web application that requires form data, it is crucial to validate the data being entered before processing it. At a minimum, we usually want to make sure that the user entered text into all the form fields.

Likewise, it is always annoying from the user's perspective if a user is sent back to a form that they missed entering a field of data, only to find out that all the data they entered in the other fields didn't persist. In this case, we want to create sticky fields that will fill in the form fields with the user's data if we have to redisplay the form.

We will take the FullName application we've been working on in the last two chapters and add validation and sticky fields for the form entries.

## Modifying FullName Behavior Based On Validation

When a user brings up the FullName application, we want to process the first and last name entries only if they enter text into both fields. Otherwise, we want to send the user back to the form.

Therefore, we want to add logic to display the form as long as any field is empty and display an appropriate error message indicating what data needs to be filled in for missing fields. If the fields validate correctly, we can output our thanks to the user for submitting their full name.

Let's start by adding conditional logic that runs when the user submits the form, or navigates to this script the first time:

```php
<?php
    if (isset($_POST['submit']))
    {
        // ...
    }
    else
    {
        // ...
    }
    // ...
```

Next create a Boolean variable called $output_form that we can set to true or false based on the success of our validation. We'll set it to true in the else clause because we want to output the FullName form when a user first navigates to this script:

```php
if (isset($_POST['submit']))
{
    // ...
}
else
{
    $output_form = true;
    // ...
}
// ...
```

# Adding Field Validation

If you remember, we named the form variables first_name and last_name:

```html
<input name="first_name"/>
...
<input name="last_name"/>
```

Working inside the condition where the user submits the form, we'll create a couple of variables for our first and last name as shown in Listing 14.1.

## Listing 14.1.

```php
1.  <?php
2.      if (isset($_POST['submit']))
3.      {
4.          $first_name = $_POST['first_name'];
5.          $last_name = $_POST['last_name'];
6.          // ...
7.      }
8.      else
9.      {
10.         $output_form = true;
11.         // ...
12.     }
```

Next, we want to add linear nested conditional logic that tests if the first name, last name, or both are empty, then output an appropriate message to the user if necessary. See Listing 14.2.

## Listing 14.2.

```
1. if (isset($_POST['submit']))
2. {
3.     $first_name = $_POST['first_name'];
4.     $last_name = $_POST['last_name'];
5.
6.     // Validate first and last name fields
7.     if (empty($first_name) && empty($last_name))
8.     {
9.         echo '<p class="text-danger">You forgot to enter first name and last name</p>';
10.        $output_form = true;
11.    }
12.    else if (empty($first_name) && !empty($last_name))
13.    {
14.        echo '<p class="text-danger">You forgot to enter first name</p>';
15.        $output_form = true;
16.    }
17.    else if (!empty($first_name) && empty($last_name))
18.    {
19.        echo '<p class="text-danger">You forgot to enter last name</p>';
20.        $output_form = true;
21.    }
22.    else
23.    {
24.        // Both first name AND last name are filled in, form entry is validated
25.    }
26. }
```

We want to add our code to insert the first and last name into the FullName table in the last else clause above. Then, we echo our message thanking the user for submitting their full name. Let's add that code now. See Listing 14.3.

## Listing 14.3.

```
1. else // Both first name AND last name are filled in, form entry is validated
2. {
3.     // Insert full name into database
4.     $dbc = mysqli_connect('localhost', 'testuser', 'testuser', 'FullName')
5.            or trigger_error("Error connecting to MySQL server.", E_USER_ERROR);
6.
7.     $query = "INSERT INTO fullName (first_name, last_name) "
8.            . "VALUES ('$first_name', '$last_name')";
9.
```

```
10.    $result = mysqli_query($dbc, $query)
11.            or trigger_error('Error querying database.', E_USER_WARNING);
12.
13.    if (!$result)
14.    {
15.        echo("Query Error description: " . mysqli_error($dbc));
16.    }
17.
18.    mysqli_close($dbc);
19.
20.    echo "<br/><br/>Hello $first_name $last_name Thanks for submitting your full name!";
21.
22.    $output_form = false;
23. }
```

The last thing we should do in the above block is to set the `$output_form` variable to `false` to prevent outputting the form again.

## Making the First and Last Name Fields Sticky

Let's go back to the `else` block that follows the `if (isset($_POST['submit'])):`

```
if (isset($_POST['submit']))
{
    // ...
}
else
{
    $output_form = true;
    // ...
}
```

We need to initialize `$first_name` and `$last_name` to empty strings. Then, when the user first navigates to the script, empty strings are displayed in the `first_name` and `last_name` form fields:

```
}
else
{
    $output_form = true;
    $first_name = "";
    $last_name = "";
}
```

The final thing we need to do is add conditional code following the previous `else` block that outputs the FullName form if the `$output_form` variable is set to `true` and make the first and last name fields sticky as in Listing 14.4.

## Listing 14.4.

```
1.  if ($output_form): ?>
2.    <h2>Enter Full Name</h2>
3.    <form action="<?= $_SERVER['PHP_SELF'] ?>" method="POST">
4.      <div class="form-group">
5.        <label for="first_name">First Name</label>
6.        <input class="form-control" id="first_name" name="first_name"
7.               value="<?= $first_name ?>" placeholder="First Name">
8.      </div>
9.      <div class="form-group">
10.       <label for="last_name">Last Name</label>
11.       <input class="form-control" id="last_name" name="last_name"
12.              value="<?= $last_name ?>" placeholder="Last Name">
13.     </div>
14.     <button type="submit" class="btn btn-primary"
15.             name="submit">Submit Name</button>
16.   </form>
17. <?php endif; ?>
```

Notice in the prior block of code that value attributes for the first_name and last_name form fields are filled in with whatever the user entered in from the previous post if validation does not pass, and we redisplay the form. Listing 14.5 shows what the complete code looks like.

## Listing 14.5.

```
1.  <?php
2.  if (isset($_POST['submit']))
3.  {
4.      $first_name = $_POST['first_name'];
5.      $last_name = $_POST['last_name'];
6.
7.      // Validate first and last name fields
8.      if (empty($first_name) && empty($last_name))
9.      {
10.         echo '<p class="text-danger">You forgot to enter first name and last name</p>';
11.         $output_form = true;
12.     }
13.     else if (empty($first_name) && !empty($last_name))
14.     {
15.         echo '<p class="text-danger">You forgot to enter first name</p>';
16.         $output_form = true;
17.     }
18.     else if (!empty($first_name) && empty($last_name))
19.     {
20.         echo '<p class="text-danger">You forgot to enter last name</p>';
21.         $output_form = true;
22.     }
```

```
23.     else
24.     {
25.         // Both first name AND last name are filled in, form entry is validated
26.         // Insert full name into database
27.         $dbc = mysqli_connect('localhost', 'testuser', 'testuser', 'FullName')
28.             or trigger_error("Error connecting to MySQL server.", E_USER_ERROR);
29.
30.         $query = "INSERT INTO fullName (first_name, last_name) "
31.             . "VALUES ('$first_name', '$last_name')";
32.
33.         $result = mysqli_query($dbc, $query)
34.             or trigger_error('Error querying database.', E_USER_WARNING);
35.
36.         if (!$result)
37.         {
38.             echo("Query Error description: " . mysqli_error($dbc));
39.         }
40.
41.         mysqli_close($dbc);
42.
43.         echo "<br/><br/>Hello $first_name $last_name Thanks for submitting your full name!";
44.
45.         $output_form = false;
46.     }
47. }
48. else
49. {
50.     $output_form = true;
51.     $first_name = "";
52.     $last_name = "";
53. }
54.
55. if ($output_form): ?>
56.     <h2>Enter Full Name</h2>
57.     <form action="<?= $_SERVER['PHP_SELF'] ?>" method="POST">
58.         <div class="form-group">
59.             <label for="first_name">First Name</label>
60.             <input class="form-control" id="first_name" name="first_name"
61.                 value="<?= $first_name ?>" placeholder="First Name">
62.         </div>
63.         <div class="form-group">
64.             <label for="last_name">Last Name</label>
65.             <input class="form-control" id="last_name" name="last_name"
66.                 value="<?= $last_name ?>" placeholder="Last Name">
67.         </div>
68.         <button type="submit" class="btn btn-primary"
69.             name="submit">Submit Name</button>
70.     </form>
71. <?php endif; ?>
```

> *Normally, once you save form data to the database, you would typically redirect the user to a separate confirmation page. Doing so prevents unintentional form submission due to page refreshes by users. For simplicity in this example, we kept this all in the same script.*

## Testing Our Script with Sticky Fields

Now we can test all the use cases for our FullName application to see if we are correctly validating our form fields and if our field data is sticky.

Figure 14.1 shows the application as it first comes up.

When we submit the form without entering anything into either the first or last name field, we should see Figure 14.2.

Notice that we redisplayed the form, and we received the correct error message: "You forgot to enter first name and last name".

When we enter a first name and then select submit, we should see something like Figure 14.3.

Again, we showed the form and received the correct error message: "You forgot to enter last name." This time our first name entry persisted—or stuck—after the submission.

Now let's delete the first name from the first_name field, enter a last name, then press **Submit Name**. Figure 14.4 shows what we should see.

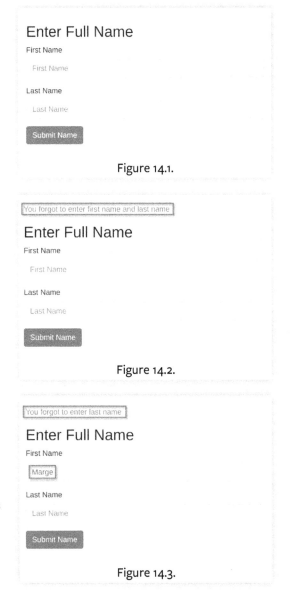

Figure 14.1.

Figure 14.2.

Figure 14.3.

Now, the code redisplayed the form. We received the correct error message: "You forgot to enter first name", and our last name entry persisted or stuck.

Finally, let's enter a first name, keep the last name, and select **Submit Name**. We should see Figure 14.5.

Once our application successfully validates all the fields, and we can insert the user's values into the database. To finish the interaction, we display a message thanking the user for submitting their full name.

## Exercise: Contact Form

1. Create the code samples adding validation to the form.
2. Create the code samples making your form fields sticky.

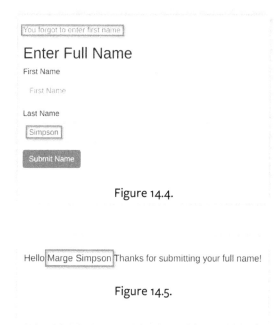

Figure 14.4.

Figure 14.5.

# Chapter

# 15

# Displaying a List of Item Details

*"Programming today is a race between software engineers striving to build bigger and better idiot-proof programs, and the universe trying to build bigger and better idiots. So far, the universe is winning."*

-Rick Cook

In this chapter, we create a database-driven movie listing web application that contains a list of items with links to another page to get more detailed information about the movie. Over the following chapters, we will be adding features to this application such as:

- Administrative ability to upload new movies
- Ability to upload a thumbnail image of a new movie
- User logins
- The ability for users to check out movies.
- The ability for users to return movies.

## Designing the Database

When thinking about the features for this application, we should consider the data we need first. Since this is an application containing information about movies, we should have the following:

- title
- rating
- director
- running time
- genre
- (eventually an image)

The opening page of our application will have a list of the movies with a link to another page for more detailed information. We can use a single table to keep our movie data in and call it movieListing. We will name our database Movie.

In our movieListing table we will have the following columns/fields:

- id for the primary key
- title
- rating
- director
- running_time_in_minutes
- genre

# Creating the Database

We will use the Adminer tool to create our database and our tables. However, before we do, it is a good and secure practice to create a separate database user for our movie database.

## Creating a Separate Database User

We will use the MySQL CLI tool to create a new user called movieguru and grant all privileges on all the tables in the Movie database.

Logging in as root in the MySQL CLI tool, execute the following commands:

```
CREATE USER 'movieguru'@'localhost' IDENTIFIED BY 'ilikemovies';

GRANT ALL PRIVILEGES ON Movie.* TO 'movieguru'@'localhost';

FLUSH PRIVILEGES;
```

Running this in the MySQL CLI tool to create a user and grant all privileges for the movie database, we see Figure 15.1.

> *We do not need to have the database created before we grant privileges on it.*

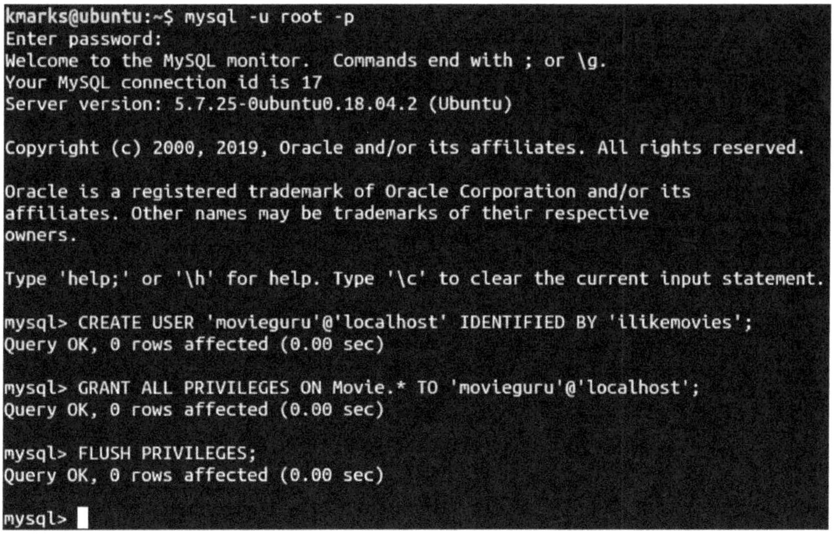

```
kmarks@ubuntu:~$ mysql -u root -p
Enter password:
Welcome to the MySQL monitor.  Commands end with ; or \g.
Your MySQL connection id is 17
Server version: 5.7.25-0ubuntu0.18.04.2 (Ubuntu)

Copyright (c) 2000, 2019, Oracle and/or its affiliates. All rights reserved.

Oracle is a registered trademark of Oracle Corporation and/or its
affiliates. Other names may be trademarks of their respective
owners.

Type 'help;' or '\h' for help. Type '\c' to clear the current input statement.

mysql> CREATE USER 'movieguru'@'localhost' IDENTIFIED BY 'ilikemovies';
Query OK, 0 rows affected (0.00 sec)

mysql> GRANT ALL PRIVILEGES ON Movie.* TO 'movieguru'@'localhost';
Query OK, 0 rows affected (0.00 sec)

mysql> FLUSH PRIVILEGES;
Query OK, 0 rows affected (0.00 sec)

mysql>
```

Figure 15.1.

## 15. Displaying a List of Item Details

### Creating Our Movie Database

Using our browser, let's log into Adminer as `movieguru` and create our database and table as in Figure 15.2.

Click on **Create database** (Figure 15.3).

Type `Movie` as the name of the database to create and select **Save** as shown in Figure 15.4

You should see the page in Figure 15.5 which shows Adminer and the `Movie` database created.

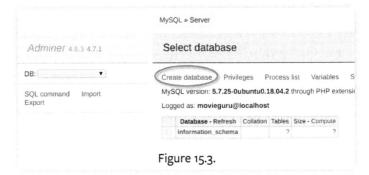

Figure 15.3.

Figure 15.2.

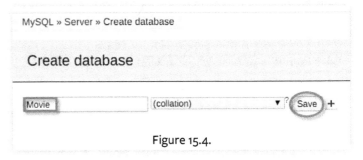

Figure 15.4.

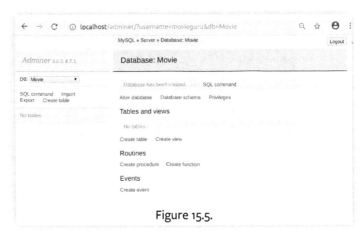

Figure 15.5.

Now we want to create our table. Select **Create table** as in Figure 15.6.

Enter movieListing for the *Table name:*

For the id Field:

1. Enter id under **Column nam***e*
2. Keep the *Type* as int
3. Select the AI radio button for auto increment

> *By naming a field* id *and making it auto-incrementing, Adminer will set this field to be the primary key for this table.*

For the title Field:

1. In the **Column name** below id, enter title
2. Select the *Type* as **varchar**
3. Enter **50** for the length

For the rating Field:

1. In the **Column name** below title, enter rating
2. Select the *Type* as **varchar**
3. Enter **10** for the length

For the director Field:

1. In the **Column name** below rating, enter director
2. Select the *Type* as **varchar**
3. Enter **25** for the length

For the running_time_in_minutes Field:

1. In the **Column name** below director, enter running_time_in_minutes
2. Select the *Type* as **int**

For the genre Field:

- In the **Column name** below running_time_in_minutes, enter genre
- Select the *Type* as **varchar**
- Enter **50** for the length

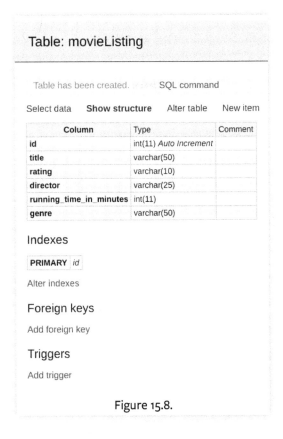

Figure 15.7.

Then select **Save**. Figure 15.7 is what the "Create Table" form should look like before saving the table.

Once you select **Save**, the table description should look like Figure 15.8.

## Table: movieListing

Table has been created.          SQL command

Select data      **Show structure**      Alter table      New item

| Column | Type | Comment |
|---|---|---|
| id | int(11) *Auto Increment* | |
| title | varchar(50) | |
| rating | varchar(10) | |
| director | varchar(25) | |
| running_time_in_minutes | int(11) | |
| genre | varchar(50) | |

### Indexes

**PRIMARY** *id*

Alter indexes

### Foreign keys

Add foreign key

### Triggers

Add trigger

Figure 15.8.

# Adding Movie Data

We can also use Adminer to add some data to our tables. For example, let's add some data for three movies. IMDB[1] is always an excellent place to find information on movies.

Select **movieListing** to get back to the movieListing table in Adminer.

To add a new movie listing, select **New item**, see Figure 15.9.

Add the following movie listing data for these titles (or any of your choosing):

- Sleepless in Seattle
- Star Wars: The Force Awakens
- Deadpool

Add the following listing data for *Sleepless in Seattle* (Figure 15.10):

- *title*: Sleepless in Seattle
- *rating*: PG
- *director*: Nora Ephron
- *running_time_in_minutes*: 105
- *genre*: Comedy, Drama, Romance

Add the following listing data for *Star Wars: The Force Awakens*:

- *title*: Star Wars: The Force Awakens
- *rating*: PG-13
- *director*: J.J. Abrams
- *running_time_in_minutes*: 135
- *genre*: Action, Adventure, Science Fiction, Fantasy

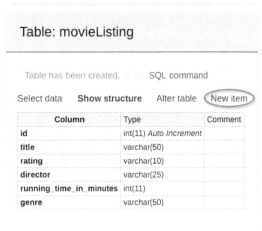

Figure 15.9.

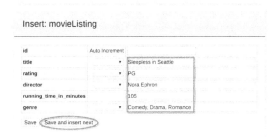

Figure 15.10.

---

[1]  IMDB: https://www.imdb.com

Add the following listing data for *Deadpool*:

- *title*: Deadpool
- *rating*: R
- *director*: Tim Miller
- *running_time_in_minutes*: 108
- *genre*: Action, Adventure, Comedy

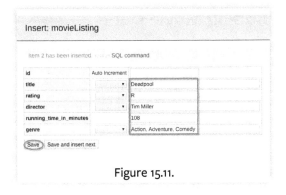

Select **Save and insert next** for the first two movie listings. Doing so saves the data and refreshes the data entry form. Press **Save** for the last one (Figure 15.11).

Figure 15.11.

After selecting *Save*, the *Select: movieListing* page is displayed (Figure 15.12), showing all the movie listings you entered.

Figure 15.12.

# Creating the Main Movie Listing Page

We start by creating an `index.php` page that lists all the movie titles in the `movieListing` table of the `Movie` database.

## Laying Out the Main Page

To make our page look clean, I use the Bootstrap[2] CSS framework and use a striped table. Figure 15.13 shows what we want our main movie listing to look like.

> *Getting familiar with the Bootstrap CSS framework*
>
> *To learn more about the Bootstrap CSS framework and get more comfortable using it, head over to https://getbootstrap.com and click the **Get Started** button. I'll be using version 4.2 in this edition of the book.*

# Movies I Like

**Movie Title**

Sleepless in Seattle

Star Wars: The Force Awakens

Deadpool

Figure 15.13.

First, let's create our main Movie Listing script and call it `index.php`. We start with a simple boilerplate that includes the necessary Bootstrap framework components and call the page title: "Movies I Like". See Listing 15.1.

## Listing 15.1.

```
1.  <html>
2.    <head>
3.      <link rel="stylesheet" href="https://stackpath.bootstrapcdn.com/bootstrap/4.2.1/css/bootstrap.min.css"
4.            integrity="sha384-GJzZqFGwb1QTTN6wy59ffF1BuGJpLSa9DkKMp0DgiMDm4iYMj70gZWKYbI706tiWS"
5.            crossorigin="anonymous">
6.      <title>Movies I Like</title>
7.    </head>
8.    <body>
9.      <script src="https://code.jquery.com/jquery-3.3.1.slim.min.js"
10.           integrity="sha384-q8i/X+965Dz00rT7abK41JStQIAqVgRVzpbzo5smXKp4YfRvH+8abtTE1Pi6jizo"
11.           crossorigin="anonymous"></script>
12.     <script src="https://cdnjs.cloudflare.com/ajax/libs/popper.js/1.14.6/umd/popper.min.js"
13.           integrity="sha384-wHAiFfRlMFy6i5SRaxvfOCifBUQy1xHdJ/yoi7FRNXMRBu5WHdZYu1hA6ZOblgut"
14.           crossorigin="anonymous"></script>
15.     <script src="https://stackpath.bootstrapcdn.com/bootstrap/4.2.1/js/bootstrap.min.js"
16.           integrity="sha384-B0UglyR+jN6CkvvICOB2joaf5I4l3gm9GU6Hc1og6Ls7i6U/mkkaduKaBhlAXv9k"
17.           crossorigin="anonymous"></script>
18.   </body>
19. </html>
```

---

[2]  Bootstrap: https://getbootstrap.com

### Storing Database Connection Definitions

Next, let's create a separate file called dbconnection.php (Listing 15.2) for our database credentials that we will create constants for. Since we'll need these values in multiple scripts, we store them in a file we can require or include across our application.

Listing 15.2.

```php
1. <?php
2.     /* dbconnection.php */
3.
4.     // Database connection constants
5.     define('DB_HOST', 'localhost');
6.     define('DB_USER', 'movieguru');
7.     define('DB_PASSWORD', 'ilikemovies');
8.     define('DB_NAME', 'Movie');
```

*Typically, you would use an environment variable to hold sensitive information, but for these examples, this is sufficient.*

### Displaying a Movie Listings Table

Now let's create our main Movie Listing script and call it index.php. Starting right after our opening <body> tag, we display our heading "Movies I Like". Next, let's switch back to our index.php page and add a couple of nested <div> tags right below our opening <body> tag to display our movies in What Bootstrap calls a "card" as shown in Listing 15.3.

Listing 15.3.

```html
1.    <body>
2.      <div class="card">
3.        <div class="card-body">
4.        </div>
5.      </div>
6.      <script ...
7.      ...
8.    </body>
9. </html>
```

Within the inner most <div> tag, add an <h1> heading called "Movies I Like":

```html
<body>
  <div class="card">
    <div class="card-body">
      <h1>Movies I Like</h1>
```

Next (right after the `<h1>` tag), we'll add some PHP code to include our database connection constants and connect to our database (Listing 15.4). We use `require_once()` to make our `dbconnection.php` values available to our script and ensure that this file is only loaded one time when our script runs.

### Listing 15.4.

```
1.  <h1>Movies I Like</h1>
2.
3.  <?php
4.  require_once('dbconnection.php');
5.
6.  $dbc = mysqli_connect(DB_HOST, DB_USER, DB_PASSWORD, DB_NAME)
7.      or trigger_error('Error connecting to MySQL server for DB_NAME.', E_USER_ERROR);
```

Then, we'll create a query string for getting the `id`, `title` fields from all the movies in the `movieListing` table and query the database:

```
$query = "SELECT id, title FROM movieListing ORDER BY title";

$result = mysqli_query($dbc, $query)
        or trigger_error('Error querying database movieListing', E_USER_ERROR);
```

Note that we will need the `id` for each movie listing when we navigate to the "Movie Details" page so we can query and retrieve the individual details for the selected movie.

At this point, we only want to display a table of the movies if there are movies in the database:

```
if (mysqli_num_rows($result) > 0):
?>
    <table class="table table-striped">
      <thead>
        <tr>
          <th scope="col">Movie Title</th>
        </tr>
      </thead>
```

Assuming we have movies to display, this `while` loop iterates and outputs through the movie titles as in Listing 15.5.

## Listing 15.5.

```
 1. <tbody>
 2. <?php
 3.     while($row = mysqli_fetch_assoc($result)):
 4. ?>
 5.             <tr>
 6.                 <td><?= $row['title'] ?></td>
 7.             </tr>
 8. <?php
 9.     endwhile;
10. ?>
```

Then we close the `<table>`:

```
            </tbody>
        </table>
```

If we do not have any movies to list, add an `else:` condition, indicate there are no movies, then close the conditional. Messages like this prevent users from wondering if the application doesn't have any databases or encountered an error or bug.

```
<?php
    else:
?>
        <h3>No Movies Found :-(</h3>
<?php
    endif;
?>
```

Listing 15.6 is what the code should look like within the `<body>` (and `<div>`) tags of the `index.php` script so far.

## Listing 15.6.

```
 1. <body>
 2.   // ...
 3.     <h1>Movies I Like</h1>
 4.
 5.     <?php
 6.         require_once('dbconnection.php');
 7.
 8.         $dbc = mysqli_connect(DB_HOST, DB_USER, DB_PASSWORD, DB_NAME)
 9.             or trigger_error('Error connecting to MySQL server for ' . DB_NAME, E_USER_ERROR);
10.
11.         $query = "SELECT id, title FROM movieListing ORDER BY title";
12.
```

```
13.        $result = mysqli_query($dbc, $query)
14.              or trigger_error('Error querying database movieListing', E_USER_ERROR);
15.
16.        if (mysqli_num_rows($result) > 0):
17.    ?>
18.            <table class="table table-striped">
19.              <thead>
20.                <tr>
21.                  <th scope="col">Movie Title</th>
22.                </tr>
23.              </thead>
24.              <tbody>
25.    <?php
26.        while($row = mysqli_fetch_assoc($result)):
27.    ?>
28.                <tr>
29.                  <td><?= $row['title'] ?></td>
30.                </tr>
31.    <?php
32.        endwhile;
33.    ?>
34.              </tbody>
35.            </table>
36.    <?php
37.        else:
38.    ?>
39.            <h3>No Movies Found :-(</h3>
40.    <?php
41.        endif;
42.    ?>
43.    // ...
44. </body>
```

## Linking Listings to Detail Pages

Now that we have our movie title listings, we want to create links for each movie that takes us to a moviedetails.php page. We want to send a query parameter containing the id field for each movie to the moviedetails.php page. Query parameters are sent to a PHP script within the $_GET superglobal variable.

### Using GET versus POST

We have two options for sending data along with our page request. Usually, this is to send form data to be saved or include information we need to lookup saved data. Many programmers use GET and POST interchangeably, but they make different assumptions about these bits of data.

POST is intended to change the state on the server. As such, POST is typically used in forms and with file uploads.

```
<form method="POST" action="doSomethingGood.php">
```

GET can be sent from a form as well (set the method attribute to GET). But it assumes the data is not being saved or persisted in any way. One typical use is a search format to send the keywords you want to find.

```
<form method="GET" action="doSomethingGreat.php">
```

When a URL includes query parameters, this is a GET request.

```
<a href="moviedetails.php?id=1&title=Sleepless%20in%20Seattle">Sleepless in Seattle</a>
```

Query parameters are sent in URLs as key-value pairs. So, in the above href example, id is the key and 1 is its value, and title is the next key, and Sleepless in Seattle is its value. When sending multiple query parameters, separate them with an ampersand (&), as is seen following 1 and preceding title. One other thing to note is that spaces are represented in a URL using the percent character (%20). Several other symbols with special meaning in a URI must also be encoded. PHP's http_build_query()[3] simplifies building complicated query strings.

Building query parameters for links in PHP from row data returned from mysqli_fetch_assoc() could look like this:

```
while($row = mysqli_fetch_assoc($result))
{
    echo "<tr><td>" .
        "<a class='nav-link' href='moviedetails.php?id=" . $row['id'] .
        "&title=" . $row['title'] . "'>" . $row['title'] . "</a></td></tr>";
}
```

When sending query parameters originating from database queries, a more secure practice is to send only the primary key field and query the other fields needed from the database within the destination script.

---

[3] http_build_query(): https://php.net/http_build_query

So, a better query of the above code would look like this:

```php
while($row = mysqli_fetch_assoc($result))
{
    echo "<tr><td>" .
        "<a class='nav-link' href='moviedetails.php?id=" . $row['id'] .
        "'>" . $row['title'] . "</a></td></tr>";
}
```

When a user clicks a link to a specific movie title, we want to send the primary key for that row in the movieListing table as a query parameter to the moviedetails.php page. Therefore, we want to send $row['id'] as the query parameter.

In index.php, replace the code in Listing 15.7

## Listing 15.7.

```php
1. <?php
2.     while($row = mysqli_fetch_assoc($result)):
3. ?>
4.     <tr>
5.       <td><?=$row['title']?></td>
6.     </tr>
7. <?php
8.     endwhile;
9. ?>
```

with:

```php
<?php
    while($row = mysqli_fetch_assoc($result))
    {
        echo "<tr><td>" .
            "<a class='nav-link' href='moviedetails.php?id=" . $row['id'] .
            "'>" . $row['title'] . "</a></td></tr>";
    }
?>
```

Listing 15.8 shows what the code should look like now within the <body> tags of the index.php file.

## Listing 15.8.

```php
1.  <body>
2.    //...
3.        <h1>Movies I Like</h1>
4.
5.        <?php
6.          require_once('dbconnection.php');
7.
8.          $dbc = mysqli_connect(DB_HOST, DB_USER, DB_PASSWORD, DB_NAME)
9.                  or trigger_error(
10.                     'Error connecting to MySQL server for ' . DB_NAME, E_USER_ERROR
11.                   );
12.
13.          $query = "SELECT id, title FROM movieListing ORDER BY title";
14.
15.          $result = mysqli_query($dbc, $query)
16.              or trigger_error('Error querying database movieListing', E_USER_ERROR);
17.
18.          if (mysqli_num_rows($result) > 0):
19.        ?>
20.              <table class="table table-striped">
21.                <thead>
22.                  <tr>
23.                    <th scope="col">Movie Title</th>
24.                  </tr>
25.                </thead>
26.                <tbody>
27.        <?php
28.              while($row = mysqli_fetch_assoc($result))
29.              {
30.                echo "<tr><td>" .
31.                     "<a class='nav-link' href='moviedetails.php?id=" . $row['id'] .
32.                     "'>" . $row['title'] . "</a></td></tr>";
33.              }
34.        ?>
35.                </tbody>
36.              </table>
37.        <?php
38.          else:
39.        ?>
40.        <h3>No Movies Found :-(</h3>
41.        <?php
42.          endif;
43.        ?>
44.    // ...
45.  </body>
```

Figure 15.14 shows what our main movie listings page looks like now.

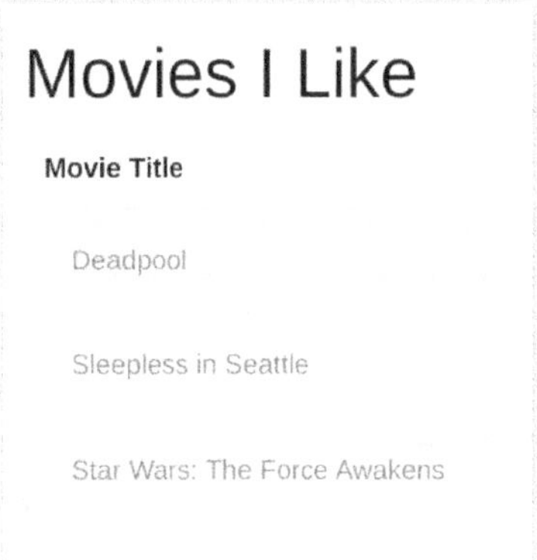

# Creating the Movie Details Page

Now we create a `moviedetails.php` page that displays the details of the movie we selected from the Movie Listings page.

### Laying Out the Details Page

Using the Bootstrap CSS framework and a striped table, Figure 15.15 displays what we want our movie details to look like.

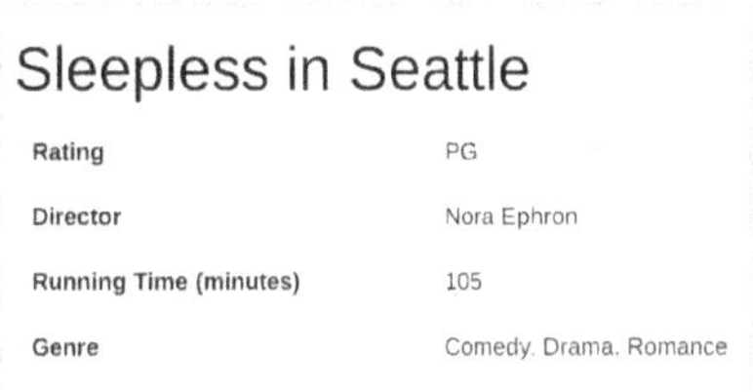

### Scripting the Details Page

Create another PHP script and call it `moviedetails.php`. Again, we will start with a simple boilerplate that includes the necessary Bootstrap framework components and call the page title: "Movie Details". We also add a couple of nested `<div>` tags right below our opening `<body>` tag to display our movies in What Bootstrap calls a "card" (Listing 15.9).

Figure 15.14.

Figure 15.15.

## Listing 15.9.

```
1.  <html>
2.  <head>
3.      <link rel="stylesheet"
4.          href="https://stackpath.bootstrapcdn.com/bootstrap/4.2.1/css/bootstrap.min.css"
5.          integrity="sha384-GJzZqFGwb1QTTN6wy59ffF1BuGJpLSa9DkKMp0DgiMDm4iYMj70gZwKYbI706tWS"
6.          crossorigin="anonymous">
7.      <title>Movie Details</title>
8.  </head>
9.  <body>
10. <div class="card">
11.     <div class="card-body">
12.     </div>
13. </div>
14. <script src="https://code.jquery.com/jquery-3.3.1.slim.min.js"
15.         integrity="sha384-q8i/X+965DzO0rT7abK41JStQIAqVgRVzpbzo5smXKp4YfRvH+8abtTE1Pi6jizo"
16.         crossorigin="anonymous"></script>
17. <script src="https://cdnjs.cloudflare.com/ajax/libs/popper.js/1.14.6/umd/popper.min.js"
18.         integrity="sha384-wHAiFfRlMFy6i5SRaxvfOCifBUQy1xHdJ/yoi7FRNXMRBu5WHdZYu1hA6ZOblgut"
19.         crossorigin="anonymous"></script>
20. <script src="https://stackpath.bootstrapcdn.com/bootstrap/4.2.1/js/bootstrap.min.js"
21.         integrity="sha384-B0UglyR+jN6CkvvICOB2joaf5I4l3gm9GU6Hc1og6Ls7i6U/mkkaduKaBhlAXv9k"
22.         crossorigin="anonymous"></script>
23. </body>
24. </html>
```

Now within the innermost <div> tag, add a nav link back to the main Movie Listings page "Movies I Like" as in Listing 15.10.

### Listing 15.10.

```
1.  <body>
2.    <div class="card">
3.      <div class="card-body">
4.        <nav class="nav">
5.          <a class="nav-link" href="index.php">Movies I Like</a>
6.        </nav>
7.      </div>
8.    </div>
```

We only want to display the details of the selected movie if the user navigated from one of the movie title links instead of just typing moviedetails.php into the URL navigation bar (Figure 15.16).

Figure 15.17 shows the incorrect navigation from Movie Listing to Movie Details.

If a user does incorrectly navigate by typing moviedetails.php into the URL navigation bar, we want to display Figure 15.18.

Therefore, we need to add an if condition that checks that we received and set the query parameter.

Before we do that, an understanding of the $_GET[] super global variable is needed.

### Super Global $_GET

Similar to a $_POST[], $_GET[] is a superglobal array variable that holds either form data when sent from a form or query parameters embedded as data in a URL.

When sending a GET request from a form, the data is automatically sent and accessed using the name attributes as indexed keys into the array.

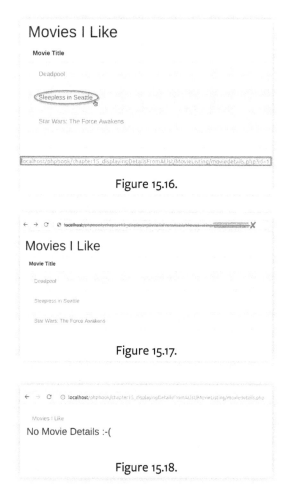

Figure 15.16.

Figure 15.17.

No Movie Details :-(

Figure 15.18.

When embedded as query parameters in a URL, the data is built as key-value pairs as part of the URL. Each value in the array is indexed using the key as mentioned earlier. See Figure 15.19.

Add the PHP conditional block from Listing 15.11 below the navigation link we just added.

Figure 15.19.

### Listing 15.11.

```
1.  <nav class="nav">
2.    <a class="nav-link" href="index.php">Movies I Like</a>
3.  </nav>
4.  <?php
5.      if (isset($_GET['id'])):
6.
7.      else:
8.  ?>
9.  <h3>No Movie Details :-(</h3>
10. <?php
11.     endif;
12. ?>
```

We only want to display the movie listing details if a user navigated to this page due to selecting a movie listing link from the main page. Therefore, we will put our code that gets and displays the movie listing details in between the if and else statements.

In between the if and else clauses, let's add code to get all the fields from the movieListing table WHERE the id field equals the value specified by $_GET['id']. We need all the usual boilerplate code to connect and query the database as in Listing 15.12.

### Listing 15.12.

```
1.  <?php
2.  if (isset($_GET['id'])):
3.
4.      require_once('dbconnection.php');
5.
6.      $id = $_GET['id'];
7.
8.      $dbc = mysqli_connect(DB_HOST, DB_USER, DB_PASSWORD, DB_NAME)
9.              or trigger_error('Error connecting to MySQL server for ' . DB_NAME, E_USER_ERROR);
10.
11.     $query = "SELECT * FROM movieListing WHERE id = $id";
12.
13.     $result = mysqli_query($dbc, $query)
14.             or trigger_error('Error querying database movieListing', E_USER_ERROR);
15. else:
16. ?>
```

This query should only return one row, and we should ensure that it always does or show no movie details if it does not. Calling the function mysqli_num_rows() on the result gives us the number of rows returned from the query.

Add the following (Listing 15.13) if and else condition clause below the mysqli_query() function, and output another no movie details within an <h3> tag set after the inner else clause before the endif:

Listing 15.13.

```
1.          $result = mysqli_query($dbc, $query)
2.              or trigger_error('Error querying database movieListing', E_USER_ERROR);
3.
4.          if (mysqli_num_rows($result) == 1):
5.
6.          else:
7.      ?>
8.  <h3>No Movie Details :-(</h3>
9.  <?php
10.         endif;
11.     else:
12. ?>
13. <h3>No Movie Details :-(</h3>
14. <?php
15.     endif;
16. ?>
```

If we do get one row back from our query, we can display a table containing the movie listing details. Add the code in Listing 15.14 below the statement:
if (mysqli_num_rows($result) == 1):.

Listing 15.14.

```
1.  <?php
2.  ...
3.          if (mysqli_num_rows($result) == 1):
4.
5.              $row = mysqli_fetch_assoc($result)
6.      ?>
7.  <h1><?= $row['title'] ?></h1>
8.  <table class="table table-striped">
9.    <tbody>
10.     <tr>
11.       <th scope="row">Rating</th>
12.       <td><?= $row['rating'] ?></td>
13.     </tr>
14.     <tr>
```

```
15.        <th scope="row">Director</th>
16.        <td><?= $row['director'] ?></td>
17.     </tr>
18.     <tr>
19.        <th scope="row">Running Time (minutes)</th>
20.        <td><?= $row['running_time_in_minutes'] ?></td>
21.     </tr>
22.     <tr>
23.        <th scope="row">Genre</th>
24.        <td><?= $row['genre'] ?></td>
25.     </tr>
26.   </tbody>
27. </table>
28.     <?php
29.         else:
30.     ?>
31. <h3>No Movie Details :-(</h3>
32. <?php
33.         endif;
34.     else:
35. ?>
36. <h3>No Movie Details :-(</h3>
37. <?php
38.     endif;
39. ?>
```

Listing 15.15 has what the code should look like within the <body> tags of the
moviedetails.php script when we are done.

## Listing 15.15.

```
1. <body>
2.   //...
3.   <nav class="nav">
4.     <a class="nav-link" href="index.php">Movies I Like</a>
5.   </nav>
6.   <?php
7.       if (isset($_GET['id'])):
8.
9.           require_once('dbconnection.php');
10.
11.          $id = $_GET['id'];
12.
13.          $dbc = mysqli_connect(DB_HOST, DB_USER, DB_PASSWORD, DB_NAME)
14.              or trigger_error('Error connecting to MySQL server for ' . DB_NAME, E_USER_ERROR);
15.
16.          $query = "SELECT * FROM movieListing WHERE id = $id";
17.
```

```
18.              $result = mysqli_query($dbc, $query)
19.                   or trigger_error('Error querying database movieListing', E_USER_ERROR);
20.
21.              if (mysqli_num_rows($result) == 1):
22.
23.                   $row = mysqli_fetch_assoc($result)
24.        ?>
25.    <h1><?= $row['title'] ?></h1>
26.    <table class="table table-striped">
27.      <tbody>
28.        <tr>
29.          <th scope="row">Rating</th>
30.          <td><?= $row['rating'] ?></td>
31.        </tr>
32.        <tr>
33.          <th scope="row">Director</th>
34.          <td><?= $row['director'] ?></td>
35.        </tr>
36.        <tr>
37.          <th scope="row">Running Time (minutes)</th>
38.          <td><?= $row['running_time_in_minutes'] ?></td>
39.        </tr>
40.        <tr>
41.          <th scope="row">Genre</th>
42.          <td><?= $row['genre'] ?></td>
43.        </tr>
44.      </tbody>
45.    </table>
46.        <?php
47.            else:
48.        ?>
49.    <h3>No Movie Details :-(</h3>
50.    <?php
51.            endif;
52.        else:
53.    ?>
54.    <h3>No Movie Details :-(</h3>
55.    <?php
56.        endif;
57.    ?>
58.    // ...
59. </body>
```

Figure 15.20 shows what our *Movie Details* page looks like now.

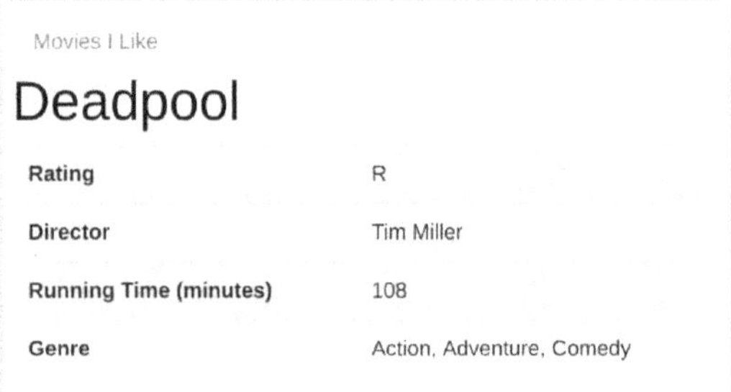

Movies I Like

# Deadpool

| | |
|---|---|
| Rating | R |
| Director | Tim Miller |
| Running Time (minutes) | 108 |
| Genre | Action, Adventure, Comedy |

Figure 15.20.

# Exercises

1. Create the database for movie listings and add data via Adminer or the mysql console.
2. Create the index page to show all movies.
3. Create the movie details page to show one movie's information. Link title on the index page to the correct detail page.

# Chapter

# 16

# Adding Data Using the Web Application

*"In My Egotistical Opinion, most people's C programs should be indented six feet downward and covered with dirt."*

*– Blair P. Houghton*

This chapter adds the ability to add movie listing data to our *Movie Listing* application we created in the last chapter.

When creating an application that lists various kinds of data, it is also a reasonable expectation to provide the ability to add data using a web interface. For example, let us create a script that allows a user to add new movie listing data.

> *Note that you generally want to limit access to who can add items to a database. In a follow-on chapter on security, I will show you how to properly limit access to a web application's ability to add data through user logins.*

## Creating a Page to Add Movies

We start by creating an addmovie.php page that displays a form to the user for entering all the movie listing data. When the user submits the form, the data will be validated and inserted into the MovieListing table of the Movie database.

### Create an "Add a Movie" Form

Figure 16.1 displays what we want our "Add a Movie" page to look like when we first navigate to it.

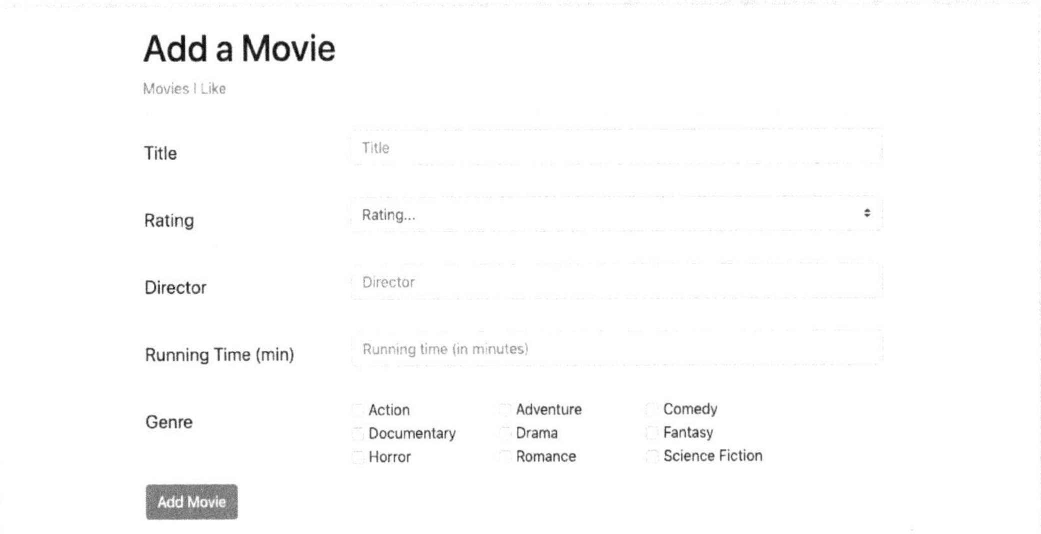

Figure 16.1.

*Initial Page Layout*

Create another PHP script and call it `addmovie.php`. Again, we will start with a simple boiler-plate that includes the necessary Bootstrap framework components and call the page title: "Add a Movie". We will also add a couple of nested `<div>` tags below our opening `<body>` tag to display our movies in a Bootstrap card. See Listing 16.1

## Listing 16.1.

```
1.  <html>
2.    <head>
3.      <link rel="stylesheet" href="https://stackpath.bootstrapcdn.com/bootstrap/4.2.1/css/bootstrap.min.css"
4.            integrity="sha384-GJzZqFGwb1QTTN6wy59ffF1BuGJpLSa9DkKMp0DgiMDm4iYMj70gZWKYbI706tWS"
5.            crossorigin="anonymous">
6.      <title>Add a Movie</title>
7.    </head>
8.    <body>
9.      <div class="card">
10.       <div class="card-body">
11.       </div>
12.     </div>
13.     <script src="https://code.jquery.com/jquery-3.3.1.slim.min.js"
14.             integrity="sha384-q8i/X+965Dz00rT7abK41JStQIAqVgRVzpbzo5smXKp4YfRvH+8abtTE1Pi6jizo"
15.             crossorigin="anonymous"></script>
16.     <script src="https://cdnjs.cloudflare.com/ajax/libs/popper.js/1.14.6/umd/popper.min.js"
17.             integrity="sha384-wHAiFfRlMFy6i5SRaxvf0CifBUQy1xHdJ/yoi7FRNXMRBu5WHdZYu1hA6ZOblgut"
18.             crossorigin="anonymous"></script>
19.     <script src="https://stackpath.bootstrapcdn.com/bootstrap/4.2.1/js/bootstrap.min.js"
20.             integrity="sha384-B0UglyR+jN6CkvvICOB2joaf5I4l3gm9GU6Hc1og6Ls7i6U/mkkaduKaBhlAXv9k"
21.             crossorigin="anonymous"></script>
22.   </body>
23. </html>
```

Now within the innermost `<div>` tag, add the title "Add a Movie" to our page in an `<h1>` tag, followed by a `<nav>` link back to the main Movie Listings page, "Movies I Like," and then a horizontal line as in Listing 16.2 and Figure 16.2.

Figure 16.2.

## Listing 16.2.

```
1.  <body>
2.    <div class="card">
3.      <div class="card-body">
4.        <h1>Add a Movie</h1>
5.        <nav class="nav">
6.          <a class="nav-link" href="index.php">Movies I Like</a>
7.        </nav>
8.        <hr/>
9.      </div>
10.   </div>
```

Next, we want to display our form. Later, we will add conditional code to display our form when we first navigate to the addmovie.php page or if there is a validation error.

You will notice I added placeholder text, shown in Figure 16.3, in the text input elements in the form. This text should not be a substitute for the use of label elements:

Figure 16.3.

```
<form ...>
  <div class="form-group row">
    <label for="movie_title"
           class="col-sm-3 col-form-label-lg">Title</label>
    <div class="col-sm-8">
      <input type="text" class="form-control" id="movie_title"
             name="movie_title" placeholder="Title" required>
      ...
```

*Bootstrap uses many div elements and class attributes for styling, especially when using its grid layout system, which is based on Flexbox[1]. See the online documentation for more information on how to use Bootstrap's grid layout[2] system (version 4.3).*

---

[1]  Flexbox: https://css-tricks.com/snippets/css/a-guide-to-flexbox/
[2]  grid layout: https://getbootstrap.com/docs/4.3/layout/grid/

*Creating an Array with Checkboxes for Genre*

A movie can fit into multiple genres. Since we want to include various selections for "Genre," we need to use checkboxes (Figure 16.4). It also cuts down on duplication of HTML markup if we create an array containing our genres.

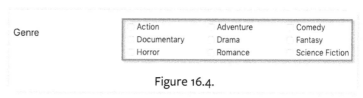

Genre

| | | |
|---|---|---|
| Action | Adventure | Comedy |
| Documentary | Drama | Fantasy |
| Horror | Romance | Science Fiction |

Figure 16.4.

Listing 16.3 shows what the PHP code and HTML markup look like for "Genre".

Listing 16.3.

```
1.  <?php
2.      $genres = [
3.          'Action', 'Adventure', 'Comedy', 'Documentary', 'Drama',
4.          'Fantasy', 'Horror', 'Romance', 'Science Fiction'
5.      ];
6.  ?>
7.  // ...
8.  <?php
9.      foreach ($genres as $genre)
10.     {
11. ?>
12.         <div class="form-check form-check-inline col-sm-3">
13.             <input class="form-check-input" type="checkbox"
14.                 id="movie_genre_checkbox_action"
15.                 name="movie_genre_checkbox[]"
16.                 value="<?= $genre ?>">
17.             <label class="form-check-label"
18.                 for="movie_genre_checkbox_action"><?= $genre ?></label>
19.         </div>
20. <?php
21.     }
22. ?>
```

The previous code and markup create a checkbox input for each item in our genres array. Every genre checked by the user gets added to the movie_genre_checkbox array (note the [] added to the name attribute). Be aware that if the user does not select any genre, the movie_genre_checkbox name attribute will not exist in the $_POST[] superglobal array.

## 16. Adding Data Using the Web Application

### PHP Code and HTML Markup for Form

Listing 16.4 is what the PHP code and HTML markup look like for the entire form.

### Listing 16.4.

```php
1.  <?php
2.     $genres = [
3.         'Action', 'Adventure', 'Comedy', 'Documentary', 'Drama',
4.         'Fantasy', 'Horror', 'Romance', 'Science Fiction'
5.     ];
6.  ?>
7.  ...
8.  <form class="needs-validation" novalidate method="POST"
9.        action="<?= $_SERVER['PHP_SELF'] ?>">
10.   <div class="form-group row">
11.     <label for="movie_title"
12.            class="col-sm-3 col-form-label-lg">Title</label>
13.     <div class="col-sm-8">
14.       <input type="text" class="form-control" id="movie_title"
15.              name="movie_title" placeholder="Title" required>
16.       <div class="invalid-feedback">
17.         Please provide a valid movie title.
18.       </div>
19.     </div>
20.   </div>
21.   <div class="form-group row">
22.     <label for="movie_rating"
23.            class="col-sm-3 col-form-label-lg">Rating</label>
24.     <div class="col-sm-8">
25.       <select class="custom-select" id="movie_rating"
26.               name="movie_rating" required>
27.       <option value="" disabled selected>Rating...</option>
28.       <option value="G">G</option>
29.       <option value="PG">PG</option>
30.       <option value="PG-13">PG-13</option>
31.       <option value="R">R</option>
32.       </select>
33.       <div class="invalid-feedback">
34.         Please select a movie rating.
35.       </div>
36.     </div>
37.   </div>
38.   <div class="form-group row">
39.     <label for="movie_director"
40.            class="col-sm-3 col-form-label-lg">Director</label>
41.     <div class="col-sm-8">
42.       <input type="text" class="form-control" id="movie_director"
43.              name="movie_director" placeholder="Director" required>
```

```
44.        <div class="invalid-feedback">
45.          Please provide a valid movie director.
46.        </div>
47.      </div>
48.    </div>
49.    <div class="form-group row">
50.      <label for="movie_running_time_in_minutes"
51.          class="col-sm-3 col-form-label-lg">Running Time (min)</label>
52.      <div class="col-sm-8">
53.        <input type="number" class="form-control"
54.            id="movie_running_time_in_minutes"
55.            name="movie_running_time_in_minutes"
56.            placeholder="Running time (in minutes)" required>
57.        <div class="invalid-feedback">
58.          Please provide a valid running time in minutes.
59.        </div>
60.      </div>
61.    </div>
62.    <div class="form-group row">
63.      <label class="col-sm-3 col-form-label-lg">Genre</label>
64.      <div class="col-sm-8">
65.      <?php
66.          foreach ($genres as $genre)
67.          {
68.      ?>
69.              <div class="form-check form-check-inline col-sm-3">
70.                  <input class="form-check-input" type="checkbox"
71.                      id="movie_genre_checkbox_action"
72.                      name="movie_genre_checkbox[]"
73.                      value="<?= $genre ?>">
74.                  <label class="form-check-label"
75.                      for="movie_genre_checkbox_action"><?= $genre ?></label>
76.              </div>
77.      <?php
78.          }
79.      ?>
80.      </div>
81.    </div>
82.    <button class="btn btn-primary" type="submit"
83.          name="add_movie_submission">Add Movie</button>
84.  </form>
```

Note that the page is self referencing as the action attribute is set to $_SERVER['PHP_SELF']:

```
<form ... action="<?= $_SERVER['PHP_SELF']; ?>">
```

*Using Bootstrap's Client Side Validation*

Also, notice that we are using Bootstrap's client-side validation. This requires we do the following:

1. Set the form's class attribute to needs-validation and add the novalidate attribute:

```
<form class="needs-validation" novalidate ...
```

2. Marking input elements with a required attribute to ensure the fields we want to be validated get validated and sent by the user's browser as part of the POST request.

```
<input type="number" ... required>
```

3. Adding <div> elements with class attributes set to invalid-feedback containing the validation text we want the user to see if they forget to fill in the field. We add these directly under the <input> elements we want validated. Listing 16.5 is the complete HTML markup for the "Running Time" input field along with the invalid feedback we want the user to see if they forget to enter a value.

Listing 16.5.

```
1.  <div class="form-group row">
2.    <label for="movie_running_time_in_minutes"
3.          class="col-sm-3 col-form-label-lg">Running Time (min)</label>
4.    <div class="col-sm-8">
5.      <input type="number" class="form-control"
6.            id="movie_running_time_in_minutes"
7.            name="movie_running_time_in_minutes"
8.            placeholder="Running time (in minutes)" required>
9.      <div class="invalid-feedback">
10.       Please provide a valid running time in minutes.
11.     </div>
12.   </div>
13. </div>
```

4. Adding the JavaScript code from Listing 16.6 in <script> tags following the form.

*A complete write-up on how to implement client-side validation using Bootstrap[3] (version 4.3) can be found online.*

---

[3] client-side validation using Bootstrap: https://getbootstrap.com/docs/4.3/components/forms/#validation

## Listing 16.6.

```
1.  </form>
2.  <script>
3.  // JavaScript for disabling form submissions if there are invalid fields
4.  (function() {
5.    'use strict';
6.    window.addEventListener('load', function() {
7.      // Fetch all the forms we want to apply custom Bootstrap validation styles to
8.      var forms = document.getElementsByClassName('needs-validation');
9.      // Loop over them and prevent submission
10.     var validation = Array.prototype.filter.call(forms, function(form) {
11.       form.addEventListener('submit', function(event) {
12.         if (form.checkValidity() === false) {
13.           event.preventDefault();
14.           event.stopPropagation();
15.         }
16.         form.classList.add('was-validated');
17.       }, false);
18.     });
19.   }, false);
20. })();
21. </script>
```

Figure 16.5 displays what our "Add a Movie" page look likes if we forget to add an entry for "Running Time."

Note that the "Title", "Rating", and "Director" have been validated successfully. However, "Running Time" failed to validate.

### Displaying the "Add a Movie" Form

The "Add a Movie" form should only be displayed when first navigating to the addmovie.php page or if there are validation errors after submitting the form. Therefore,

Figure 16.5.

we will create a Boolean variable called $display_add_movie_form immediately following the <hr/> element and set it to true:

```
<hr/>
<?php
    $display_add_movie_form = true;
```

Next, we wrap our form and JavaScript validation code in a conditional that checks this variable. See Listing 16.7.

## Listing 16.7.

```
1.     if ($display_add_movie_form)
2.     {
3.  ?>
4.  <form ...>
5.     ...
6.  </form>
7.  <script>
8.  ...
9.  </script>
10. <?php
11.     } // Display add movie form
12. ?>
```

## Inserting Movie Data Into the Database

When the user successfully enters the required data into the form fields and submits the form, we will insert the data into the movieListing table of the Movie database.

Also, even though we are validating the field inputs on the client-side, it is still important to validate the field inputs on the server-side as well. We can't trust that every browser or user visiting our site performs any validation. Therefore, we create a conditional check to ensure the required fields are present before inserting them into the database and place this code before the form markup as in Listing 16.8.

## Listing 16.8.

```
1.     // pro-tip: you can test multiple variables within a single isset() call
2.     if (isset($_POST['add_movie_submission'], $_POST['movie_title'],
3.             $_POST['movie_rating'], $_POST['movie_director'],
4.             $_POST['movie_running_time_in_minutes']))
5.     {
6.         // Code to insert new movie into database
7.         ...
8.     }
9.     ...
10.    if ($display_add_movie_form) {
11. ?>
12. <form ...>
```

In the code above, we are making sure that the fields we require to be filled in are set.

*Note that you can test multiple variables in a single* isset() *function call.*

Assuming the user enters all the required data, we can now insert the data into the database. Refer to Listing 16.9.

## Listing 16.9.

```php
1.  <?php
2.  if (isset($_POST['add_movie_submission'], $_POST['movie_title'],
3.           $_POST['movie_rating'], $_POST['movie_director'],
4.           $_POST['movie_running_time_in_minutes']))
5.  {
6.    require_once('dbconnection.php');
7.
8.    $movie_title = $_POST['movie_title'];
9.    $movie_rating = $_POST['movie_rating'];
10.   $movie_director = $_POST['movie_director'];
11.   $movie_runtime = $_POST['movie_running_time_in_minutes'];
12.   $checked_movie_genres = $_POST['movie_genre_checkbox'];
13.
14.   $movie_genre_text = "";
15.   if (isset($checked_movie_genres))
16.   {
17.       $movie_genre_text = implode(",", $checked_movie_genres);
18.   }
19.
20.   $dbc = mysqli_connect(DB_HOST, DB_USER, DB_PASSWORD, DB_NAME)
21.         or trigger_error(
22.       'Error connecting to MySQL server for ' . DB_NAME,
23.       E_USER_ERROR
24.         );
25.
26.   $query = "INSERT INTO movieListing (title, rating, director,
27.                                 running_time_in_minutes, genre) "
28.         . "VALUES ('$movie_title', '$movie_rating', '$movie_director',
29.                     '$movie_runtime', '$movie_genre_text')";
30.
31.   mysqli_query($dbc, $query)
32.       or trigger_error(
33.               'Error querying database movieListing: Failed to insert movie listing',
34.               E_USER_ERROR
35.           );
36.
37.   //
```

### Extracting the Genre from the Checkbox Array

Notice the section of code above that deals with the movie genre:

```php
$movie_genre_text = "";

if (isset($checked_movie_genres))
{
    $movie_genre_text = implode(", ", $checked_movie_genres);
}
```

Since a movie can have multiple genres, we create a comma-delimited list of the selected genres from the checkbox array. We do this by calling the implode() function ONLY if the user chose at least one genre. If the user doesn't select any genres, the checkbox array doest not exist. Therefore we need to check that it is set first before calling implode(). If the user does not select a genre, we insert an empty string into the genre field of the movieListing table.

### Preventing the Display of the "Add a Movie" Form

After inserting the new movie information into the database, we prevent the form from displaying again by setting $display_add_movie_form to false:

```php
mysqli_query($dbc, $query)
    or trigger_error(
            'Error querying database movieListing: Failed to insert movie listing',
            E_USER_ERROR
    );

$display_add_movie_form = false;
```

### Displaying the Added Details and a Link to Add Another Movie

To make this page more useful, we should let the user know their movie information was successfully added to the database. Let us do this by displaying a page and a table that looks like Figure 16.6, including a link to add another movie as shown.

Listing 16.10 lists the HTML markup and PHP code to display the added movie details.

Figure 16.6.

## Listing 16.10.

```
1.    $display_add_movie_form = false;
2.  ?>
3.    <h3 class="text-info">The Following Movie Details were Added:</h3><br/>
4.
5.    <h1><?= $movie_title ?></h1>
6.    <table class="table table-striped">
7.        <tbody>
8.        <tr>
9.            <th scope="row">Rating</th>
10.            <td><?= $movie_rating ?></td>
11.        </tr>
12.        <tr>
13.            <th scope="row">Director</th>
14.            <td><?= $movie_director ?></td>
15.        </tr>
16.        <tr>
17.            <th scope="row">Running Time (minutes)</th>
18.            <td><?= $movie_runtime ?></td>
19.        </tr>
20.        <tr>
21.            <th scope="row">Genre</th>
22.            <td><?= $movie_genre_text ?></td>
23.        </tr>
24.        </tbody>
25.    </table>
26.    <hr/>
27.    <p>Would you like to <a href='<?= $_SERVER['PHP_SELF'] ?>'> add another movie</a>?</p>
28.  <?php
29.    }
30.
31.    if ($display_add_movie_form) {
```

# Complete Code Listing

And now, Listing 16.11 is the complete source code for the addmovie.php page.

## Listing 16.11.

```
1.  <!DOCTYPE html>
2.  <html>
3.    <head>
4.      <title>Add a Movie</title>
5.      <link rel="stylesheet"
6.          href="https://stackpath.bootstrapcdn.com/bootstrap/4.2.1/css/bootstrap.min.css"
7.          integrity="sha384-GJzZqFGwb1QTTN6wy59ffF1BuGJpLSa9DkKMp0DgiMDm4iYMj70gZWKYbI706tWS"
8.          crossorigin="anonymous">
9.    </head>
```

```
10.    <body>
11.      <div class="card">
12.        <div class="card-body">
13.          <h1>Add a Movie</h1>
14.          <nav class="nav">
15.            <a class="nav-link" href="index.php">Movies I Like</a>
16.          </nav>
17.          <hr/>
18.          <?php
19.            $display_add_movie_form = true;
20.
21.            $genres = [
22.              'Action', 'Adventure', 'Comedy', 'Documentary', 'Drama',
23.              'Fantasy', 'Horror', 'Romance', 'Science Fiction'
24.            ];
25.            // pro-tip: you can test multiple variables within a single isset() call
26.            if (isset($_POST['add_movie_submission'], $_POST['movie_title'],
27.                      $_POST['movie_rating'], $_POST['movie_director'],
28.                      $_POST['movie_running_time_in_minutes']))
29.            {
30.              require_once('dbconnection.php');
31.
32.              $movie_title = $_POST['movie_title'];
33.              $movie_rating = $_POST['movie_rating'];
34.              $movie_director = $_POST['movie_director'];
35.              $movie_runtime = $_POST['movie_running_time_in_minutes'];
36.              $checked_movie_genres = $_POST['movie_genre_checkbox'];
37.
38.              $movie_genre_text = "";
39.              if (isset($checked_movie_genres))
40.              {
41.                $movie_genre_text = implode(",", $checked_movie_genres);
42.              }
43.
44.              $dbc = mysqli_connect(DB_HOST, DB_USER, DB_PASSWORD, DB_NAME)
45.                    or trigger_error(
46.                          'Error connecting to MySQL server for' . DB_NAME,
47.                          E_USER_ERROR
48.                      );
49.
50.              $query = "INSERT INTO movieListing (title, rating, director, "
51.                    . " running_time_in_minutes, genre) "
52.                    . " VALUES ('$movie_title', '$movie_rating', '$movie_director', "
53.                    . "        '$movie_runtime', '$movie_genre_text')";
54.
55.              mysqli_query($dbc, $query)
56.                  or trigger_error(
57.                      'Error querying database movieListing: Failed to insert movie listing',
58.                      E_USER_ERROR
59.                  );
60.
61.              $display_add_movie_form = false;
62.          ?>
```

```
63.              <h3 class="text-info">The Following Movie Details were Added:</h3><br/>
64.
65.              <h1><?= $movie_title ?></h1>
66.              <table class="table table-striped">
67.                  <tbody>
68.                  <tr>
69.                      <th scope="row">Rating</th>
70.                      <td><?= $movie_rating ?></td>
71.                  </tr>
72.                  <tr>
73.                      <th scope="row">Director</th>
74.                      <td><?= $movie_director ?></td>
75.                  </tr>
76.                  <tr>
77.                      <th scope="row">Running Time (minutes)</th>
78.                      <td><?= $movie_runtime ?></td>
79.                  </tr>
80.                  <tr>
81.                      <th scope="row">Genre</th>
82.                      <td><?= $movie_genre_text ?></td>
83.                  </tr>
84.                  </tbody>
85.              </table>
86.              <hr/>
87.              <p>Would you like to <a href='<?= $_SERVER['PHP_SELF'] ?>'>add another movie</a>?</p>
88.          <?php
89.            }
90.
91.          if ($display_add_movie_form)
92.            {
93.          ?>
94.      <form class="needs-validation" novalidate method="POST"
95.            action="<?= $_SERVER['PHP_SELF'] ?>">
96.        <div class="form-group row">
97.          <label for="movie_title"
98.                class="col-sm-3 col-form-label-lg">Title</label>
99.          <div class="col-sm-8">
100.            <input type="text" class="form-control" id="movie_title"
101.                name="movie_title" placeholder="Title" required>
102.            <div class="invalid-feedback">
103.              Please provide a valid movie title.
104.            </div>
105.          </div>
106.        </div>
107.        <div class="form-group row">
108.          <label for="movie_rating"
109.                class="col-sm-3 col-form-label-lg">Rating</label>
110.          <div class="col-sm-8">
111.            <select class="custom-select" id="movie_rating"
112.                name="movie_rating" required>
113.              <option value="" disabled selected>Rating...</option>
```

```
114.                    <option value="G">G</option>
115.                    <option value="PG">PG</option>
116.                    <option value="PG-13">PG-13</option>
117.                    <option value="R">R</option>
118.                </select>
119.                <div class="invalid-feedback">
120.                    Please select a movie rating.
121.                </div>
122.            </div>
123.        </div>
124.        <div class="form-group row">
125.            <label for="movie_director"
126.                    class="col-sm-3 col-form-label-lg">Director</label>
127.            <div class="col-sm-8">
128.                <input type="text" class="form-control" id="movie_director"
129.                    name="movie_director" placeholder="Director" required>
130.                <div class="invalid-feedback">
131.                    Please provide a valid movie director.
132.                </div>
133.            </div>
134.        </div>
135.        <div class="form-group row">
136.            <label for="movie_running_time_in_minutes"
137.                    class="col-sm-3 col-form-label-lg">Running Time (min)</label>
138.            <div class="col-sm-8">
139.                <input type="number" class="form-control"
140.                    id="movie_running_time_in_minutes"
141.                    name="movie_running_time_in_minutes"
142.                    placeholder="Running time (in minutes)" required>
143.                <div class="invalid-feedback">
144.                    Please provide a valid running time in minutes.
145.                </div>
146.            </div>
147.        </div>
148.        <div class="form-group row">
149.            <label class="col-sm-3 col-form-label-lg">Genre</label>
150.            <div class="col-sm-8">
151.            <?php
152.                foreach ($genres as $genre)
153.                {
154.            ?>
155.                    <div class="form-check form-check-inline col-sm-3">
156.                        <input class="form-check-input" type="checkbox"
157.                            id="movie_genre_checkbox_action"
158.                            name="movie_genre_checkbox[]"
159.                            value="<?= $genre ?>">
160.                        <label class="form-check-label"
161.                            for="movie_genre_checkbox_action"><?= $genre ?></label>
162.                    </div>
163.            <?php
164.                }
165.            ?>
```

```
166.                </div>
167.              </div>
168.              <button class="btn btn-primary" type="submit"
169.                    name="add_movie_submission">Add Movie</button>
170.            </form>
171.            <script>
172.            // JavaScript for disabling form submissions if there are invalid fields
173.            (function() {
174.              'use strict';
175.              window.addEventListener('load', function() {
176.                // Fetch all the forms we want to apply custom Bootstrap validation styles to
177.                var forms = document.getElementsByClassName('needs-validation');
178.                // Loop over them and prevent submission
179.                var validation = Array.prototype.filter.call(forms, function(form) {
180.                  form.addEventListener('submit', function(event) {
181.                    if (form.checkValidity() === false) {
182.                      event.preventDefault();
183.                      event.stopPropagation();
184.                    }
185.                    form.classList.add('was-validated');
186.                  }, false);
187.                });
188.              }, false);
189.            })();
190.            </script>
191.            <?php
192.                } // Display add movie form
193.            ?>
194.          </div>
195.        </div>
196.        <script src="https://code.jquery.com/jquery-3.3.1.slim.min.js"
197.                integrity="sha384-q8i/X+965DzO0rT7abK41JStQIAqVgRVzpbzo5smXKp4YfRvH+8abtTE1Pi6jizo"
198.                crossorigin="anonymous"></script>
199.        <script src="https://cdnjs.cloudflare.com/ajax/libs/popper.js/1.14.6/umd/popper.min.js"
200.                integrity="sha384-wHAiFfRlMFy6i5SRaxvfOCifBUQy1xHdJ/yoi7FRNXMRBu5WHdZYu1hA6ZOblgut"
201.                crossorigin="anonymous"></script>
202.        <script src="https://stackpath.bootstrapcdn.com/bootstrap/4.2.1/js/bootstrap.min.js"
203.                integrity="sha384-B0UglyR+jN6CkvvIC0B2joaf5I4l3gm9GU6Hc1og6Ls7i6U/mkkaduKaBhlAXv9k"
204.                crossorigin="anonymous"></script>
205.  </body>
206. </html>
```

## Link to the "Add a Movie" Page from the Listing Page

Now that our "Add a Movie" page is complete, let's add a link to the addmovie.php script from the main "Movies I Like" index.php script. (Figure 16.7).

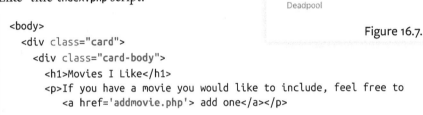

Figure 16.7.

Add the link to the addmovie.php script in the <body> element, right below the "Movies I Like" title index.php script:

```
<body>
  <div class="card">
    <div class="card-body">
      <h1>Movies I Like</h1>
      <p>If you have a movie you would like to include, feel free to
        <a href='addmovie.php'> add one</a></p>
```

## Exercises

1. Create an "Add Movie" page with a form that allows users to insert a movie in the database.
    1. Ensure users submit a title, rating, director, running time, and genre.
    2. Put an "Add Movie" button on the movie listings page.
2. Add at least one new genre of movies to the form. Ensure the data is saved to the database. Display the value (if selected) on the details page.
3. Add a field for the year the movie was released to the form. Allow years from 1900 to ten years in the future. Ensure the data is saved to the database. Display the year released on the details page.

# Chapter

# 17

# Removing Data Using the Web Application

*"Most of you are familiar with the virtues of a programmer. There are three, of course: laziness, impatience, and hubris."*

*–Larry Wall*

In this chapter, we add the ability to remove movie listing data to our *Movie Listing* application.

In addition to providing a mechanism to add movies, it also seems reasonable to provide the means for removing movies using a web interface. So, let us add a script that allows the user to remove movie listing data.

> *Note that you generally want to limit access to who can remove items from a database. In a follow-on chapter on <u>security</u>, I will show you how to properly limit access to a web application's ability to remove data through user logins.*

## Adding Deletion Links to Movie Listings

There are several ways we could design our *Movie Listing* application to include the ability to remove movies. I have chosen to add links to each movie listing on the main "Movies I Like" `index.php` page for removing each movie. If we use an icon that looks like a trashcan, the purpose of the link should be apparent as in Figure 17.1

Each trashcan link will take us to the (yet to be written) `removemovie.php` script and send over the primary key of the specified movie (from the `movieListing` table) as a query parameter.

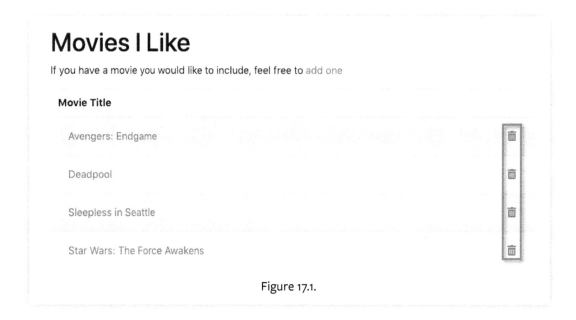

Figure 17.1.

## Adding Font Awesome

To use this trashcan link, we need to add a link to the free Font Awesome[1] stylesheet within the <head> element tag set. Font Awesome provides many icons as fonts, so we don't need to create dozens or hundreds of tiny, custom graphics.

```
<head>
  ...
  <link rel="stylesheet"
        href="https://use.fontawesome.com/releases/v5.8.1/css/all.css"
        integrity="sha384-50oBUHEmvpQ+1lW4y57PTFmhCaXp0ML5d60M1M7uH2+nqUivzIebhndOJK28
anvf"
        crossorigin="anonymous">
</head>
```

## Add a "Remove Link" Column to the Movie Listing Table

Next, we need to add a column to our movie listing table by adding a blank table head column. Then, we can add a data item for each movie listing with a link to removemovie.php and the id of the movie as a query parameter to the table row. Let us name the query parameter: id_to_delete as in Listing 17.1.

## Listing 17.1.

```
1.  <table class="table table-striped table-hover">
2.    <thead>
3.      <tr>
4.        <th scope="col">Movie Title</th>
5.        <th scope="col"></th>
6.      </tr>
7.    </thead>
8.    <tbody>
9.  <?php
10.     while($row = mysqli_fetch_assoc($result))
11.     {
12.       echo "<tr><td><a class='nav-link' href='moviedetails.php?id="
13.            . $row['id'] . "'>" . $row['title'] ."</a></td>"
14.            . "<td><a class='nav-link' href='removemovie.php?id_to_delete="
15.            . $row['id'] ."'><i class='fas fa-trash-alt'></i></a></td></tr>";
16.     }
17.  ?>
18.    </tbody>
19.  </table>
```

---

[1]  Font Awesome: https://fontawesome.com

Reload the updated index.php script in a browser. Now, when we hover our cursor over a trashcan icon of one of the movie listings, we see that our destination hyperlink is the removemovie.php script. The hyperlink includes a query parameter of id_to_delete set to the primary key of the movie we are interested in deleting. See Figure 17.2.

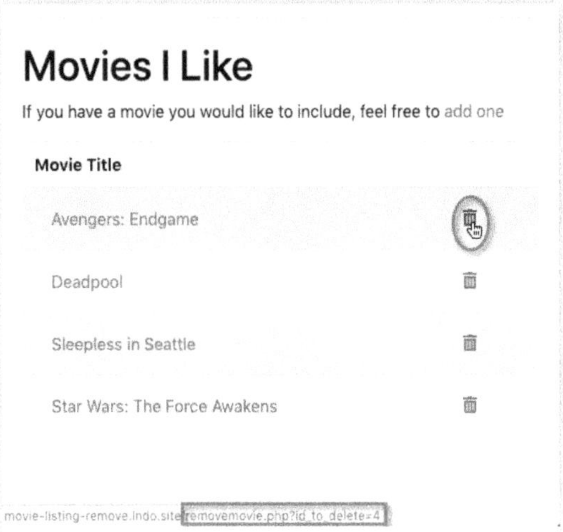

The browser sends this query parameter, and PHP parses that into the $_GET[] superglobal array.

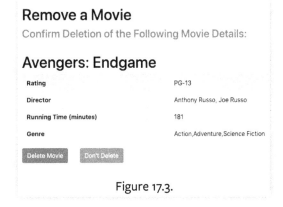

Figure 17.2.

## Creating a "Remove a Movie Page"

Any page dedicated to removing data from our application should clearly display what we want to delete. Doing so allows users to confirm if they want to delete this information or not. For example, when we select a movie we want to delete, our browser should take us to a page that looks like Figure 17.3.

Although it is not necessary, I like putting important text and actions—like selecting the "Delete Movie" submit button—in

Figure 17.3.

`<span style="color:red">red</span>`. Bootstrap also has button-specific classes we could use to differentiate it.

### Initial Page Layout

Create another PHP script and call it removemovie.php. Again, start with a simple boiler-plate that includes the necessary Bootstrap framework components and call the page title: "Remove a Movie." Next, add a couple of nested <div> tags right below our opening <body> tag to display our movies in a Bootstrap card as shown in Listing 17.2.

## Listing 17.2.

```
1.  <html>
2.  <head>
3.      <link rel="stylesheet"
4.          href="https://stackpath.bootstrapcdn.com/bootstrap/4.2.1/css/bootstrap.min.css"
5.          integrity="sha384-GJzZqFGwb1QTTN6wy59ffF1BuGJpLSa9DkKMp0DgiMDm4iYMj70gZWKYbI706tWS"
6.          crossorigin="anonymous">
7.      <title>Remove a Movie</title>
8.  </head>
9.  <body>
10. <div class="card">
11.     <div class="card-body">
12.     </div>
13. </div>
14. <script src="https://code.jquery.com/jquery-3.3.1.slim.min.js"
15.         integrity="sha384-q8i/X+965Dz00rT7abK41JStQIAqVgRVzpbzo5smXKp4YfRvH+8abtTE1Pi6jizo"
16.         crossorigin="anonymous"></script>
17. <script src="https://cdnjs.cloudflare.com/ajax/libs/popper.js/1.14.6/umd/popper.min.js"
18.         integrity="sha384-wHAiFfRlMFy6i5SRaxvfOCifBUQy1xHdJ/yoi7FRNXMRBu5WHdZYu1hA6ZOblgut"
19.         crossorigin="anonymous"></script>
20. <script src="https://stackpath.bootstrapcdn.com/bootstrap/4.2.1/js/bootstrap.min.js"
21.         integrity="sha384-B0UglyR+jN6CkvvICOB2joaf5I4l3gm9GU6Hc1og6Ls7i6U/mkkaduKaBhlAXv9k"
22.         crossorigin="anonymous"></script>
23. </body>
24. </html>
```

Within the inner most `<div>` tag, add the title "Remove a Movie" to our page in an `<h1>` tag like so:

```
<body>
  <div class="card">
    <div class="card-body">
      <h1>Remove a Movie</h1>
    </div>
  </div>
```

## Connect to the Movie Database

Since we need to access the database for the movie we want to remove, we should include our dbconnection.php script and connect to our Movie database as in Listing 17.3.

## Listing 17.3.

```
1.  <body>
2.      <div class="card">
3.       <div class="card-body">
4.         <h1>Remove a Movie</h1>
5.         <?php
6.          require_once('dbconnection.php');
7.
8.          $dbc = mysqli_connect(DB_HOST, DB_USER, DB_PASSWORD, DB_NAME)
9.              or trigger_error(
10.                 'Error connecting to MySQL server for' . DB_NAME,
11.                 E_USER_ERROR
12.             );
```

### Multiple Ways to Navigate to "Remove a Movie" Page

As you can see from Figure 17.4, the page displays the movie details of the movie to remove, along with two buttons. This gives the user a choice to remove the movie or not.

When the user selects one of the buttons ("Delete Movie" or "Don't Delete"), the removemovie.php script is called with the name attribute of the button selected. The movie id attribute is sent and parsed into the $_POST[] superglobal array.

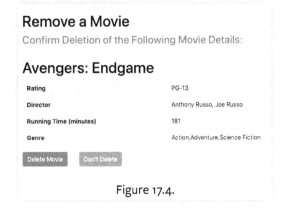

Figure 17.4.

There are two other ways a user can navigate to the removemovie.php script. First, by selecting one of the trashcan links for a movie to remove from the index.php page. Another—unintended mechanism—would be to type removemovie.php into the URL address bar of the browser. That is, without the query parameter containing the movie id.

We need to handle all of these possible methods of navigating to the removemovie.php script. So, first, we handle the expected ways of navigating to the removemovie.php script, then the unexpected ones.

The best way to deal with these choices is to create an if/elseif/else block of code as in Listing 17.4.

## Listing 17.4.

```
1.  $dbc = mysqli_connect(DB_HOST, DB_USER, DB_PASSWORD, DB_NAME)
2.          or trigger_error(
3.              'Error connecting to MySQL server for' . DB_NAME, E_USER_ERROR
4.          );
5.
6.  if (isset($_POST['delete_movie_submission']) && isset($_POST['id'])):
7.      ...
8.  elseif (isset($_POST['do_not_delete_movie_submission'])):
9.      ...
10. elseif (isset($_GET['id_to_delete'])):
11.     ...
12. else: // Unintended page link
13.     ...
14. endif;
```

The following sections will break down each condition based on how we navigated to removemovie.php.

### Navigating from index.php

This is the first intended way we will navigate to the removemovie.php page. Therefore we will be dealing with the second elseif block:

Confirm Deletion of the Following Movie Details:

Figure 17.5.

```
elseif (isset($_GET['id_to_delete'])):
```

We reach this condition when a user selects one of the trashcan icons for the movie they want to delete. They should be presented with a page like Figure 17.4.

First, I chose to display a deletion confirmation message using Bootstrap's text-danger class. See Figure 17.5

```
    elseif (isset($_GET['id_to_delete'])):
?>
        <h3 class="text-danger">Confirm Deletion of the Following Movie Details:</h3><br/>
<?php
```

## 17. REMOVING DATA USING THE WEB APPLICATION

We grab the query parameter that holds the ID of the movie we want to delete from the $_GET[] superglobal array. With it, we can query the movieListing table in the Movie database for the row of fields for the given movie id as in Listing 17.5.

Next, display the movie title in and <h1> tag set and all the movie details in a striped table (Figure 17.6 and Listing 17.6).

### Avengers: Endgame

| | |
|---|---|
| Rating | PG-13 |
| Director | Anthony Russo, Joe Russo |
| Running Time (minutes) | 181 |
| Genre | Action,Adventure,Science Fiction |

Figure 17.6.

### Listing 17.5.

```
1.          <h3 class="text-danger">Confirm Deletion of the Following Movie Details:</h3><br/>
2. <?php
3.      $id = $_GET['id_to_delete'];
4.
5.      $query = "SELECT * FROM movieListing WHERE id = $id";
6.
7.      $result = mysqli_query($dbc, $query)
8.              or trigger_error(
9.                  'Error querying database movieListing',
10.                 E_USER_ERROR
11.              );
12.
13.     if (mysqli_num_rows($result) == 1):
14.
15.         $row = mysqli_fetch_assoc($result)
16. ?>
```

### Listing 17.6.

```
1. $row = mysqli_fetch_assoc($result)
2. ?>
3. <h1><?= $row['title'] ?></h1>
4. <table class="table table-striped">
5.     <tbody>
6.     <tr>
7.         <th scope="row">Rating</th>
8.         <td><?= $row['rating'] ?></td>
9.     </tr>
10.    <tr>
11.        <th scope="row">Director</th>
12.        <td><?= $row['director'] ?></td>
13.    </tr>
14.    <tr>
15.        <th scope="row">Running Time (minutes)</th>
16.        <td><?= $row['running_time_in_minutes'] ?></td>
17.    </tr>
18.    <tr>
```

```
19.          <th scope="row">Genre</th>
20.          <td><?= $row['genre'] ?></td>
21.      </tr>
22.      </tbody>
23. </table>
```

Finally, display a form (Figure 17.7)—that self references the removemovie.php page—with two submit buttons: one for deleting the movie and another for not deleting the movie.

Figure 17.7.

## Listing 17.7.

```
1.  </table>
2.  <form method="POST" action="<?= $_SERVER['PHP_SELF'] ?>">
3.      <div class="form-group row">
4.          <div class="col-sm-2">
5.              <button class="btn btn-danger" type="submit"
6.                      name="delete_movie_submission">Delete Movie
7.              </button>
8.          </div>
9.          <div class="col-sm-2">
10.             <button class="btn btn-success" type="submit"
11.                     name="do_not_delete_movie_submission">Don't Delete
12.             </button>
13.         </div>
14.         <input type="hidden" name="id" value="<?= $id ?>">
15.     </div>
16. </form>
```

Notice the name attributes in Listing 17.7 for the two buttons are descriptive:

```
    <button class="btn btn-danger" type="submit"
            name="delete_movie_submission">Delete Movie</button>
  ...
    <button class="btn btn-success" type="submit"
            name="do_not_delete_movie_submission">Don't Delete</button>
```

*In Bootstrap, add* btn btn-danger *or* btn btn-success *to the* class *attribute of the button element to make a button red or green.*

Also, notice I created a hidden <input> element in the form and set it to the id of the movie. After the form data is POSTed back to removemovie.php when the user presses the "Delete Movie" submit button, the id is available to our PHP script in the $_POST[] superglobal array so that our code can delete it from the database.

> *THE WEB IS STATELESS! When the user selects the "Delete Movie" submit button, the action is to re-render the removemovie.php script and send new data to the page through the $_POST[] superglobal array. However, all of the previous variable data from the PHP code (as a result of the last navigation to removemovie.php from the index.php page) is gone. The definition of "Stateless" behavior is that all data is communicated in a single HTTP request and response between the client (browser) and the server. This data is only present for the current HTTP request/response. Using hidden variables in a form is one way to keep information between requests (after linking to a different or the same page). In subsequent chapters on Cookies and Sessions, we explore other techniques we can use to persist data as a user navigates between the pages in our application.*

### Clicking the "Delete Movie" Button

Pressing the "Delete Movie" button is the second intended way for user to arrive at the removemovie.php page. Therefore we are dealing with the if block:

```
if (isset($_POST['delete_movie_submission']) && isset($_POST['id'])):
```

When we reach this condition, it was because a user selected the "Delete Movie" submit button. The browser then sends a POST request to removemovie.php with the form variables delete_movie_submission and id in the $_POST[] superglobal array.

In this block, we delete the movie with the given id from the movieListing table in the Movie database. Then, we link back to the main *Movies I Like* index.php. See Listing 17.8.

### Listing 17.8.

```
 1. if (isset($_POST['delete_movie_submission']) && isset($_POST['id'])):
 2.
 3.     $id = $_POST['id'];
 4.
 5.     $query = "DELETE FROM movieListing WHERE id = $id";
 6.
 7.     $result = mysqli_query($dbc, $query)
 8.             or trigger_error('Error querying database movieListing', E_USER_ERROR);
 9.
10.     header("Location: index.php");
11.     exit;
```

Notice that once our code runs, the removed movie is no longer listed (Figure 17.8).

Figure 17.8.

### Pressing the "Don't Delete" Button

This is the third intended way to navigate to the removemovie.php page. Therefore we will be dealing with first elseif block:

```
elseif (isset($_POST['do_not_delete_movie_submission'])):
```

If this condition is true, it was because a user selected the "Don't Delete" submit button. Doing so, POSTs to removemovie.php with the form variables do_not_delete_movie_submission in the $_POST[] superglobal array.

In this block, we redirect the user automatically to the main "Movies I Like" index.php page. Using the header()[2] function, We send a Location: with the destination URL, index.php.

```
elseif (isset($_POST['do_not_delete_movie_submission'])):

    header("Location: index.php");
    exit;
```

When the page reloads, notice the movie was not removed (Figure 17.9).

Figure 17.9.

### Soft vs Hard Deletes

*Depending on your application, you may not want to delete a row from the database immediately. What if the user wants to recover a record? In that case, many programs use a "soft" delete by adding a boolean column to a table to indicate that something has been "deleted." When querying for records, exclude the rows with this field set to* true. *To recover a record, we need only flip the field to* false.

---

[2]  header(): *https://php.net/header*

### Unexpected Navigation Method

Since the HTTP request is coming from the client, in theory, unanticipated, unwanted, and malicious parameters can be in the query string. All other conditions we could navigate to the removemovie.php page are unintended. Therefore, we are dealing with the else block:

```
else: // Unintended page link
```

Since all of the above conditions are where we want the application to function in a specific way, it is common practice to put the application's response to unpredictable behavior in an else condition. In this case, we redirect to the main *Movies I Like* index.php page:

```
else: // Unintended page link -  No movie to remove, link back to index

    header("Location: index.php");
    exit;

endif;
```

## Complete Code Listing

Listing 17.9 holds the complete code for the removemovie.php page.

### Listing 17.9.

```
 1.  <html>
 2.  <head>
 3.      <title>Remove a Movie</title>
 4.      <link rel="stylesheet"
 5.          href="https://stackpath.bootstrapcdn.com/bootstrap/4.2.1/css/bootstrap.min.css"
 6.          integrity="sha384-GJzZqFGwb1QTTN6wy59ffF1BuGJpLSa9DkKMpODgiMDm4iYMj70gZWKYbI706tWS"
 7.          crossorigin="anonymous">
 8.  </head>
 9.  <body>
10.  <div class="card">
11.      <div class="card-body">
12.          <h1>Remove a Movie</h1>
13.          <?php
14.          require_once('dbconnection.php');
15.
16.          $dbc = mysqli_connect(DB_HOST, DB_USER, DB_PASSWORD, DB_NAME)
17.              or trigger_error(
18.                  'Error connecting to MySQL server for DB_NAME.',
19.                  E_USER_ERROR
20.              );
21.
22.          if (isset($_POST['delete_movie_submission']) && isset($_POST['id'])):
```

```php
23.
24.            $id = $_POST['id'];
25.
26.            $query = "DELETE FROM movieListing WHERE id = $id";
27.
28.            $result = mysqli_query($dbc, $query)
29.                or trigger_error('Error querying database movieListing', E_USER_ERROR);
30.
31.            header("Location: index.php");
32.            exit;
33.
34.        elseif (isset($_POST['do_not_delete_movie_submission'])):
35.
36.            header("Location: index.php");
37.            exit;
38.
39.        elseif (isset($_GET['id_to_delete'])):
40.            ?>
41.             <h3 class="text-danger">Confirm Deletion of the Following
42.                Movie Details:</h3><br/>
43.            <?php
44.            $id = $_GET['id_to_delete'];
45.
46.            $query = "SELECT * FROM movieListing WHERE id = $id";
47.
48.            $result = mysqli_query($dbc, $query)
49.                or trigger_error('Error querying database movieListing', E_USER_ERROR);
50.
51.            if (mysqli_num_rows($result) == 1):
52.
53.                $row = mysqli_fetch_assoc($result)
54.                ?>
55.                 <h1><?= $row['title'] ?></h1>
56.                 <table class="table table-striped">
57.                    <tbody>
58.                    <tr>
59.                        <th scope="row">Rating</th>
60.                        <td><?= $row['rating'] ?></td>
61.                    </tr>
62.                    <tr>
63.                        <th scope="row">Director</th>
64.                        <td><?= $row['director'] ?></td>
65.                    </tr>
66.                    <tr>
67.                        <th scope="row">Running Time (minutes)</th>
68.                        <td><?= $row['running_time_in_minutes'] ?></td>
69.                    </tr>
70.                    <tr>
71.                        <th scope="row">Genre</th>
72.                        <td><?= $row['genre'] ?></td>
```

```
73.                    </tr>
74.                  </tbody>
75.              </table>
76.              <form method="POST"
77.                  action="<?= $_SERVER['PHP_SELF'] ?>">
78.                  <div class="form-group row">
79.                      <div class="col-sm-2">
80.                          <button class="btn btn-danger" type="submit"
81.                              name="delete_movie_submission">
82.                              Delete Movie
83.                          </button>
84.                      </div>
85.                      <div class="col-sm-2">
86.                          <button class="btn btn-success"
87.                              type="submit"
88.                              name="do_not_delete_movie_submission">
89.                              Don't Delete
90.                          </button>
91.                      </div>
92.                      <input type="hidden" name="id"
93.                          value="<?= $id ?>">
94.                  </div>
95.              </form>
96.          <?php
97.          else:
98.              ?>
99.              <h3>No Movie Details :-(</h3>
100.          <?php
101.          endif;
102.
103.      else: // Unintended page link -  No movie to remove, go back to index
104.
105.          header("Location: index.php");
106.          exit;
107.
108.      endif;
109.      ?>
110.  </div>
111. </div>
112. <script src="https://code.jquery.com/jquery-3.3.1.slim.min.js"
113.      integrity="sha384-q8i/X+965DzO0rT7abK41JStQIAqVgRVzpbzo5smXKp4YfRvH+8abtTE1Pi6jizo"
114.      crossorigin="anonymous"></script>
115. <script src="https://cdnjs.cloudflare.com/ajax/libs/popper.js/1.14.6/umd/popper.min.js"
116.      integrity="sha384-wHAiFfRlMFy6i5SRaxvfOCifBUQy1xHdJ/yoi7FRNXMRBu5WHdZYu1hA6ZOblgut"
117.      crossorigin="anonymous"></script>
118. <script src="https://stackpath.bootstrapcdn.com/bootstrap/4.2.1/js/bootstrap.min.js"
119.      integrity="sha384-B0UglyR+jN6CkvvICOB2joaf5I4l3gm9GU6Hc1og6Ls7i6U/mkkaduKaBhlAXv9k"
120.      crossorigin="anonymous"></script>
121. </body>
122. </html>
```

# Exercises

1. Add a clickable trashcan icon (one per movie) to the movie listing page so users can delete a single movie.

2. Create the remove a movie page to show the movie details and confirmation of the deletion.

3. Bonus: Switch the behavior to use a soft delete and mark movies not to display. Update the listing and detail pages to hide movies marked as "deleted."

# Chapter

# 18

# Editing Data Using the Web Application

*"I develop for Linux for a living, I used to develop for DOS. Going from DOS to Linux is like trading a glider for an F117."*

*–Lawrence Foard, entropy@world.std.com*

In this chapter, we add the ability to edit movie listing data to our *Movie Listing* application.

Since we have an application with the ability to add and remove movies, we should probably add the ability to edit a movie listing as well. From a movie's "Movie Details" page, we want to navigate to a page with a form that allows us to modify all the movie details. After successfully editing the movie data, we want to be taken back to the "Movie Details" page for that movie to see the changes reflected immediately.

> *Note that you generally want to limit access to who can edit items in a database. A follow-on chapter on <u>security</u> shows how to properly restrict access to a web application's ability to edit data through user logins.*

## Linking Movie Details to the Edit Page

Add a horizontal line and a link to the (yet to be written) editmovie.php script in the moviedetails.php script just after the closing </table> element:

```
</table>
<hr/>
<p>If you would like to change any of the details of this movie, feel free to <a
href='editmovie.php?id_to_edit=<?=$row['id']?>'> edit it</a></p>
```

The updated "Movie Details" page should look like Figure 18.1.

When we run the updated moviedetails.php script, we can see when hovering on "edit it", our destination hyperlink is the editmovie. php script along with the query parameter of id_to_edit set to the primary key of the movie we are interested in editing as in Figure 18.2.

This query parameter is contained in $row['id'] and will get sent over in the $_GET[] superglobal array.

Movies I Like

### Avengers: Endgame

| Rating | PG-13 |
| --- | --- |
| Director | Anthony Russo, Joe Russo |
| Running Time (minutes) | 181 |
| Genre | Action,Adventure,Science Fiction |

If you would like to change any of the details of this movie, feel free to edit it

Figure 18.1.

If you would like to change any of the details of this movie, feel free to edit it

movie-listing.indo.site editmovie.php?id_to_edit=6

Figure 18.2.

# Create the Editing Page

We create an `editmovie.php` script that displays essentially the same form as the "Add a Movie" `addmovie.php` script. The difference is that we pre-populate the form inputs with the movie details from the database. Additionally, we use the same Bootstrap validation code—in the `addmovie.php` script—in case the user inadvertently deletes a required field from the form. When we select "edit it" for the movie we want to update, our browser should take us to a page that looks like Figure 18.3.

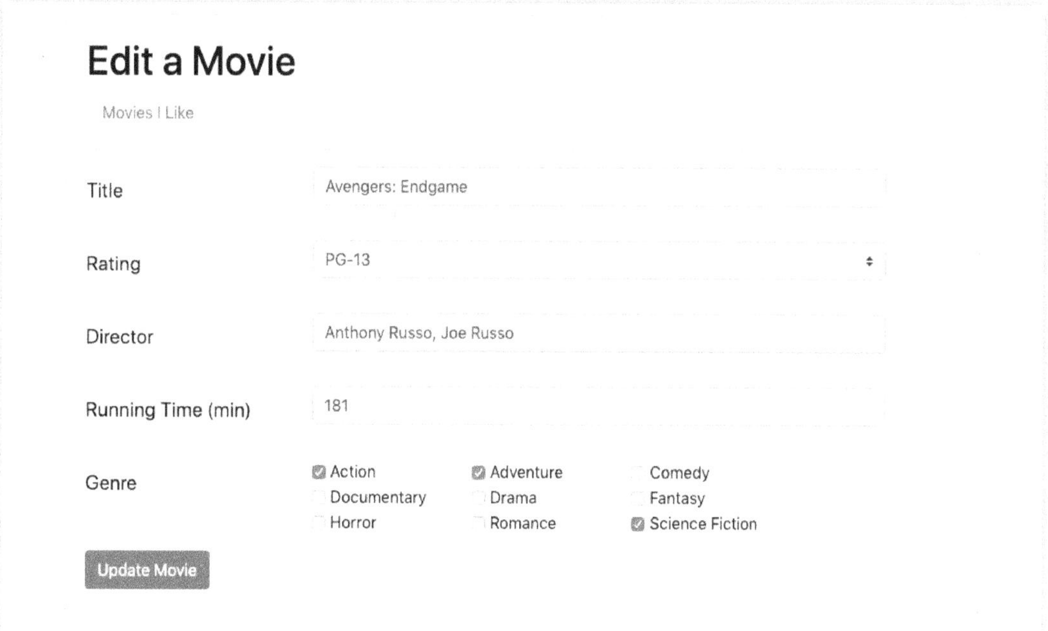

Figure 18.3.

> **DRY (Do Not Repeat Yourself)**
>
> *For easier maintenance and reduced duplication of code, you should reuse the same* `addmovie.php` *form markup and code. You can do this with PHP's* `require_once`[1] *statement in* `addmovie.php` *and* `editmovie.php` *scripts. We will leave this up to you as an exercise.*

---

[1]  `require_once`: *https://php.net/require_once*

## First Steps

First, we will display the "Edit a Movie" title in an <h1> tag set within the <body> element:

```
<body>
  <div class="card">
    <div class="card-body">
      <h1>Edit a Movie</h1>
```

Next, let's create a link back to the index.php page if the user does not want to update this movie and a horizontal line (<hr/> element):

```
<body>
  <div class="card">
    <div class="card-body">
      <h1>Edit a Movie</h1>
      <nav class="nav">
        <a class="nav-link" href="index.php">Movies I Like</a>
      </nav>
      <hr/>
```

As in the previous "Remove a Movie" page, we will need to access the database for the movie we want to edit, so we need to include our dbconnection.php script and connect to our Movie database as shown in Listing 18.1.

## Listing 18.1.

```
1.  <body>
2.    <div class="card">
3.      <div class="card-body">
4.        <h1>Edit a Movie</h1>
5.        <p><a class='nav-link' href='index.php'>Movies I Like</a></p>
6.        <hr/>
7.          <?php
8.            require_once('dbconnection.php');
9.
10.           $dbc = mysqli_connect(DB_HOST, DB_USER, DB_PASSWORD, DB_NAME)
11.             or trigger_error(
12.                 'Error connecting to MySQL server for' . DB_NAME,
13.                 E_USER_ERROR
14.               );
```

## Anticipating Paths to the Edit Page

There are two expected ways and various unanticipated ways to navigate to the editmovie.php script. The first expected way is for the user to select the "edit it" link on the "Movie Details" page as in Figure 18.4.

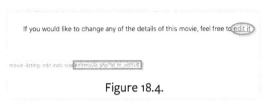

Figure 18.4.

Doing so sends a single query parameter contained in the id_to_edit element of the $_GET super global variable.

The second expected way is when the user selects "Update Movie." When the user successfully enters the required data in the form fields and submits the form, we will want to update the data for this movie in the movieListing table of the Movie database. You can find the submitted form fields in the $_POST super global variable.

All other mechanisms are unanticipated. So this essentially gives us three choices we are looking for. Therefore, the best way to deal with these three choices is to create an if/elseif/else block of code structure in Listing 18.2.

Listing 18.2.

```
1. $dbc = mysqli_connect(DB_HOST, DB_USER, DB_PASSWORD, DB_NAME)
2.          or trigger_error(
3.              'Error connecting to MySQL server for' . DB_NAME,
4.              E_USER_ERROR
5.          );
6.
7. if (isset($_GET['id_to_edit']))
8. {
9.     // ...
10. }
11. elseif (isset($_POST['edit_movie_submission'], $_POST['movie_title'],
12.         $_POST['movie_rating'], $_POST['movie_director'],
13.         $_POST['movie_running_time_in_minutes']))
14. {
15.     // ...
16. }
17. else   // Unintended page link
18. {
19.     // ...
20. }
```

*In the elseif block of code above: even though we are validating the field inputs on the client-side, it is still important to validate the field inputs on the server-side.*

## Direct Navigation

The first intended way we will navigate to the editmovie.php script is when the user selects the "edit it" link on the moviedetails.php page. The link causes an HTTP GET to be sent to the editmovie.php script with the query parameter in the $_GET superglobal variable. We deal with this in the first if block:

```
if (isset($_GET['id_to_edit']))
{
```

When we get to this condition, the primary key of the movie we want to edit is referenced by the id_to_edit query parameter.

Take a look at the form shown in Figure 18.5.

You will notice that the fields are pre-populated with the movie details. To do this, we need to query the movieListing table for the movie details before displaying the form.

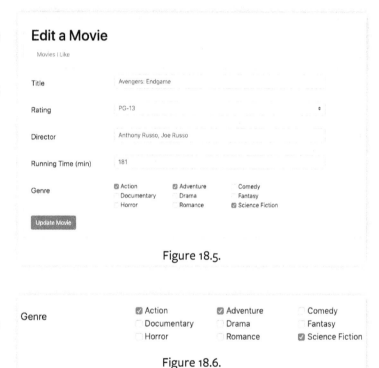

Figure 18.5.

Notice, in Figure 18.6, that the "Genre" checkboxes are correctly selected with the set movie genres.

Figure 18.6.

In order to display the checkboxes for "Genre"—just as in the addmovie.php script—we need an array to hold the names of each genre. Just above the if block, but right after the mysqli_connect() function call, add the $genres array from Listing 18.3.

## Listing 18.3.

```
 1. $dbc = mysqli_connect(DB_HOST, DB_USER, DB_PASSWORD, DB_NAME)
 2.         or trigger_error(
 3.                 'Error connecting to MySQL server for DB_NAME.', E_USER_ERROR
 4.         );
 5.
 6. $genres = [
 7.     'Action', 'Adventure', 'Comedy', 'Documentary', 'Drama',
 8.     'Fantasy', 'Horror', 'Romance', 'Science Fiction'
 9. ];
10.
11. if (isset($_GET['id_to_edit']))
12. {
13.     // ...
14. }
```

Next, inside the if block, query the movieListing table for the movie details of the movie we want to edit using the id_to_edit query parameter by adding the code from Listing 18.4.

## Listing 18.4.

```
 1. if (isset($_GET['id_to_edit']))
 2. {
 3.
 4.     $id_to_edit = $_GET['id_to_edit'];
 5.
 6.     $query = "SELECT * FROM movieListing WHERE id = $id_to_edit";
 7.
 8.     $result = mysqli_query($dbc, $query)
 9.             or trigger_error('Error querying database movieListing', E_USER_ERROR);
10.     // ...
11. }
```

If the query is successful, you only get one row back. It's a good idea to use separate descriptive variables for each field, but it is not necessary. Add the code in Listing 18.5 below the mysqli_query() function call.

## Listing 18.5.

```
1. $result = mysqli_query($dbc, $query)
2.        or trigger_error('Error querying database movieListing', E_USER_ERROR);
3.
4.    if (mysqli_num_rows($result) == 1)
5.    {
6.        $row = mysqli_fetch_assoc($result);
7.
8.        $movie_title = $row['title'];
9.        $movie_rating = $row['rating'];
10.        $movie_director = $row['director'];
11.        $movie_runtime = $row['running_time_in_minutes'];
12.        $movie_genre_text = $row['genre'];
13.
14.        $checked_movie_genres = explode(', ', $movie_genre_text);
15.    }
```

Notice that last line of code:

```
$checked_movie_genres = explode(', ', $movie_genre_text);
```

The explode()[2] function takes the comma-delimited list of genres stored for this movie and turns it into an array called $checked_movie_genres. Using it converts this string:

```
'Action,Adventure,Science Fiction'
```

into this array:

```
$checked_movie_genres[0] = 'Action'
$checked_movie_genres[1] = 'Adventure'
$checked_movie_genres[2] = 'Science Fiction'
```

So we can use it to populate the correct checkboxes for the "Genre".

The complete code for this if block looks like Listing 18.6.

---

[2]  explode(): *https://php.net/explode*

## Listing 18.6.

```php
1.  if (isset($_GET['id_to_edit']))
2.  {
3.      $id_to_edit = $_GET['id_to_edit'];
4.
5.      $query = "SELECT * FROM movieListing WHERE id = $id_to_edit";
6.
7.      $result = mysqli_query($dbc, $query)
8.              or trigger_error('Error querying database movieListing', E_USER_ERROR);
9.
10.     if (mysqli_num_rows($result) == 1)
11.     {
12.         $row = mysqli_fetch_assoc($result);
13.
14.         $movie_title = $row['title'];
15.         $movie_rating = $row['rating'];
16.         $movie_director = $row['director'];
17.         $movie_runtime = $row['running_time_in_minutes'];
18.         $movie_genre_text = $row['genre'];
19.
20.         $checked_movie_genres = explode(', ', $movie_genre_text);
21.     }
22.  }
```

### Consider a Database Relationship for Genres

*Notice above that we use* explode() *to separate a comma-delimited string of genres we store in the database. The problem with the above solution is that it denormalizes our list of genres—which incidentally is hard-coded from the* addmovie.php *script. A better and more long-term solution would be to create a database table that holds all of our genres and then create a cross-reference (or* JOIN *table) representing a many-to-many relationship between movies and genres. The advantage of this approach makes it easier to maintain/modify genres because it is contained entirely within the data model. A minor disadvantage is that it adds some complexity to your SQL queries. I leave it as a refactoring exercise for you to implement this improvement within the application.*

### Display the Edit Form

Before we add code for the other two conditions, we create the form to update the movie. We add this below the else block for the unintended condition. This form should look very similar to the form for the addmovie.php script, except that the fields are pre-populated with the data we just queried from the database. Listing 18.7 is the code for the form. Notice some of the differences between this form and the one in addmovie.php.

# 18. Editing Data Using the Web Application

## Listing 18.7.

```php
1. else // Unintended page link - No movie to edit, link back to index
2. {
3.     header("Location: index.php");
4. }
5. ?>
6. <form class="needs-validation" novalidate method="POST"
7.       action="<?= $_SERVER['PHP_SELF'] ?>">
8.     <div class="form-group row">
9.         <label for="movie_title" class="col-sm-3 col-form-label-lg">Title</label>
10.        <div class="col-sm-8">
11.            <input type="text" class="form-control" id="movie_title"
12.                name="movie_title" value='<?= $movie_title ?>'
13.                placeholder="Title" required>
14.            <div class="invalid-feedback">
15.                Please provide a valid movie title.
16.            </div>
17.        </div>
18.    </div>
19.    <div class="form-group row">
20.        <label for="movie_rating" class="col-sm-3 col-form-label-lg">Rating</label>
21.        <div class="col-sm-8">
22.            <select class="custom-select" id="movie_rating"
23.                    name="movie_rating" value='<?= $movie_rating ?>'
24.                    required>
25.            <option value="" disabled selected>Rating...</option>
26.            <option value="G" <?= $movie_rating == 'G' ? 'selected' : '' ?>>G
27.            </option>
28.            <option value="PG" <?= $movie_rating == 'PG' ? 'selected' : '' ?>>PG
29.            </option>
30.            <option value="PG-13" <?= $movie_rating == 'PG-13' ? 'selected' : '' ?>>PG-13
31.            </option>
32.            <option value="R" <?= $movie_rating == 'R' ? 'selected' : '' ?>>R
33.            </option>
34.            </select>
35.            <div class="invalid-feedback">
36.                Please select a movie rating.
37.            </div>
38.        </div>
39.    </div>
40.    <div class="form-group row">
41.        <label for="movie_director"
42.               class="col-sm-3 col-form-label-lg">Director</label>
43.        <div class="col-sm-8">
44.            <input type="text" class="form-control"
45.                id="movie_director" name="movie_director"
46.                value="<?= $movie_director ?>"
47.                placeholder="Director" required>
48.            <div class="invalid-feedback">
49.                Please provide a valid movie director.
50.            </div>
```

```
51.            </div>
52.        </div>
53.        <div class="form-group row">
54.            <label for="movie_running_time_in_minutes"
55.                    class="col-sm-3 col-form-label-lg">Running Time (min)</label>
56.            <div class="col-sm-8">
57.                <input type="number" class="form-control"
58.                        id="movie_running_time_in_minutes"
59.                        name="movie_running_time_in_minutes"
60.                        value='<?= $movie_runtime ?>'
61.                        placeholder="Running time (in minutes)" required>
62.                <div class="invalid-feedback">
63.                    Please provide a valid running time in minutes.
64.                </div>
65.            </div>
66.        </div>
67.        <div class="form-group row">
68.            <label class="col-sm-3 col-form-label-lg">Genre</label>
69.            <div class="col-sm-8">
70.                <?php
71.                foreach ($genres as $genre) {
72.                ?>
73.                    <div class="form-check form-check-inline col-sm-3">
74.                        <input class="form-check-input" type="checkbox"
75.                                id="movie_genre_checkbox_action_<?= $genre ?>"
76.                                name="movie_genre_checkbox[]"
77.                                value="<?= $genre ?>"
78.                                <?= in_array($genre, $checked_movie_genres) ? 'checked' : '' ?>>
79.                        <label class="form-check-label"
80.                                for="movie_genre_checkbox_action_<?= $genre ?>"><?= $genre ?></label>
81.                    </div>
82.                <?php
83.                }
84.                ?>
85.            </div>
86.        </div>
87.        <button class="btn btn-primary" type="submit" name="edit_movie_submission">Update Movie
88.        </button>
89.        <input type="hidden" name="id_to_update" value="<?= $id_to_edit ?>">
90. </form>
```

## Making Fields Sticky

Looking at the input text field for the movie title as an example:

```
<input type="text" class="form-control" id="movie_title"
        name="movie_title" value="<?= $movie_title ?>"
        placeholder="Title" required>
```

Notice the value attribute is set to the value of the $movie_title variable. This variable comes from the title field for this movie's row in the movieListing database table returned by our earlier query.

```
value='<?= $movie_title ?>'
```

The value attributes for these input fields need to be set for the movie title, director, and running time:

```
... name="movie_title" value= "<?= $movie_title ?>" ...
... name="movie_director" value= "<?= $movie_director ?>" ...
... name="movie_running_time_in_minutes" value="<?= $movie_runtime ?>" ...
```

The value attributes also need to be set for the rating selection and the genre checkboxes. However, they are a little trickier. First we will deal with rating selection:

```
<select class="custom-select" id="movie_rating" name="movie_rating"
        value="<?= $movie_rating ?>" required>
  <option value="" disabled selected>Rating...</option>
  <option value="G" <?= $movie_rating=='G' ? 'selected' : '' ?>>G</option>
  <option value="PG" <?= $movie_rating=='PG' ? 'selected':'' ?>>PG</option>
  <option value="PG-13" <?= $movie_rating=='PG-13' ? 'selected':''?>>PG-13</option>
  <option value="R" <?= $movie_rating=='R' ? 'selected':'' ?>>R</option>
</select>
```

In a select, only one option can be selected by default. Therefore, I used the ternary operator (?:) to check each option as it was added to the movie_rating select to test if this option was equal to the rating for this movie. If the option was equal, I set this option to selected. Otherwise, I set this option to an empty string ('').

Setting the value attributes for the genre checkboxes are also a little tricky and required the use of the ternary operator. Similar to how we displayed the checkboxes for "Genre" in addmovie.php, the code and markup in Listing 18.8 creates a checkbox input for each item in our genres array. Every genre checked by the user gets added to the movie_genre_checkbox array—note the [] added to the name attribute. Be aware that if the user does not select any genre, the movie_genre_checkbox name attribute will not exist in the $_POST[] superglobal array.

## Listing 18.8.

```php
1.  <?php
2.     foreach ($genres as $genre) {
3.  ?>
4.         <div class="form-check form-check-inline col-sm-3">
5.           <input class="form-check-input" type="checkbox"
6.              id="movie_genre_checkbox_action_<?= $genre ?>"
7.              name="movie_genre_checkbox[]"
8.              value="<?= $genre ?>" <?=in_array($genre, $checked_movie_genres) ? 'checked' : '' ?>>
9.           <label class="form-check-label"
10.             for="movie_genre_checkbox_action_<?= $genre ?>"><?= $genre ?></label>
11.        </div>
12. <?php
13.      }
14. ?>
```

Notice I added to the value attribute whether or not the genre was selected or not using the ternary operator:

```php
... value="<?= $genre ?>" <?= in_array($genre, $checked_movie_genres) ? 'checked' : '' ?> ...
```

In addmovie.php we merely have:

```php
... value="<?= $genre ?>" ...
```

However, we want to know if a particular genre is selected or not, and that information is contained in the $checked_movie_genres array we created above using the explode()function. Using the function in_array()[3] we can determine if $genre (the current genre we are processing in the foreach loop in the array $genres) is contained in the array $checked_movie_genres. in_array() returns true if $genre exists, otherwise it returns false. We can use the ternary operator to add the checked ('checked') attribute to the option for this genre if found, or an empty string ('') if not found:

```php
... <?= in_array($genre, $checked_movie_genres) ? 'checked' : '' ?> ...
```

### Using Bootstrap's Client-side Validation

As in the addmovie.php script, we are using Bootstrap's client side validation. This requires we do the following:

1. Set the form's class attribute to needs-validation and adding the novalidate attribute:

```html
<form class="needs-validation" novalidate ...
```

[3] in_array(): *https://php.net/in_array*

2. Marking `input` elements with a `required` attribute to ensure the fields we want validated get validated:

```
<input type="number" ... required>
```

3. Adding `<div>` elements with `class` attributes set to `invalid-feedback` containing the validation text we want the user to see if they forget to fill in the field. Again, we add these directly under the `<input>` elements we want validated. Listing 18.9 is the complete HTML markup for the "Running Time" input field along with the invalid feedback we want the user to see if they forget to enter a value.

## Listing 18.9.

```
1. <div class="form-group row">
2.     <label for="movie_running_time_in_minutes"
3.            class="col-sm-3 col-form-label-lg">Running Time (min)</label>
4.     <div class="col-sm-8">
5.         <input type="number" class="form-control"
6.                id="movie_running_time_in_minutes"
7.                name="movie_running_time_in_minutes"
8.                value='<?= $movie_runtime ?>'
9.                placeholder="Running time (in minutes)" required>
10.         <div class="invalid-feedback">
11.             Please provide a valid running time in minutes.
12.         </div>
13.     </div>
14. </div>
```

4. Adding the JavaScript code in Listing 18.10 to `<script>` tags following the form.

## Listing 18.10.

```
1. </form>
2. <script>
3. // JavaScript for disabling form submissions if there are invalid fields
4. (function() {
5.   'use strict';
6.   window.addEventListener('load', function() {
7.     // Fetch all the forms we want to apply custom Bootstrap validation styles to
8.     var forms = document.getElementsByClassName('needs-validation');
9.     // Loop over them and prevent submission
10.     var validation = Array.prototype.filter.call(forms, function(form) {
11.       form.addEventListener('submit', function(event) {
12.         if (form.checkValidity() === false) {
13.           event.preventDefault();
14.           event.stopPropagation();
15.         }
16.         form.classList.add('was-validated');
17.       }, false);
18.     });
19.   }, false);
20. })();
21. </script>
```

## DRY?

*This looks like we are repeating code from the* addmovie.php *script, doesn't it? In this case, since we are using boiler-plate Bootstrap validation code, it makes more sense to put the JavaScript code in an anonymous function directly below the form.*

### Pressing the Update Button

This is the second intended way we will navigate to the editmovie.php page. Therefore we will be dealing with the elseif block:

```php
elseif (isset($_POST['edit_movie_submission'], $_POST['movie_title'],
        $_POST['movie_rating'], $_POST['movie_director'],
        $_POST['movie_running_time_in_minutes'], $_POST['id_to_update'])) {
```

When we get into this condition, it is because a user selected the **Update Movie** submit button. Doing so POSTs back to editmovie.php with the form variables edit_movie_submission, movie_title, movie_rating, movie_director, movie_running_time_in_minutes, and id_to_update in the $_POST[] superglobal array. Note, because genre is optional we do not check if it is set.

Speaking of id_to_update, notice I created a hidden <input> element in the form and set it to the ID of the movie and set the name attribute to id_to_update. When the form data is posted back to editmovie.php, the ID is available in the $_POST[] superglobal array so that it can be updated in the database:

```php
<input type="hidden" name="id_to_update" value="<?= $id_to_edit ?>">
```

We need to do this to carry over the ID of the movie that was sent using a query parameter when editmovie.php was first called. Remember, HTTP requests and responses do not any state or information.

*Please see the aside in the previous chapter titled: THE WEB IS STATELESS!*

Upon first entering a condition where either form or query parameters are being passed in, I create separate variables for each. Again, this is not required and can be just as readable if you created descriptive name attributes for your form fields and access them using the $_POST super global variable. However, I find it easier to type, and the purpose of the variable stands out, assuming you use sufficiently descriptive names. Add the code in Listing 18.11 immediately under and within the elseif line.

## Listing 18.11.

```
1. elseif (isset($_POST['edit_movie_submission'], $_POST['movie_title'],
2.         $_POST['movie_rating'], $_POST['movie_director'],
3.         $_POST['movie_running_time_in_minutes'], $_POST['id_to_update']))
4. {
5.
6.     $movie_title = $_POST['movie_title'];
7.     $movie_rating = $_POST['movie_rating'];
8.     $movie_director = $_POST['movie_director'];
9.     $movie_runtime = $_POST['movie_running_time_in_minutes'];
10.    $checked_movie_genres = $_POST['movie_genre_checkbox'];
11.    $id_to_update = $_POST['id_to_update'];
```

We also need to build a comma delimited string containing the movie genre from the checkbox array. Add the following code next:

```
$movie_genre_text = "";

if (isset($checked_movie_genres))
{
    $movie_genre_text = implode(", ", $checked_movie_genres);
}
```

Just like the addmovie.php script, a movie can have multiple genres. To store them all, we create a comma-delimited list of the chosen genres from the checkbox array. We do this by calling the implode()[4] function ONLY if the user selected at least one genre. If the user doesn't choose any genres, the checkbox array does not exist. Therefore we need to check that it is set first before calling implode(). If the user does not select a genre, we insert an empty string into the genre field of the movieListing table.

Now that we have all the updated movie listing data in the form we want, we can update the movieListing table with an SQL UPDATE query.

A SQL UPDATE query looks like this:

```
UPDATE <table_name> SET <field_name> = <value_[, ...]> WHERE <condition>
```

Thus, our query string and call to mysqli_query() should look like Listing 18.12

---

[4] implode(): https://php.net/implode

## Listing 18.12.

```
1. $query = "UPDATE movieListing SET title = '$movie_title', rating = '$movie_rating', "
2.         . "director = '$movie_director', running_time_in_minutes = '$movie_runtime', "
3.         . "genre = '$movie_genre_text' "
4.         . "WHERE id = $id_to_update";
5.
6. mysqli_query($dbc, $query)
7.     or trigger_error(
8.         'Error querying database movieListing: Failed to update movie listing',
9.         E_USER_ERROR
10.     );
```

Finally, we can navigate back to the moviedetails.php using this movie's ID as a query parameter to display the updated movie details with the following lines of code:

```
$nav_link = 'moviedetails.php?id=' . $id_to_update;

header("Location: $nav_link");
exit;
```

The complete listing for this elseif block looks like Listing 18.13.

## Listing 18.13.

```
1. elseif (isset($_POST['edit_movie_submission'], $_POST['movie_title'],
2.          $_POST['movie_rating'], $_POST['movie_director'],
3.          $_POST['movie_running_time_in_minutes'], $_POST['id_to_update']))
4. {
5.
6.     $movie_title = $_POST['movie_title'];
7.     $movie_rating = $_POST['movie_rating'];
8.     $movie_director = $_POST['movie_director'];
9.     $movie_runtime = $_POST['movie_running_time_in_minutes'];
10.    $checked_movie_genres = $_POST['movie_genre_checkbox'];
11.    $id_to_update = $_POST['id_to_update'];
12.
13.    $movie_genre_text = "";
14.
15.    if (isset($checked_movie_genres))
16.    {
17.        $movie_genre_text = implode(", ", $checked_movie_genres);
18.    }
19.
20.    $query = "UPDATE movieListing SET title = '$movie_title', rating = '$movie_rating', "
21.        . "director = '$movie_director', running_time_in_minutes = '$movie_runtime', "
22.        . "genre = '$movie_genre_text' "
23.        . "WHERE id = $id_to_update";
24.
```

```
25.      mysqli_query($dbc, $query)
26.          or trigger_error(
27.              'Error querying database movieListing: Failed to update movie listing',
28.              E_USER_ERROR
29.          );
30.
31.      $nav_link = 'moviedetails.php?id=' . $id_to_update;
32.
33.      header("Location: $nav_link");
34.      exit;
35. }
```

So, let us say we want to add five minutes to a movie because IMDB[5] may not have accounted for the end credits scene. We also believe this movie fits in the "Drama" and "Fantasy" genres as well. So, our edits might look something like Figure 18.7.

The application directs the user to the "Movie Details" page, where they can immediately see the results (Figure 18.8).

Figure 18.7.

Figure 18.8.

### Unanticipated Navigation Methods

As in the last chapter, since the HTTP request is coming from the client. In theory, unanticipated or malicious parameters can be in the query string (or even field parameters from the HTTP POST). Therefore, all other conditions we could navigate to the editmovie.php page are unintended, and we will be dealing with the else block:

```
else  // Unintended page link
{
```

As in the last chapter, since all of the above conditions are the ones where we want the application to function in a specific way, it is a best practice to put the application's response to unpredictable behavior in an else condition. In this case, we just want to link back to the main "Movies I Like" index.php page:

---

[5]  IMDB: https://imdb.com

```
else // Unintended page link -  No movie to edit, redirect back to index
{
    header("Location: index.php");
    exit();
}
```

# Complete Code Listing

Listing 18.14 holds the complete listing for the editmovie.php page.

Listing 18.14.

```
1.  <html>
2.  <head>
3.     <link rel="stylesheet"
4.            href="https://stackpath.bootstrapcdn.com/bootstrap/4.2.1/css/bootstrap.min.css"
5.            integrity="sha384-GJzZqFGwb1QTTN6wy59ffF1BuGJpLSa9DkKMp0DgiMDm4iYMj70gZWKYbI706tWS"
6.            crossorigin="anonymous">
7.     <title>Edit a Movie</title>
8.  </head>
9.  <body>
10. <div class="card">
11.     <div class="card-body">
12.         <h1>Edit a Movie</h1>
13.         <nav class="nav">
14.             <a class="nav-link" href="index.php">Movies I Like</a>
15.         </nav>
16.         <hr/>
17.         <?php
18.         require_once('dbconnection.php');
19.
20.         $dbc = mysqli_connect(DB_HOST, DB_USER, DB_PASSWORD, DB_NAME)
21.                 or trigger_error(
22.                     'Error connecting to MySQL server for ' . DB_NAME,
23.                     E_USER_ERROR
24.                 );
25.
26.         $genres = [
27.             'Action', 'Adventure', 'Comedy', 'Documentary', 'Drama',
28.             'Fantasy', 'Horror', 'Romance', 'Science Fiction'
29.         ];
30.
31.         if (isset($_GET['id_to_edit'])) {
32.             $id_to_edit = $_GET['id_to_edit'];
33.
34.             $query = "SELECT * FROM movieListing WHERE id = $id_to_edit";
35.
36.             $result = mysqli_query($dbc, $query)
37.                 or trigger_error('Error querying database movieListing', E_USER_ERROR);
38.
```

```
39.            if (mysqli_num_rows($result) == 1) {
40.                $row = mysqli_fetch_assoc($result);
41.
42.                $movie_title = $row['title'];
43.                $movie_rating = $row['rating'];
44.                $movie_director = $row['director'];
45.                $movie_runtime = $row['running_time_in_minutes'];
46.                $movie_genre_text = $row['genre'];
47.
48.                $checked_movie_genres = explode(', ', $movie_genre_text);
49.            }
50.        } elseif (isset($_POST['edit_movie_submission'], $_POST['movie_title'],
51.            $_POST['movie_rating'], $_POST['movie_director'],
52.            $_POST['movie_running_time_in_minutes'])) {
53.
54.            $movie_title = $_POST['movie_title'];
55.            $movie_rating = $_POST['movie_rating'];
56.            $movie_director = $_POST['movie_director'];
57.            $movie_runtime = $_POST['movie_running_time_in_minutes'];
58.            $checked_movie_genres = $_POST['movie_genre_checkbox'];
59.            $id_to_update = $_POST['id_to_update'];
60.
61.            $movie_genre_text = "";
62.
63.            if (isset($checked_movie_genres)) {
64.                $movie_genre_text = implode(", ", $checked_movie_genres);
65.            }
66.
67.            $query = "UPDATE movieListing SET title = '$movie_title', rating = '$movie_rating', "
68.                    . "director = '$movie_director', running_time_in_minutes = '$movie_runtime', "
69.                    . "genre = '$movie_genre_text' "
70.                    . "WHERE id = $id_to_update";
71.
72.        mysqli_query($dbc, $query)
73.        or trigger_error(
74.            'Error querying database movieListing: Failed to update movie listing',
75.            E_USER_ERROR
76.        );
77.
78.        $nav_link = 'moviedetails.php?id=' . $id_to_update;
79.
80.        header("Location: $nav_link");
81.        exit;
82.        } else  // Unintended page link - No movie to edit, link back to index
83.        {
84.        header("Location: index.php");
85.        exit;
86.        }
87.    ?>
88.     <form class="needs-validation" novalidate method="POST"
89.            action="<?= $_SERVER['PHP_SELF'] ?>">
```

```
90.          <div class="form-group row">
91.              <label for="movie_title"
92.                   class="col-sm-3 col-form-label-lg">Title</label>
93.              <div class="col-sm-8">
94.                  <input type="text" class="form-control"
95.                       id="movie_title" name="movie_title"
96.                       value='<?= $movie_title ?>'
97.                       placeholder="Title" required>
98.                  <div class="invalid-feedback">
99.                      Please provide a valid movie title.
101.                 </div>
101.             </div>
102.         </div>
103.         <div class="form-group row">
104.             <label for="movie_rating"
105.                  class="col-sm-3 col-form-label-lg">Rating</label>
106.             <div class="col-sm-8">
107.                 <select class="custom-select" id="movie_rating"
108.                      name="movie_rating"
109.                      value='<?= $movie_rating ?>' required>
110.                 <option value="" disabled selected>Rating...
111.                 </option>
112.                 <option value="G" <?= $movie_rating == 'G' ? 'selected' : '' ?>>G
113.                 </option>
114.                 <option value="PG" <?= $movie_rating == 'PG' ? 'selected' : '' ?>>PG
115.                 </option>
116.                 <option value="PG-13" <?= $movie_rating == 'PG-13' ? 'selected' : '' ?>>PG-13
117.                 </option>
118.                 <option value="R" <?= $movie_rating == 'R' ? 'selected' : '' ?>>R
119.                 </option>
120.                 </select>
121.                 <div class="invalid-feedback">
122.                     Please select a movie rating.
123.                 </div>
124.             </div>
125.         </div>
126.         <div class="form-group row">
127.             <label for="movie_director"
128.                  class="col-sm-3 col-form-label-lg">Director</label>
129.             <div class="col-sm-8">
130.                 <input type="text" class="form-control"
131.                      id="movie_director" name="movie_director"
132.                      value='<?= $movie_director ?>'
133.                      placeholder="Director" required>
134.                 <div class="invalid-feedback">
135.                     Please provide a valid movie director.
136.                 </div>
137.             </div>
138.         </div>
139.         <div class="form-group row">
```

```
140.            <label for="movie_running_time_in_minutes"
141.                 class="col-sm-3 col-form-label-lg">Running Time (min)</label>
142.            <div class="col-sm-8">
143.                <input type="number" class="form-control"
144.                     id="movie_running_time_in_minutes"
145.                     name="movie_running_time_in_minutes"
146.                     value='<?= $movie_runtime ?>'
147.                     placeholder="Running time (in minutes)"
148.                     required>
149.                <div class="invalid-feedback">
150.                    Please provide a valid running time in minutes.
151.                </div>
152.            </div>
153.        </div>
155.        <div class="form-group row">
156.            <label class="col-sm-3 col-form-label-lg">Genre</label>
156.            <div class="col-sm-8">
157.                <?php
158.                foreach ($genres as $genre) {
159.                ?>
160.                    <div class="form-check form-check-inline col-sm-3">
161.                        <input class="form-check-input"
162.                             type="checkbox"
163.                             id="movie_genre_checkbox_action_<?= $genre ?>"
164.                             name="movie_genre_checkbox[]"
165.                             value="<?= $genre ?>"
166.                             <?= in_array($genre, $checked_movie_genres) ? 'checked' : '' ?>>
167.                        <label class="form-check-label"
168.                             for="movie_genre_checkbox_action_<?= $genre ?>"><?= $genre ?></label>
169.                    </div>
170.                <?php
171.                }
172.                ?>
173.            </div>
174.        </div>
175.        <button class="btn btn-primary" type="submit"
176.             name="edit_movie_submission">Update Movie
177.        </button>
178.        <input type="hidden" name="id_to_update"
179.             value="<?= $id_to_edit ?>">
180.    </form>
181.    <script>
182.        // JavaScript for disabling form submissions if there are invalid fields
183.        (function () {
184.          'use strict';
185.          window.addEventListener('load', function () {
186.            // Fetch all the forms we want to apply custom Bootstrap validation styles to
187.            var forms = document.getElementsByClassName('needs-validation');
188.            // Loop over them and prevent submission
189.            var validation = Array.prototype.filter.call(forms, function (form) {
```

```
190.                    form.addEventListener('submit', function (event) {
191.                        if (form.checkValidity() == false) {
192.                            event.preventDefault();
193.                            event.stopPropagation();
194.                        }
195.                        form.classList.add('was-validated');
196.                    }, false);
197.                });
198.            }, false);
199.        })();
200.    </script>
201.    </div>
202. </div>
203. <script src="https://code.jquery.com/jquery-3.3.1.slim.min.js"
204.         integrity="sha384-q8i/X+965Dz00rT7abK41JStQIAqVgRVzpbzo5smXKp4YfRvH+8abtTE1Pi6jizo"
205.         crossorigin="anonymous"></script>
206. <script src="https://cdnjs.cloudflare.com/ajax/libs/popper.js/1.14.6/umd/popper.min.js"
207.         integrity="sha384-wHAiFfRlMFy6i5SRaxvfOCifBUQy1xHdJ/yoi7FRNXMRBu5WHdZYu1hA6ZOblgut"
208.         crossorigin="anonymous"></script>
209. <script src="https://stackpath.bootstrapcdn.com/bootstrap/4.2.1/js/bootstrap.min.js"
210.         integrity="sha384-B0UglyR+jN6CkvvICOB2joaf5I4l3gm9GU6Hc1og6Ls7i6U/mkkaduKaBhlAXv9k"
211.         crossorigin="anonymous"></script>
212. </body>
213. </html>
```

## Exercises

1. Add an "edit a movie" page and add a button to update a movie to the details page.
2. **Bonus:** Change the Movie Genre field from a comma-separated text field to a "Genre" table. See the aside at the end of the section on "Navigating from moviedetails.php to editmovie.php"

# Chapter

# 19

# Working With Files and Feature Additions to Existing Code

*"One of my most productive days was throwing away 1000 lines of code."*

*–Ken Thompson*

In this chapter, we add the ability to upload and display an image to our *Movie Listing* application.

Let's say we have our *Movie Listing* application out in the wild, and one of our users says, "Hey, I really like the App, but it would be truly awesome if you could add a thumbnail image for each movie. Can you do that?"

As easy as that one sentence is to say regarding the addition of this feature, it does require changing quite a few PHP scripts. Furthermore, it can require modifying all the PHP scripts depending on our implementation. Therefore, it makes sense to keep your users in the loop and present them with different use cases and screenshots. However, this is beyond the scope of this book, so I will jump right in with a description of how I think it should look, work, and what needs to be modified:

1. Add a field to the `movieListing` database table for holding the file information (more on this below).

2. Create an `images/` folder for holding images for movies.

3. Modify `addmovie.php` so users can upload an image of a movie and add it to the movie details entry in the database. Also, display the image on the "Add a Movie" page after adding the movie. The uploading of an image should be optional as well.

4. Modify `index.php` to display a thumbnail image of the movie at the beginning of each movie row.

5. Modify `moviedetails.php` to display the image on the "Movie Details" page to better identify the movie.

6. Modify `editmovie.php` so that a user can upload a different image of a movie (or not) and modify the movie details entry in the database.

7. Modify `removemovie.php` to show the image on the "Remove a Movie" page to identify the movie better.

# Add a Field for File Information

In theory, we could upload an image file and store the image in the database. However, databases were designed for quick access, and image files can be large. Therefore, doing so could slow down the retrieval time when querying the database, especially when dealing with a large database.

A better solution is storing the image on the server in an images/ folder. Then, we create a string field in the movieListing table that holds the file path location to the uploaded image.

To add a new field to an existing table, we need to ALTER the the movieListing table. Let's do this using Adminer. Using our browser, log in to Adminer as movieguru and create our database and table (Figure 19.1).

Select the Movie database as in Figure 19.2.

Select the movieListing table shown in Figure 19.3

Figure 19.1.

Figure 19.2.

Figure 19.3.

Then select **Alter table** (Figure 19.4).

Select the + after the genre field to add a new field at the end of the movieListing table as in Figure 19.5

Give the image_file field the following properties as in Figure 19.6:

- In the **Column name** below genre, enter image_file.
- Select the type as **varchar**.
- Enter 100 for the **length**.

Once you press **Save**, the table description should look like Figure 19.7.

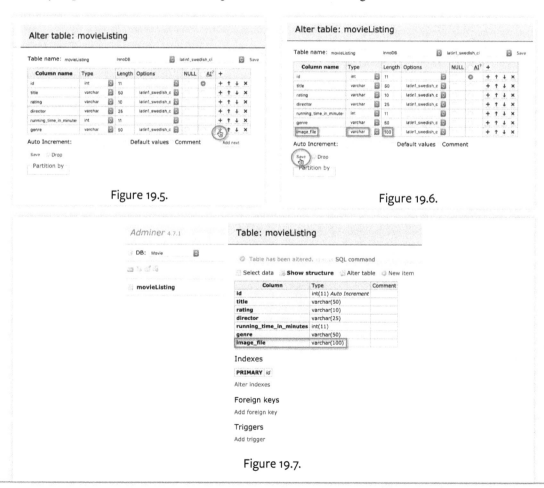

Figure 19.4.

Figure 19.5.

Figure 19.6.

Figure 19.7.

# Create a Folder for Uploaded Movie Image Files

In your main web folder, where your index.php script is located (mine is /MovieListing), create a new folder called images/ as in Figure 19.8.

Note, your web server must have privileges to write files into this folder. For example, on a *NIX system, if your webserver (i.e., Apache) runs as user www-data, make sure this folder is writeable by the same user.

Figure 19.8.

```
$ cd /var/www/public/html/MovieListing
$ sudo chown www-data images
$ sudo chmod u+w images
```

It is also good to have a generic image you can use for movie listings that do not have an image. I called mine generic_movie.jpg.

# Adding File Upload Capability

We want to modify the addmovie.php script so a user can (optionally) upload an image of a movie and add it to the movie details entry in the database. Then, we can display the image on the page after the user adds the new movie. Here is how we want it to work.

When first navigating to our "Add a Movie" page, our modified form should look like Figure 19.9

Figure 19.9.

Let's say I want to add the movie "Serenity." Figure 19.10 shows the details so far.

Assuming I already downloaded an image, when I select **Choose File** as in Figure 19.11, I should get a file browser window that pops up, and I can navigate to the image file I want to upload, select it, then select **Open** (Figure 19.12).

The name of the selected file is now displayed (Figure 19.13) after the "Choose File" button (instead of "No file chosen").

Once we press **Add Movie** (Figure 19.16), We want to see the added movie details modified with the image we uploaded on a page that looks like Figure 19.15.

Figure 19.10.

Movie Image File    Choose File   No file chosen

Figure 19.11.

Add Movie

Figure 19.14.

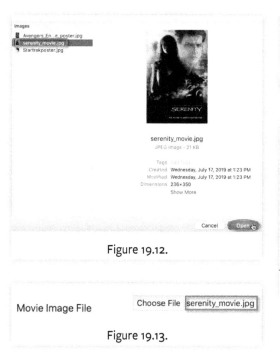

Figure 19.12.

Movie Image File    Choose File   serenity_movie.jpg

Figure 19.13.

Add a Movie

Movies I Like

The Following Movie Details were Added:

**Serenity**

| | | |
|---|---|---|
| Rating | | PG-13 |
| Director | | Joss Whedon |
| Running Time (minutes) | | 119 |
| Genre | | Action, Adventure, Science Fiction |

Would you like to add another movie?

Figure 19.15.

## Modifying the Form to Allow Uploads

We need to add two main things to our `addmovie.php` form to enable the uploading of files. First we need to add the `enctype` attribute_to the `<form>` element and set it to `multipart/form-data`:

```
<form enctype="multipart/form-data" ...>
```

When files are uploaded using a form, the file data is contained in the form data. By setting the `enctype` attribute of the `<form>` element to `multipart/form-data`, the browser knows to include the file data in the form data when sent to the webserver.

Secondly, we must add a file input element to the form:

```
<input type="file" class="form-control-file"
        id="movie_image_file" name="movie_image_file">
```

Add the file input element within a Bootstrap `form-group row` right before the submit button in your form like in Listing 19.1.

### Listing 19.1.

```
 1. </div>
 2. <div class="form-group row">
 3.     <label for="movie_image_file"
 4.             class="col-sm-3 col-form-label-lg">Movie Image File</label>
 5.     <div class="col-sm-8">
 6.         <input type="file" class="form-control-file"
 7.                 id="movie_image_file" name="movie_image_file">
 8.     </div>
 9. </div>
10. <button class="btn btn-primary" type="submit"
11.         name="add_movie_submission">Add Movie</button>
12. </form>
```

Adding file upload capability adds a bit of code to our script. Therefore, it would be best to decouple as much of the file handling capability from the `addmovie.php` script as possible and put this capability into its own set of functions. This separation is a good design decision since we will utilize this functionality in our "Edit a Movie" page as well. Therefore, create a separate script for holding image file functionality.

## Create Separate Functions for Handling Image File Uploads

When uploading an image file to the server, there are two things we need to take into consideration:

1. what type(s) of image files we want to allow,
2. and how big of a file do we want to allow.

For security, we want to ensure users only upload image files (of the image types we support) so users do not upload any executable files. Also, we want to limit the size so that we do not run out of storage space and the web server does not crash. Before saving an uploaded file to our images/ folder, we should validate the file meets these considerations, and there were no errors in the file upload. The $_FILES super global variable contains all of the information about an uploaded file.

### The $_FILES Superglobal Variable

The ability to upload files is typically done with a form. All the information about and including the file is contained in the $_FILES super global variable. The $_FILES superglobal variable is a two-dimensional associative array. The first dimension is set to the name attribute of the file input element, which is movie_image_file in this case. PHP sets the second dimension to different attributes about the uploaded file.

Here are the following attributes and their values:

| Attribute Name | Attribute Meaning | Attribute Value |
|---|---|---|
| $_FILES['movie_image_file']['name'] | the name of file | serenity_movie.jpg |
| $_FILES['movie_image_file']['type'] | the image type | image/jpg |
| $_FILES['movie_image_file']['size'] | the image size in bytes | 21480 |
| $_FILES['movie_image_file']['tmp_name'] | the temporary storage location of the file on the server | /tmp/phpV9CAHI |
| $_FILES['movie_image_file']['error'] | the error code for the file upload; 0 is good[1] | 0 |

---

[1]   The PHP documentation has a complete explanation of all the error codes that can be found in $_FILES['movie_image_file']['error'] as a result of uploading a file, see: https://php.net/features.file-upload.errors

## Validating Uploaded Movie Image Files

As mentioned earlier, we want to limit the size and the image type of the uploaded image file. We want to restrict our images to either JPEGs, PNGs, or GIFs. We also want to make sure the file is uploaded without error. Since we will often refer to the size limit, it is best to create a constant for this maximum file size and put it in a separate file that other scripts can include.

Create a new PHP script called movielistingfileconstants.php and add the following code:

```php
<?php
// Movie Listing File Constants
define('ML_MAX_FILE_SIZE', 524288);
```

*In the php.ini configuration file, a couple of settings affect file uploads. By default, these settings should already be enabled:*

- post_max_size = (some number)M
- upload_max_filesize = (some number)M
- file_uploads = TRUE

post_max_size *controls the total size of your post request while* upload_max_filesize *controls the max size of each file uploaded. The sum of file sizes can't exceed the maximum size of the post request. The* M *suffix signifies megabytes.*

*In the* apache2.conf *configuration file ensure the following setting is enabled correctly:*

- LimitRequestBody *sets a limit on how large a post request can be.*

*So, in order to have working uploads for your PHP scripts, these three numbers have to be set correctly:* LimitRequestBody = post_max_size > upload_max_filesize

Next, create another new PHP script called movieimagefileutil.php. This file is where we put functions that work with movie image files.

Add the following require_once() statement to movieimagefileutil.php to include movielistingfileconstants.php:

```php
<?php
require_once 'movielistingfileconstants.php';
```

Now, let's create a function called `validateMovieImageFile()`:

```php
<?php
require_once 'movielistingfileconstants.php';

function validateMovieImageFile()
{
}
```

## PHP DocBlocks

Although not required, a standard practice is to add PHP DocBlock comments to the beginning of functions. It is a great way to document how a function works, which is helpful for developers using and maintaining your function. It is also a great way to flesh out the design of your function and serves as a roadmap when implementing it. Based on the description above on how we are validating uploaded movie image files, here is what a good *Doc Block* for this function should look like:

```php
/**
 * Purpose:        Validates an uploaded movie image file
 *
 * Description:    Validates an uploaded movie image file is not greater than ML_MAX_FILE_SIZE (1/2 MB),
 *                 and is either a jpg or png image type, and has no errors. If the image file
 *                 validates to these constraints, an error message containing an empty string is
 *                 returned. If there is an error, a string containing constraints the file failed
 *                 to validate to are returned.
 *
 * @return string  Empty if validation is successful, otherwise error string containing
 *                 constraints the image file failed to validate to.
 */
function validateMovieImageFile()
{
}
```

> *There are no parameters in this function. However, if you don't use type hints, parameters are noted using the @param tag, one for each parameter. For more information, see Docblocks in PHP[2] on their proper usage.*

## Handling Errors

We know we will return a string containing an error message if there are errors or an empty string if there are none. Let's create a variable called `error_message` initialized to an empty string at the start of our function. At the end of the function, return it:

---

[2]   Docblocks in PHP: https://docs.phpdoc.org/guides/docblocks.html

```
function validateMovieImageFile()
{
    $error_message = "";
    // ...
    return $error_message;
}
```

There are two top-level conditions we need to check before we can do anything with the uploaded file. We need to check that the $_FILES super global variable exists—it does not exist if the user chose not to select a file for upload. Also, we need to check there were no errors uploading the file. We can combine these checks in a single if statement, joining them with a logical AND (&&). Add the following code after $error_message = "":

```
$error_message = "";

// Check for $_FILES being set and no errors.
if (isset($_FILES) && $_FILES['movie_image_file']['error'] == UPLOAD_ERR_OK)
{
    // ...
}
```

There is one other elseif condition that we need to check if the above if condition is false. We need to check if there was an error uploading the file. Since we do not know whether the condition failed because the $_FILES super global was not set or because the error was not equal to UPLOAD_ERR_OK, we need to check if the $_FILES is set before we can check to see if there was an error uploading the file. We also need to check that the user did upload a file. Again, we can combine all these into one elseif condition check combining these clauses using &&. PHP provides several constants to describe file errors. For our purposes, we can catch all the error conditions by testing that 'error' in our $_FILES array is NOT UPLOAD_ERR_OK. If we get into this elseif condition, it was because there was an error uploading the image file. if so, we need to set error_message to an appropriate error message stating there was an error uploading the file:

```
elseif (isset($_FILES) && $_FILES['movie_image_file']['error'] != UPLOAD_ERR_NO_FILE
    && $_FILES['movie_image_file']['error'] != UPLOAD_ERR_OK)
{
    $error_message = "Error uploading movie image file.";
}
```

So, our function looks like Listing 19.2 so far.

## Listing 19.2.

```
1. function validateMovieImageFile()
2. {
3.     $error_message = "";
4.
5.
6.     // Check for $_FILES being set and no errors.
7.     if (isset($_FILES) && $_FILES['movie_image_file']['error'] == UPLOAD_ERR_OK)
8.     {
9.         ...
10.    }
11.    elseif (isset($_FILES) && $_FILES['movie_image_file']['error'] != UPLOAD_ERR_NO_FILE
12.            && $_FILES['movie_image_file']['error'] != UPLOAD_ERR_OK)
13.    {
14.        $error_message = "Error uploading movie image file.";
15.    }
16.
17.    return $error_message;
18. }
```

If neither of the above conditions is true, the user did not upload a file and there is no error.

If we enter the first condition (the if condition), the user uploaded a file, and there were no errors. Now we can check if the file meets the size constraints. Add the following condition to see if the file is too large inside and just below the if condition, and if it is, set error_message to an appropriate error message stating the file exceeds the maximum size as in Listing 19.3.

## Listing 19.3.

```
1. // Check for $_FILES being set and no errors.
2. if (isset($_FILES) && $_FILES['movie_image_file']['error'] == UPLOAD_ERR_OK)
3. {
4.     // Check for uploaded file < Max file size AND an acceptable image type
5.     if ($_FILES['movie_image_file']['size'] > ML_MAX_FILE_SIZE)
6.     {
7.         $error_message = "The movie file image must be less than " . ML_MAX_FILE_SIZE . " Bytes";
8.     }
9.     //...
10. }
```

Next, we need to make sure the type of image file uploaded is either a JPEG, PNG, or GIF type of image. There are five strings that can be set in $_FILES['movie_image_file']['type'] that meet this constraint: image/jpg, image/jpeg, image/pjpeg, image/png, and image/gif. Again, we can combine these checks into a single condition check by joining the conditional clauses with &&. If the uploaded image type is not one of these images, we need to add an appropriate error message string stating the acceptable types of images allowed. Also, the error message will be slightly different depending on if the uploaded file also exceeds the maximum file size or not. Add the code in Listing 19.4, just after the maximum file size condition code you just added.

## Listing 19.4.

```
1.  // Check for $_FILES being set and no errors.
2.  if (isset($_FILES) && $_FILES['movie_image_file']['error'] == UPLOAD_ERR_OK)
3.  {
4.      // ...
5.      $image_type = $_FILES['movie_image_file']['type'];
6.
7.      if ($image_type != 'image/jpg' && $image_type != 'image/jpeg' && $image_type != 'image/pjpeg'
8.          && $image_type != 'image/png' && $image_type != 'image/gif')
9.      {
10.         if (empty($error_message))
11.         {
12.             $error_message = "The movie file image must be of type jpg, png, or gif.";
13.         }
14.         else
15.         {
16.             $error_message .= ", and be an image of type jpg, png, or gif.";
17.         }
18.     }
19. }
```

Our completed `validateMovieImageFile()` function looks like Listing 19.5.

## Listing 19.5.

```
1.  function validateMovieImageFile()
2.  {
3.      $error_message = "";
4.
5.      // Check for $_FILES being set and no errors.
6.      if (isset($_FILES) && $_FILES['movie_image_file']['error'] == UPLOAD_ERR_OK)
7.      {
8.          // Check for uploaded file < Max file size AND an acceptable image type
9.          if ($_FILES['movie_image_file']['size'] > ML_MAX_FILE_SIZE)
10.         {
11.             $error_message = "The movie file image must be less than " . ML_MAX_FILE_SIZE . " Bytes";
12.         }
13.
14.         $image_type = $_FILES['movie_image_file']['type'];
15.
16.         if ($image_type != 'image/jpg' && $image_type != 'image/jpeg' && $image_type != 'image/pjpeg'
17.             && $image_type != 'image/png' && $image_type != 'image/gif')
18.         {
19.             if (empty($error_message))
```

```
20.            {
21.                $error_message = "The movie file image must be of type jpg, png, or gif.";
22.            }
23.            else
24.            {
25.                $error_message .= ", and be an image of type jpg, png, or gif.";
26.            }
27.        }
28.    }
29.    elseif (isset($_FILES) && $_FILES['movie_image_file']['error'] != UPLOAD_ERR_NO_FILE
30.        && $_FILES['movie_image_file']['error'] != UPLOAD_ERR_OK)
31.    {
32.        $error_message = "Error uploading movie image file.";
33.    }
34.
35.    return $error_message;
36. }
```

### Consider Preventing Uploading of generic_movie.jpg

In the above implementation, nothing is preventing the user from uploading an image named generic_movie.jpg. It would be a good idea to prevent this by checking the name of the uploaded file. Otherwise, anyone could overwrite the default image we use for movies. In general, you should handle file uploads carefully and consider how someone might abuse them. I leave this as an exercise for you to do.

### Consider in_array() to Check Image Types

In the code in Listing 19.5, we have the following if clause for validating legal image types:

```
if ($image_type != 'image/jpg' && $image_type != 'image/jpeg' && $image_type != 'image/pjpeg'
    && $image_type != 'image/png' && $image_type != 'image/gif')
```

This kind of code gets messy and is difficult to maintain. A better solution for picking out a legal image type is to use the built-in PHP function in_array()[3]. To use it, create an array of the allowed image types, then check to see if the set image type is found in the array:

```
$allowed_image_types = [
    'image/jpg', 'image/jpeg', 'image/pjpeg', 'image/png', 'image/gif'
];

if (in_array($image_type, $allowed_image_types))
{
    // ...
}
```

---

[3]  in_array(): https://php.net/in-array

## Moving Image Files

Assuming the uploaded movie image file validates, we want to move the file from the temporary location on the webserver to our `images/` folder. Once that's done, we should return the path location of the file to store with the other movie details in the database. If a user does not upload a file—or there was an error uploading the file—we return an empty string for the path location. This empty string serves later as an indicator to show the generic file icon.

Since we will be referring to the `images/` folder often, it is best to create a constant for this upload path and put it in a separate file that can be included by other scripts. Therefore, add `define('ML_UPLOAD_PATH', 'images/');` to `movielistingfileconstants.php`. We also need a constant for a default image file in case the user does not upload an image. Here is what the complete constants file should look like now:

```php
<?php
// Movie Listing File Constants
define('ML_UPLOAD_PATH', 'images/');
define('ML_MAX_FILE_SIZE', 524288);
define('ML_DEFAULT_MOVIE_FILE_NAME', 'generic_movie.jpg');
```

Always use descriptive names for functions, a good one is: `addMovieImageFileReturnPathLocation()`. Below the `validateMovieImageFile()` function, let's create our new function with a good descriptive DocBlock as in Listing 19.6.

## Listing 19.6.

```
1.  /**
2.   * Purpose:        Moves an uploaded movie image file to the ML_UPLOAD_PATH (images/)
3.   *                 folder and return the path location.
4.   *
5.   * Description:    Moves an uploaded movie image file from the temporary server location
6.   *                 to the ML_UPLOAD_PATH (images/) folder IF a movie image file was uploaded
7.   *                 and returns the path location of the uploaded file by appending the file
8.   *                 name to the ML_UPLOAD_PATH (e.g. images/movie_image.png). IF a movie image
9.   *                 file was NOT uploaded, an empty string will be returned for the path.
10.  *
11.  * @return string  Path to movie image file IF a file was uploaded AND moved to the
12.  *                 ML_UPLOAD_PATH (images/) folder, otherwise and empty string.
13.  */
14. function addMovieImageFileReturnPathLocation()
15. {
16. }
```

Since we know we are going to return a string containing the path location or an empty string if no file was uploaded or there were errors, create a variable called $movie_file_path set to an empty string and return it:

```
function addMovieImageFileReturnPathLocation()
{
    $movie_file_path = "";
    // ...
    return $movie_file_path;
}
```

Before we move the uploaded file, we need to check that the user actually uploaded a file and there are no errors. Add the following code after $movie_file_path = "":

```
$movie_file_path = "";

// Check for $_FILES being set and no errors.
if (isset($_FILES) && $_FILES['movie_image_file']['error'] == UPLOAD_ERR_OK)
{
    // ...
}
```

If we reach this condition, we can start building the path. Add the following code just below the if condition:

```
if (isset($_FILES) && $_FILES['movie_image_file']['error'] == UPLOAD_ERR_OK)
{
    $movie_file_path = ML_UPLOAD_PATH . $_FILES['movie_image_file']['name'];
}
```

Next, we need to move the file from its temporary location on the webserver to our images/ folder. We do that using the move_uploaded_file()[4] function. This function takes two arguments:

1. the first is the source path location of the file we want to move,
2. and the second is the destination path location of where we want to move the file to

---

[4] move_uploaded_file(): *https://php.net/move_uploaded_file*

Note the file path locations also must include the name of the files. `move_uploaded_file()` returns `true` if successful, otherwise `false`. We will put the call in an `if` condition and reset `movie_file_path` to an empty string if it fails. Add the following code below the line where we previously set `movie_file_path`:

```
$movie_file_path = ML_UPLOAD_PATH . $_FILES['movie_image_file']['name'];

if (!move_uploaded_file($_FILES['movie_image_file']['tmp_name'], $movie_file_path))
{
    $movie_file_path = "";
}
```

The above code moves the uploaded movie image file from the temporary location on the webserver to the `images/` folder. Our completed `addMovieImageFileReturnPathLocation()` function looks like Listing 19.7.

## Listing 19.7.

```
1. function addMovieImageFileReturnPathLocation()
2. {
3.     $movie_file_path = "";
4.
5.     // Check for $_FILES being set and no errors.
6.     if (isset($_FILES) && $_FILES['movie_image_file']['error'] == UPLOAD_ERR_OK) {
7.         $movie_file_path =
8.             ML_UPLOAD_PATH . $_FILES['movie_image_file']['name'];
9.
10.         if (!move_uploaded_file($_FILES['movie_image_file']['tmp_name'], $movie_file_path)) {
11.             $movie_file_path = "";
12.         }
13.     }
14.
15.     return $movie_file_path;
16. }
```

## Complete Movie Image File Script

Our completed `movieimagefileutil.php` script including our `validateMovieImageFile()` and `addMovieImageFileReturnPathLocation()` functions looks like Listing 19.8.

### Listing 19.8.

```php
1.  <?php
2.  require_once 'movielistingfileconstants.php';
3.
4.  /**
5.   * Purpose:     Validates an uploaded movie image file
6.   *
7.   * Description: Validates an uploaded movie image file is not greater than
8.   *              ML_MAX_FILE_SIZE (1/2 MB), and is either a jpg or png image type, and
9.   *              has no errors. If the image file validates to these constraints,
10.  *              an error message containing an empty string is returned. If
11.  *              there is an error, a string containing constraints the file failed
12.  *              to validate to are returned.
13.  *
14.  * @return string  Empty if validation is successful, otherwise error string containing
15.  *                 constraints the image file failed to validate to.
16.  */
17. function validateMovieImageFile()
18. {
19.     $error_message = "";
20.
21.     // Check for $_FILES being set and no errors.
22.     if (isset($_FILES) && $_FILES['movie_image_file']['error'] == UPLOAD_ERR_OK)
23.     {
24.         // Check for uploaded file < Max file size AND an acceptable image type
25.         if ($_FILES['movie_image_file']['size'] > ML_MAX_FILE_SIZE)
26.         {
27.             $error_message = "The movie file image must be less than "
28.                             . ML_MAX_FILE_SIZE . " Bytes";
29.         }
30.
31.         $image_type = $_FILES['movie_image_file']['type'];
32.
33.         if ($image_type != 'image/jpg' && $image_type != 'image/jpeg'
34.             && $image_type != 'image/pjpeg' && $image_type != 'image/png'
35.             && $image_type != 'image/gif')
36.         {
37.             if (empty($error_message))
38.             {
39.                 $error_message = "The movie file image must be of type jpg, png, or gif.";
40.             }
41.             else
42.             {
43.                 $error_message .= ", and be an image of type jpg, png, or gif.";
```

```
44.                 }
45.             }
46.         }
47.     elseif (isset($_FILES)
48.             && $_FILES['movie_image_file']['error'] != UPLOAD_ERR_NO_FILE
49.             && $_FILES['movie_image_file']['error'] != UPLOAD_ERR_OK)
50.     {
51.         $error_message = "Error uploading movie image file.";
52.     }
53.
54.     return $error_message;
55. }
56.
57. /**
58.  * Purpose:     Moves an uploaded movie image file to the
59.  *              ML_UPLOAD_PATH (images/) folder and return the path location.
60.  *
61.  * Description: Moves an uploaded movie image file from the temporary
62.  *              server location to the ML_UPLOAD_PATH (images/) folder
63.  *              IF a movie image file was uploaded and returns the path
64.  *              location of the uploaded file by appending the file
65.  *              name to the ML_UPLOAD_PATH (e.g. images/movie_image.png).
66.  *              IF a movie image file was NOT uploaded, an empty string
67.  *              is returned for the path.
68.  *
69.  * @return string  Path to movie image file IF a file was uploaded
70.  *                  AND moved to the ML_UPLOAD_PATH (images/) folder,
71.  *                  otherwise and empty string.
72.  */
73. function addMovieImageFileReturnPathLocation()
74. {
75.     $movie_file_path = "";
76.
77.     // Check for $_FILES being set and no errors.
78.     if (isset($_FILES) && $_FILES['movie_image_file']['error'] == UPLOAD_ERR_OK)
79.     {
80.         $movie_file_path = ML_UPLOAD_PATH . $_FILES['movie_image_file']['name'];
81.
82.         if (!move_uploaded_file($_FILES['movie_image_file']['tmp_name'],
83.                                 $movie_file_path))
84.         {
85.             $movie_file_path = "";
86.         }
87.     }
88.
89.     return $movie_file_path;
90. }
```

## Using the File Uploading Functions on addmovie.php

Now that we have our two functions for validating and adding our uploaded movie image file, we can get back to modifying addmovie.php to use these functions.

You should have already modified the form element and added an input file element for uploading a movie image file. If not, see above for how to do that.

Figure 19.16.

After the user submits the form data by selecting the **Add Movie** button shown in Figure 19.16, the form data is available within the if block checking to see if the form data is set in the $_POST superglobal variable:

```
if (isset($_POST['add_movie_submission'], $_POST['movie_title'],
        $_POST['movie_rating'], $_POST['movie_director'],
        $_POST['movie_running_time_in_minutes']))
{
```

We want to validate the file inside this if block, move it to the images/ folder, and save the path to the database.

First, add a require_once for the movieimagefileutil.php script immediately after the require_once for the dbconnection.php script so we can use the two functions we created:

```
if (isset($_POST['add_movie_submission'], $_POST['movie_title'],
        $_POST['movie_rating'], $_POST['movie_director'],
        $_POST['movie_running_time_in_minutes']))
{
    require_once('dbconnection.php');
    require_once('movieimagefileutil.php');
```

We will validate the uploaded movie image file right after checking if checked_movie_genres is set and before the call to connect to the database. So it might be a good idea to add an appropriate comment here, something like Listing 19.9.

## Listing 19.9.

```
 1. if (isset($checked_movie_genres))
 2. {
 3.     $movie_genre_text = implode(", ", $checked_movie_genres);
 4. }
 5.
 6. /*
 7. Here is where we will deal with the file by calling validateMovieImageFile().
 8. This function will validate that the movie image file is the right image type
 9. (jpg/png/gif), and not greater than 512KB. This function will return an empty
10. string ('') if the file validates successfully, otherwise, the string will
11. contain error text to be output to the web page before redisplaying the form.
12. */
```

Next, we make our call to validateMovieImageFile() and set the return value to a new variable that captures the file error message:

```
successfully. Otherwise, the string will contain error text to be output to
the web page before redisplaying the form.
*/
$file_error_message = validateMovieImageFile();
```

If validateMovieImageFile() returns anything but an empty string, there was an error uploading the file. We want to display this error message and redisplay the form instead of storing the data in the database, allowing the user to correct the error. The two common reasons for the error are: the image is too big, or the image is the wrong file type. This also means we need to make the fields the user already entered sticky, so they do not have to reenter them into the form (unless they want to change them).

> *See section: on setting the value of the fields <u>making them sticky</u> in Chapter 18, Editing Data Using the Web Application to review how to make the input fields sticky.*

Create an if condition for file_error_message being empty, and move all the database code, the table results and the link to add another movie into this new if block. The new if block should look like Listing 19.10.

## Listing 19.10.

```
1.   $file_error_message = validateMovieImageFile();
2.
3.   if (empty($file_error_message))
4.   {
5.       $dbc = mysqli_connect(DB_HOST, DB_USER, DB_PASSWORD, DB_NAME)
6.               or trigger_error(
7.                   'Error connecting to MySQL server for' . DB_NAME,
8.                   E_USER_ERROR
9.               );
10.
11.      $query = "INSERT INTO movieListing (title, rating, director, "
12.          . " running_time_in_minutes, genre) "
13.          . "VALUES ('$movie_title', '$movie_rating', '$movie_director',"
14.          . "'$movie_runtime', '$movie_genre_text')";
15.
16.      mysqli_query($dbc, $query)
17.              or trigger_error(
18.                  'Error querying database movieListing: Failed to insert movie listing',
19.                  E_USER_ERROR
20.              );
21.
22.      $display_add_movie_form = false;
23.  ?>
24.      <h3 class="text-info">The Following Movie Details were Added:</h3><br/>
25.
26.      <h1><?= $movie_title ?></h1>
27.      <table class="table table-striped">
28.        <tbody>
29.        <tr>
30.          <th scope="row">Rating</th>
31.          <td><?= $movie_rating ?></td>
32.        </tr>
33.        <tr>
34.          <th scope="row">Director</th>
35.          <td><?= $movie_director ?></td>
36.        </tr>
37.        <tr>
38.          <th scope="row">Running Time (minutes)</th>
39.          <td><?= $movie_runtime ?></td>
40.        </tr>
41.        <tr>
42.          <th scope="row">Genre</th>
43.          <td><?= $movie_genre_text ?></td>
44.        </tr>
45.        </tbody>
46.      </table>
47.      <hr/>
48.      <p>Would you like to <a href="<?= $_SERVER['PHP_SELF'] ?>"> add another movie</a>?</p>
49.      <?php
50.  }
51. }
```

*Handling File Upload Errors*

To handle errors encountered when a user tries to upload a file, we need to modify the above code. But, first, let's add an `else` condition after the `if` so we can output the error message as in Listing 19.11.

## Listing 19.11.

```
1. if (empty($file_error_message))
2. {
3.     //...
4. }
5. else
6. {
7.     // echo error message
8.     echo "<h5><p class='text-danger'>" . $file_error_message . "</p></h5>";
9. }
```

Note that the form is redisplayed if this `else` executes because `display_add_movie_form` will already be set to `true`.

Before we get back to modifying the code in the `if` block, let's make the form sticky to handle the error condition in the `else` block. Near the top of the script, just below the line initializing `$display_add_movie_form = true;`, add the following variables Listing 19.12 initialized to empty strings and `null`.

## Listing 19.12.

```
1. // Initialization
2. $display_add_movie_form = true;
3.
4. $movie_title = "";
5. $movie_rating = "";
6. $movie_director = "";
7. $movie_runtime = "";
8. $movie_genre_text = "";
9. $checked_movie_genres = null;
```

These values get set after the user submits the form in the `if` condition in Listing 19.13 that checks the $_POST form variables are set.

## Listing 19.13.

```php
1.  if (isset($_POST['add_movie_submission'], $_POST['movie_title'],
2.              $_POST['movie_rating'], $_POST['movie_director'],
3.              $_POST['movie_running_time_in_minutes']))
4.  {
5.      ...
6.      $movie_title = $_POST['movie_title'];
7.      $movie_rating = $_POST['movie_rating'];
8.      $movie_director = $_POST['movie_director'];
9.      $movie_runtime = $_POST['movie_running_time_in_minutes'];
10.     $checked_movie_genres = $_POST['movie_genre_checkbox'];
11.
12.     $movie_genre_text = "";
13.
14.     if (isset($checked_movie_genres))
15.     {
16.         $movie_genre_text = implode(", ", $checked_movie_genres);
17.     }
```

As mentioned earlier, the two common reasons for the error are: the image is too big, or the image is the wrong file type. So this gives us three error conditions we can test:

1. The file is the right image type but too big.

2. The file is the wrong image type but less than ML_MAX_FILE_SIZE.

3. The file is the wrong image type AND too big.

Implementing these tests is left as an exercise for you. You'll want to write one error message for each of these cases.

We can now make the title, rating, director, running time, and genre sticky back down in the form. Since this is identical to what we did for the "Edit a Movie" page, I only show the updated form in Listing 19.14.

## Listing 19.14.

```html
1.  <form enctype="multipart/form-data" class="needs-validation"
2.      novalidate method="POST" action="<?= $_SERVER['PHP_SELF'] ?>">
3.      <div class="form-group row">
4.          <label for="movie_title" class="col-sm-3 col-form-label-lg">Title</label>
5.          <div class="col-sm-8">
6.              <input type="text" class="form-control" id="movie_title"
7.                  name="movie_title" value='<?= $movie_title ?>'
8.                  placeholder="Title" required>
9.              <div class="invalid-feedback">
10.                 Please provide a valid movie title.
11.             </div>
```

```
12.            </div>
13.        </div>
14.        <div class="form-group row">
15.            <label for="movie_rating" class="col-sm-3 col-form-label-lg">Rating</label>
16.            <div class="col-sm-8">
17.                <select class="custom-select" id="movie_rating"
18.                        name="movie_rating" value='<?= $movie_rating ?>'
19.                        required>
20.                  <option value="" disabled selected>Rating...</option>
21.                  <option value="G" <?= $movie_rating == 'G' ?
22.                      'selected' : '' ?>>G
23.                  </option>
24.                  <option value="PG" <?= $movie_rating == 'PG' ?
25.                      'selected' : '' ?>>PG
26.                  </option>
27.                  <option value="PG-13" <?= $movie_rating == 'PG-13' ?
28.                      'selected' : '' ?>>PG-13
29.                  </option>
30.                  <option value="R" <?= $movie_rating == 'R' ?
31.                      'selected' : '' ?>>R
32.                  </option>
33.                </select>
34.                <div class="invalid-feedback">
35.                    Please select a movie rating.
36.                </div>
37.            </div>
38.        </div>
39.        <div class="form-group row">
40.            <label for="movie_director"
41.                    class="col-sm-3 col-form-label-lg">Director</label>
42.            <div class="col-sm-8">
43.                <input type="text" class="form-control"
44.                        id="movie_director" name="movie_director"
45.                        value='<?= $movie_director ?>'
46.                        placeholder="Director" required>
47.                <div class="invalid-feedback">
48.                    Please provide a valid movie director.
49.                </div>
50.            </div>
51.        </div>
52.        <div class="form-group row">
53.            <label for="movie_running_time_in_minutes"
54.                    class="col-sm-3 col-form-label-lg">Running Time (min)</label>
55.            <div class="col-sm-8">
56.                <input type="number" class="form-control"
57.                        id="movie_running_time_in_minutes"
58.                        name="movie_running_time_in_minutes"
59.                        value='<?= $movie_runtime ?>'
60.                        placeholder="Running time (in minutes)" required>
61.                <div class="invalid-feedback">
```

```
62.                    Please provide a valid running time in minutes.
63.                  </div>
64.              </div>
65.          </div>
66.          <div class="form-group row">
67.              <label class="col-sm-3 col-form-label-lg">Genre</label>
68.              <div class="col-sm-8">
69.                  <?php
70.                  foreach ($genres as $genre) {
71.                      ?>
72.                      <div class="form-check form-check-inline col-sm-3">
73.                          <input class="form-check-input" type="checkbox"
74.                                 id="movie_genre_checkbox_action_<?= $genre ?>"
75.                                 name="movie_genre_checkbox[]"
76.                                 value="<?= $genre ?>"<?= in_array($genre, $checked_movie_genres) ?
77.                                 'checked' : '' ?>>
78.                          <label class="form-check-label"
79.                                 for="movie_genre_checkbox_action_<?= $genre ?>"><?= $genre ?></label>
80.                      </div>
81.                      <?php
82.                  }
83.                  ?>
84.              </div>
85.          </div>
86.          <div class="form-group row">
87.              <label for="movie_image_file"
88.                     class="col-sm-3 col-form-label-lg">Movie Image File</label>
89.              <div class="col-sm-8">
90.                  <input type="file" class="form-control-file"
91.                         id="movie_image_file" name="movie_image_file">
92.              </div>
93.          </div>
94.          <button class="btn btn-primary" type="submit"
95.                  name="add_movie_submission">Add Movie
96.          </button>
97.  </form>
```

## Handling Successful Validation

Now, let's get back to modifying the code in the `if` block where there are no errors validating the uploaded file:

```
if (empty($file_error_message))
{
    // ...
}
```

Since we know the uploaded file is valid, we need to call addMovieImageFileReturnPathLocation().
This function adds the uploaded movie image to the images/ folder and returns the path we
need to store in the database. We'll do this just below where we connect to the database, setting
the path returned to a new variable movie_image_file_path:

```php
1. if (empty($file_error_message))
2. {
3.     $dbc = mysqli_connect(DB_HOST, DB_USER, DB_PASSWORD, DB_NAME)
4.             or trigger_error(
5.                 'Error connecting to MySQL server for' . DB_NAME, E_USER_ERROR
6.             );
7.
8.     $movie_image_file_path = addMovieImageFileReturnPathLocation();
9. }
```

Remember, the user may not have uploaded a movie image file, so movie_image_file_path
may be an empty string (which is OK).

We need to modify our SQL INSERT query to include the new field image_file we added to the
movieListing table in the Movie database and set it to movie_image_file_path before performing
the query. It should look like Listing 19.15.

## Listing 19.15.

```php
1. $movie_image_file_path = addMovieImageFileReturnPathLocation();
2.
3. $query = "INSERT INTO movieListing (title, rating, director, running_time_in_minutes,
4.                                     genre, image_file) "
5.         . "VALUES ('$movie_title', '$movie_rating', '$movie_director', "
6.         . "'$movie_runtime', '$movie_genre_text', '$movie_image_file_path')";
7.
8. mysqli_query($dbc, $query)
9.         or trigger_error(
10.             'Error querying database movieListing: Failed to insert movie listing',
11.             E_USER_ERROR
12.         );
```

Next, if the user did not upload a file, we need to set movie_image_file_path to the generic—or
default—image we used earlier. This file is found at the path: images/generic_movie.jpg. Add
the following code after the query:

```
 1.  mysqli_query($dbc, $query)
 2.          or trigger_error(
 3.              'Error querying database movieListing: Failed to insert movie listing',
 4.              E_USER_ERROR
 5.          );
 6.
 7.  if (empty($movie_image_file_path))
 8.  {
 9.      $movie_image_file_path = ML_UPLOAD_PATH . ML_DEFAULT_MOVIE_FILE_NAME;
10.  }
```

The next line should already be set to not display the form:

```
if (empty($movie_image_file_path))
{
    $movie_image_file_path = ML_UPLOAD_PATH . ML_DEFAULT_MOVIE_FILE_NAME;
}

$display_add_movie_form = false;
```

Finally, we need to add the movie image file (or the default image) to the table to display the added movie details.

Since we are using Bootstrap's Flexbox grid implementation, it is best to encapsulate the image and table in separate columns and put them both in a single row, all just below the movie title located in the <h1> element as in Listing 19.16.

## Listing 19.16.

```
 1.  <h1><?= $movie_title ?></h1>
 2.  <div class="row">
 3.    <div class="col-2">
 4.      <img src="<?= $movie_image_file_path ?>"
 5.            class="img-thumbnail" style="max-height: 200px;" alt="Movie image">
 6.    </div>
 7.    <div class="col">
 8.      <table class="table table-striped">
 9.        ...
10.      </table>
11.    </div>
12.  </div>
```

Notice we set the style attribute to a maximum height of 200 pixels.

## Complete addmovie.php Code Listing

### Listing 19.17.

```
1.  <!DOCTYPE html>
2.  <html>
3.    <head>
4.      <title>Add a Movie</title>
5.      <link rel="stylesheet"
6.            href="https://stackpath.bootstrapcdn.com/bootstrap/4.2.1/css/bootstrap.min.css"
7.            integrity="sha384-GJzZqFGwb1QTTN6wy59ffF1BuGJpLSa9DkKMp0DgiMDm4iYMj70gZWKYbI706tWS"
8.            crossorigin="anonymous">
9.    </head>
10.   <body>
11.    <div class="card">
12.      <div class="card-body">
13.        <h1>Add a Movie</h1>
14.        <nav class="nav">
15.          <a class="nav-link" href="index.php">Movies I Like</a>
16.        </nav>
17.        <hr/>
18.        <?php
19.          // Initialization
20.          $display_add_movie_form = true;
21.          $movie_title = "";
22.          $movie_rating = "";
23.          $movie_director = "";
24.          $movie_runtime = "";
25.          $movie_genre_text = "";
26.          $checked_movie_genres = null;
27.
28.          $genres = [
29.              'Action', 'Adventure', 'Comedy', 'Documentary', 'Drama',
30.              'Fantasy', 'Horror', 'Romance', 'Science Fiction'
31.          ];
32.
33.          if (isset($_POST['add_movie_submission'], $_POST['movie_title'],
34.                  $_POST['movie_rating'], $_POST['movie_director'],
35.                  $_POST['movie_running_time_in_minutes']))
36.          {
37.              require_once('dbconnection.php');
38.              require_once('movieimagefileutil.php');
39.
40.              $movie_title = $_POST['movie_title'];
41.              $movie_rating = $_POST['movie_rating'];
42.              $movie_director = $_POST['movie_director'];
43.              $movie_runtime = $_POST['movie_running_time_in_minutes'];
44.              $checked_movie_genres = $_POST['movie_genre_checkbox'];
45.
46.              $movie_genre_text = "";
47.
48.              if (isset($checked_movie_genres))
```

```php
49.                  {
50.                      $movie_genre_text = implode(", ", $checked_movie_genres);
51.                  }
52.
53.                  /*
54.                  Here is where we will deal with the file by calling validateMovieImageFile().
55.                  This function will validate that the movie image file is not greater than 128
56.                  characters, is the right image type (jpg/png/gif), and not greater than 512KB.
57.                  This function will return an empty string ('') if the file validates successfully,
58.                  otherwise, the string will contain error text to be output to the web page before
59.                  redisplaying the form.
60.                  */
61.
62.                  $file_error_message = validateMovieImageFile();
63.
64.                  if (empty($file_error_message))
65.                  {
66.                      $dbc = mysqli_connect(DB_HOST, DB_USER, DB_PASSWORD, DB_NAME)
67.                          or trigger_error(
68.                                  'Error connecting to MySQL server for' . DB_NAME,
69.                              E_USER_ERROR
70.                          );
71.
72.                      $movie_image_file_path = addMovieImageFileReturnPathLocation();
73.
74.                      $query = "INSERT INTO movieListing (title, rating, director,"
75.                          . "running_time_in_minutes, genre, image_file) "
76.                          . "VALUES ('$movie_title', '$movie_rating', '$movie_director', "
77.                          . "'$movie_runtime', '$movie_genre_text', '$movie_image_file_path')";
78.
79.                      mysqli_query($dbc, $query)
80.                          or trigger_error(
81.                              'Error querying database movieListing: Failed to insert movie listing',
82.                              E_USER_ERROR
83.                          );
84.
85.                      if (empty($movie_image_file_path))
86.                      {
87.                          $movie_image_file_path = ML_UPLOAD_PATH . ML_DEFAULT_MOVIE_FILE_NAME;
88.                      }
89.
90.                      $display_add_movie_form = false;
91.                  ?>
92.                  <h3 class="text-info">The Following Movie Details were Added:</h3><br/>
93.
94.                  <h1><?= $movie_title ?></h1>
95.                  <div class="row">
96.                      <div class="col-2">
97.                          <img src="<?= $movie_image_file_path ?>" class="img-thumbnail"
98.                              style="max-height: 200px;" alt="Movie image">
99.                      </div>
100.                     <div class="col">
101.                         <table class="table table-striped">
```

```
102.                        <tbody>
103.                          <tr>
104.                            <th scope="row">Rating</th>
105.                            <td><?= $movie_rating ?></td>
106.                          </tr>
107.                          <tr>
108.                            <th scope="row">Director</th>
109.                            <td><?= $movie_director ?></td>
110.                          </tr>
111.                          <tr>
112.                            <th scope="row">Running Time (minutes)</th>
113.                            <td><?= $movie_runtime ?></td>
114.                          </tr>
115.                          <tr>
116.                            <th scope="row">Genre</th>
117.                            <td><?= $movie_genre_text ?></td>
118.                          </tr>
119.                        </tbody>
120.                      </table>
121.                    </div>
122.                  </div>
123.                  <hr/>
124.                  <p>Would you like to <a href='<?= $_SERVER['PHP_SELF']; ?>'> add another movie</a>?</p>
125.                  <?php
126.                }
127.                else
128.                {
129.                    // echo error message
130.                    echo "<h5><p class='text-danger'>" . $file_error_message . "</p></h5>";
131.                }
132.            }
133.
134.            if ($display_add_movie_form)
135.            {
136.                ?>
137.        <form enctype="multipart/form-data" class="needs-validation" novalidate
138.            method="POST" action="<?= $_SERVER['PHP_SELF'] ?>">
139.          <div class="form-group row">
140.            <label for="movie_title"
141.                    class="col-sm-3 col-form-label-lg">Title</label>
142.            <div class="col-sm-8">
143.              <input type="text" class="form-control" id="movie_title"
144.                    name="movie_title" value="<?= $movie_title ?>"
145.                    placeholder="Title" required>
146.              <div class="invalid-feedback">
147.                Please provide a valid movie title.
148.              </div>
149.            </div>
150.          </div>
151.          <div class="form-group row">
152.            <label for="movie_rating" class="col-sm-3 col-form-label-lg">Rating</label>
153.            <div class="col-sm-8">
154.            <select class="custom-select" id="movie_rating"
155.                    name="movie_rating" value="<?= $movie_rating ?>" required>
```

```
156.            <option value="" disabled selected>Rating...</option>
157.            <option value="G" <?= $movie_rating == 'G' ? 'selected' : '' ?>>G</option>
158.            <option value="PG" <?= $movie_rating == 'PG' ? 'selected' : '' ?>>PG</option>
159.            <option value="PG-13" <?= $movie_rating == 'PG-13' ? 'selected' : '' ?>>PG-13</option>
160.            <option value="R" <?= $movie_rating == 'R' ? 'selected' : '' ?>>R</option>
161.          </select>
162.          <div class="invalid-feedback">
163.            Please select a movie rating.
164.          </div>
165.        </div>
166.      </div>
167.      <div class="form-group row">
168.        <label for="movie_director" class="col-sm-3 col-form-label-lg">Director</label>
169.        <div class="col-sm-8">
170.          <input type="text" class="form-control" id="movie_director"
171.              name="movie_director" value="<?= $movie_director ?>"
172.              placeholder="Director" required>
173.          <div class="invalid-feedback">
174.            Please provide a valid movie director.
175.          </div>
176.        </div>
177.      </div>
178.      <div class="form-group row">
179.        <label for="movie_running_time_in_minutes"
180.              class="col-sm-3 col-form-label-lg">Running Time (min)</label>
181.        <div class="col-sm-8">
182.          <input type="number" class="form-control"
183.              id="movie_running_time_in_minutes"
184.              name="movie_running_time_in_minutes"
185.              value="<?= $movie_runtime ?>"
186.              placeholder="Running time (in minutes)" required>
187.          <div class="invalid-feedback">
188.            Please provide a valid running time in minutes.
189.          </div>
190.        </div>
191.      </div>
192.      <div class="form-group row">
193.        <label class="col-sm-3 col-form-label-lg">Genre</label>
194.        <div class="col-sm-8">
195.          <?php
196.            foreach ($genres as $genre)
197.            {
198.              ?>
199.              <div class="form-check form-check-inline col-sm-3">
200.                <input class="form-check-input" type="checkbox"
201.                    id="movie_genre_checkbox_action_<?= $genre ?>"
202.                    name="movie_genre_checkbox[]"
203.          value="<?= $genre ?>"<?= in_array($genre, $checked_movie_genres) ? 'checked' : '' ?>>
204.                <label class="form-check-label"
205.                    for="movie_genre_checkbox_action_<?= $genre ?>"><?= $genre ?></label>
206.              </div>
207.              <?php
208.            }
```

```
209.                    ?>
210.                  </div>
211.                </div>
212.                <div class="form-group row">
213.                  <label for="movie_image_file"
214.                         class="col-sm-3 col-form-label-lg">Movie Image File</label>
215.                  <div class="col-sm-8">
216.                    <input type="file" class="form-control-file"
217.                           id="movie_image_file" name="movie_image_file">
218.                  </div>
219.                </div>
220.                <button class="btn btn-primary" type="submit"
221.                        name="add_movie_submission">Add Movie</button>
222.              </form>
223.              <script>
224.              // JavaScript for disabling form submissions if there are invalid fields
225.              (function() {
226.                'use strict';
227.                window.addEventListener('load', function() {
228.                  // Fetch all the forms we want to apply custom Bootstrap validation styles to
229.                  var forms = document.getElementsByClassName('needs-validation');
230.                  // Loop over them and prevent submission
231.                  var validation = Array.prototype.filter.call(forms, function(form) {
232.                    form.addEventListener('submit', function(event) {
233.                      if (form.checkValidity() == false) {
234.                        event.preventDefault();
235.                        event.stopPropagation();
236.                      }
237.                      form.classList.add('was-validated');
238.                    }, false);
239.                  });
240.                }, false);
241.              })();
242.              </script>
243.              <?php
244.                } // Display add movie form
245.              ?>
246.            </div>
247.          </div>
248.          <script src="https://code.jquery.com/jquery-3.3.1.slim.min.js"
249.                  integrity="sha384-q8i/X+965Dz00rT7abK41JStQIAqVgRVzpbzo5smXKp4YfRvH+8abtTE1Pi6jizo"
250.                  crossorigin="anonymous"></script>
251.          <script src="https://cdnjs.cloudflare.com/ajax/libs/popper.js/1.14.6/umd/popper.min.js"
252.                  integrity="sha384-wHAiFfRlMFy6i5SRaxvfOCifBUQy1xHdJ/yoi7FRNXMRBu5WHdZYu1hA6ZOblgut"
253.                  crossorigin="anonymous"></script>
254.          <script src="https://stackpath.bootstrapcdn.com/bootstrap/4.2.1/js/bootstrap.min.js"
255.                  integrity="sha384-B0UglyR+jN6CkvvICOB2joaf5I4l3gm9GU6Hc1og6Ls7i6U/mkkaduKaBhlAXv9k"
256.                  crossorigin="anonymous"></script>
257.      </body>
258. </html>
```

## Displaying Thumbnail Images of Movies on Main Page

Now that we can add images to our movies let's modify the main "Movies I Like" page (index.php) to display a thumbnail image of the movie at the beginning of each movie row or a default image (generic_movie.jpg) if the user did not upload an image for the movie. We want our modified "Movies I Like" page to look like Figure 19.17.

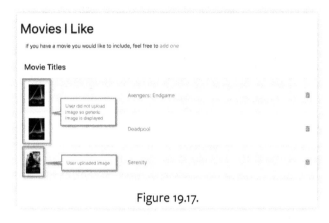

Figure 19.17.

The modifications are relatively simple since all we need to do is modify our query to get the new image_file field from the movieListing database table and add a column to our HTML table for displaying a thumbnail image at the beginning of each row of the table.

So let's get to it. First, add a reference to the movielistingfileconstants.php script by adding the following require_once() following the reference to dbconnection.php:

```
require_once('dbconnection.php');
require_once('movielistingfileconstants.php');
```

Next, modify the SQL query statement (that follows the connection to the database) to include the image_file field in the movieListing database table:

```
$dbc = mysqli_connect(DB_HOST, DB_USER, DB_PASSWORD, DB_NAME)
        or trigger_error(
                'Error connecting to MySQL server for' . DB_NAME,
                E_USER_ERROR
        );

$query = "SELECT id, title, image_file FROM movieListing ORDER BY title";
```

Down where the HTML table is displayed, we need to add a column for our thumbnail image. First, add an HTML table header field (so there are three columns instead of two) as in Listing 19.18.

## Listing 19.18.

```
1.  <table class="table table-striped table-hover">
2.    <thead>
3.      <tr>
4.        <th scope="col"><h4>Movie Titles</h4></th>
5.        <th scope="col"></th>
6.        <th scope="col"></th>
7.      </tr>
8.    </thead>
9.    <tbody>
```

Next, we need to modify the display of each HTML table row so that three columns (instead of just two) are output, with a thumbnail image for the first column. Also, we need to make sure that if the user did not upload an image for a movie, the default image (generic_movie.jpg) is displayed instead. All of this is done in the while loop and looks like Listing 19.19.

## Listing 19.19.

```
1.  while ($row = mysqli_fetch_assoc($result))
2.  {
3.      $movie_image_file = $row['image_file'];
4.
5.      if (empty($movie_image_file))
6.      {
7.          $movie_image_file = ML_UPLOAD_PATH . ML_DEFAULT_MOVIE_FILE_NAME;
8.      }
9.
10.     echo "<tr><td><img src=" . $movie_image_file . " class='img-thumbnail'" .
11.         "style='max-height: 75px;' alt='Movie image'></td>" .
12.         "<td class='align-middle'><a class='nav-link' href='moviedetails.php?id=" .
13.         $row['id'] . "'>" . $row['title'] ."</a></td>" .
14.         "<td class='align-middle'><a class='nav-link' href='removemovie.php?id_to_delete=" .
15.         $row['id'] ."'><i class='fas fa-trash-alt'></i></a></td></tr>";
16. }
```

Note that if the image_file field is an empty string, we set the image to display to images/generic_movie.jpg.

## Complete Code Listing for index.php

## Listing 19.20.

```
1.  <html>
2.   <head>
3.    <title>Movies I Like</title>
4.    <link rel="stylesheet"
5.        href="https://stackpath.bootstrapcdn.com/bootstrap/4.2.1/css/bootstrap.min.css"
6.        integrity="sha384-GJzZqFGwb1QTTN6wy59ffF1BuGJpLSa9DkKMp0DgiMDm4iYMj70gZWKYbI706tiWS"
7.        crossorigin="anonymous">
8.    <link rel="stylesheet"
9.        href="https://use.fontawesome.com/releases/v5.8.1/css/all.css"
10.       integrity="sha384-50oBUHEmvpQ+1lW4y57PTFmhCaXp0ML5d60M1M7uH2+nqUivzIebhndOJK28anvf"
11.       crossorigin="anonymous">
12.  </head>
13.  <body>
14.   <div class="card">
15.    <div class="card-body">
16.     <h1>Movies I Like</h1>
17.     <p class='nav-link'>If you have a movie you would like to include, feel free to <a
href="addmovie.php"> add one</a></p>
18.     <?php
19.       require_once('dbconnection.php');
20.       require_once('movielistingfileconstants.php');
21.
22.       $dbc = mysqli_connect(DB_HOST, DB_USER, DB_PASSWORD, DB_NAME)
23.           or trigger_error(
24.           'Error connecting to MySQL server for' . DB_NAME,
25.           E_USER_ERROR
26.             );
27.
28.       $query = "SELECT id, title, image_file FROM movieListing ORDER BY title";
29.
30.       $result = mysqli_query($dbc, $query)
31.           or trigger_error(
32.           'Error querying database movieListing',
33.           E_USER_ERROR
34.             );
35.
36.       if (mysqli_num_rows($result) > 0):
37.
38.     ?>
39.     <table class="table table-striped table-hover">
40.       <thead>
41.         <tr>
42.           <th scope="col"><h4>Movie Titles</h4></th>
```

```php
43.                  <th scope="col"></th>
44.                  <th scope="col"></th>
45.               </tr>
46.            </thead>
47.            <tbody>
48.         <?php
49.            while($row = mysqli_fetch_assoc($result))
50.            {
51.               $movie_image_file = $row['image_file'];
52.
53.               if (empty($movie_image_file))
54.               {
55.                  $movie_image_file = ML_UPLOAD_PATH . ML_DEFAULT_MOVIE_FILE_NAME;
56.               }
57.
58.               echo "<tr><td><img src=" . $movie_image_file . " class='img-thumbnail'"
59.                     . "style='max-height: 75px;' alt='Movie image'></td>"
60.                     . "<td class='align-middle'><a class='nav-link' href='moviedetails.php?id="
61.                     . $row['id'] . "'>" . $row['title'] ."</a></td>"
62.                     . "<td class='align-middle'><a class='nav-link' href='removemovie.php?id_to_delete="
63.                     . $row['id'] ."'><i class='fas fa-trash-alt'></i></a></td></tr>";
64.            }
65.         ?>
66.            </tbody>`
67.         </table>
68.         <?php
69.            else:
70.         ?>
71.         <h3>No Movies Found :-(</h3>
72.         <?php
73.            endif;
74.         ?>
75.      </div>
76.   </div>
77.   <script src="https://code.jquery.com/jquery-3.3.1.slim.min.js"
78.           integrity="sha384-q8i/X+965Dz00rT7abK41JStQIAqVgRVzpbzo5smXKp4YfRvH+8abtTE1Pi6jizo"
79.           crossorigin="anonymous"></script>
80.   <script src="https://cdnjs.cloudflare.com/ajax/libs/popper.js/1.14.6/umd/popper.min.js"
81.           integrity="sha384-wHAiFfRlMFy6i5SRaxvfOCifBUQy1xHdJ/yoi7FRNXMRBu5WHdZYu1hA6Z0blgut"
82.           crossorigin="anonymous"></script>
83.   <script src="https://stackpath.bootstrapcdn.com/bootstrap/4.2.1/js/bootstrap.min.js"
84.           integrity="sha384-B0UglyR+jN6CkvvICOB2joaf5I4l3gm9GU6Hc1og6Ls7i6U/mkkaduKaBhlAXv9k"
85.           crossorigin="anonymous"></script>
86.   </body>
87. </html>
```

## Displaying Movie Image on Details Page

Now we need to modify moviedetails.php so that the movie's image is displayed on the "Movie Details" page to identify the movie better. This process will be very similar to the modifications we made to addmovie.php that displays the movie details after the user selected "Add a Movie" and look like Figure 19.18.

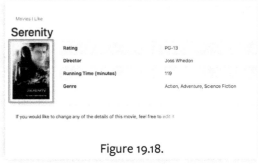

Figure 19.18.

First, add a reference to the movielistingfileconstants.php script by adding the following require_once() following the reference to dbconnection.php inside the condition if (isset($_GET['id'])):

```
if (isset($_GET['id'])):

    require_once('dbconnection.php');
    require_once('movielistingfileconstants.php');
```

Next, just inside the condition if (mysqli_num_rows($result) == 1), right after the line: $row = mysqli_fetch_assoc($result);, we need to add code that displays the default image if the image_file field is an empty string. See Listing 19.21.

### Listing 19.21.

```
1. if (mysqli_num_rows($result) == 1):
2.     $row = mysqli_fetch_assoc($result);
3.
4.     $movie_image_file = $row['image_file'];
5.
6.     if (empty($movie_image_file)):
7.         $movie_image_file = ML_UPLOAD_PATH . ML_DEFAULT_MOVIE_FILE_NAME;
8.
9.     endif;
```

Finally, as we did in addmovie.php, we need to add the movie image file (or the default image) to the table to display the movie details.

Since we are using Bootstrap's Flexbox grid implementation, it is best to encapsulate the image and table in separate columns and put them both in a single row, all just below the movie title located in the <h1> element:

## Listing 19.22.

```
1.  <h1><?= $row['title'] ?></h1>
2.  <div class="row">
3.    <div class="col-2">
4.      <img src="<?= $movie_image_file ?>" class="img-thumbnail"
5.           style="max-height: 200px;" alt="Movie image">
6.    </div>
7.    <div class="col">
8.      <table class="table table-striped">
9.          ...
10.     </table>
11.   </div>
12. </div>
```

Again, notice we set the style attribute to a maximum height of 200 pixels.

## Complete moviedetails.php Code Listing

## Listing 19.23.

```
1.  <html>
2.  <head>
3.    <link rel="stylesheet"
4.          href="https://stackpath.bootstrapcdn.com/bootstrap/4.2.1/css/bootstrap.min.css"
5.          integrity="sha384-GJzZqFGwb1QTTN6wy59ffF1BuGJpLSa9DkKMp0DgiMDm4iYMj70gZwKYbI706tWS"
6.          crossorigin="anonymous">
7.    <title>Movie Details</title>
8.  </head>
9.  <body>
10. <div class="card">
11.   <div class="card-body">
12.     <nav class="nav">
13.       <a class="nav-link" href="index.php">Movies I Like</a>
14.     </nav>
15.     <?php
16.     if (isset($_GET['id'])):
17.
18.       require_once('dbconnection.php');
19.       require_once('movielistingfileconstants.php');
20.
21.       $id = $_GET['id'];
```

```php
22.
23.        $dbc = mysqli_connect(DB_HOST, DB_USER, DB_PASSWORD, DB_NAME)
24.            or trigger_error(
25.                'Error connecting to MySQL server for' . DB_NAME,
26.                E_USER_ERROR
27.        );
28.
29.        $query = "SELECT * FROM movieListing WHERE id = $id";
30.
31.        $result = mysqli_query($dbc, $query)
32.            or trigger_error(
33.                'Error querying database movieListing',
34.                E_USER_ERROR
35.        );
36.
37.        if (mysqli_num_rows($result) == 1):
38.          $row = mysqli_fetch_assoc($result);
39.
40.          $movie_image_file = $row['image_file'];
41.
42.          if (empty($movie_image_file)):
43.            $movie_image_file = ML_UPLOAD_PATH . ML_DEFAULT_MOVIE_FILE_NAME;
44.          endif;
45.          ?>
46.          <h1><?= $row['title'] ?></h1>
47.          <div class="row">
48.              <div class="col-2">
49.                  <img src="<?= $movie_image_file ?>" class="img-thumbnail"
50.                      style="max-height: 200px;" alt="Movie image">
51.              </div>
52.              <div class="col">
53.                  <table class="table table-striped">
54.                      <tbody>
55.                      <tr>
56.                          <th scope="row">Rating</th>
57.                          <td><?= $row['rating'] ?></td>
58.                      </tr>
59.                      <tr>
60.                          <th scope="row">Director</th>
61.                          <td><?= $row['director'] ?></td>
62.                      </tr>
63.                      <tr>
64.                          <th scope="row">Running Time (minutes)</th>
65.                          <td><?= $row['running_time_in_minutes'] ?></td>
66.                      </tr>
67.                      <tr>
```

```
69.                              <th scope="row">Genre</th>
70.                                <td><?= $row['genre'] ?></td>
71.                        </tr>
72.                        </tbody>
73.                    </table>
74.                </div>
75.            </div>
76.            <hr/>
77.            <p class='nav-link'>
78.                If you would like to change any of the details of
79.                this movie, feel free to
80.                <a href="editmovie.php?id_to_edit=<?= $row['id'] ?>">edit it</a>
81.            </p>
82.        <?php
83.        else:
84.            ?>
85.            <h3>No Movie Details :-(</h3>
86.        <?php
87.        endif;
88.    else:
89.        ?>
90.        <h3>No Movie Details :-(</h3>
91.    <?php
92.    endif;
93.    ?>
94.    </div>
95. </div>
96. <script src="https://code.jquery.com/jquery-3.3.1.slim.min.js"
97.         integrity="sha384-q8i/X+965DzO0rT7abK41JStQIAqVgRVzpbzo5smXKp4YfRvH+8abtTE1Pi6jizo"
98.         crossorigin="anonymous"></script>
99. <script src="https://cdnjs.cloudflare.com/ajax/libs/popper.js/1.14.6/umd/popper.min.js"
100.         integrity="sha384-wHAiFfRlMFy6i5SRaxvfOCifBUQy1xHdJ/yoi7FRNXMRBu5WHdZYu1hA6ZOblgut"
101.         crossorigin="anonymous"></script>
102. <script src="https://stackpath.bootstrapcdn.com/bootstrap/4.2.1/js/bootstrap.min.js"
103.         integrity="sha384-B0UglyR+jN6CkvvICOB2joaf5I4l3gm9GU6Hc1og6Ls7i6U/mkkaduKaBhlAXv9k"
104.         crossorigin="anonymous"></script>
105. </body>
106. </html>
```

## Add Image File Uploads to the Editing Page

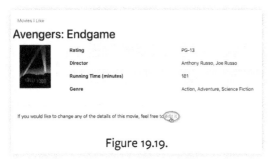

Figure 19.19.

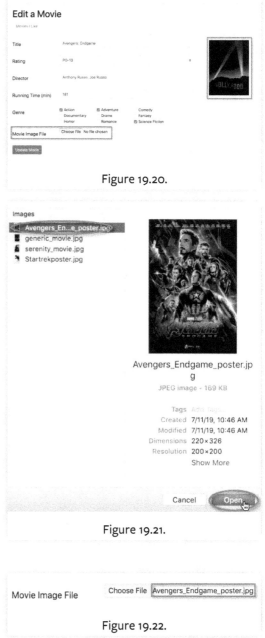

Figure 19.20.

Figure 19.21.

Figure 19.22.

Now, new movies can have a custom file image. We need to add to the editmovie. php script the same ability to upload a movie image and any other details for the movie. That way, users can update existing file images with a new one or add a movie thumbnail to existing entries.

When we navigate to the "Edit a Movie" page, as a result of selecting the **edit it** link on the "Movie Details" page, we should see Figure 19.19

We want to add an image of the movie to the right of the form and add a "Choose File" button towards the bottom of the form (Figure 19.20).

When choosing an image to update, a file browser window pops up. Then, users can navigate to the image file they want to upload, select it, then press **Open** as in Figure 19.21.

The name of the selected file displays after the "Choose File" button, instead of "No file chosen". See Figure 19.22.

Once we select "Update Movie" (Figure 19.23), we want to see the updated movie details modified with the image we uploaded on the "Movie Details" as shown in Figure 19.24.

Figure 19.23.

First, open the editmovie.php script and add a reference to the movieimagefileutil.php script by adding the following require_once() just after the reference to dbconnection.php towards the top of the script:

```
require_once('dbconnection.php');
require_once('movieimagefileutil.php');
```

Figure 19.24.

## Displaying Movie Image Details when Editing

When first browsing to the "Edit a Movie" page (editmovie.php), it was because of an HTTP GET request/response when navigating from the "Movie Details" page. Therefore, we need to make the modifications in Listing 19.24 to add the movie image file details in the if (isset($_GET['id_to_edit'])) block of code:

## Listing 19.24.

```
 1. if (isset($_GET['id_to_edit']))
 2. {
 3.     // ...
 4.     if (mysqli_num_rows($result) == 1)
 5.     {
 6.         // ...
 7.         $movie_genre_text = $row['genre'];
 8.         $movie_image_file = $row['image_file'];
 9.
10.         if (empty($movie_image_file))
11.         {
12.             $movie_image_file_displayed = ML_UPLOAD_PATH . ML_DEFAULT_MOVIE_FILE_NAME;
13.         }
14.         else
15.         {
16.             $movie_image_file_displayed = $movie_image_file;
17.         }
18.
19.         $checked_movie_genres = explode(', ', $movie_genre_text);
20.     }
21. }
```

Note that if $movie_image_file is empty, we need to set $movie_image_file_displayed to the default movie file image. $movie_image_file_displayed is used to display the movie image on the page to the right of the form.

Since we are using Bootstrap's Flexbox grid implementation, it is best to encapsulate the form and image in separate columns and put them both in a single row. Make the modifications in Listing 19.25 to display the form on the left, and the image on the right.

Listing 19.25.

```
1. <div class="row">
2.   <div class="col">
3.     <form ...>
4.       // ...
5.     </form>
6.   </div>
7.   <div class="col-3">
8.     <img src="<?= $movie_image_file_displayed ?>" class="img-thumbnail"
9.          style="max-height: 400px;" alt="Movie image">
10.  </div>
11. </div>
```

Notice we set the style attribute to a maximum height of 400 pixels.

## Modifying the Form to Allow File Uploading

Just like we did in addmovie.php, there are two things we need to add to our form in editmovie.php to enable file uploads. First, we need to add the enctype attribute to the <form> element and set it to multipart/form-data:

```
<form enctype="multipart/form-data" ...>
```

Then we need to add a file input element to the form:

```
<input type="file" class="form-control-file" id="movie_image_file"
       name="movie_image_file">
```

Add the file input element within a Bootstrap form-group row right before the submit button in your form as in Listing 19.26.

## Listing 19.26.

```
1.    </div>
2.    <div class="form-group row">
3.      <label for="movie_image_file"
4.             class="col-sm-3 col-form-label-lg">Movie Image File</label>
5.      <div class="col-sm-8">
6.        <input type="file" class="form-control-file" id="movie_image_file"
7.               name="movie_image_file">
8.      </div>
9.    </div>
10.   <button class="btn btn-primary" type="submit"
11.          name="edit_movie_submission">Update Movie</button>
12. </form>
```

In regards to $movie_image_file, just like the hidden <input> element for id_to_update, I created another hidden <input> element in the form and set it to the value of $movie_image_file and set the name attribute to movie_image_file. When the form data is posted back to editmovie.php as a result of the user pressing the **Update Movie** submit button, the name of the existing file name (prior to updating) will be available in the $_POST[] super-global array so that it can be removed (if not empty) if the user selected a new file:

```
<input type="hidden" name="id_to_update" value="<?= $id_to_edit ?>">
<input type="hidden" name="movie_image_file" value="<?= $movie_image_file ?>">
```

*Please see the aside in chapter 17 titled: THE WEB IS STATELESS!*

## Modifying Edit Code to Store Files

After the user submits the form data by selecting the "Update Movie" button in Figure 19.25, the form data is available within the elseif block checking to see if the form data is set in the $_POST super global variable. Notice we added movie_image_file hidden field to the condition.

```
elseif (isset($_POST['edit_movie_submission'], $_POST['movie_title'],
        $_POST['movie_rating'], $_POST['movie_director'],
        $_POST['movie_running_time_in_minutes'], $_POST['id_to_update'],
        $_POST['movie_image_file']))
{
```

Inside this elseif block is where we want to validate the file, move it to the images/ folder, and modify the image_file field in the movieListing table in the database.

First, right after setting $id_to_update from the form data, create a variable named $movie_image_file and set it to the hidden variable now within the $_POST superglobal:

```php
elseif (isset($_POST['edit_movie_submission'], $_POST['movie_title'],
        $_POST['movie_rating'], $_POST['movie_director'],
        $_POST['movie_running_time_in_minutes'], $_POST['id_to_update'],
        $_POST['movie_image_file']))
{
    // ...
    $id_to_update = $_POST['id_to_update'];
    $movie_image_file = $_POST['movie_image_file'];
```

We need to test if an image file was previously set for the movie right after checking if checked_movie_genres is set and before connecting to the database. If not, set the previously displayed movie to the default image (Listing 19.27).

## Listing 19.27.

```php
1.  if (isset($checked_movie_genres))
2.  {
3.      $movie_genre_text = implode(", ", $checked_movie_genres);
4.  }
5.
6.  if (empty($movie_image_file))
7.  {
8.      $movie_image_file_displayed = ML_UPLOAD_PATH . ML_DEFAULT_MOVIE_FILE_NAME;
9.  }
10. else
11. {
12.     $movie_image_file_displayed = $movie_image_file;
13. }
```

Just as with addmovie.php, we will validate the uploaded movie image file right before the call connecting to the database. It might be a good idea to add an appropriate comment here, something like I have in Listing 19.28.

## Listing 19.28.

```php
1.  else
2.  {
3.      $movie_image_file_displayed = $movie_image_file;
4.  }
5.
6.  /*
7.  Here is where we will deal with the file by calling validateMovieImageFile().
8.  This function will validate that the movie image file is not greater than 128
```

```
 9. characters, is the right image type (jpg/png/gif), and not greater than 512KB.
10. This function will return an empty string ('') if the file validates successfully,
11. otherwise, the string will contain error text to be output to the web page before
12. redisplaying the form.
13. */
```

Next, we make our call to validateMovieImageFile() and set the return value to a new variable that captures the file error message:

```
otherwise, the string will contain error text to be output to the web page before
redisplaying the form.
*/

$file_error_message = validateMovieImageFile();
```

Just as we did in addmovie.php, if validateMovieImageFile() returns anything but an empty string, there was an error uploading the file. We want to display this error message and redisplay the form instead of updating the data in the database, allowing the user to correct the error. The two common reasons for the error are: the image is too big, or the image is the wrong file type.

Create an if condition for file_error_message being empty, and move all the database code into this new if block. The new if block should now look like Listing 19.29.

## Listing 19.29.

```
 1. $file_error_message = validateMovieImageFile();
 2.
 3. if (empty($file_error_message))
 4. {
 5.    $query = "UPDATE movieListing SET title = '$movie_title', rating = '$movie_rating', "
 6.          . "director = '$movie_director', running_time_in_minutes = '$movie_runtime', "
 7.          . "genre = '$movie_genre_text' WHERE id = $id_to_update";
 8.
 9.    mysqli_query($dbc, $query)
10.          or trigger_error(
11.              'Error querying database movieListing: Failed to update movie listing',
12.              E_USER_ERROR
13.          );
14.
15.    $nav_link = 'moviedetails.php?id=' . $id_to_update;
16.
17.    header("Location: $nav_link");
18.    exit();
19. }
```

Next, we have to do three more things before updating the database:

1. Move the image file to the images/ folder and get the path location by calling addMovieImageFileReturnPathLocation().

```
$movie_image_file_path = addMovieImageFileReturnPathLocation();
```

2. Remove the old image file from the images/ folder if there was a previously set image by calling removeMovieImageFile().

```
// IF new image selected, set it to be updated in the database.
if (!empty($movie_image_file_path))
{
    // IF replacing an image (other than the default), remove it
    if (!empty($movie_image_file))
    {
        removeMovieImageFile($movie_image_file);
    }

    $movie_image_file = $movie_image_file_path;
}
```

3. Update the query to the database to update the image_file field in the movieListing database table.

```
$query = "UPDATE movieListing SET title = '$movie_title', rating = '$movie_rating', "
    . "director = '$movie_director', running_time_in_minutes = '$movie_runtime', "
    . "genre = '$movie_genre_text', image_file = '$movie_image_file' "
    .  "WHERE id = $id_to_update";
```

The complete code block looks like Listing 19.30.

## Listing 19.30.

```
1. if (empty($file_error_message))
2. {
3.     $movie_image_file_path = addMovieImageFileReturnPathLocation();
4.
5.     // IF new image selected, set it to be updated in the database.
6.     if (!empty($movie_image_file_path))
7.     {
8.         // IF replacing an image (other than the default), remove it
9.         if (!empty($movie_image_file))
10.        {
11.            removeMovieImageFile($movie_image_file);
12.        }
13.
14.        $movie_image_file = $movie_image_file_path;
15.    }
```

```
16.
17.    $query = "UPDATE movieListing SET title = '$movie_title', rating = '$movie_rating', "
18.            . "director = '$movie_director', running_time_in_minutes = '$movie_runtime', "
19.            . "genre = '$movie_genre_text', image_file = '$movie_image_file' " .
20.            . "WHERE id = $id_to_update";
21.
22.    mysqli_query($dbc, $query)
23.            or trigger_error(
24.                'Error querying database movieListing: Failed to update movie listing',
25.                E_USER_ERROR
26.            );
27.
28.    $nav_link = 'moviedetails.php?id=' . $id_to_update;
29.
30.    header("Location: $nav_link");
31.    exit();
32. }
```

If there is an error validating the uploaded movie image file, you will want to output the
error to the web page and redisplay the form as in Listing 19.31.

## Listing 19.31.

```
1. $file_error_message = validateMovieImageFile();
2.
3. if (empty($file_error_message))
4. {
5.     // ...
6. }
7. else
8. {
9.     // echo error message
10.    echo "<h5><p class='text-danger'>" . $file_error_message . "</p></h5>";
11. }
```

## Complete "Edit a Movie" Code Listing

## Listing 19.32.

```
1. <!DOCTYPE html>
2. <html>
3. <head>
4.     <title>Edit a Movie</title>
5.     <link rel="stylesheet"
6.         href="https://stackpath.bootstrapcdn.com/bootstrap/4.2.1/css/bootstrap.min.css"
7.         integrity="sha384-GJzZqFGwb1QTTN6wy59ffF1BuGJpLSa9DkKMp0DgiMDm4iYMj70gZWKYbI706tWS"
8.         crossorigin="anonymous">
9. </head>
```

```php
10. <body>
11. <div class="card">
12.     <div class="card-body">
13.         <h1>Edit a Movie</h1>
14.         <nav class="nav">
15.             <a class="nav-link" href="index.php">Movies I Like</a>
16.         </nav>
17.         <hr/>
18.         <?php
19.         require_once('dbconnection.php');
20.         require_once('movieimagefileutil.php');
21.
22.         $dbc = mysqli_connect(DB_HOST, DB_USER, DB_PASSWORD, DB_NAME)
23.             or trigger_error(
24.                 'Error connecting to MySQL server for ' . DB_NAME,
25.                 E_USER_ERROR
26.             );
27.
28.         $genres = [
29.             'Action', 'Adventure', 'Comedy', 'Documentary', 'Drama',
30.             'Fantasy', 'Horror', 'Romance', 'Science Fiction'
31.         ];
32.
33.         if (isset($_GET['id_to_edit'])) {
34.             $id_to_edit = $_GET['id_to_edit'];
35.
36.             $query = "SELECT * FROM movieListing WHERE id = $id_to_edit";
37.
38.             $result = mysqli_query($dbc, $query)
39.                 or trigger_error(
40.                     'Error querying database movieListing',
41.                     E_USER_ERROR
42.                 );
43.
44.             if (mysqli_num_rows($result) == 1) {
45.                 $row = mysqli_fetch_assoc($result);
46.
47.                 $movie_title = $row['title'];
48.                 $movie_rating = $row['rating'];
49.                 $movie_director = $row['director'];
50.                 $movie_runtime = $row['running_time_in_minutes'];
51.                 $movie_genre_text = $row['genre'];
52.                 $movie_image_file = $row['image_file'];
53.
54.                 if (empty($movie_image_file)) {
55.                     $movie_image_file_displayed = ML_UPLOAD_PATH . ML_DEFAULT_MOVIE_FILE_NAME;
56.                 } else {
57.                     $movie_image_file_displayed = $movie_image_file;
58.                 }
59.
```

```
60.              $checked_movie_genres = explode(', ', $movie_genre_text);
61.          }
62.      } elseif (isset($_POST['edit_movie_submission'], $_POST['movie_title'],
63.          $_POST['movie_rating'], $_POST['movie_director'],
64.          $_POST['movie_running_time_in_minutes'], $_POST['id_to_update'],
65.          $_POST['movie_image_file'])) {
66.          $movie_title = $_POST['movie_title'];
67.          $movie_rating = $_POST['movie_rating'];
68.          $movie_director = $_POST['movie_director'];
69.          $movie_runtime = $_POST['movie_running_time_in_minutes'];
70.          $checked_movie_genres = $_POST['movie_genre_checkbox'];
71.          $id_to_update = $_POST['id_to_update'];
72.          $movie_image_file = $_POST['movie_image_file'];
73.
74.          $movie_genre_text = "";
75.
76.          if (isset($checked_movie_genres)) {
77.              $movie_genre_text = implode(", ", $checked_movie_genres);
78.          }
79.
80.          if (empty($movie_image_file)) {
81.              $movie_image_file_displayed = ML_UPLOAD_PATH . ML_DEFAULT_MOVIE_FILE_NAME;
82.          } else {
83.              $movie_image_file_displayed = $movie_image_file;
84.          }
85.
86.          /*
87.          Here is where we will deal with the file by calling validateMovieImageFile().
88.          This function will validate that the movie image file is the right image type
89.          (jpg/png/gif), and not greater than 512KB. This function will return an empty
90.          string ('') if the file validates successfully, otherwise, the string will contain
91.          error text to be output to the web page before redisplaying the form.
92.          */
93.
94.          $file_error_message = validateMovieImageFile();
95.
96.          if (empty($file_error_message)) {
97.              $movie_image_file_path = addMovieImageFileReturnPathLocation();
98.
99.              // IF new image selected, set it to be updated in the database.
100.             if (!empty($movie_image_file_path)) {
101.                 // IF replacing an image (other than the default), remove it
102.                 if (!empty($movie_image_file)) {
103.                     removeMovieImageFile($movie_image_file);
104.                 }
105.
106.                 $movie_image_file = $movie_image_file_path;
107.             }
108.
109.             $query = "UPDATE movieListing SET title = '$movie_title', rating = '$movie_rating', "
110.                   . "director = '$movie_director', running_time_in_minutes = '$movie_runtime', "
```

```php
111.                        . "genre = '$movie_genre_text', image_file = '$movie_image_file' "
112.                        . "WHERE id = $id_to_update";
113.
114.                mysqli_query($dbc, $query)
115.                    or trigger_error(
116.                        'Error querying database movieListing: Failed to update movie listing',
117.                        E_USER_ERROR
118.                    );
119.
120.                $nav_link = 'moviedetails.php?id=' . $id_to_update;
121.
122.                header("Location: $nav_link");
123.                exit();
124.            } else {
125.                // echo error message
126.                echo "<h5><p class='text-danger'>" . $file_error_message . "</p></h5>";
127.            }
128.
129.        } else // Unintended page link -  No movie to edit, link redirect to index
130.        {
131.            header("Location: index.php");
132.            exit();
133.        }
134.        ?>
135.        <div class="row">
136.            <div class="col">
137.                <form enctype="multipart/form-data"
138.                    class="needs-validation" novalidate
139.                    method="POST"
140.                    action="<?= $_SERVER['PHP_SELF'] ?>">
141.                    <div class="form-group row">
142.                        <label for="movie_title"
143.                            class="col-sm-3 col-form-label-lg">Title</label>
144.                        <div class="col-sm-9">
145.                            <input type="text" class="form-control"
146.                                id="movie_title" name="movie_title"
147.                                value="<?= $movie_title ?>"
148.                                placeholder="Title" required>
149.                            <div class="invalid-feedback">
150.                                Please provide a valid movie title.
151.                            </div>
152.                        </div>
153.                    </div>
154.                    <div class="form-group row">
155.                        <label for="movie_rating"
156.                            class="col-sm-3 col-form-label-lg">Rating</label>
157.                        <div class="col-sm-9">
158.                            <select class="custom-select"
159.                                id="movie_rating"
160.                                name="movie_rating"
```

```
161.                              value='<?= $movie_rating ?>'
162.                              required>
163.                          <option value="" disabled selected>
164.                              Rating...
165.                          </option>
166.                          <option value="G" <?= $movie_rating == 'G' ? 'selected' : '' ?>>G
167.                          </option>
168.                          <option value="PG" <?= $movie_rating == 'PG' ? 'selected' : '' ?>>PG
169.                          </option>
170.                          <option value="PG-13" <?= $movie_rating == 'PG-13' ? 'selected' : '' ?>>PG-13
171.                          </option>
172.                          <option value="R" <?= $movie_rating == 'R' ? 'selected' : '' ?>>R
173.                          </option>
174.                      </select>
175.                      <div class="invalid-feedback">
176.                          Please select a movie rating.
177.                      </div>
178.                  </div>
179.              </div>
180.              <div class="form-group row">
181.                  <label for="movie_director"
182.                      class="col-sm-3 col-form-label-lg">Director</label>
183.                  <div class="col-sm-9">
184.                      <input type="text" class="form-control" id="movie_director"
185.                          name="movie_director" value="<?= $movie_director ?>"
186.                          placeholder="Director" required>
187.                      <div class="invalid-feedback">
188.                          Please provide a valid movie director.
189.                      </div>
190.                  </div>
191.              </div>
192.              <div class="form-group row">
193.                  <label for="movie_running_time_in_minutes"
194.                      class="col-sm-3 col-form-label-lg">Running Time (min)</label>
195.                  <div class="col-sm-9">
196.                      <input type="number" class="form-control"
197.                          id="movie_running_time_in_minutes"
198.                          name="movie_running_time_in_minutes"
199.                          value="'<?= $movie_runtime ?>"
200.                          placeholder="Running time (in minutes)"
201.                          required>
202.                      <div class="invalid-feedback">
203.                          Please provide a valid running time in minutes.
204.                      </div>
205.                  </div>
206.              </div>
207.              <div class="form-group row">
208.                  <label class="col-sm-3 col-form-label-lg">Genre</label>
209.                  <div class="col-sm-9">
210.                      <?php
```

```
211.                         foreach ($genres as $genre) {
212.                             ?>
213.                             <div class="form-check form-check-inline col-sm-3">
214.                                 <input class="form-check-input"
215.                                         type="checkbox"
216.                                         id="movie_genre_checkbox_action_<?= $genre ?>"
217.                                         name="movie_genre_checkbox[]"
218.                                         value="<?= $genre ?>"
219.                                     <?= in_array($genre, $checked_movie_genres) ? 'checked' : '' ?>>
220.                                 <label class="form-check-label"
221.                                         for="movie_genre_checkbox_action_<?= $genre ?>"
222.                                 ><?= $genre ?></label>
223.                             </div>
224.                             <?php
225.                         }
226.                         ?>
227.                     </div>
228.                 </div>
229.                 <div class="form-group row">
230.                     <label for="movie_image_file"
231.                             class="col-sm-3 col-form-label-lg">Movie Image File</label>
232.                     <div class="col-sm-8">
233.                         <input type="file" class="form-control-file" id="movie_image_file"
234.                                 name="movie_image_file">
235.                     </div>
236.                 </div>
237.                 <button class="btn btn-primary" type="submit"
238.                         name="edit_movie_submission">Update Movie
239.                 </button>
240.                 <input type="hidden" name="id_to_update" value="<?= $id_to_edit ?>">
241.                 <input type="hidden" name="movie_image_file"
242.                         value="<?= $movie_image_file ?>">
243.             </form>
244.         </div>
245.         <div class="col-3">
246.             <img src="<?= $movie_image_file_displayed ?>" class="img-thumbnail"
247.                 style="max-height: 400px;" alt="Movie image">
248.         </div>
249.     </div>
250.     <script>
251.         // JavaScript for disabling form submissions if there are invalid fields
252.         (function () {
253.             'use strict';
254.             window.addEventListener('load', function () {
255.                 // Fetch all the forms we want to apply custom Bootstrap validation styles to
256.                 var forms = document.getElementsByClassName('needs-validation');
257.                 // Loop over them and prevent submission
258.                 var validation = Array.prototype.filter.call(forms, function (form) {
259.                     form.addEventListener('submit', function (event) {
260.                         if (form.checkValidity() === false) {
```

```
261.                          event.preventDefault();
262.                          event.stopPropagation();
263.                        }
264.                        form.classList.add('was-validated');
265.                  }, false);
266.                });
267.              }, false);
268.            })();
269.          </script>
270.      </div>
271.    </div>
272.    <script src="https://code.jquery.com/jquery-3.3.1.slim.min.js"
273.            integrity="sha384-q8i/X+965Dz00rT7abK41JStQIAqVgRVzpbzo5smXKp4YfRvH+8abtTE1Pi6jizo"
274.            crossorigin="anonymous"></script>
275.    <script src="https://cdnjs.cloudflare.com/ajax/libs/popper.js/1.14.6/umd/popper.min.js"
276.            integrity="sha384-wHAiFfRlMFy6i5SRaxvfOCifBUQy1xHdJ/yoi7FRNXMRBu5WHdZYu1hA6ZOblgut"
277.            crossorigin="anonymous"></script>
278.    <script src="https://stackpath.bootstrapcdn.com/bootstrap/4.2.1/js/bootstrap.min.js"
279.            integrity="sha384-B0UglyR+jN6CkvvICOB2joaf5I4l3gm9GU6Hc1og6Ls7i6U/mkkaduKaBhlAXv9k"
280.            crossorigin="anonymous"></script>
281. </body>
282. </html>
```

# Displaying Image on Deletion Page

Finally, we need to modify removemovie.php so that the movie's image is displayed on the "Remove a Movie" page for better identification of the movie. We need to delete the image file from the database and filesystem on confirmation of delete. We will add the image to the left side of the table so that it looks like Figure 19.26.

Open removemovie.php and add a reference to the movieimagefileutil.php script by adding the following require_once() following the reference to dbconnection.php towards the top of the script:

```php
<?php
    require_once('dbconnection.php');
    require_once('movieimagefileutil.php');
```

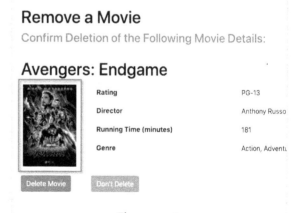

Figure 19.26.

## Displaying the Image on removemovie.php

When first linking to the "Remove a Movie" page (removemovie.php), it was because of an HTTP GET request/response when navigating from the index.php script as a result of selecting the trash can icon. Therefore, we need to make the following modifications to display movie image file details in the elseif (isset($_GET['id_to_delete'])) block of code:

```
elseif (isset($_GET['id_to_delete'])):
```

First, we query the movieListing database table for all the fields for this movie. Then, inside the if (mysqli_num_rows($result) == 1) condition block, just below fetching the row, create a variable named $movie_image_file and set it to the image_file field. Finally, change it to the path of the default movie image file if it is empty as in Listing 19.33.

### Listing 19.33.

```
1. elseif (isset($_GET['id_to_delete'])):
2.     // ...
3.     if (mysqli_num_rows($result) == 1)
4.     {
5.         $row = mysqli_fetch_assoc($result);
6.
7.         $movie_image_file = $row['image_file'];
8.
9.         if (empty($movie_image_file))
10.        {
11.            $movie_image_file = ML_UPLOAD_PATH . ML_DEFAULT_MOVIE_FILE_NAME;
12.        }
```

As we did in addmovie.php and editmovie.php, we need to add the movie image file (or the default image) to the left of the table to display the movie details.

Since we use Bootstrap's Flexbox grid implementation, we can encapsulate the image and table in separate columns and put them both in a single row. All this is just below the movie tile located in the <h1> element as in Listing 19.34.

### Listing 19.34.

```
1. <h1><?= $row['title'] ?></h1>
2. <div class="row">
3.     <div class="col-2">
4.         <img src="<?= $movie_image_file ?>" class="img-thumbnail"
5.             style="max-height: 200px;" alt="Movie image">
6.     </div>
7.     <div class="col">
```

```
8.      <table class="table table-striped">
9.          ...
10.     </table>
11.   </div>
12. </div>
13. </p>
14. <form ... >
```

Again, notice we set the style attribute to a maximum height of 200 pixels.

## Removing the Movie Image On Delete

After the user submits the form data by selecting the **Delete Movie** button (Figure 19.27), the following condition is true. This is because the user selected the "Delete Movie" submit button, which posts back to removemovie.php with the form variables delete_movie_submission and id in the $_POST[] superglobal array.

Figure 19.27.

```
if (isset($_POST['delete_movie_submission']) && isset($_POST['id'])):
```

In this block, before we query to delete this movie, we need to query the image_file field from the movieListing database table and delete the image from the images/ folder—only if the image_file field is not empty by calling removeMovieImageFile(). Make the code modifications in Listing 19.35.

## Listing 19.35.

```
1.  if (isset($_POST['delete_movie_submission']) && isset($_POST['id'])):
2.
3.      $id = $_POST['id'];
4.
5.      // Query image file from DB
6.      $query = "SELECT image_file FROM movieListing WHERE id = $id";
7.
8.      $result = mysqli_query($dbc, $query)
9.              or trigger_error(
10.                 'Error querying database movieListing', E_USER_ERROR
11.             );
12.
13.     if (mysqli_num_rows($result) == 1)
14.     {
15.         $row = mysqli_fetch_assoc($result);
16.
17.         $movie_image_file = $row['image_file'];
18.
19.         if (!empty($movie_image_file))
```

```
20.        {
21.            removeMovieImageFile($movie_image_file);
22.        }
23.    }
24.
25.    $query = "DELETE FROM movieListing WHERE id = $id";
26.
27.    $result = mysqli_query($dbc, $query)
28.        or trigger_error(
29.            'Error querying database movieListing', E_USER_ERROR
30.        );
31.
32.    header("Location: index.php");
33.    exit;
```

## Complete removemovie.php Listing

## Listing 19.36.

```
1.  <html>
2.  <head>
3.      <title>Remove a Movie</title>
4.      <link rel="stylesheet"
5.          href="https://stackpath.bootstrapcdn.com/bootstrap/4.2.1/css/bootstrap.min.css"
6.          integrity="sha384-GJzZqFGwb1QTTN6wy59ffF1BuGJpLSa9DkKMp0DgiMDm4iYMj70gZWKYbI706tWS"
7.          crossorigin="anonymous">
8.      <link rel="stylesheet"
9.          href="https://use.fontawesome.com/releases/v5.8.1/css/all.css"
10.         integrity="sha384-50oBUHEmvpQ+1lW4y57PTFmhCaXp0ML5d60M1M7uH2+nqUivzIebhnd0JK28anvf"
11.         crossorigin="anonymous">
12. </head>
13. <body>
14. <div class="card">
15.     <div class="card-body">
16.         <h1>Remove a Movie</h1>
17.         <?php
18.         require_once('dbconnection.php');
19.         require_once('movieimagefileutil.php');
20.
21.         $dbc = mysqli_connect(DB_HOST, DB_USER, DB_PASSWORD, DB_NAME)
22.         or trigger_error(
23.             'Error connecting to MySQL server for' . DB_NAME,
24.             E_USER_ERROR
25.         );
26.
27.         if (isset($_POST['delete_movie_submission']) && isset($_POST['id'])):
28.
29.             $id = $_POST['id'];
30.
```

```
31.          // Query image file from DB
32.          $query =
33.             "SELECT image_file FROM movieListing WHERE id = $id";
34.
35.          $result = mysqli_query($dbc, $query)
36.             or trigger_error(
37.                'Error querying database movieListing',
38.                E_USER_ERROR
39.             );
40.
41.          if (mysqli_num_rows($result) == 1) {
42.             $row = mysqli_fetch_assoc($result);
43.
44.             $movie_image_file = $row['image_file'];
45.
46.             if (!empty($movie_image_file)) {
47.                removeMovieImageFile($movie_image_file);
48.             }
49.          }
50.
51.          $query = "DELETE FROM movieListing WHERE id = $id";
52.
53.          $result = mysqli_query($dbc, $query)
54.          or trigger_error(
55.                'Error querying database movieListing',
56.                E_USER_ERROR
57.             );
58.
59.          header("Location: index.php");
60.          exit;
61.
62.      elseif (isset($_POST['do_not_delete_movie_submission'])):
63.
64.          header("Location: index.php");
65.          exit;
66.
67.      elseif (isset($_GET['id_to_delete'])):
68.          ?>
69.           <h3 class="text-danger">Confirm Deletion of the Following
70.              Movie Details:</h3><br/>
71.          <?php
72.          $id = $_GET['id_to_delete'];
73.
74.          $query = "SELECT * FROM movieListing WHERE id = $id";
75.
76.          $result = mysqli_query($dbc, $query)
77.             or trigger_error(
78.                'Error querying database movieListing',
79.                E_USER_ERROR
80.             );
81.
```

```php
82.         if (mysqli_num_rows($result) == 1) {
83.             $row = mysqli_fetch_assoc($result);
84.
85.             $movie_image_file = $row['image_file'];
86.
87.             if (empty($movie_image_file)) {
88.                 $movie_image_file =
89.                     ML_UPLOAD_PATH . ML_DEFAULT_MOVIE_FILE_NAME;
90.             }
91.
92.         ?>
93.         <h1><?= $row['title'] ?></h1>
94.         <div class="row">
95.             <div class="col-2">
96.                 <img src="<?= $movie_image_file ?>"
97.                     class="img-thumbnail"
98.                     style="max-height: 200px;"
99.                     alt="Movie image">
100.            </div>
101.            <div class="col">
102.                <table class="table table-striped">
103.                    <tbody>
104.                    <tr>
105.                        <th scope="row">Rating</th>
106.                        <td><?= $row['rating'] ?></td>
107.                    </tr>
108.                    <tr>
109.                        <th scope="row">Director</th>
110.                        <td><?= $row['director'] ?></td>
111.                    </tr>
112.                    <tr>
113.                        <th scope="row">Running Time (minutes)
114.                        </th>
115.                        <td><?= $row['running_time_in_minutes'] ?></td>
116.                    </tr>
117.                    <tr>
118.                        <th scope="row">Genre</th>
119.                        <td><?= $row['genre'] ?></td>
120.                    </tr>
121.                    </tbody>
122.                </table>
123.            </div>
124.        </div>
125.        <p>
126.        <form method="POST"
127.            action="<?= $_SERVER['PHP_SELF'] ?>">
128.            <div class="form-group row">
129.                <div class="col-sm-2">
130.                    <button class="btn btn-danger" type="submit"
131.                        name="delete_movie_submission">
132.                        Delete Movie
133.                    </button>
```

```
134.                        </div>
135.                        <div class="col-sm-2">
136.                            <button class="btn btn-success"
137.                                    type="submit"
138.                                    name="do_not_delete_movie_submission">
139.                                Don't Delete
140.                            </button>
141.                        </div>
142.                        <input type="hidden" name="id"
143.                               value="<?= $id ?>;">
144.                    </div>
145.                </form>
146.            <?php
147.        } else {
148.            ?>
149.            <h3>No Movie Details :-(</h3>
150.            <?php
151.        }
152.
153.    else: // Unintended page link. No movie to remove, redirect to index
154.
155.        header("Location: index.php");
156.        exit;
157.
158.    endif;
159.    ?>
160.    </div>
161. </div>
162. <script src="https://code.jquery.com/jquery-3.3.1.slim.min.js"
163.         integrity="sha384-q8i/X+965Dz00rT7abK41JStQIAqVgRVzpbzo5smXKp4YfRvH+8abtTE1Pi6jizo"
164.         crossorigin="anonymous"></script>
165. <script src="https://cdnjs.cloudflare.com/ajax/libs/popper.js/1.14.6/umd/popper.min.js"
166.         integrity="sha384-wHAiFfRlMFy6i5SRaxvfOCifBUQy1xHdJ/yoi7FRNXMRBu5WHdZYu1hA6ZOblgut"
167.         crossorigin="anonymous"></script>
168. <script src="https://stackpath.bootstrapcdn.com/bootstrap/4.2.1/js/bootstrap.min.js"
169.         integrity="sha384-B0UglyR+jN6CkvvICOB2joaf5I4l3gm9GU6Hc1og6Ls7i6U/mkkaduKaBhlAXv9k"
170.         crossorigin="anonymous"></script>
171. </body>
172. </html>
```

## Exercises

1. Add the capability to upload an image file for a movie by modifying the database and source files as indicated in this chapter. Make sure users can only upload a valid image file type.

2. Refactor the code to use in_array() to check if an uploaded file is in the list of allowed image types.

3. Display the movie image on the details page for the movie.

4. The "Default" image is intentionally unprotected from user manipulation. Update the upload case so that users can't overwrite the default image with something else. For example, don't allow users to upload a file named generic_movie.jpg.

5. Fix a bug: anyone can replace another movie's file by using the same filename—if a user knows it. So after upload and before saving the data, rename the file name to be unique to the movie it references.

# Chapter

# 20

# Basic HTTP Authentication

*"First, solve the problem. Then, write the code."*

*–John Johnson*

Currently, our *MovieListing* application has no protection from someone simply deleting all of our movies in our database or adding movie entries that we might not approve of.

In this chapter, we implement basic HTTP authentication that adds a level of protection for features of our application we do not want to expose to everyone.

In a follow-on chapter covering Security, I will discuss authentication and authorization further. Basic HTTP Authentication is a simple way to control who can use particular web pages.

The question is, what features do we want to require authentication for? Given that our application allows anyone to access the whole website, we need to add basic authentication to any feature that modifies or deletes data from the application. This limits who can change the database to trusted users who know a valid username and password combination. Therefore we will require authentication to:

- addmovie.php
- removemovie.php
- editmovie.php

## Password Protection with HTTP Authentication

Users should be able to add a movie by clicking on the link shown in Figure 20.1, remove a movie (Figure 20.2), or edit movie details via the link in Figure 20.3. Before carrying out any of these operations, we want to display the authorization dialog shown in Figure 20.4, or something similar, to verify their identity. The exact dialog you see varies depending on your browser and operating system.

Figure 20.1.

Figure 20.2.

Figure 20.3.

This dialog continues to pop up as long as the user enters the incorrect credentials. A user can add, edit, or remove movie details only if they sign in with the correct credentials.

If the user presses **Cancel**, the message in Figure 20.5 shows on the page.

Figure 20.4.

## How Does HTTP Authentication Work?

HTTP Authentication is sent using HTTP headers. Every time a user requests a webpage, headers to verify the user's identity are sent from the server to the client before returning any HTML. You should be aware that while you can use basic authentication

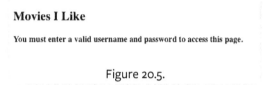

Figure 20.5.

with HTTP, the username and password are not encrypted and can be intercepted. If you must use basic authentication, make sure you're using HTTPS on your live site.

Headers control how and what kind of information passes between the client and the server. Headers usually (but not always) consist of a name/value pair separated by a colon (:).

> NOTE: For more information on HTTP Request and Response Headers, please see
> _Chapter 1: HTTP Request/Response_

In PHP, we use the header()[1] function to create HTTP headers and send them from a script.

Because headers must be sent before any HTML markup, it must be the first thing in your PHP code. There cannot be any blank lines before the <?php tag. Also, any other file you've included or required before the header() call must not send any output to the browser.

---

[1]  header(): _https://php.net/header_

## Headers Required for Authentication

As long as the password and username are incorrect or missing, our script sends these two headers:

```
header('HTTP/1.1 401 Unauthorized');
header('WWW-Authenticate: Basic realm="Movies I Like"');
```

*Note that the* Basic realm *is used to identify this authentication. Thus, it is possible to protect different web pages with separate credentials as long as the* Basic realm *is set differently. You can use whatever text you want here, but make sure it's clear to the user.*

*That said, once a page has been successfully authenticated, any other web page in the application that uses the same* Basic realm *will be automatically authenticated and not require re-credentialing.*

## Credentials in $_SERVER Superglobal

When the user enters their username and password into the authentication request dialog, the browser sends the credentials to your PHP script. They're parsed and added to the superglobal variable $_SERVER (Figure 20.6). Our code then uses these values to validate the credentials:

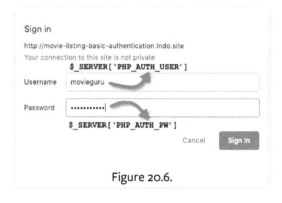

Figure 20.6.

- The username is held in $_SERVER['PHP_AUTH_USER']
- The password is in $_SERVER['PHP_AUTH_PW']

# Create authorizeaccess.php

Since we will only use one Basic realm, it makes sense to create a single PHP script that will handle our authorization. Therefore, we will create a script called authorizeaccess.php.

Since HTTP authentication is sent over in a Header, we need to make sure we have no blank lines before sending the authorization headers. So make sure your opening <?php script tag is at the top of your script and flush to the left margin:

```
<?php
```

Next, we create a couple of variables to hold the correct username and password:

```php
<?php
$username = 'movieguru';
$password = 'ilikemovies';
```

> *For a professional implementation, usernames and passwords would never be hard-coded into the source code. A more secure practice is to either use environment variables or the database. The latter allows you to give every user separate usernames and passwords. This example is for educational demonstration only.*

Every time the `authorizeaccess.php` script runs, we want to compare `$_SERVER['PHP_AUTH_USER']` to `$username` and `$_SERVER['PHP_AUTH_PW']` to `$password`. As long as either superglobal is not set or not equal to the expected values, we want to continue to post the authorization dialog.

Add the conditional shown in Listing 20.1 to the new file.

## Listing 20.1.

```php
 1. <?php
 2. $username = 'movieguru';
 3. $password = 'ilikemovies';
 4.
 5. // IF Password OR Username are empty
 6. //   OR Password  OR Username don't match
 7. // send HTTP authentication headers
 8. if (!isset($_SERVER['PHP_AUTH_USER']) || !isset($_SERVER['PHP_AUTH_PW'])
 9.     || $_SERVER['PHP_AUTH_USER'] !== $username
10.     || $_SERVER['PHP_AUTH_PW'] !== $password) {
11.
12.
13.
14. }
```

Add the following two `header()` lines of code inside of the `if` conditional statement:

```php
if (!isset($_SERVER['PHP_AUTH_USER']) || !isset($_SERVER['PHP_AUTH_PW'])
    || $_SERVER['PHP_AUTH_USER'] !== $username
    || $_SERVER['PHP_AUTH_PW'] !== $password) {

    header('HTTP/1.1 401 Unauthorized');
    header('WWW-Authenticate: Basic realm="Movies I Like"');

}
```

## 20. BASIC HTTP AUTHENTICATION

Figure 20.7.                                           Figure 20.8.

The first time this script is called, neither $_SERVER['PHP_AUTH_USER'] nor $_SERVER['PHP_AUTH_PW'] is set, so the authorization dialog is shown. If the user enters in the wrong credentials and then presses **Sign In** (Figure 20.7), the authorizeaccess.php script is called again. The code again meets the if statement conditions because the credentials do not match, and the authorization headers are sent again.

When the user submits the correct credentials, the authorizeaccess.php script is called again. This time, the previous if statement doesn't trigger, and the script continues execution.

The last case we need to handle is the user selecting **Cancel** from the authorization dialog (Figure 20.8).

We want to display a message to the page that they need to enter a valid username and password and exit our application. Therefore, add the following code after the two header() lines of code:

```
header('HTTP/1.1 401 Unauthorized');
header('WWW-Authenticate: Basic realm="Movies I Like"');

$invalid_response = "<h2>Movies I Like</h2><h4>You must enter a "
        . "valid username and password to access this page.</h4>";
exit($invalid_response);
```

If the user selects **Cancel**, their page request does not include any access credentials. Doing so invokes the exit() function, exits the application, and displays contents of $invalid_response.

## Complete Code Listing for authorizeaccess.php

### Listing 20.2.

```php
1.  <?php
2.  $username = 'movieguru';
3.  $password = 'ilikemovies';
4.
5.  // IF Password OR Username are empty
6.  //   OR Password  OR Username don't match
7.  // send HTTP authentication headers
8.  if (!isset($_SERVER['PHP_AUTH_USER']) || !isset($_SERVER['PHP_AUTH_PW'])
9.      || $_SERVER['PHP_AUTH_USER'] !== $username
10.     || $_SERVER['PHP_AUTH_PW'] !== $password) {
11.
12.     header('HTTP/1.1 401 Unauthorized');
13.     header('WWW-Authenticate: Basic realm="Movies I Like"');
14.     $invalid_response = "<h2>Movies I Like</h2><h4>You must enter a "
15.                         . "valid username and password to access this page.</h4>";
16.     exit($invalid_response);
17. }
```

# Adding Authorization to Pages

Adding our new authorization requirements to the addmovie.php, removemovie.php, and editmovie.php scripts is straightforward. Simply include the authorizeaccess.php script with a require_once() call just before the opening <html> element tag:

```php
<?php
require_once('authorizeaccess.php');
?>
<!DOCTYPE html>
<html>
  <head>
```

On any page that needs authentication, requiring authorizeaccess.php should be the first thing in the script. That way, authentication must happen before a user tries to do anything that changes your database.

## Exercises

1.  Create an `authorizeaccess.php` script to handle authentication and add it to the pages that require an authenticated user.

2.  Modify `authorizeaccess.php` to accept two or more username and password combinations.

3.  Modify `authorizeaccess.php` to accept two or more username and password combinations.

# Chapter

# 21

# Persistence

*"Measuring programming progress by lines of code is like measuring aircraft building progress by weight."*

–Bill Gates

Persistence. That's a big word. What if we need to remember the user's name and whether they're logged in? Back in chapter 18, I mentioned that the web is <u>stateless</u>. To carry over data from a previous HTTP request, so far, we have needed to save this data in a hidden variable in the form. This approach is a fragile form of persistence because if we want that data to stay around for another HTTP GET or POST, we must remember always to include our hidden variable in future requests. Wouldn't it be nice to have a better mechanism to persist our data with less work so we could use it across multiple HTTP GETs or POSTs? In web development, there are three mechanisms we can use to persist data: cookies, session variables, and the database. We have already been using the database. This chapter focuses on cookies and session variables, how they are used, and the best practices for using them.

## Cookies

Cookies allow the persistence of small pieces of string data on the client's browser, have a time limit and can be deleted at will. The components (Figure 21.1) of a cookie are:

- Name: The unique name of the cookie
- Value: The value stored in the cookie
- Expiration Date: The date and time when the cookie expires

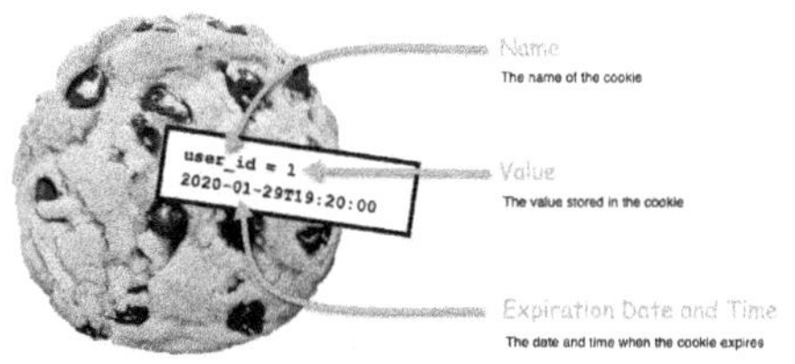

Figure 21.1.

A cookie lasts as long as its set expiration date and time. If you don't set a cookie's expiration date and time, it lasts until the user dismisses the browser session. A cookie can only be read or modified by the site that sets it for security and privacy.

> *What do we mean by small? Most browsers limit the maximum size of a cookie to 4096 bytes.*

## Using Cookies with PHP

To create a cookie in PHP, use the function setcookie()[1]. To specify the expiration date, we use the time() function to specify it as a UNIX timestamp.

```php
// Expires when browser session ends
setcookie('user_id', '1');
// Expires 1 hour from now
setcookie('user_name', 'kenmarks', time() + 3600);
```

> In the above code snippet, time() is a function that returns the current time. This value is the number of seconds since midnight on January 1st, 1970—known as a UNIX timestamp. Therefore, by adding 3600 (one hour in seconds) to the result of the time() function, we get one hour from now.

To use the cookie, you use the superglobal $_COOKIE[2] to retrieve its value. One thing to keep in mind, since it is populated from the user's request data, you can't access a value saved by setcookie() immediately via $_COOKIE. Instead, you must wait for the user to make another page request.

```php
<p class="login">You are logged in as <?= $_COOKIE['user_name'] ?>.</p>;
```

To delete a cookie, use setcookie() to set a time in the past. Doing so tells the user's browser to remove it.

```php
setcookie('username', 'kenmarks', time() - 3600); // Set the time back one hour from now
```

## Demonstrating the Use of Cookies

Let's create a simple single-page web application that asks a couple of questions and uses cookies to save the user's response. When the page is first displayed, it should look like Figure 21.2.

After entering your name and pressing the **Submit** button, the code saves the entered name to a cookie. You should see the page in Figure 21.3.

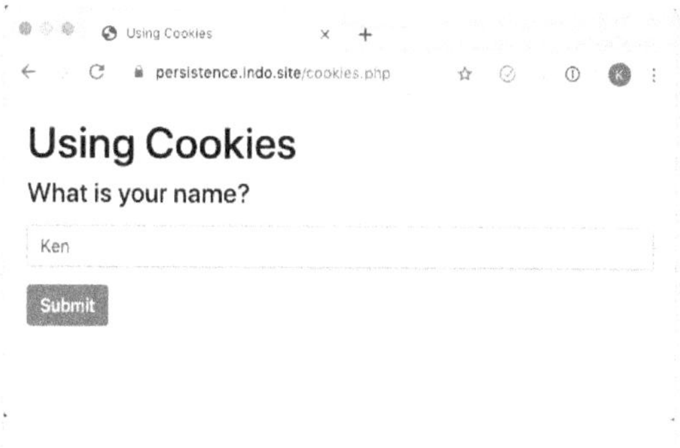

Figure 21.2.

---

[1]  setcookie(): *https://php.net/setcookie*

[2]  $_COOKIE: *https://php.net/reserved.variables.cookies*

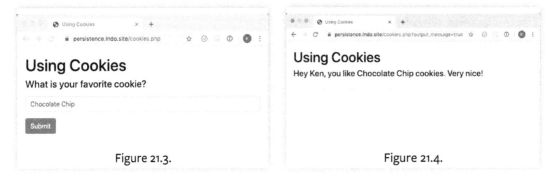

Figure 21.3.                    Figure 21.4.

After entering your favorite cookie and pressing the **Submit** button, the user's favorite cookie is saved to a cookie. We can then display the cookie values on the web page in a phrase. The page should look like Figure 21.4.

Create a PHP script called: cookies.php, and let's use the conditional logic in Listing 21.1 for progressing from the first form, to the next form, to the last page with the output phrase that uses the saved cookies.

Listing 21.1.

```
1.  <body>
2.  <div class="card">
3.    <div class="card-body">
4.      <h1>Using Cookies</h1>
5.      <?php
6.      // User entered name. Save name to Cookie and display form
7.      if (isset($_POST['name_submission']) && isset($_POST['entered_name'])) {
8.        setcookie('name', $_POST['entered_name']);
9.        // ...
10.     } // User entered favorite cookie, save favorite cookie and redirect to this page
11.     elseif (isset($_POST['cookie_submission']) && isset($_POST['entered_cookie'])) {
12.       setcookie('favorite_cookie', $_POST['entered_cookie']);
13.
14.       header("Location: {$_SERVER['PHP_SELF']}");
15.       exit;
16.     } // Output message displaying saved Cookies then delete the Cookies
17.     elseif (isset($_COOKIE['name']) && isset($_COOKIE['favorite_cookie'])) {
18.       // ...
19.       setcookie('name', '', time() - 3600);
20.       setcookie('favorite_cookie', '', time() - 3600);
21.     } // Initial navigation to this page, display form asking for name
22.     else {
23.       // ...
24.     }
25.     ?>
26.   </div>
27. </div>
28. ...
29. </body>
```

The last else clause is where initial navigation to this page begins, so here is where we want to display our form for asking for a name with the code in Listing 21.2.

Listing 21.2.

```
1. else
2. {
3.     ?>
4.     <form class="needs-validation" novalidate method="POST"
5.         action="<?= $_SERVER['PHP_SELF'] ?>">
6.       <div class="form-group">
7.         <label for="name"><h4>What is your name?</h4></label>
8.         <input type="test" class="form-control" id="entered_name"
9.             name="entered_name" placeholder="Enter your name" required>
10.       </div>
11.       <button type="submit" class="btn btn-primary"
12.             name="name_submission">Submit</button>
13.     </form>
14.     <?php
15. }
```

Since this script contains multiple forms and they will all be POSTing to $_SERVER['PHP_SELF'], we use different name attributes for the submit button on each of the forms.

Once the user has submitted this form, execution starts up in the if clause where we will set a cookie for the entered name:

```
if (isset($_POST['name_submission']) && isset($_POST['entered_name']))
{
    setcookie('name', $_POST['entered_name']);
}
```

Following the setcookie() function in the if clause, we want to display the following form that asks the user for their favorite cookie. See Listing 21.3

Listing 21.3.

```
1. if (isset($_POST['name_submission']) && isset($_POST['entered_name']))
2. {
3.     setcookie('name', $_POST['entered_name']);
4. ?>
5. <form class="needs-validation" novalidate method="POST"
6.     action="<?= $_SERVER['PHP_SELF'] ?>">
7.   <div class="form-group">
8.     <label for="name"><h4>What is your favorite cookie?</h4></label>
```

```
 9.      <input type="test" class="form-control" id="entered_cookie"
10.             name="entered_cookie" placeholder="Enter a cookie you like to eat"
11.             required>
12.   </div>
13.   <button type="submit" class="btn btn-primary"
14.             name="cookie_submission">Submit</button>
15. </form>
16. <?php
17. }
```

Again, notice we are POSTing to $_SERVER['PHP_SELF'], so we use different name attributes for the submit button for this form. Doing so lets us track which form the user is submitting.

Once the user has submitted this form, execution starts up in the first elseif clause where we set a cookie named favorite_cookie for the entered favorite cookie:

```
elseif (isset($_POST['cookie_submission']) && isset($_POST['entered_cookie']))
{
    setcookie('favorite_cookie', $_POST['entered_cookie']);
    header("Location: {$_SERVER['PHP_SELF']}");
    exit;
}
```

This code saves the favorite cookie and redirects the browser to $_SERVER['PHP_SELF']. Remember, until we send our response to the user's browser, the cookie is not set, and the value does not exist in the $_COOKIE superglobal. We can differentiate from direct navigation to this script which displays the first form by checking for the existence of the two cookies.

Next, execution starts in the second elseif clause where we want to output the phrase that uses the saved cookies:

```
elseif (isset($_COOKIE['name']) && isset($_COOKIE['favorite_cookie']))
{
    // ...
    setcookie('name', '', time() - 3600);
    setcookie('favorite_cookie', '', time() - 3600);
}
```

Notice the two calls to setcookie(). These calls set the time back one hour (in seconds), which tells the browser to delete the cookies.

Directly above the calls to setcookie(), we want to output a phrase that includes the entered name and favorite cookie saved in the cookies. Since we're outputting user-supplied strings, we must escape them to prevent cross-site scripting attacks, which we cover later in the Security chapter.

Listing 21.4.

```
1. elseif (isset($_COOKIE['name']) && isset($_COOKIE['favorite_cookie']))
2. {
3. ?>
4. <h4>
5.   Hey <?= htmlspecialchars($_COOKIE['name']) ?>, you like
6.   <?= htmlspecialchars($_COOKIE['favorite_cookie']) ?> cookies. Very nice!
7. </h4>
8. <?php
9.     setcookie('name', '', time() - 3600);
10.     setcookie('favorite_cookie', '', time() - 3600);
11. }
```

## Complete cookies.php Code Listing

*This script uses Bootstrap's client-side validation for forms and requires special CSS classes and a JavaScript function. For more information on using Bootstrap's client-side validation, please see Chapter 16: Using Bootstrap's Client-Side Validation*

Listing 21.5.

```
1. <html>
2. <head>
3.     <title>Using Cookies</title>
4.     <link rel="stylesheet"
5.         href="https://stackpath.bootstrapcdn.com/bootstrap/4.2.1/css/bootstrap.min.css"
6.         integrity="sha384-GJzZqFGwb1QTTN6wy59ffF1BuGJpLSa9DkKMp0DgiMDm4iYMj70gZWKYbI706tWS"
7.         crossorigin="anonymous">
8. </head>
9. <body>
10. <div class="card">
11.     <div class="card-body">
12.         <h1>Using Cookies</h1>
13.         <?php
14.         // User entered name, save name to Cookie and display form asking for favorite cookie
15.         if (isset($_POST['name_submission']) && isset($_POST['entered_name'])) {
16.             setcookie('name', $_POST['entered_name']);
```

```
17.             ?>
18.               <form class="needs-validation" novalidate method="POST"
19.                   action="<?= $_SERVER['PHP_SELF']; ?>">
20.                 <div class="form-group">
21.                   <label for="name"><h4>What is your favorite
22.                       cookie?</h4></label>
23.                   <input type="test" class="form-control"
24.                       id="entered_cookie" name="entered_cookie"
25.                       placeholder="Enter a cookie you like to eat"
26.                       required>
27.                 </div>
28.                 <button type="submit" class="btn btn-primary"
29.                     name="cookie_submission">Submit
30.                 </button>
31.               </form>
32.             <?php
33.         } // User entered favorite cookie, save favorite cookie to Cookie and redirect to this page
34.         elseif (isset($_POST['cookie_submission']) && isset($_POST['entered_cookie'])) {
35.             setcookie('favorite_cookie', $_POST['entered_cookie']);
36.
37.             header("Location: {$_SERVER['PHP_SELF']}");
38.             exit;
39.         } // Output message displaying saved Cookies then delete the Cookies
40.         elseif (isset($_COOKIE['name']) && isset($_COOKIE['favorite_cookie'])) {
41.             ?>
42.               <h4>
43.                   Hey <?= htmlspecialchars($_COOKIE['name']) ?>, you
44.                   like <?= htmlspecialchars($_COOKIE['favorite_cookie']) ?>
45.                   cookies. Very nice!
46.               </h4>
47.             <?php
48.             setcookie('name', '', time() - 3600);
49.             setcookie('favorite_cookie', '', time() - 3600);
50.         } // Initial navigation to this page, display form asking for name
51.         else {
52.             ?>
53.               <form class="needs-validation" novalidate method="POST"
54.                   action="<?= $_SERVER['PHP_SELF'] ?>">
55.                 <div class="form-group">
56.                   <label for="name"><h4>What is your name?</h4></label>
57.                   <input type="test" class="form-control"
58.                       id="entered_name" name="entered_name"
59.                       placeholder="Enter your name" required>
60.                 </div>
61.                 <button type="submit" class="btn btn-primary"
62.                     name="name_submission">Submit
```

```
63.              </button>
64.            </form>
65.          <?php
66.        }
67.      ?>
68.    </div>
69.  </div>
70.  <script>
71.    // JavaScript for disabling form submissions if there are invalid fields
72.    (function () {
73.      'use strict';
74.      window.addEventListener('load', function () {
75.        // Fetch all the forms we want to apply custom Bootstrap validation styles to
76.        var forms = document.getElementsByClassName('needs-validation');
77.        // Loop over them and prevent submission
78.        var validation = Array.prototype.filter.call(forms, function (form) {
79.          form.addEventListener('submit', function (event) {
80.            if (form.checkValidity() == false) {
81.              event.preventDefault();
82.              event.stopPropagation();
83.            }
84.            form.classList.add('was-validated');
85.          }, false);
86.        });
87.      }, false);
88.    })();
89.  </script>
90.  <script src="https://code.jquery.com/jquery-3.3.1.slim.min.js"
91.          integrity="sha384-q8i/X+965Dz00rT7abK41JStQIAqVgRVzpbzo5smXKp4YfRvH+8abtTE1Pi6jizo"
92.          crossorigin="anonymous"></script>
93.  <script src="https://cdnjs.cloudflare.com/ajax/libs/popper.js/1.14.6/umd/popper.min.js"
94.          integrity="sha384-wHAiFfRlMFy6i5SRaxvfOCifBUQy1xHdJ/yoi7FRNXMRBu5WHdZYu1hA6ZOblgut"
95.          crossorigin="anonymous"></script>
96.  <script src="https://stackpath.bootstrapcdn.com/bootstrap/4.2.1/js/bootstrap.min.js"
97.          integrity="sha384-B0UglyR+jN6CkvvICOB2joaf5I4l3gm9GU6Hc1og6Ls7i6U/mkkaduKaBhlAXv9k"
98.          crossorigin="anonymous"></script>
99.  </body>
100. </html>
```

## Session Variables

Session variables also allow the persistence of small pieces of data. However, instead of storing them on the client's browser, they are stored on the server, giving them an added security benefit in preventing users from altering the data. They are also not limited to storing string data. You can persist arrays, variables, and serializable objects, and the PHP interpreter automatically converts them between scripts. However, session variables only last as long as the current web browsing session. In other words, the session ends when the user closes the browser. When the session ends, the $_SESSION variables are destroyed.

To use session variables, you must indicate when your session starts by using the function session_start()[3]:

```
session_start();
```

When first calling session_start(), there is no data saved. It only indicates that the PHP interpreter can start storing and accessing session variables and internally sets a unique identifier for this session. The web browser and our application use this unique identifier to associate a session with multiple web pages.

The session identifier is not destroyed until the session is closed. This happens when the web browser is closed or when you call the session_destroy() function:

```
session_destroy();
```

If you close a session yourself by using the session_destroy()[4] function, it does not delete the session variables. Instead, it only ends the session.

To create session variables, you use the $_SESSION[] superglobal:

```
$_SESSION['user_name'] = 'kenmarks';
```

You use the session variable by accessing the $_SESSION superglobal[5] using the assigned index to retrieve it's value:

```
<p class="login">You are logged in as <?= $_SESSION['user_name'] ?>.</p>;
```

---

[3]  session_start(): https://php.net/session_start
[4]  session_destroy(): https://php.net/session_destroy
[5]  $_SESSION superglobal: https://php.net/reserved.variables.session

There are a few interesting things about using session variables. First, you must call the session_start() before creating and accessing session variables. Second, when hyperlinking from one page to another (or to the same page), you must remember that the web is stateless. To access any session variables you have created, you must call the session_start() function again.

> *The naming of* session_start() *is unfortunate. When developers first learn how to use session variables in PHP, they often assume that once they call* session_start(), *they do not need to call it again—even though the web is stateless. They wonder why they do not have access to their session variables in subsequent requests. A more accurate name for this function might be:* session_start_or_resume().

Third, as mentioned above, calling session_destroy() only ends the session but does not delete the session variables. Until the user closes their browser and PHP's session garbage collector deletes expired session data, you can't depend on any data being deleted. To ensure session variables are deleted, set the $_SESSION[] superglobal to an empty array right after you destroy the session:

```
session_destroy();
$_SESSION = []; // Destroy all session variables in the current session
```

## A Session Example

To show how to use sessions, let's rewrite our favorite cookie application to use session variables instead of cookies.

Copy cookies.php and name it sessionvariables.php. Change the content in the <title> element within the <head> element section and the <h1> content within the <body> element section from Using Cookies to Using Session Variables:

Add a call to start_session() at the top of the script. You should call this function early and before sending any HTML output to prevent web server warnings.

```
<?php
    session_start(); // Start or resume the current session so we can access session
variables
?>

<title>Using Session Variables</title>

    <h1>Using Session Variables</h1>
```

Right above the first `if` clause, change the comment to reference the `$_SESSION` variable instead of `$_COOKIE`:

```php
<?php
    // User entered name, save name to Session variable and display form asking for favorite cookie
    if (isset($_POST['name_submission']) && isset($_POST['entered_name']))
    {
```

Once you've called session_start, setting a session variable doesn't require calling a special function. Next, replace the call to `setcookie()` with the creation of a session variable.

```php
// User entered name, save name to Session variable and display form asking for favorite cookie
if (isset($_POST['name_submission']) && isset($_POST['entered_name']))
{
    $_SESSION['name'] = $_POST['entered_name'];
```

Right before the first `elseif` clause, change the comment to reference session variable instead of cookie. Within this `elseif` clause, replace the call to `setcookie()` with the creation of a session variable:

```php
// User entered favorite cookie, save favorite cookie to Session variable and route to this page
elseif (isset($_POST['cookie_submission']) && isset($_POST['entered_cookie']))
{
    $_SESSION['favorite_cookie'] = $_POST['entered_cookie'];
```

Before the final `elseif` clause, add the following comment to replace the one referencing cookies:

```php
// Output message displaying saved Session variables
// then end the current session and delete the Session variables
elseif (isset($_SESSION['name']) && isset($_SESSION['favorite_cookie']))
{
```

And replace the references to `$_COOKIE[]` within the `isset()` calls to use `$_SESSION[]`.

Within this `elseif` clause replace the reference to the `$_COOKIE` to use the `$_SESSION` variables instead for the phrase being output:

```php
    elseif (isset($_SESSION['name']) && isset($_SESSION['favorite_cookie']))
    {
?>
<h4>
  Hey <?= $_SESSION['name'] ?>, you like
  <?= $_SESSION['favorite_cookie'] ?> cookies. Very nice!
</h4>
```

Finally, to clear the responses, replace the calls to setcookie() that delete the cookies with a call to session_destroy(). Then, delete the contents of the $_SESSION[] superglobal. See Listing 21.6.

## Listing 21.6.

```
1.      elseif (isset($_SESSION['name']) && isset($_SESSION['favorite_cookie']))
2.      {
3.  ?>
4.  <h4>
5.    Hey <?= $_SESSION['name'] ?>, you like
6.    <?= $_SESSION['favorite_cookie'] ?> cookies. Very nice!
7.  </h4>
8.  <?php
9.        session_destroy();  // End the current session
10.       $_SESSION = []; // Destroy all session variables in the current session
11.     }
```

## Complete sessionvariables.php Code Listing

## Listing 21.7.

```
1. <?php
2. session_start(); // Start or resume the current session so we can access session variables
3. ?>
4. <html>
5. <head>
6.     <title>Using Session Variables</title>
7.     <link rel="stylesheet"
8.         href="https://stackpath.bootstrapcdn.com/bootstrap/4.2.1/css/bootstrap.min.css"
9.         integrity="sha384-GJzZqFGwb1QTTN6wy59ffF1BuGJpLSa9DkKMp0DgiMDm4iYMj70gZWKYbI706tWS"
10.         crossorigin="anonymous">
11. </head>
12. <body>
13. <div class="card">
14.     <div class="card-body">
15.         <h1>Using Session Variables</h1>
16.         <?php
17.         // User entered name, save name and display form asking for favorite cookie
18.         if (isset($_POST['name_submission']) && isset($_POST['entered_name'])) {
19.             $_SESSION['name'] = $_POST['entered_name'];
20.         ?>
21.           <form class="needs-validation" novalidate method="POST"
22.                 action="<?= $_SERVER['PHP_SELF']; ?>">
23.               <div class="form-group">
24.                   <label for="name"><h4>What is your favorite
25.                       cookie?</h4></label>
26.                   <input type="test" class="form-control"
27.                       id="entered_cookie" name="entered_cookie"
```

```
28.                     placeholder="Enter a cookie you like to eat"
29.                     required>
30.             </div>
31.             <button type="submit" class="btn btn-primary"
32.                     name="cookie_submission">Submit
33.             </button>
34.         </form>
35.         <?php
36.     } // User entered favorite cookie, save session variable and redirect to this page
37.     elseif (isset($_POST['cookie_submission']) && isset($_POST['entered_cookie'])) {
38.         $_SESSION['favorite_cookie'] = $_POST['entered_cookie'];
39.
40.         header("Location: {$_SERVER['PHP_SELF']}");
41.         exit;
42.     }
43.     // Output message displaying saved Session variables
44.     // then end the current session and delete the Session variables
45.     elseif (isset($_SESSION['name']) && isset($_SESSION['favorite_cookie'])) {
46.         ?>
47.         <h4>
48.             Hey <?= $_SESSION['name'] ?>, you like
49.             <?= $_SESSION['favorite_cookie'] ?> cookies. Very nice!
50.         </h4>
51.         <?php
52.         session_destroy();  // End the current session
53.         $_SESSION =
54.             []; // Destroy all session variables in the current session
55.     } // Initial navigation to this page, display form asking for name
56.     else {
57.         ?>
58.         <form class="needs-validation" novalidate method="POST"
59.             action="<?= $_SERVER['PHP_SELF'] ?>">
60.             <div class="form-group">
61.                 <label for="name"><h4>What is your name?</h4>
62.                 </label>
63.                 <input type="test" class="form-control"
64.                         id="entered_name" name="entered_name"
65.                         placeholder="Enter your name" required>
66.             </div>
67.             <button type="submit" class="btn btn-primary"
68.                     name="name_submission">Submit
69.             </button>
70.         </form>
71.         <?php
72.     }
73.     ?>
74.     </div>
75. </div>
76. <script>
77.     // JavaScript for disabling form submissions if there are invalid fields
```

```
78.    (function () {
79.        'use strict';
80.        window.addEventListener('load', function () {
81.            // Fetch all the forms we want to apply custom Bootstrap validation styles to
82.            var forms = document.getElementsByClassName('needs-validation');
83.            // Loop over them and prevent submission
84.            var validation = Array.prototype.filter.call(forms, function (form) {
85.                form.addEventListener('submit', function (event) {
86.                    if (form.checkValidity() === false) {
87.                        event.preventDefault();
88.                        event.stopPropagation();
89.                    }
90.                    form.classList.add('was-validated');
91.                }, false);
92.            });
93.        }, false);
94.    })();
95.  </script>
96.  <script src="https://code.jquery.com/jquery-3.3.1.slim.min.js"
97.          integrity="sha384-q8i/X+965Dz00rT7abK41JStQIAqVgRVzpbzo5smXKp4YfRvH+8abtTE1Pi6jizo"
98.          crossorigin="anonymous"></script>
99.  <script src="https://cdnjs.cloudflare.com/ajax/libs/popper.js/1.14.6/umd/popper.min.js"
100.          integrity="sha384-wHAiFfRlMFy6i5SRaxvfOCifBUQy1xHdJ/yoi7FRNXMRBu5WHdZYu1hA6ZOblgut"
101.          crossorigin="anonymous"></script>
102.  <script src="https://stackpath.bootstrapcdn.com/bootstrap/4.2.1/js/bootstrap.min.js"
103.          integrity="sha384-B0UglyR+jN6CkvvICOB2joaf5I4l3gm9GU6Hc1og6Ls7i6U/mkkaduKaBhlAXv9k"
104.          crossorigin="anonymous"></script>
105.  </body>
106.  </html>
```

# Cookies and Session Variables

Cookies and session variables can coexist. One reason is that cookies can persist longer than session variables. However, since cookies live on the browser, they can be a security risk. One cookie that makes sense to have when using sessions is the session identifier (ID). This is because a user can have multiple tabs open into an application. When you call session_start(), the session ID is sent as a cookie to the browser using a generated session name as the key. You get access to this session name for the current session by calling the session_name() function. When you are finished using any cookies, and you are ready to delete them, you also want to delete the session cookie using the session_name() function:

```php
if (isset($_COOKIE[session_name()]))
{
    setcookie(session_name(), '', time() - 3600);
}
```

## The Database

Of course, the database is one of the best tools we have for persisting data for as long as we want. I do not need to go into how to use the database here since you already know how to do that. Therefore, remember many of our persistence problems can be solved using the database.

## Best Practices in Solving the Persistence Problem

It is essential to recognize the reason cookies and session variables were created in the first place. They were designed to solve the persistence problem due to the stateless behavior of the web. They're still helpful for saving bits of data between pages for a short amount of time that we don't need to save permanently to the database.

The problem with cookies is that they live on the browser and are therefore insecure, or at least not trustworthy. The next option is session variables. Since these live on the server, they are more secure. However, they only last as long as the session is active. So for small pieces of data that you want to retain for the session's life, session variables make sense.

So how do we solve the problem of wanting to log out of a tax preparation application, and then when we log in, we want to resume right where we left off? This case is where using the database is a superior solution. Nothing stops us from having a database table tied to a user that identifies where they are in the workflow of their tax preparation, for example.

One thing to note is that when you use session variables, you create a cookie on the browser that stores the session ID. This result is necessary since a user may have multiple tabs open to the same application, and we need a practical way to tie a user's browser to a session.

## Exercises

1. Create `cookies.php` to ask a user their favorite cookie and store it in their browser.
2. Add a field to ask a user their favorite flavor of ice cream and store it in a cookie. Display their ice cream preference below the form.
3. Create `sessionvariables.php` to store the favorite cookie for a user.
4. Create a select menu with the four seasons, Spring, Summer, Winter, and Fall. Ask a user to pick their preferred season, store it as a session var, and display the choice.

# Chapter

# 22

# Creating Secure Web Applications

*"Complexity kills. It sucks the life out of developers, it makes products difficult to plan, build and test, it introduces security challenges and it causes end-user and administrator frustration."*

–Ray Ozzie

Since this is a book on web development, I would be remiss if I did not spend time on web application security. Most people—developer or not—have heard about the horrific data breaches that occurred over the past ten or so years. The most significant breach to date was the Equifax data breach reported in September of 2017, where hundreds of millions of customer credit records were stolen—basically, more than 70% of all adults in the U.S. Ironically, the Equifax breach was a result of a vulnerability in the Apache webserver having to do with the Java Struts framework that was not patched. However, there are plenty of vulnerabilities that can be prevented by developers properly securing their web applications.

Web security is a deep topic, and I can only scratch its surface. At the end of this chapter, I list some references you can read to dive deeper into the subject. That said, a reference that every developer must become familiar with is the *Open Web Application Security Project*[1] (OWASP) site. The two resources I find most useful on it are the OWASP Top Ten[2] and the OWASP Cheat Sheet Series[3]. The "OWASP Top Ten" lists the top ten security risks present in web applications today and has helpful links describing the vulnerability and how to mitigate the risk effectively. The "OWASP Cheat Sheet Series" has a collection of security information organized by topic. Each article explains the vulnerability and gives recommendations for how to mitigate the risks.

This chapter discusses the more common vulnerabilities, what they look like, and how to mitigate them in your application.

## Secure Password Protection for Authenticating

This scenario is a subset of the third top application security risk (ASR) from the "OWASP Top Ten".

### SHA-1 is Not Secure

I taught one of my PHP web development courses from a book that used the example of securing user passwords with Secure Hash Algorithm 1 SHA-1. Unfortunately, since 2005, SHA-1 was no longer considered secure for protecting data. SHA-1 hashed passwords, once obtained by an attacker, can be cracked offline with sufficient processing power. In 2017, Google successfully cracked the SHA-1 algorithm using a collision attack. The bad thing about using hashing algorithms like SHA-1 or even SHA-256, which has not been cracked, for storing passwords is that an attacker can generate the hashes quickly. As a result, hashes are

---

[1]   Open Web Application Security Project: https://owasp.org
[2]   OWASP Top Ten: https://owasp.org/www-project-top-ten/
[3]   OWASP Cheat Sheet Series: https://cheatsheetseries.owasp.org

generated from dictionaries of potential passwords and stored in online databases known as "Rainbow Tables."

Let me give you an example. Let's say I have an account for a web application. The password I use for my login is: ilikebananas. Let us also suppose the developer of this application is using SHA-256 to hash passwords. If I navigate in

Figure 22.1.

my web browser to the website https://passwordsgenerator.net/sha256-hash-generator/ and generate a SHA-256 hash of my password as in Figure 22.1, I get the following hash.

06855FBBC5079369B8240F7ED71093ED8203994521A715ED96546FA4B4CE31B7

## CrackStation Can Crack Unsalted Passwords

Next, if we navigate to the website https://crackstation.net and enter the same hash, I can successfully crack the password. See Figure 22.2.

This site maintains a database of reverse lookups for unsalted hashes to a dictionary of possible passwords. Here's a quote from CrackStation on how they create their lookup tables:

Figure 22.2.

> *Crackstation's lookup tables were created by extracting every word from the Wikipedia databases and adding it with every password list we could find. We also applied intelligent word mangling (brute force hybrid) to our wordlists to make them much more effective. For MD5 and SHA1 hashes, we have a 190GB, 15-billion-entry lookup table, and for other hashes, we have a 19GB 1.5-billion-entry lookup table.*

This is why everyone tells you to create strong, random passwords and use a password generator tool like LastPass or 1Password.

Let me try to crack a password I generated with my password management tool 1Password:

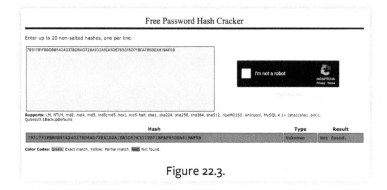

Figure 22.3.

```
RbkboCLYoPKisqKFKV2ikXvV
```

This results in the generated SHA-256 hash of:

```
7931791FBBDB854240378D6AD728A1D2A1EA5DE763315D71BFAF85DEA819AF5B
```

When I head over to CrackStation and try to crack this hash, it fails, as shown in Figure 22.3.

> *What about MD5? Everything in this section applies doubly to another commonly abused hashing function, md5(). Many older PHP articles on building login systems use this hashing function. However, it is eminently crackable because it is designed to generate hashes quickly. Therefore, no one should ever use MD5 for passwords.*

## Salted Passwords

These rainbow tables only work on hashed values that are unsalted. What is a "salt," and how does this apply to password hashes? A salt is a string added to make a password hash output unique. Randomly generated salts make the hash output unique even if multiple users use the same password. Every user must have a unique salt for this to work.

Let's say two users of my web application choose the same password: ilikebananas. To avoid the problems of this password ending up in a rainbow table, I want to use a password hashing algorithm that generates a unique hash for each of these users. First, this algorithm generates a random salt value. Then, when the first user signs up, we get a salt value similar to the following:

```
saEEWZTmyiIklQ0U2MLw9e
```

Next, the password hashing algorithm takes this salt value along with the user's password and creates a hash from concatenating these values. So the salt saEEWZTmyiIklQ0U2MLw9e and the password ilikebananas might get combined into a hash of:

```
VN.Ccp7weRXV/zln7XevGny2AO7MLMO
```

The password algorithm will then (typically) return the password hash along with the salt prepended to the hash:

```
saEEWZTmyiIklQ0U2MLw9eVN.Ccp7weRXV/zln7XevGny2AO7MLMO
```

This string is called a salted hash.

So if another user signs up and uses the same password of ilikebananas, they might get a salted hash of:

```
jDLyqNAsHEGJk19xGirRqeZNuz7VXwNw.239c4JwY3I/HBfIGukwG
```

As you can see, even if a user selects the same password, a unique hash is generated when using salted passwords. Thus, an attacker who knows what one version of ilikebananas looks like when hashed can't find other accounts using the same password. This defense is necessary given we live in a world where many users still pick password123 as their password.

When we are ready to authenticate either user, the salt prepended to the hash is used along with the entered password to verify that the stored hash matches for this user.

## Using password_hash() and password_verify()

When creating web applications in PHP requiring user authentication, always use functions that generate and validate salted hashes relying upon strong encryption algorithms. PHP offers built-in functions to make this process straightforward and less error-prone. You should not roll your own.

When signing up a new user, we use the password_hash()[4] function to generate a salted hash. The standard way to use this function is to pass a single string argument containing the user's password and the constant PASSWORD_DEFAULT, and a salted hash is returned as a string:

```
$salted_hashed_password = password_hash($password, PASSWORD_DEFAULT);
```

We can save this hashed value to the database.

---

[4]  password_hash(): *https://php.net/password_hash*

One thing to note is that passwords are truncated to 72 characters if they are over 72 characters in length. Another thing is that the current default length of a hashed password using `password_hash()` is 60 characters in length. Therefore, when storing hashed passwords in a database, make this field a `VARCHAR(255)` to account for updates to the encryption algorithms available in these functions.

When authenticating a user logging in with their password, use the `password_verify()`[5] function. This function takes two arguments, the first is the user-entered password, and the second is the hashed password you retrieve from the database. The function returns `true` if the password is verified—you've successfully authenticated the user. Otherwise, it returns `false`.

```php
if (password_verify($password, $salted_hashed_password))
{
    echo "You're Legit!";
}
```

# Guarding Against SQL Injection

SQL injection is the number one security risk for web applications and is listed as the number one ASR from the "OWASP Top Ten." An SQL injection attack inserts data directly into an SQL query without first sanitizing the input. Therefore, any source of data passed to a query can be a vector of attack and must be appropriately escaped. However, for this discussion, I focus on form field data as an attack vector into our web application and how to prevent it.

### What a SQL Injection Attack Looks Like

All the code we have written so far has been vulnerable to SQL injection. Let's look at an example of how bad this can be. Let's say I have an ecommerce application with a page that allows users to browse the inventory of stuff I'm selling as in Figure 22.4.

As we can see, if a user enters nothing into the search field, we get all the inventory displayed in an HTML table of three columns.

Figure 22.4.

---

[5] `password_verify()`:
   https://php.net/password_verify

We can assume the SQL query to produce this output might be structured like this:

```
SELECT <some fields> FROM <a table> WHERE <search field> LIKE '%<search term>%';
```

Since this is a LIKE query, the % are wildcards. If we search the inventory for anything with sir in it, we get output in Figure 22.5.

To detect if the application is directly inserting data from entered form fields into an SQL query, we can insert a single quote (') to create a malformed SQL query like in Figure 22.6.

This output is faulty and indicates our application is vulnerable to SQL injection. It's even worse because we can manipulate the application into returning information in the database. Let me show you how.

> **Do not** *perform any of what I am about to show you on any website unless you are explicitly contracted and qualified to perform penetration testing for said website!*

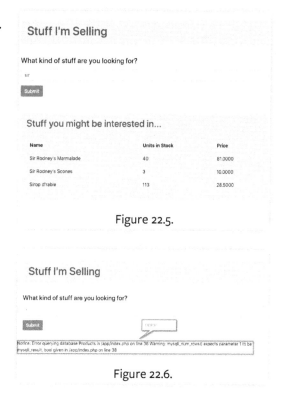

Figure 22.5.

Figure 22.6.

We need to understand that the only part of the query we can control is what is entered in between the two percent signs (%%). We can imagine that our PHP code that performs the query might look something like this:

```
$search_term = isset($_POST['search']) ? $_POST['search'] : '';

$query = "SELECT some_field_1, some_field_2, some_field_3 FROM SomeTable "
       . "WHERE some_field_n LIKE '%$search_term%'";
```

I can now manipulate the query to return almost anything I want. I can test that by entering the following into the search field:

```
';--
```

When expanded out, the complete query might look like this:

```
SELECT some_field_1, some_field_2, some_field_3 FROM SomeTable WHERE some_field_n LIKE '%';-- %';
```

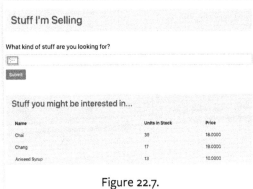

Figure 22.7.

I'll try the following entry and get these results (Figure 22.7).

Since we now know this application is vulnerable to SQL injection, I want to figure out which database technology the application uses. MySQL uses SLEEP() as a command to wait a specified number of milliseconds. If this works, I know the database technology is MySQL.

Next, I enter this into the search field:

```
sir%' AND 0 = SLEEP(2);--
```

This search therm gives me all the inventory having "sir" in the name, and for each entry, it waits two seconds before rendering the table. Since there are three entries, it should take six seconds (and it does). I get the output shown in Figure 22.8.

Then returns something like Figure 22.9.

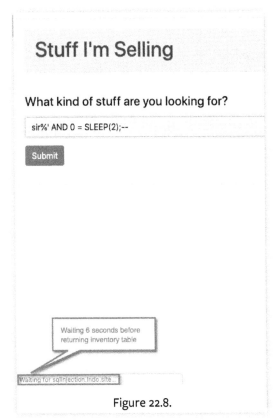

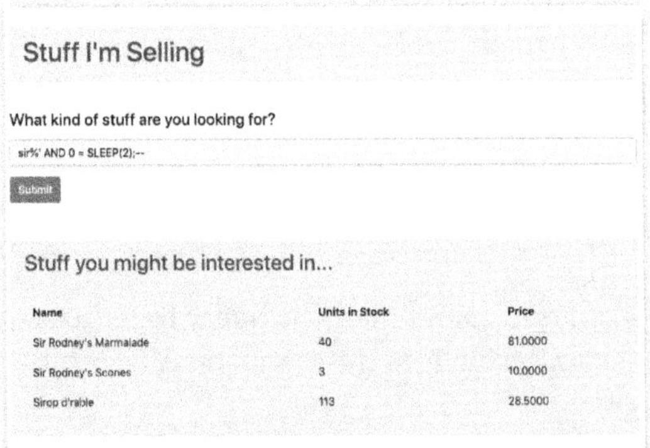

Figure 22.8.

Figure 22.9.

Now, I know I can manipulate the query through the search field and that it is a MySQL database. So, let's see if we can display some dummy data at the bottom of the table. MySQL has a dummy table called DUAL. Using the UNION command with a sub-query in SQL, we can add three columns of fake information to the end of the table.

Let's enter this into the search field:

```
sir%' UNION (SELECT 1, 2, 3 FROM dual);--
```

And we get Figure 22.10.

This is no longer a blind attack as we can harvest information out of the database.

MySQL has a database called information_schema containing meta-information about all the databases and their tables. The information_schema.tables table contains information about all the tables in the current database. The fields TABLE_NAME and TABLE_SCHEMA give us the names of each table and the database containing them.

Figure 22.10.

Figure 22.11.

Let's enter this into the search field to harvest some information from this database:

```
sir%' UNION (SELECT TABLE_NAME, TABLE_SCHEMA, 3 FROM information_schema.tables);--
```

We should get output shown in Figure 22.11 and Figure 22.12. There is a lot of interesting information here we can mine. However, I am particularly interested in the Login table within the SQLInjection database. The COLUMN_NAME field within the columns table of the information_schema database will list all

| | | |
|---|---|---|
| Customers | SQLInjection | 3.0000 |
| EmployeeTerritories | SQLInjection | 3.0000 |
| Employees | SQLInjection | 3.0000 |
| Invoices | SQLInjection | 3.0000 |
| Login | SQLInjection | 3.0000 |
| Order Details | SQLInjection | 3.0000 |
| Order Details Extended | SQLInjection | 3.0000 |
| Order Subtotals | SQLInjection | 3.0000 |
| Orders | SQLInjection | 3.0000 |

Figure 22.12.

the fields for any table I am interested in. The fields are contained within the COLUMN_NAME field.

Let's enter the following into the search field to find out what fields are in the Login table:

```
sir%' UNION (SELECT COLUMN_NAME, 2, 3 FROM information_schema.columns WHERE TABLE_NAME = 'Login');--
```

And we get this (Figure 22.13). UserName, HashedPassword, and Access look very promising!

I now know the database, table, and columns I want to interrogate. Let's see if I can get some user names and passwords! Enter this into the search field:

```
sir%' UNION (SELECT UserName, HashedPassword, Access FROM Login);--
```

This gets us the information in Figure 22.14. I'm particularly interested in the user that has admin access, and it looks like the hashes might not be salted (uh oh)! In fact, when I run the hash through https://crackstation.net, I get Figure 22.15 (next page).

In all seriousness, this is very scary. On average (year over year), 20% to 30% of websites are vulnerable to SQL injections.

> *https://edgescan.com puts out a vulnerability report every year that breaks down the statistics of vulnerabilities that have been found. Here's a link to their 2020 report[6].*

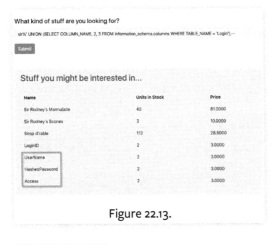

Figure 22.13.

Figure 22.14.

[6]   2020 report: http://phpa.me/edgescan-2020

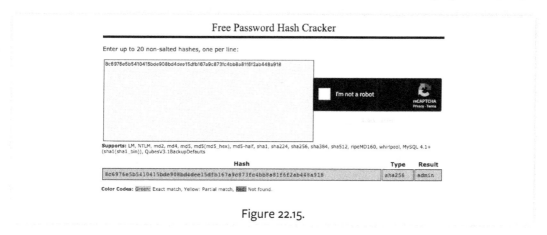

Figure 22.15.

Thankfully, SQL injection attacks are straightforward to mitigate.

## Using mysqli_real_escape_string()

mysqli_real_escape_string()[7] is a bandaid, but it's better than nothing. The easiest way to sanitize form field inputs is to use the mysqli_real_escape_string() function. Listing 22.1 shows how you would use it.

### Listing 22.1.

```php
1.  <?php
2.  $dbc = mysqli_connect(DB_HOST, DB_USER, DB_PASSWORD, DB_NAME)
3.          or trigger_error(
4.              'Error connecting to MySQL server for' . DB_NAME,
5.              E_USER_ERROR
6.          );
7.
8.  $search_term = isset($_POST['search']) ? $_POST['search'] : '';
9.
10. $search_term = mysqli_real_escape_string($dbc, $search_term);
11.
12. $query = "SELECT some_field_1, some_field_2, some_field_3 FROM SomeTable "
13.         . "WHERE some_field_n LIKE '%$search_term%'";
14.
15. $result = mysqli_query($dbc, $query)
16.     or trigger_error(
17.         'Error querying database Products', E_USER_ERROR
18.     );
```

---

[7] mysqli_real_escape_string(): *https://php.net/mysqli_real_escape_string*

The issue with using mysqli_real_escape_string() is that it escapes the form field entry without the context of the underlying SQL query using it. The reasons why this fails sometimes are pretty technical. However, take a look at http://phpa.me/so-sqli-edgecase for an edge case that fails sanitation.

## Prepared Statements

Prepared Statements are a better guard against SQL injection. A more robust method for mitigating SQL injections is to use prepared statements, also known as parameterized queries. The problem with mysqli_real_escape_string() is that it doesn't separate your input from the query itself, but in effect, it inserts it into the query. However, prepared statements will separate your database inputs from your queries and not allow you to insert SQL commands (like subqueries). Let's look at prepared statements and how to use them.

The PHP language, via the mysqli extension, provides two functions to parameterize our database inputs: mysqli_prepare()[8] and mysqli_stmt_bind_param()[9]. We can use these functions together to parameterize database queries. mysqli_prepare() is used to parameterize the SQL query into a statement that will be bound to the input parameters using the mysqli_stmt_bind_param()[10] function.

Listing 22.2 shows how to use these functions.

### Listing 22.2.

```php
1.  <?php
2.  $dbc = mysqli_connect(DB_HOST, DB_USER, DB_PASSWORD, DB_NAME)
3.          or trigger_error(
4.              'Error connecting to MySQL server for' . DB_NAME,
5.              E_USER_ERROR
6.          );
7.
8.  $search_term = isset($_POST['search']) ? $_POST['search'] : '';
9.
10. $sql = "SELECT some_field_1, some_field_2, some_field_3 "
11.        . " FROM SomeTable WHERE some_field_n LIKE ?";
12.
13. $stmt = mysqli_prepare($dbc, $sql);
14.
15. $search_term = '%' . $search_term . '%';
16.
17. mysqli_stmt_bind_param($stmt, 's', $search_term);
```

---

[8] mysqli_prepare(): https://php.net/mysqli_prepare
[9] mysqli_stmt_bind_param(): https://php.net/mysqli_stmt_bind_param
[10] mysqli_stmt_bind_param(): https://php.net/mysqli_stmt_bind_param

The next step is to invoke or execute the prepared SQL statement with mysqli_stmt_
execute()[11] and then get the results of the executed prepared SQL statement using
mysqli_stmt_get_result()[12].

```php
mysqli_stmt_execute($stmt);

$result = mysqli_stmt_get_result($stmt);
```

Putting it all together with some reasonable conditional logic looks like Listing 22.3. Note, a
? is used as a placeholder for query parameters.

## Listing 22.3.

```php
1.  <?php
2.  $dbc = mysqli_connect(DB_HOST, DB_USER, DB_PASSWORD, DB_NAME)
3.          or trigger_error(
4.              'Error connecting to MySQL server for' . DB_NAME,
5.              E_USER_ERROR
6.          );
7.
8.  $search_term = isset($_POST['search']) ? $_POST['search'] : '';
9.
10. $sql = 'SELECT some_field_1, some_field_2, some_field_3'
11.     . ' FROM SomeTable WHERE some_field_n LIKE ?';
12.
13. if ($stmt = mysqli_prepare($dbc, $sql))
14. {
15.     // the % is part of our query parameter not the SQL statement
16.     $search_term = '%' . $search_term . '%';
17.
18.     mysqli_stmt_bind_param($stmt, 's', $search_term);
19.
20.     mysqli_stmt_execute($stmt);
21.
22.     $result = mysqli_stmt_get_result($stmt);
23.
24.     while ($row = mysqli_fetch_assoc($result))
25.     {
26.         // ...
27.     }
28. }
```

This code is certainly more to write than mysqli_real_escape_string() and mysqli_query().
However, it is the safest procedural-based code to write for mitigating SQL injection attacks.

---

[11] mysqli_stmt_execute(): *https://php.net/mysqli_stmt_execute*
[12] mysqli_stmt_get_result(): *https://php.net/mysqli_stmt_get_result*

# Leaking Information to Hackers

Speaking in security lingo, it is essential to know what the attack vectors are for any application you write. These are cookies, query parameters, and form fields typically sent via POST for web applications. Another thing to consider is what information we make available—like the database schema or file system paths—that hackers can use to penetrate our application. These happen to be closely related to the attack vectors. Let's take a look at each of these.

## Cookies

Web applications can use cookies to store all kinds of information. However, they reside on a client's browser, and as such, they are viewable and vulnerable to modification. I could spend a lot of time talking about what should and should not be stored in cookies (e.g., you should never store personal information in cookies). However, the debate is moot; along with the database, use session variables and only use a single cookie to store the session ID. Doing so avoids most problems with using cookies. Remember, cookies are only one solution to the problem of the web being stateless. We have much better tools available to solve the persistence problem: the database and session variables.

## Query Parameters

Query parameters are sent over in the URL of an HTTP GET request, after the ?:

```
http://example.com?term=elephant&page=3
```

The user or a potential hacker can see this. Query parameters can be used as a persistence mechanism (similar to hidden variables in a form). This practice exposes details about the application and how it runs. Often we only need to send a single query parameter which can be an ID that maps to a primary key in a database table which can be queried in the script after processing the GET request.

```
http://example.com?id=840938
```

Since query parameters are user-supplied data, they should be parameterized when used in queries and escaped when displayed in HTML.

## Form Fields

Form fields are a gold mine of information for hackers trying to guess field names in a database schema. Unfortunately, this has been a common practice for developers and makes the process of guessing the database schema much easier in a blind SQL injection attack.

I live in an area with many insurance companies, and they typically have development requirements for obfuscating the column names in database tables used in form fields. This is an excellent practice every developer should follow.

## Preventing Cross-Site Scripting Attacks

Cross-Site Scripting (XSS) is listed as the number seven ASR from the "OWASP Top Ten." According to OWASP:

> *XSS flaws occur whenever an application includes untrusted data in a new web page without proper validation or escaping, or updates an existing web page with user-supplied data using a browser API that can create HTML or JavaScript. XSS allows attackers to execute scripts in the victim's browser which can hijack user sessions, deface web sites, or redirect the user to malicious sites.*

Sounds scary! Well, all this stuff is scary. There are three vectors of XSS attacks targeting browsers: Reflected XSS, Stored XSS, and DOM XSS:

Here is what the OWASP says about these:

- **Reflected XSS:** *The application or API includes unvalidated and unescaped user input as part of HTML output. A successful attack can allow the attacker to execute arbitrary HTML and JavaScript in the victim's browser. Typically, the user will need to interact with some malicious link that points to an attacker-controlled page, such as malicious watering hole websites, advertisements, or similar.*
- **Stored XSS:** *The application or API stores unsanitized user input that is viewed at a later time by another user or an administrator. Stored XSS is often considered high or critical risk.*
- **DOM XSS:** *JavaScript frameworks, single-page applications, and APIs that dynamically include attacker-controllable data to a page are vulnerable to DOM XSS. Ideally, the application would not send attacker-controllable data to unsafe JavaScript APIs.*

I will deal with the first two since mitigating the third type of attack is done outside of PHP.

The mechanics of how XSS works are pretty involved due to the number of actors. An excellent reference is *Security Principles for PHP Applications* by Eric Mann for a more in-depth discussion. In Chapter 7, Eric explains XSS and how to prevent it. Another great reference is https://excess-xss.com. The authors have a comprehensive tutorial with diagrams explaining XSS and mitigation strategies.

XSS involves three actors at its core: the attacker, the victim, and the vulnerable website. To mitigate the vulnerability, our code must sanitize all inputs to the website of JavaScript and HTML entities before outputting it.

### Reflected XSS

Let's take the application we wrote above to test an SQL Injection attack and add an output of our search term to the web page as in Figure 22.16.

Even though we've parameterized our search term input to the database query, let's see if this web application is exploitable to a reflected XSS attack. We'll know it can be exploited if we can execute a JavaScript command or render some additional HTML.

Let's start by entering `<script>alert('XSS Attack')</script>` into the search field as shown in Figure 22.17. We get the results shown in Figure 22.18. Uh oh! Unfortunately, this indicates our application is vulnerable to XSS attacks.

Figure 22.16.

Figure 22.17.

Figure 22.18.

Let's do one more test to see if we can render the following HTML form:

```
<h4>Clickbait Login</h4>
<form action=http://iwantyourcredentials.info method=POST>
  Username:
  <input type='text' name='username'><br/>
  Password:
  <input type='password' name='password'><br/>
  <input type='submit' value='Submit'>
</form>
```

When we enter the HTML into the search field in Figure 22.19 and press **Submit,** we get the results in Figure 22.20.

If I fill this form out and submit it (Figure 22.21), I'll be in a world of hurt! We're allowing any attacker on the web to host a form on our site. In this case, they can use it to harvest our users' credentials.

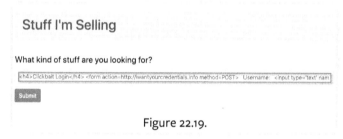

Figure 22.19.

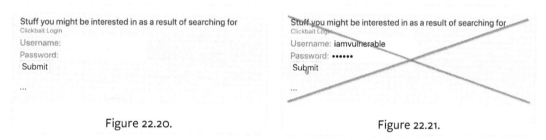

Figure 22.20.            Figure 22.21.

Let's take a look at a portion of the vulnerable code:

```
    $search_term = isset($_POST['search']) ? $_POST['search'] : '';
?>
<h2>Stuff you might be interested in as a result of searching for
<span class="text-danger"><?= $search_term ?></span>...</h2>
```

We're not sanitizing the input from our search field of HTML entities like <, >, ", and other special symbols. As a result, we allow HTML markup and JavaScript code to execute.

Thankfully, the solution is straightforward and requires using the function `filter_var()`[13]. Since we expect a string for our search term, this is how we can sanitize our application from XSS:

```
$search_term = isset($_POST['search']) ? $_POST['search'] : '';
$search_term = filter_var($search_term, FILTER_SANITIZE_STRING);
?>
<h2>Stuff you might be interested in as a result of searching for
<span class="text-danger"><?= $search_term?></span>...</h2>
```

Now when we enter `<script>alert('XSS Attack')</script>` into the search field we no longer get the `alert()`, but instead get the output you see in Figure 22.22. And when we enter our

form into the search field, we no longer get the login form, but instead get what is shown in Figure 22.23.

Note that if you receive an email address as an input, you should use `FILTER_SANITIZE_EMAIL` as it removes all characters except those allowed in an email address. For more information on the list of filters for sanitization, see https://php.net/filter.filters.sanitize.

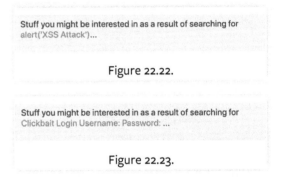

Stuff you might be interested in as a result of searching for
alert('XSS Attack')...

Figure 22.22.

Stuff you might be interested in as a result of searching for
Clickbait Login Username: Password: ...

Figure 22.23.

> *You may see older articles using the functions* `htmlentites()`[14] *and* `htmlspecialchars()` *to guard against XSS. While they may work, they don't protect against directory traversal attacks. Also, the default parameters don't protect you from all XSS attacks.*

## Stored XSS

Regarding stored XSS, you should be super paranoid and make sure you run the `filter_var()` function on everything you query out of your database that you plan to display on a web page. If you're sending the output in a CSV file, PDF document, or another format, you may need to escape it differently.

You should couple this approach with validating and sanitizing everything coming into the web application. This means filtering every input from a form or a query parameter using `filter_var()` and then parameterizing all your queries from these inputs as well.

---

[13] `filter_var()`: *https://php.net/filter_var*
[14] `htmlentites()`: *https://php.net/htmlentities*

# File Uploads

Another source of attack is uploaded files. The OWASP has a lot of detailed information regarding the risks of uploaded files and various mitigation strategies. My recommendation is always to follow the guidance from the OWASP. Still, here are the minimal things you must consider to allow for securely uploading files.

For this example, let's say we are asking a user to upload an image file using this form:

```
<form method="POST" enctype="multipart/form-data" action="upload.php">
    File: <input type="file" name="picture">
    <input type="submit" value="Submit">
</form>
```

## Validate the Uploaded File

There are a few steps you need to follow to validate an uploaded file. For example, you want to guard against a directory path traversal attack, only accept uploaded files using POST, check the file type, and check the file size.

### Protect Against a Path Traversal Attack

An attacker can try and acquire passwords from our web server or access a file that wasn't meant to be accessed by setting the file's name as a relative path (e.g. ../../../etc/passwd).

To guard against this attack, use the basename()[15] function to strip off unwanted characters:

```
$file_name = basename($_FILES['picture']['name']);
```

### Only Accept Uploaded Files Using HTTP POST

As an extension to not being able to manipulate the web application to work on files it should not, you should verify the file was actually uploaded using HTTP POST with the is_uploaded_file()[16] function:

```
if (is_uploaded_file($_FILES['picture']['tmp_name']) === true)
{
    // You're good to go!
}
else
{
    // We've got a problem!
}
```

---

[15] basename(): https://php.net/basename
[16] is_uploaded_file(): https://php.net/is_uploaded_file

### Check the MIME File Type

We also want to prevent attackers from uploading files our application is not interested in (e.g. executable files). Rather than relying on the file extension contained in `$_FILES['picture']['type']`, it is best to use the `finfo_open()`[17] and `finfo_file()`[18] functions that interrogate the actual file for it's MIME file type:

```
$file_info = finfo_open(FILEINFO_MIME_TYPE);
$file_mime_type = finfo_file($file_info, $_FILES['picture']['tmp_name']);
finfo_close($file_info);
```

If you are expecting an image type, in addition to explicitly validating the MIME file type, you should also use the function `getimagesize()`[19] as shown in Listing 22.4

### Listing 22.4.

```
 1. if (is_readable($_FILES['picture']['tmp_name']))
 2. {
 3.    $file_size = getimagesize($_FILES['picture']['tmp_name']);
 4.    if (!empty($file_size) && ($file_size[0] !== 0) && ($file_size[1] !== 0))
 5.    {
 6.        // You're good to go!
 7.    }
 8.    else
 9.    {
10.        // We've got a problem!
11.    }
12. }
```

### Check the File Size

It is always a best practice to limit the maximum file size of uploaded files. We typically do that by setting a hidden input element with the name attribute set to `max_file_size` inside the form. However, an attacker can manipulate this value.

The web server also has an INI file directive called `upload_max_filesize` that limits the maximum file that a browser can upload to the server.

A file will not be uploaded if it exceeds either the `max_file_size` or `upload_max_filesize` (whichever is smaller). In this case, `UPLOAD_ERR_FORM_SIZE` will be set for `$_FILES['picture']['error']` To further limit the size (in bytes) of the uploaded file to the application by checking `$_FILES['picture']['size']`:

---

[17] `finfo_open()`: *https://php.net/finfo_open*
[18] `finfo_file()`: *https://php.net/finfo_file*
[19] `getimagesize()`: *https://php.net/getimagesize*

```php
if ($_FILES['pictures']['size'] <= 1000000)
{
    // You're good to go!
}
else
{
    // Too big!
}
```

# Securing Your Session

The last attack I'll cover is session hijacking. An attacker can steal your session if they can get a hold of your session ID. This frequently happens as a result of an XSS or man-in-the-middle attack and not using an encrypted connection.

## Use HTTP-Only Session Cookies

You can prevent session hijacking by making sure to set the web server's INI directive `session.cookie_httponly=On`. This will refuse access to the session cookie from JavaScript.

Another INI directive to consider is `session.use_strict_mode=On`. It prevents the session module from accepting session IDs that were not generated by the session module and can prevent using an attacker-initialized session ID.

For more information on securing sessions and INI settings, see https://php.net/session.security.ini.

## HTTPS Uses Encrypted Communication

Another way to prevent a session from being hijacked is to make your web application available only using an encrypted connection (i.e., HTTPS). The HTTP protocol is communicated in cleartext. In contrast, HTTPS encrypts the HTTP using the Transport Layer Security (TLS) protocol. In the past, browsers used their predecessor, the Secure Socket Layer (SSL). Setting up a webserver to use the HTTPS protocol involves using TLS/SSL certificates that contain a private key for the webserver and a public key that client browsers use to connect to the secure server. The public and private keys handle encryption and decryption.

If your site uses HTTPS, you can further protect your sessions by setting `session.cookie_secure=On`. This setting only allows accessing the session ID cookie over HTTPS.

Let's Encrypt[20] is a nonprofit Certificate Authority that provides TLS certificates free of charge.

---

[20] Let's Encrypt: https://letsencrypt.org

## Final Thoughts

Given this book concerns developing web applications using PHP and MySQL, this chapter only scratches the surface of what it takes to create a secure web application. When writing web applications that you will release in the wild (i.e., deployed and accessible on the internet), it is essential to follow the guidelines laid out in the *Open Web Application Security Project* (OWASP) site at: https://owasp.org. Web site security is an ongoing process. As I mentioned earlier, another excellent resource is the book *Security Principles for PHP Applications* by Eric Mann. When you deploy a web application, make sure it is safe and keep your users' information safe.

## Exercises

1. Go back to our Movie Database application, rewrite queries to use prepared statements, particularly if they have user-supplied data.

2. In the Movie Application, test some text fields to see if you can inject the following value: `<script>alert('oh no!')</script>`. If you get an alert box, change the code to escape the user's input before displaying it.

3. In the Favorite Cookies application, test some text fields to see if you can inject the following value: `<script>alert('oh no!')</script>`. If you get an alert box, change the code to escape the user's input before displaying it.

4. Review the Movie Database application and ensure any user-supplied data about a movie is properly escaped on output.

# Chapter

# 23

# Adding User Logins

*"Haskell is faster than C++, more concise than Perl, more regular than Python, more flexible than Ruby, more typeful than C#, more robust than Java, and has absolutely nothing in common with PHP."*

–Autrijus Tang

## 23. ADDING USER LOGINS

Now that we are armed with proper techniques for securing our web applications let's get back to our *Movie Listing* application. We need to make three significant changes to the application. First, we add individual logins with the ability to sign new users up. Second, we add a navigation menu to increase the ease of use of the application. And third, we incorporate a reservation system to allow users to check out movies and return them. We will also modify the application to only allow administrators to add, edit, and remove movies. Here is a detailed list of the modifications that we need to make to turn the *Movie Listing* application into a *Movie Reservations* application:

1. **Adding Individual User Logins**
    1. Create a database table to hold information for users and their access privileges
    2. Create signup, login, and logout scripts for individual users
    3. Modify the authorizeaccess.php script to only allow users with admin access privileges to add, edit, and remove movies

2. **Add a Navigation Menu to Increase Ease of Use**
    1. Create and integrate a navigation bar script to be used by multiple pages

3. **Adding Reservation Features**
    1. Create a database table to hold information for movie reservations
    2. Add fields to the movieListing database table to keep track of the number of copies and reserved movies for each movie
    3. Modify the add and edit movie scripts to include the number of copies of a movie
    4. Modify the Movie listings page to show a link for reserving a movie for logged in users
    5. Modify the Movie listings page to show a link for removing a movie for users logged in with admin privileges
    6. Add a reservation script for users to check out movies
    7. Add a script for a shopping cart that allows users to reserve movies in their cart and remove them from their cart
    8. Add a shopping cart icon that allows users to view their cart
    9. Add a reserved movies script allowing users to check movies back in
    10. Add a reservations icon that allows users to view their reservations

In this chapter, we modify the application to add individual user logins. We add the other features in the following two chapters.

# Create a user Table

To add user logins, we need to create another table in the Movie database to hold user information. Let's create a user table that holds the following fields:

| Column Name | Type | Default |
|---|---|---|
| id | int(11) *Auto Increment* | |
| user_name | varchar(50) | |
| password_hash | varchar(255) | |
| access_privileges | varchar(25) | [user] |
| date_created | datetime | [CURRENT_TIMESTAMP] |

> *The PHP Manual entry for* password_hash()[1] *recommends allowing for hash lengths between 60 and 255 characters to allow for the hash to expand over time as the algorithm is updated.*
>
> *In a professional application, you would want to capture more demographic information (contact info, etc.).*

Using Adminer, create a new table in the Movie database containing the columns (and associated data types) listed above. We will have two types of access privileges: user and admin. When we sign up a new user, we want to set the default access privileges to user. Any user account you want to have admin privileges must be altered manually in the database table. We also want a default value of CURRENT_TIMESTAMP set for the date_created field, which also gets set when we sign up a new user.

---

[1] password_hash(): *https://php.net/password_hash*

# 23. Adding User Logins

## Create a Signup.php script

To allow new users to access our application, we need to create a signup.php script. Figure 23.1 shows what we want our signup page to look like.

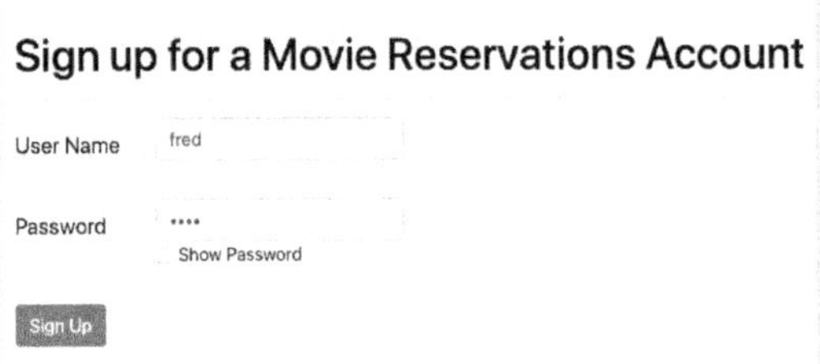

Sign up for a Movie Reservations Account

User Name: fred

Password: ••••  Show Password

Sign Up

Figure 23.1.

To make our application more secure, we might implement a CAPTCHA[2] feature on our "Sign Up" form to lower the risk of automated scripts signing up for an account. CAPTCHAs are annoying for the user, so a better implementation is like Google's reCAPTCHA shown in Figure 23.2.

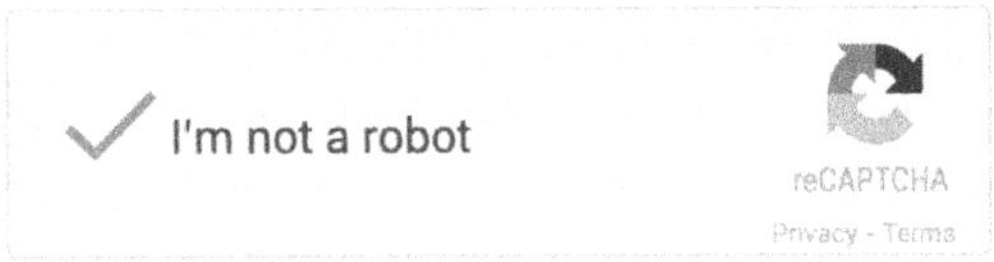

✓ I'm not a robot

reCAPTCHA
Privacy - Terms

Figure 23.2.

Google has a new version, v3[3] that minimizes user interaction using analytics to better determine if a user or an automated script is interacting with the website.

### Create a Signup Form

Let's start by creating a basic Bootstrap page and name it signup.php as in Listing 23.1.

### Listing 23.1.

```
1. <!DOCTYPE html>
2. <?php
3.    require_once('pagetitles.php');
4.    $page_title = MR_SIGNUP_PAGE;
5. ?>
6. <html>
7. <head>
8.    <title><?= $page_title ?></title>
9.    <link rel="stylesheet"
10.       href="https://stackpath.bootstrapcdn.com/bootstrap/4.5.0/css/bootstrap.min.css"
11.       integrity="sha384-9aIt2nRpC12Uk9gS9baDl411NQApFmC26EwAOH8WgZl5MYYxFfc+NcPb1dKGj7Sk"
12.       crossorigin="anonymous">
13. </head>
14. <body>
15. <script src="https://code.jquery.com/jquery-3.5.1.slim.min.js"
16.       integrity="sha384-DfXdz2htPH0lsSSs5nCTpuj/zy4C+OGpamoFVy38MVBnE+IbbVYUew+OrCXaRkfj"
17.       crossorigin="anonymous"></script>
```

[2] CAPTCHA: https://en.wikipedia.org/wiki/CAPTCHA
[3] version, v3: https://www.google.com/recaptcha/intro/v3.html

```
18. <script src="https://cdn.jsdelivr.net/npm/popper.js@1.16.0/dist/umd/popper.min.js"
19.         integrity="sha384-Q6E9RHvbIyZFJoft+2mJbHaEWldlvI9IOYy5n3zV9zzTtmI3UksdQRVvoxMfooAo"
20.         crossorigin="anonymous"></script>
21. <script src="https://stackpath.bootstrapcdn.com/bootstrap/4.5.0/js/bootstrap.min.js"
22.         integrity="sha384-OgVRvuATP1z7JjHLkuOU7Xw704+h835Lr+6QL9UvYjZE3Ipu6Tp75j7Bh/kR0JKI"
23.         crossorigin="anonymous"></script>
24. </body>
25. </html>
```

Notice, I added a definition for the page title that is included from a script called pagetitles.php:

```
<!DOCTYPE html>
<?php
  require_once('pagetitles.php');
  $page_title = MR_SIGNUP_PAGE;
?>
```

This code helps us later when we add a navigation bar to display links to specific pages based on access privileges and when we want application functionality available. I'll cover that in more detail later.

For now, create a new script called pagetitles.php and add the definition for the sign up page:

```
<?php
  // Page Titles
  define('MR_SIGNUP_PAGE', 'Movie Reservations - Sign Up');
```

Now back to our signup.php script. At the beginning of the <body> tag, we'll add some descriptive text and form for signing up new users as in Listing 23.2.

## Listing 23.2.

```
1.  <body>
2.  <div class="card">
3.      <div class="card-body">
4.          <h1>Sign up for a Movie Reservations Account</h1>
5.          <hr/>
6.          <form class="needs-validation" novalidate method="POST"
7.              action="<?= $_SERVER['PHP_SELF'] ?>">
8.              <div class="form-group row">
9.                  <label for="user_name"
10.                         class="col-sm-2 col-form-label-lg">User Name</label>
11.                  <div class="col-sm-4">
12.                      <input type="text" class="form-control"
13.                             id="user_name" name="user_name"
14.                             placeholder="Enter a user name" required>
15.                      <div class="invalid-feedback">
16.                          Please provide a valid user name.
```

```
18.                     </div>
19.                 </div>
20.             </div>
21.             <div class="form-group row">
22.                 <label for="password"
23.                        class="col-sm-2 col-form-label-lg">Password</label>
24.                 <div class="col-sm-4">
25.                     <input type="password" class="form-control"
26.                            id="password" name="password"
27.                            placeholder="Enter a password" required>
28.                     <div class="form-group form-check">
29.                         <input type="checkbox"
30.                                class="form-check-input"
31.                                id="show_password_check"
32.                                onclick="togglePassword()">
33.                         <label class="form-check-label"
34.                                for="show_password_check">Show Password</label>
35.                     </div>
36.                     <div class="invalid-feedback">
37.                         Please provide a valid password.
38.                     </div>
39.                 </div>
40.             </div>
41.             <button class="btn btn-primary" type="submit"
42.                     name="signup_submission">Sign Up
43.             </button>
44.         </form>
45.     </div>
46. </div>
47. // ...
48. </body>
```

Similar to previous forms we've created for this application, you'll notice I've added Bootstrap's validation for the password and user_name fields. Hence, we get Figure 23.3 when a user doesn't enter any data into these form fields.

To enable this behavior, as in previous forms we've created requiring validation, we need to include the JavaScript function in Listing 23.3 in a <script> element tag set in our HTML <body> (right before the other <script> tags).

| User Name | Enter a user name ⓘ |
|---|---|
| | Please provide a valid user name. |
| Password | Enter a password ⓘ |
| | ☐ Show Password |
| | Please provide a valid password. |

Figure 23.3.

## Listing 23.3.

```
1.  <body>
2.  <div class="card">
3.      <div class="card-body">
4.          <h1>Sign up for a Movie Reservations Account</h1>
5.          <hr/>
6.          <form ...>
7.              ...
8.          </form>
9.      </div>
10. </div>
11. <script>
12.     // JavaScript for disabling form submissions if there are invalid fields
13.     (function () {
14.         'use strict';
15.         window.addEventListener('load', function () {
16.             // Fetch all the forms we want to apply custom Bootstrap validation styles to
17.             var forms = document.getElementsByClassName('needs-validation');
18.             // Loop over them and prevent submission
19.             var validation = Array.prototype.filter.call(forms, function (form) {
20.                 form.addEventListener('submit', function (event) {
21.                     if (form.checkValidity() === false) {
22.                         event.preventDefault();
23.                         event.stopPropagation();
24.                     }
25.                     form.classList.add('was-validated');
26.                 }, false);
27.             });
28.         }, false);
29.     })();
30. </script>
31. <script src="https://code.jquery.com/jquery-3.5.1.slim.min.js"
32.         integrity="sha384-DfXdz2htPH0lsSSs5nCTpuj/zy4C+0GpamoFVy38MVBnE+IbbVYUew+OrCXaRkfj"
33.         crossorigin="anonymous"></script>
```

Also, notice I added a checkbox to show the password as you type it in as in Figure 23.4. Figure 23.5 shows it when checked.

Figure 23.4.                              Figure 23.5.

The checkbox field is set to call a JavaScript function called `togglePassword()` when the `onclick` event occurs:

```
<input type="checkbox" class="form-check-input"
       id="show_password_check" onclick="togglePassword()">
```

Add JavaScript function `togglePassword()` from Listing 23.4 below the form field validation function we just added before the closing `</script>` tag.

## Listing 23.4.

```
1.    <script>
2.        // Disable form submissions if there are invalid fields
3.        (function() {
4.            ...
5.        })();
6.        // Toggles between showing and hiding the entered password
7.        function togglePassword() {
8.            var password_entry = document.getElementById("password");
9.            if (password_entry.type === "password") {
10.               password_entry.type = "text";
11.           } else {
12.               password_entry.type = "password";
13.           }
14.       }
15.   </script>
```

When the user submits the form, we'll validate the credentials and either create an account or redirect them to correct their entries. Therefore, we need to add conditional logic to ensure the form only displays when we want it to.

Right before the form, add the Boolean variable (Listing 23.5) set to display the form, and move the form within an `if()` statement that checks this condition.

## Listing 23.5.

```
1.  <h1>Sign up for a Movie Reservations Account</h1>
2.  <hr/>
3.    <?php
4.      $show_sign_up_form = true;
5.
6.      if ($show_sign_up_form):
7.    ?>
8.  <form ...>
9.    ...
10. </form>
11.   <?php
12.     endif;
13.   ?>
```

## Create a New User

Let's add code to create a new user in the Movie database when successfully signing up a new user. Right after setting $show_sign_up_form to true, add a condition for when the user submits the form:

```php
<?php
  $show_sign_up_form = true;

  if (isset($_POST['signup_submission']))
  {
  }
```

Inside this condition, grab the user_name and password fields from the $_POST superglobal, and add a condition verifying the user entered values for the fields, otherwise output and error that they need to fill out the form correctly as in Listing 23.6

## Listing 23.6.

```php
1.  if (isset($_POST['signup_submission']))
2.  {
3.      // Get user name and password
4.      $user_name = $_POST['user_name'];
5.      $password = $_POST['password'];
6.
7.      if (!empty($user_name) && !empty($password))
8.      {
9.      }
10.     else
11.     {
12.         // Output error message
13.         echo "<h4><p class='text-danger'>You must enter both a "
14.             . "user name and password.</p></h4><hr/>";
15.     }
16. }
```

Inside the condition where the $user_name and $password are not empty, we must first query if the user already exists in the database. However, we need to practice safe database parameterization, and as I mentioned in the last chapter on securing our web applications, this is quite a bit more code to write. This is an excellent opportunity to abstract out the common calls we would need to make for parameterized queries by creating a helper function.

### Create a *parameterizedQuery()* Function

Let's take a slight detour and create a function we can use to parameterize all our inputs to our database queries. This function safeguards our SQL queries by using prepared statements. Create a new script called queryutils.php we can include in our scripts where we will need to query the database.

First, we need to identify all the PHP functions and their input parameters to parameterize our queries. They would be:

| Function | Parameters | Return | Reference |
|---|---|---|---|
| mysqli_prepare() | connection, string query | statement | https://php.net/mysqli.prepare |
| mysqli_stmt_bind_param() | statement, string data types, variables (specified by their types) | true or false | https://php.net/mysqli-stmt.bind-param |
| mysqli_stmt_execute() | statement | true or false | https://php.net/mysqli-stmt.execute |
| mysqli_stmt_get_result() | statement | true or false | https://php.net/mysqli-stmt.get-result |
| mysqli_errno() | connection | error code | https://php.net/mysqli.errno |

Another thing to consider when creating queries is that we can have a varying number of query parameters that need to be parameterized. A cool thing about PHP is that we can create functions that take a variable number of parameters by preceding the last variable in an argument list with .... See the online documentation for more information on variable length parameters[4].

Whenever you create a function, it is a good practice to have a function header that describes the function, any input parameters, and any return values. It serves as excellent documentation on how to use your function, primarily if you use DocBlocks[5] to describe the parameters and return values. Keep in mind that you must update this comment if you change the parameters to your function or how it works.

> *Another option afforded by PHP 7 is to use scalar and class type hints to indicate what kinds of arguments your function expects and what values it returns.*

---

[4]  *variable length parameters: https://php.net/functions.arguments.php#functions.variable-arg-list*
[5]  *DocBlocks: https://docs.phpdoc.org/3.0/guide/guides/docblocks.html*

In the script `queryutils.php`, here is a function header I wrote for this function along with the function signature:

Listing 23.7.

```php
1.  <?php
2.
3.  /**
4.   * Purpose:      Parameterizes a database query
5.   *
6.   * Description:  Parameterizes an SQL query given a database connection, a query string, a data
7.   *               types string, and a variable number of parameters to be used in the query. If
8.   *               the query is successful, the database results object will be returned (or TRUE
9.   *               if no results set and the query was successful), otherwise FALSE will be returned
10.  *               and the connection will have to be queried for the last error.
11.  *
12.  * @param        $dbc database connection
13.  * @param        $sql_query SQL statement
14.  * @param        $data_types string containing one character for each parameter's type
15.  * @param        $query_parameters a variable list of parameters representing each query parameter
16.  *
17.  * @return string Database results set, otherwise false if there is a database error, or true if successful.
18.  */
19. function parameterizedQuery($dbc, $sql_query, $data_types, ...$query_parameters)
20. {
21. }
```

`$data_types` is a string that must contain one character representing the data type for each query parameter. Consider a query with two parameters where both parameters are integers. The `$data_types` parameter must be the string: `'ii'`. You would pass two variables into the function for `...$query_parameters`. Here's our example using these two parameters:

```php
$query = "DELETE FROM reservation WHERE user_id = ? AND movieListing_id = ?";

$result = parameterizedQuery($dbc, $query, 'ii', $user_id, $movie_to_delete);
```

Another helpful thing about using DocBlock function headers is that most Integrated Development Environments (IDEs), like Visual Studio Code, PhpStorm, etc., display the info in a tooltip when you call the function as in Figure 23.6. So let's fill in the guts of this function with the code from Listing 23.8.

Figure 23.6.

## Listing 23.8.

```
1. function parameterizedQuery($dbc, $sql_query, $data_types, ...$query_parameters)
2. {
3.    $ret_val = false;  // Assume failure
4.
5.    if ($stmt = mysqli_prepare($dbc, $sql_query))
6.    {
7.        if (mysqli_stmt_bind_param($stmt, $data_types, ...$query_parameters)
8.            && mysqli_stmt_execute($stmt))
9.        {
10.           $ret_val = mysqli_stmt_get_result($stmt);
11.
12.           if (!mysqli_errno($dbc) && !$ret_val)
13.           {
14.              $ret_val = true;
15.           }
16.       }
17.    }
18.    return $ret_val;
19. }
```

This code is essentially a repeat of what I covered in the last chapter, just a little more efficient. Notice that the mysqli_stmt_bind_param() function conveniently takes the passed in $data_types and ...$query_parameters variable parameters. Our new function returns the results of our query or false if there is an error.

Now let's get back to using this new function to check if the user trying to sign up already exists before creating a new user. If you recall, in our signup.php script, we are in the condition where we know the user has entered in their user name and password.

```
// Get user name and password
$user_name = $_POST['user_name'];
$password = $_POST['password'];

if (!empty($user_name) && !empty($password))
{
}
```

Since we are querying the database, we must include our dbconnection.php. We also require our queryutils.php script to connect to our Movie database as in Listing 23.9.

## Listing 23.9.

```
1. if (!empty($user_name) && !empty($password))
2. {
3.     require_once('dbconnection.php');
4.     require_once('queryutils.php');
5.
6.     $dbc = mysqli_connect(DB_HOST, DB_USER, DB_PASSWORD, DB_NAME)
7.             or trigger_error(
8.                 'Error connecting to MySQL server for' . DB_NAME,
9.                 E_USER_ERROR
10.             );
11. }
```

Next (Listing 23.10), create a parameterized SQL string to see if this user already exists and call our parameterizedQuery() function.

## Listing 23.10.

```
1.  if (!empty($user_name) && !empty($password))
2.  {
3.      // ...
4.
5.      $dbc = mysqli_connect(DB_HOST, DB_USER, DB_PASSWORD, DB_NAME)
6.              or trigger_error(
7.                  'Error connecting to MySQL server for' . DB_NAME,
8.                  E_USER_ERROR
9.              );
10.
11.     // Check if user already exists
12.     $query = "SELECT * FROM user WHERE user_name = ?";
13.
14.     $results = parameterizedQuery($dbc, $query, 's', $user_name)
15.             or trigger_error(mysqli_error($dbc), E_USER_ERROR);
16. }
```

If this user does not exist, no rows are returned. We can use this condition to create a new user account. Otherwise, we let the user know an account with this user name exists in Listing 23.11.

Listing 23.11.

```
1. if (!empty($user_name) && !empty($password))
2. {
3.     // ...
4.     $results = parameterizedQuery($dbc, $query, 's', $user_name)
5.             or trigger_error(mysqli_error($dbc), E_USER_ERROR);
6.
7.     // IF user does not exist, create an account for them
8.     if (mysqli_num_rows($results) == 0)
9.     {
10.    }
11.    else // An account already exists for this user
12.    {
13.        echo "<h4><p class='text-danger'>An account already exists
14.        for this username:<span class='font-weight-bold'> ($user_name)</span>.
15.        Please use a different user name.</p></h4><hr/>";
16.    }
17. }
```

Within the if condition (where we know this user does not exist in the table), we hash the user's entered password and insert the new credentials into the user table using a parameterized query (Listing 23.12). Then we display a confirmation message that we created the user's account, show a link to the login.php script, and skip rendering the signup form.

Listing 23.12.

```
1. // IF user does not exist, create an account for them
2. if (mysqli_num_rows($results) == 0)
3. {
4.     $salted_hashed_password = password_hash($password, PASSWORD_DEFAULT);
5.
6.     $query = "INSERT INTO user (`user_name`, `password_hash`)
7.             VALUES (?, '$salted_hashed_password')";
8.     $results = parameterizedQuery($dbc, $query, 's', $user_name)
9.             or trigger_error(mysqli_error($dbc), E_USER_ERROR);
10.
11.    // Direct the user to the login page
12.    echo "<h4><p class='text-success'>Thank you for signing up <strong>$user_name</strong>! "
13.        . "Your new account has been successfully created.<br/>"
14.        . "You're now ready to <a href='login.php'>log in</a>.</p></h4>";
15.
16.    $show_sign_up_form = false;
17. }
```

## Complete Code Listings

Listing 23.13 is the complete listing for the `queryutils.php` page.

## Listing 23.13.

```php
1.  <?php
2.
3.  /**
4.   * Purpose:       Parameterizes a database query
5.   *
6.   * Description:   Parameterizes an SQL query given a database connection,
7.   *                a query string, a data types string, and a variable number
8.   *                of parameters to be used in the query. If the query is
9.   *                successful, the database results object will be returned
10.  *                (or TRUE if no results set and the query was successful),
11.  *                otherwise FALSE is returned  and the connection has to be
12.  *                queried for the last error.
13.  *
14.  * @param  $dbc          database connection
15.  * @param  $sql_query    SQL statement
16.  * @param  $data_types string containing one character for each parameter type
17.  * @param  $query_parameters variable list of parameters representing each query parameter
18.  * @return string   Database results set, false if there is an error, or true if successful.
19.  */
20. function parameterizedQuery($dbc, $sql_query, $data_types, ...$query_parameters)
21. {
22.     $ret_val = false;  // Assume failure
23.
24.     if ($stmt = mysqli_prepare($dbc, $sql_query))
25.     {
26.         if (mysqli_stmt_bind_param($stmt, $data_types, ...$query_parameters)
27.             && mysqli_stmt_execute($stmt))
28.         {
29.             $ret_val = mysqli_stmt_get_result($stmt);
30.
31.             if (!mysqli_errno($dbc) && !$ret_val)
32.             {
33.                 $ret_val = true;
34.             }
35.         }
36.     }
37.     return $ret_val;
38. }
```

Listing 23.14 shows the complete listing for the `signup.php` page.

## Listing 23.14.

```
1.  <!DOCTYPE html>
2.  <?php
3.  require_once('pagetitles.php');
4.  $page_title = MR_SIGNUP_PAGE;
5.  ?>
6.  <html>
7.  <head>
8.      <title><?= $page_title ?></title>
9.      <link rel="stylesheet"
10.           href="https://stackpath.bootstrapcdn.com/bootstrap/4.5.0/css/bootstrap.min.css"
11.           integrity="sha384-9aIt2nRpC12Uk9gS9baDl411NQApFmC26EwAOH8WgZl5MYYxFfc+NcPb1dKGj7Sk"
12.           crossorigin="anonymous">
13. </head>
14. <body>
15. <div class="card">
16.     <div class="card-body">
17.         <h1>Sign up for a Movie Reservations Account</h1>
18.         <hr/>
19.         <?php
20.         $show_sign_up_form = true;
21.
22.         if (isset($_POST['signup_submission'])) {
23.             // Get user name and password
24.             $user_name = $_POST['user_name'];
25.             $password = $_POST['password'];
26.
27.             if (!empty($user_name) && !empty($password)) {
28.                 require_once('dbconnection.php');
29.
30.                 require_once('queryutils.php');
31.
32.                 $dbc = mysqli_connect(DB_HOST, DB_USER, DB_PASSWORD, DB_NAME)
33.                     or trigger_error(
34.                         'Error connecting to MySQL server for DB_NAME.',
35.                         E_USER_ERROR
36.                     );
37.
38.                 // Check if user already exists
39.                 $query = "SELECT * FROM user WHERE user_name = ?";
40.
41.                 $results =
42.                     parameterizedQuery($dbc, $query, 's', $user_name)
43.                 or trigger_error(mysqli_error($dbc), E_USER_ERROR);
44.
45.                 // IF user does not exist, create an account for them
46.                 if (mysqli_num_rows($results) == 0) {
47.                     $salted_hashed_password =
48.                         password_hash($password, PASSWORD_DEFAULT);
49.
```

```
50.            $query = "INSERT INTO user (`user_name`, `password_hash`)
51.                    VALUES (?, '$salted_hashed_password')";
52.            $results = parameterizedQuery($dbc, $query, 's', $user_name)
53.                    or trigger_error(mysqli_error($dbc), E_USER_ERROR);
54.
55.            // Direct the user to the login page
56.            echo "<h4><p class='text-success'>Thank you for signing up <strong>$user_name</strong>! "
57.                . "Your new account has been successfully created.<br/>"
58.                . "You're now ready to <a href='login.php'>log in</a>.</p></h4>";
59.
60.            $show_sign_up_form = false;
61.          } else // An account already exists for this user
62.          {
63.            echo "<h4><p class='text-danger'>An account already exists for this username:
64.                <span class='font-weight-bold'> ($user_name)</span>. Please use
65.                a different user name.</p></h4><hr/>";
66.
67.          }
68.        } else {
69.          // Output error message
70.          echo "<h4><p class='text-danger'>You must enter both a user name
71.              and password.</p></h4><hr/>";
72.        }
73.      }
74.      if ($show_sign_up_form):
75.        ?>
76.         <form class="needs-validation" novalidate method="POST"
77.             action="<?= $_SERVER['PHP_SELF'] ?>">
78.          <div class="form-group row">
79.            <label for="user_name"
80.                class="col-sm-2 col-form-label-lg">User Name</label>
81.            <div class="col-sm-4">
82.              <input type="text" class="form-control" id="user_name"
83.                  name="user_name" placeholder="Enter a user name" required>
84.              <div class="invalid-feedback">Please provide a valid user name.</div>
85.            </div>
86.          </div>
87.          <div class="form-group row">
88.            <label for="password"
89.                class="col-sm-2 col-form-label-lg">Password</label>
90.            <div class="col-sm-4">
91.              <input type="password" class="form-control"
92.                  id="password" name="password" placeholder="Enter a password" required>
93.              <div class="form-group form-check">
94.                <input type="checkbox" class="form-check-input" id="show_password_check"
95.                    onclick="togglePassword()">
96.                <label class="form-check-label"
97.                    for="show_password_check">Show Password</label>
98.              </div>
99.              <div class="invalid-feedback">Please provide a valid password.</div>
```

```
100.                        </div>
101.                    </div>
102.                    <button class="btn btn-primary" type="submit" name="signup_submission">Sign Up
103.                    </button>
104.                </form>
105.            <?php
106.            endif;
107.            ?>
108.        </div>
109.    </div>
110.    <script>
111.        // JavaScript for disabling form submissions if there are invalid fields
112.        (function () {
113.            'use strict';
114.            window.addEventListener('load', function () {
115.                // Fetch all the forms we want to apply custom Bootstrap validation styles to
116.                var forms = document.getElementsByClassName('needs-validation');
117.                // Loop over them and prevent submission
118.                var validation = Array.prototype.filter.call(forms, function (form) {
119.                    form.addEventListener('submit', function (event) {
120.                        if (form.checkValidity() == false) {
121.                            event.preventDefault();
122.                            event.stopPropagation();
132.                        }
124.                        form.classList.add('was-validated');
125.                    }, false);
126.                });
127.            }, false);
128.        })();
129.
130.        function togglePassword() {
131.            var password_entry = document.getElementById("password");
132.            if (password_entry.type == "password") {
133.                password_entry.type = "text";
134.            } else {
135.                password_entry.type = "password";
136.            }
137.        }
138.    </script>
139.    <script src="https://code.jquery.com/jquery-3.5.1.slim.min.js"
140.            integrity="sha384-DfXdz2htPH0lsSSs5nCTpuj/zy4C+OGpamoFVy38MVBnE+IbbVYUew+OrCXaRkfj"
141.            crossorigin="anonymous"></script>
142.    <script src="https://cdn.jsdelivr.net/npm/popper.js@1.16.0/dist/umd/popper.min.js"
143.            integrity="sha384-Q6E9RHvbIyZFJoft+2mJbHaEWldlvI9IOYy5n3zV9zzTmI3UksdQRVvoxMfooAo"
144.            crossorigin="anonymous"></script>
145.    <script src="https://stackpath.bootstrapcdn.com/bootstrap/4.5.0/js/bootstrap.min.js"
146.            integrity="sha384-OgVRvuATP1z7JjHLkuOU7Xw704+h835Lr+6QL9UvYjZE3Ipu6Tp75j7Bh/kR0JKI"
147.            crossorigin="anonymous"></script>
148. </body>
149. </html>
```

# Create a login.php Script

Now that we have a Sign Up page, we need to create a login.php script to allow users to log in to our application. Here is what we want our login page to look like Figure 23.7

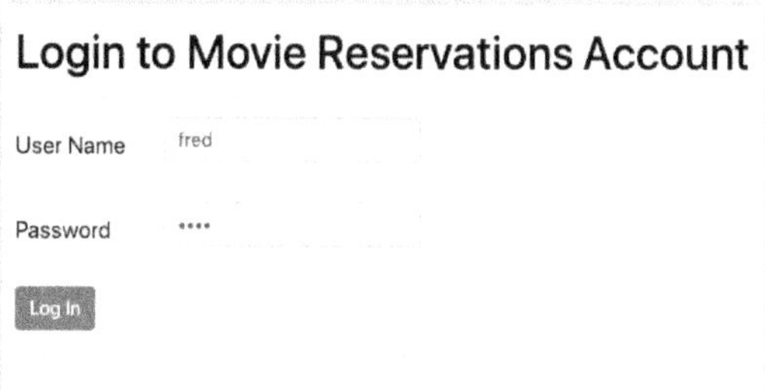

## Login to Movie Reservations Account

User Name    fred

Password    ****

Log In

Figure 23.7.

*When creating a professional application with user signup and login capabilities, it is a good idea to include a "Forgot my Password" link in your application. Otherwise, your admins won't like you very much. I leave that as an exercise for you.*

## Create a Login Form

Again, let's start by creating a basic Bootstrap page and name it login.php (Listing 23.15)

## Listing 23.15.

```php
1.  <?php
2.  session_start();
3.  require_once('pagetitles.php');
4.  $page_title = MR_LOGIN_PAGE;
5.  ?>
6.  <!DOCTYPE html>
7.  <html>
8.  <head>
9.      <title><?= $page_title ?></title>
10.     <link rel="stylesheet"
11.         href="https://stackpath.bootstrapcdn.com/bootstrap/4.5.0/css/bootstrap.min.css"
12.         integrity="sha384-9aIt2nRpC12Uk9gS9baDl411NQApFmC26EwAOH8WgZl5MYYxFfc+NcPb1dKGj7Sk"
13.         crossorigin="anonymous">
14. </head>
15. <body>
16. <script src="https://code.jquery.com/jquery-3.5.1.slim.min.js"
17.         integrity="sha384-DfXdz2htPH0lsSSs5nCTpuj/zy4C+OGpamoFVy38MVBnE+IbbVYUew+OrCXaRkfj"
18.         crossorigin="anonymous"></script>
19. <script src="https://cdn.jsdelivr.net/npm/popper.js@1.16.0/dist/umd/popper.min.js"
20.         integrity="sha384-Q6E9RHvbIyZFJoft+2mJbHaEWldlvI9IOYy5n3zV9zzTtmI3UksdQRVvoxMfooAo"
21.         crossorigin="anonymous"></script>
22. <script src="https://stackpath.bootstrapcdn.com/bootstrap/4.5.0/js/bootstrap.min.js"
23.         integrity="sha384-OgVRvuATP1z7JjHLkuOU7Xw704+h835Lr+6QL9UvYjZE3Ipu6Tp75j7Bh/kR0JKI"
24.         crossorigin="anonymous"></script>
25. </body>
26. </html>
```

Notice, I call the `session_start()`[6] function since we will be creating session variables for a user after a successful login. Also notice I added a definition for the page title that is included from the script called `pagetitles.php`:

```php
<!DOCTYPE html>
<?php
  session_start();
  require_once('pagetitles.php');
  $page_title = MR_LOGIN_PAGE;
?>
```

Add the definition for the Login page to `pagetitles.php`:

```php
<?php
    // Page Titles
    define('MR_SIGNUP_PAGE', 'Movie Reservations - Sign Up');
    define('MR_LOGIN_PAGE', 'Movie Reservations - Login');
```

Now back to our `login.php` script. At the beginning of the `<body>` tag, we'll add some descriptive text and our form for logging in users as in Listing 23.16.

## Listing 23.16.

```html
 1. <body>
 2. <div class="card">
 3.     <div class="card-body">
 4.         <h1>Login to Movie Reservations Account</h1>
 5.         <hr/>
 6.         <form class="needs-validation" novalidate method="POST"
 7.             action="<?= $_SERVER['PHP_SELF'] ?>">
 8.             <div class="form-group row">
 9.                 <label for="user_name" class="col-sm-2 col-form-label-lg">User
10.                     Name</label>
11.                 <div class="col-sm-4">
12.                     <input type="text" class="form-control" id="user_name"
13.                         name="user_name" placeholder="Enter a user name" required>
14.                     <div class="invalid-feedback">
15.                         Please provide a valid user name.
16.                     </div>
17.                 </div>
18.             </div>
19.             <div class="form-group row">
20.                 <label for="password" class="col-sm-2 col-form-label-lg">Password</label>
21.                 <div class="col-sm-4">
22.                     <input type="password" class="form-control" id="password"
23.                         name="password" placeholder="Enter a password" required>
24.                     <div class="invalid-feedback">
25.                         Please provide a valid password.
```

[6]  session_start(): https://php.net/session_start

```
26.                    </div>
27.                  </div>
28.                </div>
29.                <button class="btn btn-primary" type="submit"
30.                        name="login_submission">Log In
31.                </button>
32.            </form>
33.        </div>
34.    </div>
35.  </body>
```

Like the Signup form, we will add Bootstrap's validation for the password and user_name fields, so we see Figure 23.8 when a user doesn't enter any data into these form fields.

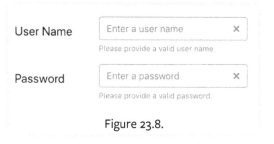

Figure 23.8.

Just like the Signup form we need to include the JavaScript function (Listing 23.17) in a <script> element tag set in our HTML <body> (right before the other <script> tags):

## Listing 23.17.

```
1.  <body>
2.  <div class="card">
3.      <div class="card-body">
4.          <h1>Login to Movie Reservations Account</h1>
5.          <hr/>
6.          <form ...>
7.              ...
8.          </form>
9.      </div>
10. </div>
11. <script>
12.     // JavaScript for disabling form submissions if there are invalid fields
13.     (function () {
14.         'use strict';
15.         window.addEventListener('load', function () {
16.             // Fetch all the forms we want to apply custom Bootstrap validation styles to
17.             var forms = document.getElementsByClassName('needs-validation');
18.             // Loop over them and prevent submission
19.             var validation = Array.prototype.filter.call(forms, function (form) {
20.                 form.addEventListener('submit', function (event) {
21.                     if (form.checkValidity() === false) {
22.                         event.preventDefault();
23.                         event.stopPropagation();
24.                     }
25.                     form.classList.add('was-validated');
26.                 }, false);
```

```
27.                 });
28.             }, false);
29.         })();
30. </script>
31. <script src="https://code.jquery.com/jquery-3.5.1.slim.min.js"
32.         integrity="sha384-DfXdz2htPH0lsSSs5nCTpuj/zy4C+OGpamoFVy38MVBnE+IbbVYUew+OrCXaRkfj"
33.         crossorigin="anonymous"></script>
```

When the user submits the form, we validate the credentials and either log them in or redirect them to correct their entries. To be successfully logged in, the user has to exist in the user table of the Movie database, and their password has to be correct. Once we've validated the user's credentials in the database, we note they are authenticated by setting a session variable for the user's user_id and user_name. After setting the session variables, we will redirect the user to the index.php page. If the user navigates to the login.php script, we display that they have logged in rather than showing the form.

Therefore, add the following conditional logic so that the form only displays when the user_id session variable is empty. Then, move the form within the if condition. Also, add an elseif condition that displays the user is logged in if the user_name session variable is set as in Listing 23.18.

## Listing 23.18.

```
1. <h1>Login to Movie Reservations Account</h1>
2. <hr/>
3.   <?php
4.     if (empty($_SESSION['user_id'])):
5.   ?>
6. <form>
7.   <!- ... -->
8. </form>
9.   <?php
10.    elseif (isset($_SESSION['user_name'])):
11.        echo "<h4><p class='text-success'>You are logged in as:
12.            <strong>{$_SESSION['user_name']}</strong>.</p></h4>";
13.    endif;
14.  ?>
```

## Log the User In

Let's add code to log the user in upon successful validation of their credentials.

Right before the `if (empty($_SESSION['user_id'])):`, add a condition that checks for the `user_id` session variable being empty and the user submitted the form (Listing 23.19).

### Listing 23.19.

```
1. <h1>Login to Movie Reservations Account</h1>
2. <hr/>
3.   <?php
4.     if (empty($_SESSION['user_id']) && isset($_POST['login_submission']))
5.     {
6.     }
7.
8.     if (empty($_SESSION['user_id'])):
9.   ?>
10. <form ...>
```

Inside this condition (Listing 23.20), grab the `user_name` and `password` fields from the `$_POST` superglobal, and add a condition verifying the user entered values for the fields, otherwise output an error that they need to fill out the form correctly:

### Listing 23.20.

```
1. if (empty($_SESSION['user_id']) && isset($_POST['login_submission']))
2. {
3.     // Get user name and password
4.     $user_name = $_POST['user_name'];
5.     $password = $_POST['password'];
6.
7.     if (!empty($user_name) && !empty($password))
8.     {
9.     }
10.    else
11.    {
12.       // Output error message
13.       echo "<h4><p class='text-danger'>You must enter both a user name
14.             and password.</p></h4><hr/>";
15.    }
16. }
```

Inside the if() condition that verifies the user_name and password were set, we can query the Movie database for our user. We need to include our dbconnection.php and now our queryutils.php scripts and connect to our Movie database as in Listing 23.21.

### Listing 23.21.

```
 1. if (!empty($user_name) && !empty($password))
 2. {
 3.    require_once('dbconnection.php');
 4.    require_once('queryutils.php');
 5.
 6.    $dbc = mysqli_connect(DB_HOST, DB_USER, DB_PASSWORD, DB_NAME)
 7.          or trigger_error(
 8.              'Error connecting to MySQL server for' . DB_NAME,
 9.              E_USER_ERROR
10.    );
11. }
```

Next, create a SQL string for this user's id, user_name, password_hash, and access_privileges to see if this user exists and call the parameterizedQuery() function as shown in Listing 23.22.

### Listing 23.22.

```
 1. if (!empty($user_name) && !empty($password))
 2. {
 3.    //...
 4.
 5.    $dbc = mysqli_connect(DB_HOST, DB_USER, DB_PASSWORD, DB_NAME)
 6.          or trigger_error(
 7.              'Error connecting to MySQL server for' . DB_NAME, E_USER_ERROR
 9.          );
10.
11.    // Check if user already exists
12.    $query = "SELECT id, user_name, password_hash, access_privileges
13.          FROM user WHERE user_name = ?";
14.
15.    $results = parameterizedQuery($dbc, $query, 's', $user_name)
16.              or trigger_error(mysqli_error($dbc), E_USER_ERROR);
17. }
```

If the user exists, we get a single row from the query, and we can validate the password hashes matches. Otherwise, we need to output a message that this user does not exist. Add the code in Listing 23.23. We should either get one or no rows back from the query. If we get more than one row back, this means we have more than one user with the same user name—which is horribly wrong!

## Listing 23.23.

```
1. if (!empty($user_name) && !empty($password))
2. {
3.     // ...
4.
5.     $results = parameterizedQuery($dbc, $query, 's', $user_name)
6.                 or trigger_error(mysqli_error($dbc), E_USER_ERROR);
7.
8.     // IF user was found, validate password
9.     if (mysqli_num_rows($results) == 1)
10.     {
11.     }
12.     else if(mysqli_num_rows($results) == 0) // User does not exist
13.     {
14.         echo "<h4><p class='text-danger'>An account does not exist for this username:"
15.             . "<span class='font-weight-bold'> ($user_name)</span>. "
16.             . "Please use a different user name.</p></h4><hr/>";
17.     }
18.     else
19.     {
20.         echo "<h4><p class='text-danger'>Something went terribly wrong!</p></h4><hr/>";
21.     }
22. }
```

*To reduce the information you might leak to a potential attacker, a better practice is indicating that the login credentials are not valid without saying explicitly that the user name or passwords are invalid. Otherwise, someone could build a list of valid and invalid usernames and then target the valid ones to try to crack the password. This is another good exercise to follow up on.*

Within the if condition where we found the user's credentials, we need to verify the supplied password matches the stored password hash. If verified, we can set user_id, user_name, and user_access_privileges session variables for the user. Then, we redirect them to the home page. If the password hash verification fails, we need to output a message that an incorrect password was entered and have the user try again. Add the code from Listing 23.24.

### Listing 23.24.

```php
1.  // IF user was found, validate password
2.  if (mysqli_num_rows($results) == 1)
3.  {
4.      $row = mysqli_fetch_array($results);
5.
6.      if (password_verify($password, $row['password_hash']))
7.      {
8.          $_SESSION['user_id'] = $row['id'];
9.          $_SESSION['user_name'] = $row['user_name'];
10.         $_SESSION['user_access_privileges'] = $row['access_privileges'];
11.
12.         // Redirect to the home page
13.         $home_url = dirname($_SERVER['PHP_SELF']);
14.         header('Location: ' . $home_url);
15.         exit;
16.     }
17.     else
18.     {
19.         echo "<h4><p class='text-danger'>An incorrect user name or password was entered.</p></h4><hr/>";
20.     }
21. }
22. else if (mysqli_num_rows($results) == 0) // User does not exist
23. {
24.     ...
25. }
```

## Complete Code Listing

Listing 23.25 has the complete listing for the login.php page.

### Listing 23.25.

```php
1.  <?php
2.  session_start();
3.  require_once('pagetitles.php');
4.  $page_title = MR_LOGIN_PAGE;
5.  ?>
6.  <!DOCTYPE html>
7.  <html>
8.  <head>
9.      <title><?= $page_title ?></title>
10.     <link rel="stylesheet"
11.         href="https://stackpath.bootstrapcdn.com/bootstrap/4.2.1/css/bootstrap.min.css"
12.         integrity="sha384-GJzZqFGwb1QTTN6wy59ffF1BuGJpLSa9DkKMp0DgiMDm4iYMj70gZwIKYbI706tWS"
13.         crossorigin="anonymous">
14. </head>
15. <body>
```

```
16. <div class="card">
17.     <div class="card-body">
18.         <h1>Login to Movie Reservations Account</h1>
19.         <hr/>
20.         <?php
21.         if (empty($_SESSION['user_id']) && isset($_POST['login_submission'])) {
22.             // Get user name and password
23.             $user_name = $_POST['user_name'];
24.             $password = $_POST['password'];
25.
26.             if (!empty($user_name) && !empty($password)) {
27.                 require_once('dbconnection.php');
28.
29.                 require_once('queryutils.php');
30.
31.                 $dbc = mysqli_connect(DB_HOST, DB_USER, DB_PASSWORD, DB_NAME)
32.                 or trigger_error(
33.                     'Error connecting to MySQL server for' . DB_NAME,
34.                     E_USER_ERROR
35.                 );
36.
37.                 // Check if user already exists
38.                 $query = "SELECT id, user_name, password_hash, access_privileges
39.                         FROM user WHERE user_name = ?";
40.
41.                 $results = parameterizedQuery($dbc, $query, 's', $user_name)
42.                 or trigger_error(mysqli_error($dbc), E_USER_ERROR);
43.
44.                 // IF user was found, validate password
45.                 if (mysqli_num_rows($results) == 1) {
46.                     $row = mysqli_fetch_array($results);
47.
48.                     if (password_verify($password, $row['password_hash'])) {
49.                         $_SESSION['user_id'] = $row['id'];
50.                         $_SESSION['user_name'] = $row['user_name'];
51.                         $_SESSION['user_access_privileges'] = $row['access_privileges'];
52.
53.                         // Redirect to the home page
54.                         $home_url = dirname($_SERVER['PHP_SELF']);
55.                         header('Location: ' . $home_url);
56.                     } else {
57.                         echo "<h4><p class='text-danger'>An incorrect user name
58.                                 or password was entered.</p></h4><hr/>";
59.                     }
60.                 } else if (mysqli_num_rows($results) == 0) // User does not exist
61.                 {
62.                     echo "<h4><p class='text-danger'>An account does not exist for this username:"
63.                         . "<span class='font-weight-bold'> ($user_name)</span>. "
64.                         . "Please use a different user name.</p></h4><hr/>";
65.                 } else {
```

```
66.                    echo "<h4><p class='text-danger'>Something went terribly
67.                        wrong!</p></h4><hr/>";
68.                }
69.            } else {
70.                // Output error message
71.                echo "<h4><p class='text-danger'>You must enter both a user name
72.                    and password.</p></h4><hr/>";
73.            }
74.        }
75.        if (empty($_SESSION['user_id'])):
76.            ?>
77.        <form class="needs-validation" novalidate method="POST"
78.            action="<?= $_SERVER['PHP_SELF'] ?>">
79.            <div class="form-group row">
80.                <label for="user_name" class="col-sm-2 col-form-label-lg">User Name</label>
81.                <div class="col-sm-4">
82.                    <input type="text" class="form-control" id="user_name"
83.                        name="user_name" placeholder="Enter a user name" required>
84.                    <div class="invalid-feedback">
85.                        Please provide a valid user name.
86.                    </div>
87.                </div>
88.            </div>
89.            <div class="form-group row">
92.                <label for="password" class="col-sm-2 col-form-label-lg">Password</label>
93.                <div class="col-sm-4">
94.                    <input type="password" class="form-control"
95.                        id="password" name="password" placeholder="Enter a password" required>
96.                    <div class="invalid-feedback">Please provide a valid password.</div>
97.                </div>
98.            </div>
99.            <button class="btn btn-primary" type="submit" name="login_submission">Log In</button>
100.        </form>
101.        <?php
102.        elseif (isset($_SESSION['user_name'])):
103.            echo "<h4><p class='text-success'>You are logged in as:
104.                <strong>{$_SESSION['user_name']}</strong>.</p></h4>";
105.        endif;
106.        ?>
107.    </div>
108. </div>
109. <script>
110.    // JavaScript for disabling form submissions if there are invalid fields
111.    (function () {
112.        'use strict';
113.        window.addEventListener('load', function () {
114.            // Fetch all the forms we want to apply custom Bootstrap validation styles to
115.            var forms = document.getElementsByClassName('needs-validation');
116.            // Loop over them and prevent submission
117.            var validation = Array.prototype.filter.call(forms, function (form) {
```

```
118.                     form.addEventListener('submit', function (event) {
119.                         if (form.checkValidity() == false) {
120.                             event.preventDefault();
121.                             event.stopPropagation();
122.                         }
123.                         form.classList.add('was-validated');
124.                     }, false);
125.                 });
126.             }, false);
127.         })();
128. </script>
129. <script src="https://code.jquery.com/jquery-3.3.1.slim.min.js"
130.         integrity="sha384-q8i/X+965Dz00rT7abK41JStQIAqVgRVzpbzo5smXKp4YfRvH+8abtTE1Pi6jizo"
131.         crossorigin="anonymous"></script>
132. <script src="https://cdnjs.cloudflare.com/ajax/libs/popper.js/1.14.6/umd/popper.min.js"
133.         integrity="sha384-wHAiFfRlMFy6i5SRaxvfOCifBUQy1xHdJ/yoi7FRNXMRBu5WHdZYu1hA6ZOblgut"
134.         crossorigin="anonymous"></script>
135. <script src="https://stackpath.bootstrapcdn.com/bootstrap/4.2.1/js/bootstrap.min.js"
136.         integrity="sha384-B0UglyR+jN6CkvvICOB2joaf5I4l3gm9GU6Hc1og6Ls7i6U/mkkaduKaBhlAXv9k"
137.         crossorigin="anonymous"></script>
128. </body>
139. </html>
```

# Create a logout.php Script

To allow users to log out of our application, we need to create a logout.php script. It's a straightforward script. All it does is delete all the session variables and redirect the user to the homepage after logging out. Create a new PHP script called logout.php and enter code in Listing 23.26.

## Listing 23.26.

```php
1.  <?php
2.      session_start();
3.
4.      // If the user is logged in, delete session variables and redirect to the home page
5.      if (isset($_SESSION['user_id']))
6.      {
7.          $_SESSION = array();
8.          session_destroy();
9.      }
10.
11.     // Redirect to the home page
12.     $home_url = dirname($_SERVER['PHP_SELF']);
13.     header('Location: ' . $home_url);
14.     exit;
```

> *This application will have a shopping cart feature for users to add movies to a cart they can then reserve. It would be a good idea to add a check before logging out if a user still has movies in their cart to redirect them to their shopping cart or delete the movies out of their cart.*

## Allow Users with Administrative Access

We also need to modify the `authorizeaccess.php` script to allow users with administrative access and redirect users without it to an `unauthorizedaccess.php` page. If someone without administrative privileges tries to access the scripts that add, modify, or remove a movie, they should see a page that looks like Figure 23.9.

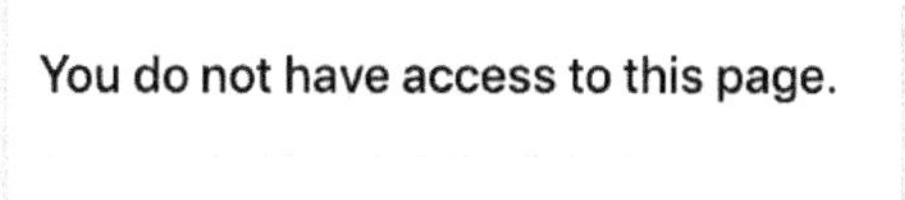

You do not have access to this page.

Figure 23.9.

> *In reality, you should route a user who is not logged in to the login page and show an unauthorized page for someone who is logged in but lacks privileges. Again, this is an exercise for you to do on your own.*

Recall that our `authorizeaccess.php` script (Listing 23.27) is currently using HTTP authentication.

Listing 23.27.

```php
1.  <?php
2.      // User name and password for basic HTTP authentication
3.      // NOTE:    For a professional implementation, usernames
4.      //          and passwords would never be hard-coded into
5.      //          the source code. Best practice is to either
6.      //          use an environment variable, or the database.
7.      //          This example is for educational demonstration
8.      //          only.
9.      $username = 'movieguru';
10.     $password = 'ilikemovies';
11.
12.     // IF Password OR Username are empty OR Password  OR Username don't match
13.     // send HTTP authentication headers
14.     if (!isset($_SERVER['PHP_AUTH_USER']) || !isset($_SERVER['PHP_AUTH_PW'])
15.         || $_SERVER['PHP_AUTH_USER'] !== $username
16.         || $_SERVER['PHP_AUTH_PW'] !== $password):
17.
18.         header('HTTP/1.1 401 Unauthorized');
19.         header('WWW-Authenticate: Basic realm="Movies I Like"');
20.         $invalid_response = "<h2>Movies I Like</h2><h4>You must enter a "
21.             . "valid username and password to access this page.</h4>";
22.         exit($invalid_response);
23.     endif;
```

Since we are now authenticating users through the login.php script, we only need to look at the session variables user_id and user_access_privileges to determine if a user is logged in, and if so, what access privileges they have.

We are going to rewrite the entire authorizeaccess.php script and start from scratch. Start by deleting everything in authorizeaccess.php and making a call to the session_start() function:

```php
<?php
    session_start();
```

Next, we want to take care of the case where a visitor is not authenticated. When not logged in, the session variables user_id or user_access_privileges are not set. Add the following code (Listing 23.28), which redirects the user to unauthorizedaccess.php if they are not logged in.

### Listing 23.28.

```php
1.  <?php
2.      session_start();
3.
4.      // Not logged in, redirect to unauthorizedaccess.php script
5.      if (!isset($_SESSION['user_id']) || !isset($_SESSION['user_access_privileges']))
6.      {
7.          header("Location: unauthorizedaccess.php");
8.          exit();
9.      }
```

If we make it past this conditional, then we know the user is logged in. Now, we need a condition to check if they have admin rights. Add the code in Listing 23.29 which redirects the user to unauthorizedaccess.php if they don't have admin privileges.

### Listing 23.29.

```php
1.  <?php
2.      // ...
3.
4.      // IF NOT admininstrative access redirect to unauthorizedaccess.php script
5.      if ($_SESSION['user_access_privileges'] != 'admin')
6.      {
7.          header("Location: unauthorizedaccess.php");
8.          exit();
9.      }
```

## Complete Code Listing

Listing 23.30 is the complete listing for the `authorizeaccess.php` page:

### Listing 23.30.

```php
1.  <?php
2.      session_start();
3.
4.      // Not logged in, redirect to unauthorizedaccess.php script
5.      if (!isset($_SESSION['user_id']) || !isset($_SESSION['user_access_privileges']))
6.      {
7.          header("Location: unauthorizedaccess.php");
8.          exit();
9.      }
10.
11.     // IF NOT admininstrative access redirect to unauthorizedaccess.php script
12.     if ($_SESSION['user_access_privileges'] != 'admin')
13.     {
14.         header("Location: unauthorizedaccess.php");
15.         exit();
16.     }
```

## Create an unauthorizedaccess.php Script

Now we need to create the `unauthorizedaccess.php` script we route unauthorized users to. Start by creating a basic Bootstrap page and name it `unauthorizedaccess.php`, see Listing 23.31.

### Listing 23.31.

```php
1.  <!DOCTYPE html>
2.  <?php
3.      require_once('pagetitles.php');
4.      $page_title = MR_UNAUTHORIZED_ACCESS_PAGE;
5.  ?>
6.  <html>
7.  <head>
8.      <title><?= $page_title ?></title>
9.      <link rel="stylesheet"
10.           href="https://stackpath.bootstrapcdn.com/bootstrap/4.5.0/css/bootstrap.min.css"
11.           integrity="sha384-9aIt2nRpC12Uk9gS9baDl411NQApFmC26EwAOH8WgZl5MYYxFfc+NcPb1dKGj7Sk"
12.           crossorigin="anonymous">
13. </head>
14. <body>
15. <script src="https://code.jquery.com/jquery-3.5.1.slim.min.js"
16.         integrity="sha384-DfXdz2htPH0lsSSs5nCTpuj/zy4C+OGpamoFVy38MVBnE+IbbVYUew+OrCXaRkfj"
17.         crossorigin="anonymous"></script>
```

```
18. <script src="https://cdn.jsdelivr.net/npm/popper.js@1.16.0/dist/umd/popper.min.js"
19.        integrity="sha384-Q6E9RHvbIyZFJoft+2mJbHaEWldlvI9IOYy5n3zV9zzTtmI3UksdQRVvoxMfooAo"
20.        crossorigin="anonymous"></script>
21. <script src="https://stackpath.bootstrapcdn.com/bootstrap/4.5.0/js/bootstrap.min.js"
22.        integrity="sha384-OgVRvuATP1z7JjHLkuOU7Xw704+h835Lr+6QL9UvYjZE3Ipu6Tp75j7Bh/kR0JKI"
23.        crossorigin="anonymous"></script>
24. </body>
25. </html>
```

Notice I added a definition for the page title that is included from the script called `pagetitles.php`:

```
<!DOCTYPE html>
<?php
   require_once('pagetitles.php');
   $page_title = MR_UNAUTHORIZED_ACCESS_PAGE;
?>
```

Add the definition for the Login page to `pagetitles.php`:

```
<?php
   // Page Titles
   define('MR_SIGNUP_PAGE', 'Movie Reservations - Sign Up');
   define('MR_LOGIN_PAGE', 'Movie Reservations - Login');
   define('MR_UNAUTHORIZED_ACCESS_PAGE', 'Movie Reservations - Unauthorized Access');
```

Now back to our `unauthorizedaccess.php` script. At the beginning of the `<body>` tag in Listing 23.32, we'll add some descriptive text telling visitors they are unauthorized to access this page:

## Listing 23.32.

```
1. <body>
2.   <div class="card">
3.     <div class="card-body">
4.       <h3>You do not have access to this page.</h3>
5.     </div>
6.   </div>
7. </body>
```

## Complete Code Listing

Finally, Listing 23.33 is the complete listing for the unauthorizedaccess.php page.

### Listing 23.33.

```
1.  <!DOCTYPE html>
2.  <?php
3.    require_once('pagetitles.php');
4.    $page_title = MR_UNAUTHORIZED_ACCESS_PAGE;
5.  ?>
6.  <html>
7.  <head>
8.      <title><?= $page_title ?></title>
9.      <link rel="stylesheet"
10.         href="https://stackpath.bootstrapcdn.com/bootstrap/4.2.1/css/bootstrap.min.css"
11.         integrity="sha384-GJzZqFGwb1QTTN6wy59ffF1BuGJpLSa9DkKMp0DgiMDm4iYMj70gZWKYbI706tWS"
12.         crossorigin="anonymous">
13.     <link rel="stylesheet"
14.         href="https://use.fontawesome.com/releases/v5.8.1/css/all.css"
15.         integrity="sha384-50oBUHEmvpQ+1lW4y57PTFmhCaXp0ML5d60M1M7uH2+nqUivzIebhndOJK28anvf"
16.         crossorigin="anonymous">
17. </head>
18. <body>
19. <div class="card">
20.     <div class="card-body">
21.         <h3>You do not have access to this page.</h3>
22.     </div>
23. </div>
24. <script src="https://code.jquery.com/jquery-3.3.1.slim.min.js"
25.         integrity="sha384-q8i/X+965Dz00rT7abK41JStQIAqVgRVzpbzo5smXKp4YfRvH+8abtTE1Pi6jizo"
26.         crossorigin="anonymous"></script>
27. <script src="https://cdnjs.cloudflare.com/ajax/libs/popper.js/1.14.6/umd/popper.min.js"
28.         integrity="sha384-wHAiFfRlMFy6i5SRaxvfOCifBUQy1xHdJ/yoi7FRNXMRBu5WHdZYu1hA6Z0blgut"
29.         crossorigin="anonymous"></script>
30. <script src="https://stackpath.bootstrapcdn.com/bootstrap/4.2.1/js/bootstrap.min.js"
31.         integrity="sha384-B0UglyR+jN6CkvvICOB2joaf5I4l3gm9GU6Hc1og6Ls7i6U/mkkaduKaBhlAXv9k"
32.         crossorigin="anonymous"></script>
33. </body>
34. </html>
```

# Exercises

1. In the Movie Database application, add Individual User Logins.

   1. Create a user with admin access privileges and confirm they can edit, add, or delete movies.

   2. Confirm regular logged-in users can not edit, add, or delete movies.

# Chapter

# 24

# Adding a Navigation Menu

*"Program testing can be a very effective way to show the presence of bugs, but is hopelessly inadequate for showing their absence."*

*–Edsger W. Dijkstra*

This chapter adds a navigation bar (otherwise known as a "navbar") to the top of our *Movie Reservations* application. A navbar makes it much more user-friendly to navigate around the application. With a few exceptions, we want our navbar to display on all the pages in our application. Additionally, we want our navbar to be context-sensitive. That is, it should indicate or hint what page we are on and display

Figure 24.1.

links we have access to based on our privileges. When we first navigate to the Home page, without being logged in, this is what we want our navbar to look like Figure 24.1.

## Create Navbar Logic

Since almost every page in our application will be displaying a navbar, we will create a script to be included by these pages. Create a script called navmenu.php and add this PHP code at the very top that checks the $page_title variable of the page that included this script:

```php
<?php
    $page_title = isset($page_title) ? $page_title : "";
?>
```

> *It is crucial that the opening PHP tag* <?php *is the first thing in your file (no spaces preceding) as this code runs before HTML headers are sent.*

Remember we set the variable $page_title to one of the definitions created in pagetitles.php in the scripts that include navmenu.php (e.g. index.php, login.php, etc.).

Since we are using session variables in our application and navmenu.php will be included by most every script, let's add the following code after the $page_title check that starts or resumes our session:

```php
<?php
    $page_title = isset($page_title) ? $page_title : "";

    if (session_status() == PHP_SESSION_NONE)
    {
        session_start();
    }
?>
```

Notice, we call `session_start()` only after checking to see that none already exists. You could certainly make the call with error suppression (e.g. `@session_start()`), however, I usually frown on that sort of behavior.

> *The navbar is part of the HTML <body>, so we assume the Bootstrap style sheet was already included in the <head> section of the including script.*

Add the code in Listing 24.1 after the closing PHP tag (?>), and I will explain it in the following paragraphs.

## Listing 24.1.

```php
1.  <?php
2.  $page_title = isset($page_title) ? $page_title : "";
3.
4.  // ...
5.  session_start();
6.  }
7.  ?>
8.  <nav class="navbar sticky-top navbar-expand-md navbar-dark"
9.        style="background-color: #569f32;">
10.     <a class="navbar-brand" href=<?= dirname($_SERVER['PHP_SELF']) ?>>
11.         <img src="resources/movie_rental_icon.png" width="30" height="30"
12.             class="d-inline-block align-top" alt="">
13.         <?= MR_HOME_PAGE ?>
14.     </a>
15.     <button class="navbar-toggler" type="button" data-toggle="collapse"
16.             data-target="#navbarNavAltMarkup" aria-controls="navbarNavAltMarkup"
17.             aria-expanded="false" aria-label="Toggle navigation">
18.         <span class="navbar-toggler-icon"></span>
19.     </button>
20.     <div class="collapse navbar-collapse" id="navbarNavAltMarkup">
21.         <div class="navbar-nav">
22.             <a class="nav-item nav-link<?= $page_title == MR_HOME_PAGE ? ' active' : '' ?>"
23.                 href=<?= dirname($_SERVER['PHP_SELF']) ?>>Home </a>
24.         </div>
25.     </div>
26. </nav>
```

## 24. Adding a Navigation Menu

The <nav> element has these Bootstrap class attributes set for the following purpose:

| Class Property | Purpose |
| --- | --- |
| .navbar | Specifies this is a navbar |
| .sticky-top | Sticks to the top as the page scrolls |
| .navbar-expand-md | For responsive collapsing |
| .navbar-dark | For white text on dark color backgrounds |

Also, notice I set the style attribute to a background-color. If you omit this, you will have white text on a black background for the menu.

Next is a standard <a href> link with the class attribute set to navbar-brand with the href set to the home folder location, along with an image icon referencing MR_HOME_PAGE, which must be defined in pagetitles.php. Create a folder under the Movie Listing folder called resources to store your image icons. I called this one movie_rental_icon.png.

> The movie projector icon is free to use with Creative Commons attribution, which I found here[1].

Before we forget, let's define MR_HOME_PAGE. Open pagetitles.php and add the following MR_HOME_PAGE definition right before the MR_SIGNUP_PAGE definition:

```php
<?php
    // Page Titles
    define('MR_HOME_PAGE', 'Movie Reservations');
    define('MR_SIGNUP_PAGE', 'Movie Reservations - Sign Up');
    define('MR_LOGIN_PAGE', 'Movie Reservations - Login');
    define('MR_UNAUTHORIZED_ACCESS_PAGE', 'Movie Reservations - Unauthorized Access');
```

Getting back to navmenu.php, we then have a <button> element with a class attribute set to navbar-toggler for the button to collapse for responsive design. This class collapses the navigation menu on mobile devices under a hamburger icon as in Figure 24.2

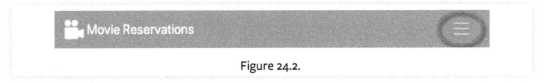

Figure 24.2.

---

[1]  here: https://iconfinder.com/icons/753134/festival_film_icon

Then we have a `<div>` tag with a `class` set to `collapse navbar-collapse` to group and hide/collapse menu items. In this `<div>`, we put `navbar-nav` item links to our home, login, and signup pages. In fact, we already have a navigation link to our Home page here. Let's take a closer look at it in Listing 24.2.

Listing 24.2.

```
1.  <nav ...>
2.    <!-- ... -->
3.    <div class="collapse navbar-collapse" id="navbarNavAltMarkup">
4.      <div class="navbar-nav">
5.        <a class="nav-item nav-link<?= $page_title == MR_HOME_PAGE ? ' active' : '' ?>"
6.            href=<?= dirname($_SERVER['PHP_SELF']) ?>>Home </a>
7.      </div>
8.    </div>
9.  </nav>
```

To create a navigation item, you need to create a child `<div>` tag container with the `class` attribute set to `navbar-nav`. Next, you create a child `<a href>` link with the class set to `nav-item nav-link`. However, you will notice I added some PHP code with a ternary operator before the `href` attribute. This link is for the home page. However, we want the navigation link for the current page we are on to be highlighted (e.g., active):

```
"nav-item nav-link<?= $page_title == MR_HOME_PAGE ? ' active' : '' ?>"
```

If the home page is being displayed (i.e. `index.php`) the `class` attribute will be set as:

```
class="nav-item nav-link active"
```

Otherwise, it is set as:

```
class="nav-item nav-link"
```

We use this mechanism for all pages that include `navmenu.php` and have a link to its page.

For more details, see the documentation on how Bootstrap's Navbar[2] works.

[2]  Bootstrap's Navbar: https://getbootstrap.com/docs/4.0/components/navbar/

## Add the Navigation Bar

Now that we have our `navmenu.php` script, let's make some modifications to `index.php` and include the `navmenu.php` script. Open the `index.php` script and add the following PHP code to the very top of the script, before the `<!DOCTYPE html>` element:

```php
<?php
  require_once('pagetitles.php');
  $page_title = MR_HOME_PAGE;
?>
<!DOCTYPE html>
<html>
```

This properly sets our `$page_title` variable for use in `navmenu.php` which we include from `pagetitles.php` and changes our page title from "Movies I Like" to "Movie Reservations". Next, in the `<head>` element, modify the `<title>` element with this code:

```php
<html>
  <head>
    <link >
    <title><?= $page_title ?></title>
  </head>
  <body>
```

This changes our `<title>` element from `Movies I Like` to `Movie Reservations`. Next, right below the `<body>` element, include the `navmenu.php` script:

```php
<body>
<?php
  require_once('navmenu.php');
?>
  <div class="card">
    <div class="card-body">
```

Next, inside the `<div class="card-body">` element, modify the `<h1>` element to reference the `$page_title` instead of `Movies I Like`:

```php
<div class="card">
  <div class="card-body">
    <h1><?= $page_title ?></h1>
```

> *Later, when we add more of the reservation system features, we will remove the link to add a movie (since it will be in the navigation menu). We also hide the trash can icon unless a user is logged in with admin privileges.*

## Add Navigation Bar to Details Page

When users select a movie, they are taken to the "Movie Details" page for that movie. The user either needs to press the back button in the browser or select the Movies I Like link to get back to the home page. It would be better to include the navbar and remove the extra link for a consistent user experience throughout the application. We want our "Movie Details" page to look like Figure 24.3.

Figure 24.3.

Notice that the "Home" menu item is not active because we are on the "Movie Details" page instead of the home page. Open pagetitles.php and add the following MR_DETAILS_PAGE definition right after the MR_HOME_PAGE definition:

```php
<?php
    // Page Titles
    define('MR_HOME_PAGE', 'Movie Reservations');
    define('MR_DETAILS_PAGE', 'Movie Reservations - Details');
    define('MR_SIGNUP_PAGE', 'Movie Reservations - Sign Up');
    define('MR_LOGIN_PAGE', 'Movie Reservations - Login');
    define('MR_UNAUTHORIZED_ACCESS_PAGE', 'Movie Reservations - Unauthorized Access');
```

Open the moviedetails.php script and add the following PHP code to the very top of the script, before the <!DOCTYPE html> element:

```php
<?php
    require_once('pagetitles.php');
    $page_title = MR_DETAILS_PAGE;
?>
<!DOCTYPE html>
<html>
```

This code properly sets our $page_title variable for use in navmenu.php, which we include from pagetitles.php.

Next, in the <head> element, modify the <title> element with this code:

```
<html>
  <head>
    <link ...>
    <title><?= $page_title ?></title>
      ...
  </head>
  <body>
```

Next, right below the <body> element, include the navmenu.php script:

```
<body>
<?php
  require_once('navmenu.php');
?>
  <div class="card">
    <div class="card-body">
```

Next, inside the <div class="card-body"> element, remove the <nav class="nav"> link to the index.php page and replace it with <h1>Movie Details</h1> and a horizontal line (<hr/>) as in Listing 24.3.

## Listing 24.3.

```
 1.    Unchanged Lines
 2.    <div class="card">
 3.      <div class="card-body">
 4.  - Removed Lines
 5.  -      <nav class="nav">
 6.  -        <a class="nav-link" href="index.php">Movies I Like</a>
 7.  -      </nav>
 8.  + Added Lines
 9.  +      <h1>Movie Details</h1>
10.  +      <hr/>
```

> *When we start to add more of the reservation system features, we will hide the link to edit a movie unless a user is logged in with admin privileges.*

# Add Login Link to Navigation Bar

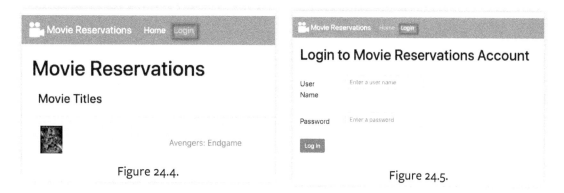

Figure 24.4.                                    Figure 24.5.

We need to add a nav link item to the login.php page and have login.php include navmenu.php. When we are on the home page and not logged in, we want our nav menu to look like Figure 24.4.

Notice that the Login link is not active, indicating we are not on the login.php page. When we navigate to the Login page, we want our nav menu to look like Figure 24.5

Notice now that the Login link is active, indicating we are on the login.php page.

Open up the login.php script and include the navmenu.php script right after the <body> element:

```
<body>
<?php
  require_once('navmenu.php');
?>
  <div class="card">
    <div class="card-body">
```

Now open the navmenu.php script. We will add a child <a href> link with the class set to nav-item nav-link for our *Login* page right below the link to the *Home* page. Add the code in Listing 24.4, and I will explain it below.

Listing 24.4.

```
1.  <nav ...>
2.    <!-- ... -->
3.    <div class="collapse navbar-collapse" id="navbarNavAltMarkup">
4.      <div class="navbar-nav">
5.        <a class="nav-item nav-link<?= $page_title == MR_HOME_PAGE ? ' active' : '' ?>"
6.          href="<?= dirname($_SERVER['PHP_SELF']) ?>">Home </a>
7.        <?php if (!isset($_SESSION['user_name'])): ?>
8.          <a class="nav-item nav-link<?= $page_title == MR_LOGIN_PAGE ? ' active' : '' ?>"
9.            href="login.php">Login</a>
10.       <?php endif; ?>
11.     </div>
12.   </div>
13. </nav>
```

Let's break this down on its own:

```
<?php if (!isset($_SESSION['user_name'])): ?>
  <a class="nav-item nav-link<?= $page_title == MR_LOGIN_PAGE ? ' active' : '' ?>" href="login.php">Login</a>
<?php endif; ?>
```

We have two conditions here. The outer condition checks to see if the user is not logged in. If you recall from login.php three session variables get set when a user gets logged in:

```
$_SESSION['user_id'] = $row['id'];
$_SESSION['user_name'] = $row['user_name'];
$_SESSION['user_access_privileges'] = $row['access_privileges'];
```

If the user is already logged in, there is no need to show a link to the "Login" page. Assuming the user is not logged in, we display a link to the "Login" page and then evaluate the ternary condition. It—similar to the link for the home page—evaluates whether the user is currently on the "Login" page or not.

# Add Logout Link to Navigation Bar

Let's add a nav link item for users to log out. Also, let's display the user name when a user is logged in to the navigation menu. When we are on the homepage and logged in, we want our nav menu to look like Figure 24.6.

Figure 24.6.

Open up the navmenu.php script. Add a child `<a href>` link with the class set to nav-item nav-link for our "Logout" page right below the link to the "Login" page. Add the code in Listing 24.5 on lines 9–10, and I will explain it below.

Listing 24.5.

```
1.  <nav ...>
2.    ...
3.    <div class="collapse navbar-collapse" id="navbarNavAltMarkup">
4.      <div class="navbar-nav">
5.        <a class="nav-item nav-link...">Home </a>
6.        <?php if (!isset($_SESSION['user_name'])): ?>
7.          <a class="nav-item nav-link...">Login</a>
8.        <?php else: ?>
9.          <a class='nav-item nav-link'
10.             href='logout.php'>Logout (<?= $_SESSION['user_name'] ?>)</a>
11.       <?php endif; ?>
12.     </div>
13.   </div>
14. </nav>
```

Again, let's look at this on its own:

```
<?php else: ?>
  <a class='nav-item nav-link'
     href='logout.php'>Logout (<?=$_SESSION['user_name'] ?>)</a>
<?php endif; ?>
```

We'll add an else clause after the if check (line 8 previous listing) to handle logged-in users. We display a link to the logout.php script and display the user's name (held in $_SESSION['user_name']).

## Add Sign Up Link to Navigation Bar

Figure 24.7.                                   Figure 24.8.

Next, we need to add a nav link item to the signup.php page and have signup.php include navmenu.php. When we are on the homepage and not logged in, we want our nav menu to look like Figure 24.7.

Notice that the "Sign Up" link is not active (indicating we are not on the signup.php page). When we navigate to the "Sign Up" page, we want our nav menu to look like Figure 24.8.

Now, notice that the "Sign Up" link is active (indicating we are on the signup.php page). Open up the signup.php script and include the navmenu.php script right after the <body> element:

```
<body>
<?php
  require_once('navmenu.php');
?>
  <div class="card">
    <div class="card-body">
```

Now open the navmenu.php script. We will add a child <a href> link with the class set to nav-item nav-link for our *Sign Up* page right below the link to the *Login* page. Add line 9–10. Since we already have a condition for users not logged in, we can add the signup link in Listing 24.6.

### Listing 24.6.

```
 1. <nav ...>
 2.   <!-- ... -->
 3.   <div class="collapse navbar-collapse" id="navbarNavAltMarkup">
 4.     <div class="navbar-nav">
 5.       <a class="nav-item nav-link...">Home </a>
 6.       <?php if (!isset($_SESSION['user_name'])): ?>
 7.         <a class="nav-item nav-link<?= $page_title == MR_LOGIN_PAGE ? ' active' : '' ?>"
 8.            href="login.php">Login</a>
 9.         <a class="nav-item nav-link<?= $page_title == MR_SIGNUP_PAGE ? ' active' : '' ?>"
10.            href="signup.php">Sign Up</a>
11.       <?php else: ?>
12.         <a class="nav-item nav-link"
13.            href="logout.php">Logout (<?=$_SESSION['user_name'] ?>)</a>
14.       <?php endif; ?>
15.     </div>
16.   </div>
17. </nav>
```

# Add Navigation Bar to addmovie.php

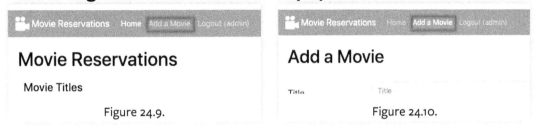

Figure 24.9.

Figure 24.10.

Now we need to add a nav link item to the addmovie.php page and have addmovie.php include navmenu.php. We only want to display a link to the "Add a Movie" page when logged in as a user with admin privileges. We want our nav menu to look like Figure 24.9 when we are on the home page and have admin privileges. And when we are on the "Add a Movie" page, we want our menu to look like Figure 24.10.

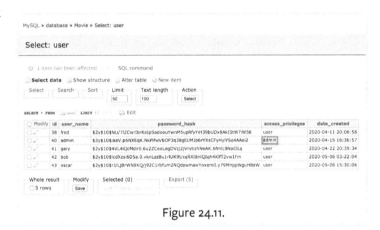

Figure 24.11.

You will need to create a user with access_privileges set to admin to test this. The easiest way to do this is to create a user and change the access_privileges field of the user table in the Movie database from user to admin (see Figure 24.11).

Open pagetitles.php and add the following MR_ADD_MOVIE_PAGE definition right after the MR_UNAUTHORIZED_ACCESS_PAGE definition.

```php
<?php
  // Page Titles
  // ...
  define('MR_UNAUTHORIZED_ACCESS_PAGE', 'Movie Reservations - Unauthorized Access');
  define('MR_ADD_MOVIE_PAGE', 'Movie Reservations - Add Movie');
```

Open the addmovie.php script and include the pagetitles.php script and set $page_title to MR_ADD_MOVIE_PAGE, right after the include for the authorizeaccess.php script:

```
<?php
  require_once('authorizeaccess.php');
  require_once('pagetitles.php');
  $page_title = MR_ADD_MOVIE_PAGE;
?>
<!DOCTYPE html>
<html>
```

This code properly sets our $page_title variable for use in navmenu.php which we include from pagetitles.php. Next, in the <head> element, modify the <title> element to remove "Add a Movie" and replace it with the $page_title (Listing 24.7).

## Listing 24.7.

```
1.    Unchanged Lines
2.       <html>
3.         <head>
4.           <link ...>
5. - Removed Line
6. -      <title>Add a Movie</title>
7. + Added Line
8. +      <title><?= $page_title ?></title>
9. Unchanged Lines
10.        </head>
11.        <body>
```

Next, right below the <body> element, include the navmenu.php script:

```
<body>
<?php
  require_once('navmenu.php');
?>
  <div class="card">
    <div class="card-body">
```

Since we're including the navbar, let's remove the link right below <h1>Add a Movie</h1> that takes us back to the home page. See Listing 24.8,

## Listing 24.8.

```
1.    Unchanged Lines
2.       <div class="card">
3.         <div class="card-body">
4.           <h1>Add a Movie</h1>
5. - Removed Lines
6. -         <nav class="nav">
7. -           <a class="nav-link" href="index.php">Movies I Like</a>
8. -         </nav>
9. Unchanged Lines
10.          <hr/>
```

Open up the `navmenu.php` script. Add a child `<a href>` link with the class set to `nav-item nav-link` for our "Add a Movie" page right below the link to the home page. Add the code in Listing 24.9.

## Listing 24.9.

```
 1.  <nav ...>
 2.     <!-- ... -->
 3.     <div class="collapse navbar-collapse" id="navbarNavAltMarkup">
 4.         <div class="navbar-nav">
 5.             <a class="nav-item nav-link...">Home </a>
 6.        <?php if (isset($_SESSION['user_access_privileges'])
 7.             && $_SESSION['user_access_privileges'] == 'admin'): ?>
 8.         <a class=" nav-item
 9.             nav-link<?= $page_title == MR_ADD_MOVIE_PAGE ? ' active' : '' ?>"
10.         href="addmovie.php">Add a Movie</a>
11.        <?php endif; ?>
12.        <?php if (!isset($_SESSION['user_name'])): ?>
13.             <a ...>Login</a>
14.             <a ...>Sign Up</a>
15.        <?php else: ?>
16.             <a class='nav-item nav-link' href='logout.php'>Logout
17.                 (<?= $_SESSION['user_name'] ?>)</a>
18.        <?php endif; ?>
19.             <!-- ... -->
20.         </div>
21.     </div>
22.  </nav>
```

Again, let's look at this on its own:

```
<?php if (isset($_SESSION['user_access_privileges'])
        && $_SESSION['user_access_privileges'] == 'admin'): ?>
  <a class="nav-item nav-link<?= $page_title == MR_ADD_MOVIE_PAGE ? ' active' : '' ?>"
     href="addmovie.php">Add a Movie</a>
<?php endif; ?>
```

As in a previous example, we have two conditions here. The first (outer condition) checks to see if the user has admin privileges.

> *Incidently, this condition also checks to see if the user is logged in, as* `$_SESSION['user_access_privileges']` *is only set when the user logs in.*

If the user is not logged in OR the user is logged in but doesn't have admin privileges, the link to the "Add a Movie" page will not be displayed. Assuming the user is logged in AND has admin privileges, we show a link to the "Add a Movie" page and then evaluate the ternary condition, which evaluates whether or not the "Add a Movie" page is active.

## Add Navigation Bar to Unauthorizedaccess.php

Since it is plausible for someone to navigate to a page they do not have access to, let's add the navbar to the unauthorizedaccess.php script. Our page will look like Figure 24.12.

Open up the unauthorizedaccess.php script and include the navmenu.php script right after the <body> element:

```
<body>
<?php
  require_once('navmenu.php');
?>
  <div class="card">
    <div class="card-body">
```

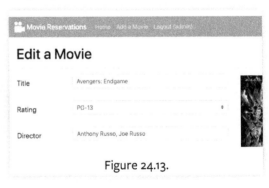

Figure 24.12.

## Add Navigation Bar to editmovie.php

Let's add the navbar to the editmovie.php script. We want our menu to look like Figure 24.13.

> You will need to log in as a user with
> access_privileges *set to* admin *to test this.*

Open pagetitles.php and add the following MR_EDIT_MOVIE_PAGE definition right after the MR_ADD_MOVIE_PAGE definition:

Figure 24.13.

```
<?php
  // Page Titles
  // ...
  define('MR_ADD_MOVIE_PAGE', 'Movie Reservations - Add Movie');
  define('MR_EDIT_MOVIE_PAGE', 'Movie Reservations - Edit Movie');
```

Open the `editmovie.php` script and include the `pagetitles.php` script and set `$page_title` to `MR_EDIT_MOVIE_PAGE`, right after the include for the `authorizizeaccess.php` script:

```php
<?php
  require_once('authorizeaccess.php');
  require_once('pagetitles.php');
  $page_title = MR_EDIT_MOVIE_PAGE;
?>
<!DOCTYPE html>
<html>
```

Doing so properly sets our `$page_title` variable for use in `navmenu.php`, which we include from `pagetitles.php`. Next, in the `<head>` element, modify the `<title>` element to remove `Edit a Movie` and replace it with the `$page_title` as in Listing 24.10.

## Listing 24.10.

```
  1.    Unchanged Lines
  2.       <html>
  3.          <head>
  4.             <link ...>
  5. - Removed Line
  6. -      <title>Edit a Movie</title>
  7. + Added Line
  8. +      <title><?= $page_title ?></title>
  9. Unchanged Lines
 10.         </head>
 11.       <body>
 12.         ...
```

Next, right below the `<body>` element, include the `navmenu.php` script:

```php
<body>
<?php
  require_once('navmenu.php');
?>
  <div class="card">
    <div class="card-body">
```

Since we include the navbar, let's remove the link right below `<h1>Edit a Movie</h1>` that takes us back to the home page. See Listing 24.11.

## Listing 24.11.

```
1.    Unchanged Lines
2.        <div class="card">
3.          <div class="card-body">
4.            <h1>Edit a Movie</h1>
5.  - Removed Lines
6.  -          <nav class="nav">
7.  -            <a class="nav-link" href="index.php">Movies I Like</a>
8.  -          </nav>
9.    Unchanged Lines
10.            <hr/>
```

## Only Show the Edit Link to Administrators

Let's go back to the moviedetails.php script and add a condition that only allows a user with administrative privileges to see the link to the editmovie.php script. Add the code at lines 4-7 and 13 in Listing 24.12 below the table starting after the right after the second closing </div> tag.

## Listing 24.12.

```
1.              </table>
2.            </div>
3.          </div>
4.            <?php
5.                  if (isset($_SESSION['user_access_privileges'])
6.                      && $_SESSION['user_access_privileges'] == 'admin'):
7.            ?>
8.          <hr/>
9.          <p class='nav-link'>If you would like to change any of the details
10.         of this movie feel free to
11.           <a href='editmovie.php?id_to_edit=<?= $row['id'] ?>'> edit it</a></p>
12.           <?php
13.                  endif;
14.              else:
15.            ?>
16.          <h3>No Movie Details :-(</h3>
17.          <?php
18.                  endif;
19.              else:
20.            ?>
21.          <h3>No Movie Details :-(</h3>
22.          <?php
23.              endif;
24.            ?>
25.          </div>
26.        </div>
27.        <script ...></script>
```

# Add Navigation Bar to removemovie.php

Finally, we'll add the navbar to the removemovie.php script. We want our menu to look like Figure 24.14.

Figure 24.14.

> *You need to be logged in as a user with* access_privileges *set to* admin *to test this.*

Open pagetitles.php and add the following MR_REMOVE_MOVIE_PAGE definition right after the MR_EDIT_MOVIE_PAGE definition:

```php
<?php
    // Page Titles
    // ...
    define('MR_EDIT_MOVIE_PAGE', 'Movie Reservations - Edit Movie');
    define('MR_REMOVE_MOVIE_PAGE', 'Movie Reservations - Remove Movie');
```

Open the removemovie.php script and include the pagetitles.php script and set $page_title to MR_REMOVE_MOVIE_PAGE, right after the include for the authorizeaccess.php script:

```php
<?php
  require_once('authorizeaccess.php');
  require_once('pagetitles.php');
  $page_title = MR_REMOVE_MOVIE_PAGE;
?>
<!DOCTYPE html>
<html>
```

This properly sets our $page_title variable for use in navmenu.php which we include from pagetitles.php. Next, in the <head> element, modify the <title> element to remove the text "Remove a Movie" and replace it with the $page_title (see Listing 24.13).

### Listing 24.13.

```
1.    Unchanged Lines
2.       ...
3.       <html>
4.         <head>
5.            <link ...>
6.  - Removed Line
7.  -      <title>Remove a Movie</title>
8.  + Added Line
9.  +      <title><?= $page_title ?></title>
10. Unchanged Lines
11.         </head>
12.         <body>
13.            ...
```

Next, right below the <body> element, include the navmenu.php script:

```
<body>
<?php
  require_once('navmenu.php');
?>
  <div class="card">
    <div class="card-body">
```

# Complete Code Listings

Listing 24.14 is the complete listing for the pagetitles.php page.

### Listing 24.14.

```
1.  <?php
2.     // Page Titles
3.     define('MR_HOME_PAGE', 'Movie Reservations');
4.     define('MR_DETAILS_PAGE', 'Movie Reservations - Details');
5.     define('MR_SIGNUP_PAGE', 'Movie Reservations - Sign Up');
6.     define('MR_LOGIN_PAGE', 'Movie Reservations - Login');
7.     define('MR_UNAUTHORIZED_ACCESS_PAGE', 'Movie Reservations - Unauthorized Access');
8.     define('MR_ADD_MOVIE_PAGE', 'Movie Reservations - Add Movie');
9.     define('MR_EDIT_MOVIE_PAGE', 'Movie Reservations - Edit Movie');
10.    define('MR_REMOVE_MOVIE_PAGE', 'Movie Reservations - Remove Movie');
```

Listing 24.15 is the complete listing for the navmenu.php page.

## Listing 24.15.

```php
1.  <?php
2.  $page_title = isset($page_title) ? $page_title : "";
3.
4.  if (session_status() == PHP_SESSION_NONE) {
5.      session_start();
6.  }
7.  ?>
8.  <nav class="navbar sticky-top navbar-expand-md navbar-dark"
9.      style="background-color: #569f32;">
10.     <a class="navbar-brand" href="<?= dirname($_SERVER['PHP_SELF']) ?>">
11.         <img src="resources/movie_rental_icon.png" width="30" height="30"
12.             class="d-inline-block align-top" alt="">
13.         <?= MR_HOME_PAGE ?>
14.     </a>
15.     <button class="navbar-toggler" type="button" data-toggle="collapse"
16.             data-target="#navbarNavAltMarkup" aria-controls="navbarNavAltMarkup"
17.             aria-expanded="false" aria-label="Toggle navigation">
18.         <span class="navbar-toggler-icon"></span>
19.     </button>
20.     <div class="collapse navbar-collapse" id="navbarNavAltMarkup">
21.         <div class="navbar-nav">
22.             <a class="nav-item nav-link<?= $page_title == MR_HOME_PAGE ? ' active' : '' ?>"
23.                 href="<?= dirname($_SERVER['PHP_SELF']) ?>">Home </a>
24.             <?php if (isset($_SESSION['user_access_privileges'])
25.                 && $_SESSION['user_access_privileges'] == 'admin'): ?>
26.                 <a class="nav-item nav-link<?= $page_title == MR_ADD_MOVIE_PAGE ? ' active' : '' ?>"
27.                     href="addmovie.php">Add a Movie</a>
28.             <?php endif; ?>
29.             <?php if (!isset($_SESSION['user_name'])): ?>
30.                 <a class="nav-item nav-link<?= $page_title == MR_LOGIN_PAGE ? ' active' : '' ?>"
31.                     href="login.php">Login</a>
32.                 <a class="nav-item nav-link<?= $page_title == MR_SIGNUP_PAGE ? ' active' : '' ?>"
33.                     href="signup.php">Sign Up</a>
34.             <?php else: ?>
35.                 <a class="nav-item nav-link"
36.                     href="logout.php">Logout (<?= $_SESSION['user_name'] ?>)</a>
37.             <?php endif; ?>
38.         </div>
39.     </div>
40. </nav>
```

## Exercises

1.  Create navmenu.php script to hold Navbar logic and add it to the required pages.

    1. Display the logged-in user's name in the navbar, next to the Login link.

2.  Add the "Add Movie" link that only admin users can use.

    1. Confirm admin users can see the link.

    2. Confirm regular site users do not see the link.

# Chapter

# 25

# Adding Reservation Features

*"For all the folks getting excited about my quotes. Here is another - Yes, I am a terrible coder, but I am probably still better than you :)"*

-Rasmus Lerdorf

Finally, we are ready to add the movie reservation features to our *Movie Reservations* application. This chapter will focus on adding reservation features to the *Movie Reservations* application so that users can reserve and return movies. Again, here is the list of modifications we need to make to finally turn the *Movie Listing* application into a *Movie Reservations* application:

1. **Adding Reservation Features**
    1. Create a database table to hold information for movie reservations
    2. Add fields to the movieListing database table to keep track of the number of copies and reserved movies for each movie
    3. Modify the add, edit, remove, and movie details movie scripts to include the number of copies of a movie
    4. Modify the Movie listings page to show a link for reserving a movie for logged in users
    5. Modify the Movie listings page to show a link for removing a movie for users logged in with admin privileges
    6. Add a reservation script for users to check out movies
    7. Add a script for a shopping cart that allows users to reserve movies in their cart and remove them from their cart
    8. Add a shopping cart icon that allows users to view their cart
    9. Add a reserved movies script allowing users to check movies back in
    10. Add a reservations icon that allows users to view their reservations

## Add Number of Copies and Number Reserved

To turn our movie listing application into a movie reservation application, we need to know how many copies of a movie title we have and how many of those copies are reserved. We will modify the database and add movie checkout features.

### Add Number of Copies and Reserved Database Fields

Let's add two fields to our movieListing table in the Movie database. One for the number of copies, and another for the number reserved. We'll use Adminer to alter our table as in Figure 25.1.

Select the + after the image_file field to add two new fields to the end of the movieListing table.

For the number_of_copies field:

- In the **Column name** below image_file, enter number_of_copies
- Select the "Type" as int
- Enter **11** for the "Length"
- Check the box and enter **1** for "Default value"

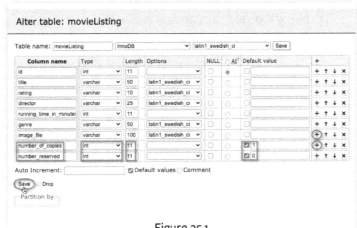

Figure 25.1.

And for the number_reserved field:

- In the **Column name** below number_of_copies, enter number_reserved
- Select the "Type" as **int**
- Enter **11** for the "Length"
- Check the box and enter **0** for "Default value"

Once you press **Save**, the table description should look like Figure 25.2. Now all the movies in our movieListing table have number_of_copies set to 1, and number_of_reserved set to 0 as shown in Figure 25.3.

Figure 25.2.

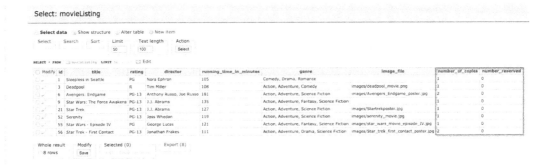

Figure 25.3.

## Tracking Copies for Movies Added

We need to add a form field to the "Add a Movie" page to set the number of copies of the movie we want to add. See Figure 25.4.

Open the addmovie.php script and add a <div class="form-group row"> for "Number of Copies" with the name attribute set to movie_copies_number just below the "Movie Image File" form field" as in Listing 25.1.

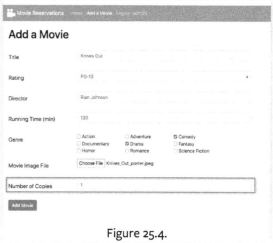

Figure 25.4.

### Listing 25.1.

```
1.    Unchanged Lines
2.    ...
3.    <div class="form-group row">
4.      <label for="movie_image_file"
5.            class="col-sm-3 col-form-label-lg">Movie Image File</label>
6.      <div class="col-sm-8">
7.        <input type="file" class="form-control-file" id="movie_image_file"
8.            name="movie_image_file">
9.      </div>
10.   </div>
11. + Added Lines
12. +   <div class="form-group row">
13. +     <label for="movie_copies_number="
14.           class="col-sm-3 col-form-label-lg">Number of Copies</label>
15. +     <div class="col-sm-8">
16. +       <input type="number" class="form-control" id="movie_copies_number"
17.             name="movie_copies_number" min="0" max="10" value="1">
18. +     </div>
19. +   </div>
20.   Unchanged Lines
21.   </div>
22.   <button class="btn btn-primary" type="submit"
23.         name="add_movie_submission">Add Movie</button>
24.   </form>
25.   <script>
```

Now let's head back up to the `// Initialization` comment and add a line below it of code that defaults `$number_of_copies` to 1 as shown in Listing 25.2.

## Listing 25.2.

```
1.    Unchanged Lines
2.        ...
3.        <div class="card">
4.          <div class="card-body">
5.            <h1>Add a Movie</h1>
6.            <hr/>
7.              <?php
8.                // Initialization
9.                $display_add_movie_form = true;
10.               $movie_title = "";
11.               $movie_rating = "";
12.               $movie_director = "";
13.               $movie_runtime = "";
14.               $movie_genre_text = "";
15.               $checked_movie_genres = null;
16. + Added Line
17. +             $number_of_copies = 1;
18.   Unchanged Lines
19.
20.               $genres = [...];
```

Next, in the `if (isset($_POST[...],...))` condition that checks if the form was submitted, add a check that `$_POST['movie_copies_number']` is set (Listing 25.3).

## Listing 25.3.

```
1.    Unchanged Lines
2.        ...
3.        $genres = [...];
4.
5.        if (isset($_POST['add_movie_submission'], $_POST['movie_title'],
6.                $_POST['movie_rating'], $_POST['movie_director'],
7.                $_POST['movie_running_time_in_minutes']
8. + Added Line
9. +              , $_POST['movie_copies_number']
10.   Unchanged Lines
11.               ))
12.               {
13.                   require_once('dbconnection.php');
14.                   ...
```

Within this if() condition, just below setting $checked_movie_generes, add a line of code to set $number_of_copies to $_POST['movie_copies_number'] and cast it to an (int). Casting it ensures we are working with a valid number and not a random user-supplied string like "100 movies".

## Listing 25.4.

```
1.    Unchanged Lines
2.       if (isset($_POST[...],...))
3.       {
4.           ...
5.           $movie_runtime = $_POST['movie_running_time_in_minutes'];
6.           $checked_movie_genres = $_POST['movie_genre_checkbox'];
7. + Added Line
8. +         $number_of_copies = (int) $_POST['movie_copies_number'];
9.    Unchanged Lines
10.
11.          $movie_genre_text = "";
```

We need to modify all of our queries to the database to be parameterized queries, so we need to include the queryutils.php script. A little further down the code, within the condition for checking there is no file error message (if (empty($file_error_message))), add the following line of code right after the opening curly brace ({):

## Listing 25.5.

```
1.    Unchanged Lines
2.       ...
3.       if (empty($file_error_message))
4.       {
5. + Added Line
6. +       require_once('queryutils.php');
7. +
8.    Unchanged Lines
9.           $dbc = mysqli_connect(DB_HOST, DB_USER, DB_PASSWORD, DB_NAME)
10.              or trigger_error(
11.                  'Error connecting to MySQL server for' . DB_NAME, E_USER_ERROR
12.              );
```

We need to modify the SQL insert into the
movieListing table to use the number_of_copies
field. We also need to change it to a parameterized query like in Listing 25.6. Finally,
we need to add a row to our table that shows
the value of the "number of copies" field
after adding a movie as in Figure 25.5

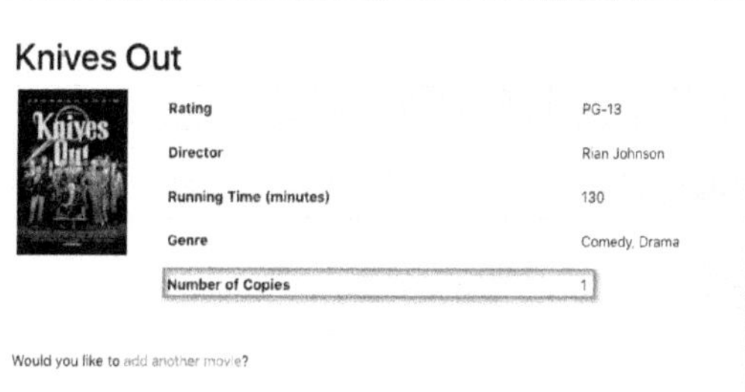

**Knives Out**

| | |
|---|---|
| Rating | PG-13 |
| Director | Rian Johnson |
| Running Time (minutes) | 130 |
| Genre | Comedy, Drama |
| Number of Copies | 1 |

Would you like to add another movie?

Listing 25.6.

Figure 25.5.

```
1.   Unchanged Lines
2.      ...
3.      if (empty($file_error_message))
4.      {
5.          ...
6.          $movie_image_file_path = addMovieImageFileReturnPathLocation();
7.
8.  - Removed Lines
9.  -       $query = "INSERT INTO movieListing (title, rating, director, running_time_in_minutes, "
10. -           . "genre, image_file) VALUES ('$movie_title', '$movie_rating', '$movie_director', "
11. -           . "'$movie_runtime', '$movie_genre_text', '$movie_image_file_path')";
12. -
13. -       mysqli_query($dbc, $query)
14. -            or trigger_error('Error querying database movieListing: Failed to insert movie listing',
15. -                   E_USER_ERROR);
16. + Added Lines
17. +       $query = "INSERT INTO movieListing (title, rating, director, running_time_in_minutes, "
18. +           . "genre, image_file, number_of_copies) VALUES (?, ?, ?, ?, ?, ?, ?)";
19. +
20. +       $results = parameterizedQuery($dbc, $query, 'sssssssi', $movie_title, $movie_rating,
21. +           $movie_director, $movie_runtime, $movie_genre_text, $movie_image_file_path,
22. +           $number_of_copies);
23. +
24. +       if (mysqli_errno($dbc))
25. +       {
26. +           trigger_error('Error querying database movieListing', E_USER_ERROR);
27. +       }
28.   Unchanged Lines
29.
30.       if (empty($movie_image_file_path))
31.       {
32.           $movie_image_file_path = ML_UPLOAD_PATH . ML_DEFAULT_MOVIE_FILE_NAME;
33.       }
```

Add an HTML table row at the end of the table showing the number of copies of the movie we added as in Listing 25.7

## Listing 25.7.

```
1.    Unchanged Lines
2.      ...
3.      <table class="table table-striped">
4.        <tbody>
5.          ...
6.          <tr>
7.            <th scope="row">Running Time (minutes)</th>
8.            <td><?= $movie_runtime ?></td>
9.          </tr>
10.         <tr>
11.           <th scope="row">Genre</th>
12.           <td><?= $movie_genre_text ?></td>
13.         </tr>
14. + Added Lines
15. +       <tr>
16. +         <th scope="row">Number of Copies</th>
17. +         <td><?= $number_of_copies ?></td>
18. +       </tr>
19.     Unchanged Lines
20.         </tbody>
21.       </table>
```

*You need to be logged in as a user with* `admin` *privileges to test this.*

## Add Number of Copies to Editing Page

Let's add a form field to the "Edit a Movie" page to set the number of copies of the movie we're editing. See Figure 25.6.

Open the `editmovie.php` script and add a `<div class="form-group row">` for "Number of Copies" with the `name` attribute set to `movie_copies_number` just below the "Movie Image File" form field as shown in Listing 25.8.

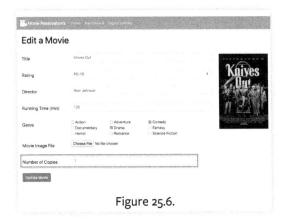

Figure 25.6.

## Listing 25.8.

```
1.    Unchanged Lines
2.      ...
3.      <div class="form-group row">
4.        <label for="movie_image_file"
5.               class="col-sm-3 col-form-label-lg">Movie Image File</label>
6.        <div class="col-sm-8">
7.          <input type="file" class="form-control-file" id="movie_image_file"
8.                 name="movie_image_file">
9.        </div>
10.     </div>
11. +  Added Lines
12. +    <div class="form-group row">
13. +      <label for="movie_copies_number="
14. +             class="col-sm-3 col-form-label-lg">Number of Copies</label>
15. +      <div class="col-sm-8">
16. +        <input type="number" class="form-control" id="movie_copies_number"
17. +               name="movie_copies_number" min="0" max="10" value="1">
18. +      </div>
19. +    </div>
20.    Unchanged Lines
21.      </div>
22.      <button class="btn btn-primary" type="submit"
23.              name="add_movie_submission">Add Movie</button>
24.    </form>
25.    <script>
26.      ...
```

We need to modify all of our queries to the database to be parameterized and include the queryutils.php script. Head back up to the where we include dbconnection.php and movieimagefileutil.php and add an include for queryutils.php:

```php
<?php
    require_once('dbconnection.php');
    require_once('movieimagefileutil.php');
    require_once('queryutils.php');
```

Now head down to the construction of the first query where we are selecting all of the movieListing fields located within the if (isset($_GET[id_to_edit'])) condition:

```php
if (isset($_GET['id_to_edit']))
{
    // ...
    $query = "SELECT * FROM movieListing WHERE id = $id_to_edit";
    // ...
}
```

Make the modifications shown in Listing 25.9.

## Listing 25.9.

```
1.    Unchanged Lines
2.      if (isset($_GET['id_to_edit']))
3.      {
4.          $id_to_edit = $_GET['id_to_edit'];
5.  - Removed Lines
6.  -       $query = "SELECT * FROM movieListing WHERE id = $id_to_edit";
7.  -
8.  -       $result = mysqli_query($dbc, $query)
9.  -               or trigger_error('Error querying database movieListing', E_USER_ERROR);
10. + Added Lines
11. +       $query = "SELECT * FROM movieListing WHERE id = ?";
12. +
13. +       $result = parameterizedQuery($dbc, $query, 'i', $id_to_edit)
14.   Unchanged Lines
15.       if (mysqli_num_rows($result) == 1)
16.       {
```

Within the if (mysqli_num_rows($result) == 1) condition, just below setting $movie_image_file, add a line of code to set $number_of_copies to $row['number_of_copies']. Doing so shows the stored value of number_of_copies on the editing form (Listing 25.10).

## Listing 25.10.

```
1.    Unchanged Lines
2.      if (mysqli_num_rows($result) == 1)
3.      {
4.          $row = mysqli_fetch_assoc($result);
5.
6.          $movie_title = $row['title'];
7.          ...
8.          $movie_image_file = $row['image_file'];
9.  + Added Line
10. +        $number_of_copies = $row['number_of_copies'];
11.   Unchanged Lines
12.
13.          if (empty($movie_image_file))
14.          {
```

Next, in the elseif (isset($_POST[...],...)) condition shown in Listing 25.11 that checks if the form was submitted, add a check for $_POST['movie_copies_number'].

## Listing 25.11.

```
1.    Unchanged Lines
2.      ...
3.      elseif (isset($_POST['add_movie_submission'], $_POST['movie_title'],
4.              $_POST['movie_rating'], $_POST['movie_director'],
5.              $_POST['movie_running_time_in_minutes']
6. + Added Line
7. +           , $_POST['movie_copies_number']
8.    Unchanged Lines
9.          ))
10.         {
11.             $movie_title = $_POST['movie_title'];
```

Within this elseif() condition, just below setting $movie_image_file (Listing 25.12), add a line of code to set $number_of_copies to $_POST['movie_copies_number'] and cast it to an (int). Now, $number_of_copies holds the updated value submitted by the user.

## Listing 25.12.

```
1.    Unchanged Lines
2.      elseif (isset($_POST[...],...))
3.      {
4.          $movie_title = $_POST['movie_title'];
5.          ...
6.          $movie_image_file = $_POST['movie_image_file'];
7. + Added Line
8. +        $number_of_copies = (int)$_POST['movie_copies_number'];
9.    Unchanged Lines
10.
11.         $movie_genre_text = "";
```

Finally, within if (empty($file_error_message)), just below the condition to check if a new image file was selected, make the following modifications (Listing 25.13) to parameterize the UPDATE to the movieListing table.

## Listing 25.13.

```
1.    Unchanged Lines
2.      if (empty($file_error_message))
3.      {
4.          $movie_image_file_path = addMovieImageFileReturnPathLocation();
5.
6.          // IF new image selected, set it to be updated in the database.
7.          if (!empty($movie_image_file_path))
8.          {
9.              ...
10.
11.             $movie_image_file = $movie_image_file_path;
12.         }
13.
14.  -  Removed Lines
15.  -      $query = "UPDATE movieListing SET title = '$movie_title', rating = '$movie_rating', "
16.  -            . "director = '$movie_director', running_time_in_minutes = '$movie_runtime', "
17.  -            . "genre = '$movie_genre_text', image_file = '$movie_image_file' "
18.  -            . "WHERE id = $id_to_update";
19.  -
20.  -      mysqli_query($dbc, $query)
21.  -              or trigger_error(
22.  -                  'Error querying database movieListing: Failed to update movie listing',
23.  -                  E_USER_ERROR
24.  -              );
25.  + Added Lines
26.  +      $query = "UPDATE movieListing SET title = ?, rating = ?, director = ?,
27.  +                  running_time_in_minutes = ?, genre = ?, image_file = ?,
28.  +                  number_of_copies = ?
29.  +              WHERE id = $id_to_update";
30.  +      parameterizedQuery($dbc, $query, 'sssssii', $movie_title, $movie_rating,
31.  +                  $movie_director, $movie_runtime, $movie_genre_text,
32.  +                  $movie_image_file, $number_of_copies, $id_to_update);
33.  +
34.  +      if(mysqli_errno($dbc))
35.  +      {
36.  +          trigger_error(
37.  +              'Error querying database movieListing: Failed to update movie listing',
38.  +              E_USER_ERROR
39.  +          );
40.  +      }
41.    Unchanged Lines
42.
43.          $nav_link = 'moviedetails.php?id=' . $id_to_update;
```

## Add Number of Copies to Removing Movies

Let's add a row to the "Remove a Movie" page that shows the number of copies as shown in Figure 25.7.

Open the removemovie.php script. We need to modify all of our queries to the database to be parameterized queries, so we need to include the queryutils.php script. Right below the include for movieimagefileutil.php add a require_once('queryutils.php'); as shown in Listing 25.14.

Figure 25.7.

### Listing 25.14.

```
1.    Unchanged Lines
2.      ...
3.      require_once('dbconnection.php');
4.      require_once('movieimagefileutil.php');
5.  + Added Line
6.  +   require_once('queryutils.php');
7.    Unchanged Lines
8.
9.        $dbc = mysqli_connect(DB_HOST, DB_USER, DB_PASSWORD, DB_NAME)
10.              or trigger_error(
11.                 'Error connecting to MySQL server for' . DB_NAME,
12.                 E_USER_ERROR
13.              );
```

Next, we parameterize the query for the image file located within the if (isset($_POST['delete_movie_submission'])...): condition (Listing 25.15).

### Listing 25.15.

```
1.    Unchanged Lines
2.      ...
3.      if (isset($_POST['delete_movie_submission']) && isset($_POST['id'])):
4.
5.          $id = $_POST['id'];
6.
7.          // Query image file from DB
8.  - Removed Lines
9.  -       $query = "SELECT image_file FROM movieListing WHERE id = $id";
10. -
11. -       $result = mysqli_query($dbc, $query)
```

```
12.  + Added Lines
13.  +        $query = "SELECT image_file FROM movieListing WHERE id = ?";
14.  +
15.  +        $result = parameterizedQuery($dbc, $query, 'i', $id)
16.     Unchanged Lines
17.                   or trigger_error('Error querying database movieListing', E_USER_ERROR);
18.
19.          if (mysqli_num_rows($result) == 1)
20.          {
21.              //...
22.          }
```

Now, let's parameterize the deletion of the movie from the database as in Listing 25.16.

## Listing 25.16.

```
1.     Unchanged Lines
2.          ...
3.          if (mysqli_num_rows($result) == 1)
4.          {
5.              ...
6.          }
7.  - Removed Lines
8.  -       $query = "DELETE FROM movieListing WHERE id = $id";
9.  -
10. -       $result = mysqli_query($dbc, $query)
11. + Added Lines
12. +       $query = "DELETE FROM movieListing WHERE id = ?";
13. +
14. +       $result = parameterizedQuery($dbc, $query, 'i', $id)
15.    Unchanged Lines
16.                   or trigger_error('Error querying database movieListing', E_USER_ERROR);
17.
18.          header("Location: " . dirname($_SERVER['PHP_SELF']));
19.
20.      elseif (isset($_POST['do_not_delete_movie_submission'])):
```

Down in the `elseif (isset($_GET['id_to_delete'])):` condition, make the modifications shown in Listing 25.17 to parameterize the query for the movie.

## Listing 25.17.

```
1.    Unchanged Lines
2.          elseif (isset($_GET['id_to_delete'])):
3.      ?>
4.              <h3 class="text-danger">Confirm Deletion of the Following Movie:</h3><br/>
5.      <?php
6.              $id = $_GET['id_to_delete'];
7.
8.  - Removed Lines
9.  -           $query = "SELECT * FROM movieListing WHERE id = $id";
10. -
11. -           $result = mysqli_query($dbc, $query)
12. + Added Lines
13. +           $query = "SELECT * FROM movieListing WHERE id = ?";
14. +
15. +           $result = parameterizedQuery($dbc, $query, 'i', $id)
16.    Unchanged Lines
17.                  or trigger_error('Error querying database movieListing', E_USER_ERROR);
18.
19.             if (mysqli_num_rows($result) == 1)
20.             {
21.                 ...
```

Finally, add an HTML table row for the number of copies with the table data set to $row['number_of_copies'] just below the row for "Genre". See Listing 25.18.

## Listing 25.18.

```
1.    Unchanged Lines
2.      <table class="table table-striped">
3.        <tbody>
4.          <tr>
5.            <th scope="row">Rating</th>
6.            <td><?= $row['rating'] ?></td>
7.          </tr>
8.            ...
9.          <tr>
10.           <th scope="row">Genre</th>
11.           <td><?= $row['genre'] ?></td>
12.         </tr>
13. + Added Lines
14. +        <tr>
15. +          <th scope="row">Number of Copies</th>
16. +          <td><?= $row['number_of_copies'] ?></td>
17. +        </tr>
18.    Unchanged Lines
19.        </tbody>
20.      </table>
```

### Add Number_of_copies and Number Available to Movie Details

We'll add a row to the "Movie Details" page that shows the number available and the number in inventory. See Figure 25.8.

> *You will need to be logged in with admin privileges to see the number in inventory.*

Open the moviedetails.php script. We need to modify the query for this movie to the database to be parameterized, so we need to include the queryutils.php script. Within the if (isset($_GET['id'])) condition, right below the include for movielistingfileconstants.php add a require_once('queryutils.php'); from Listing 25.19.

Figure 25.8.

### Listing 25.19.

```
 1.   Unchanged Lines
 2.      ...
 3.      if (isset($_GET['id'])):
 4.
 5.          require_once('dbconnection.php');
 6.          require_once('movielistingfileconstants.php');
 7. + Added Line
 8. +         require_once('queryutils.php');
 9.   Unchanged Lines
10.
11.          $id = $_GET['id'];
12.
13.          $dbc = mysqli_connect(DB_HOST, DB_USER, DB_PASSWORD, DB_NAME)
14.              or trigger_error(
15.                  'Error connecting to MySQL server for' . DB_NAME,
16.                  E_USER_ERROR
17.              );
```

Next, parameterize the query for the movie details (Listing 25.20).

## Listing 25.20.

```
1.    Unchanged Lines
2.      ...
3.      $dbc = mysqli_connect(DB_HOST, DB_USER, DB_PASSWORD, DB_NAME)
4.              or trigger_error(
5.                  'Error connecting to MySQL server for' . DB_NAME,
6.                  E_USER_ERROR
7.              );
8.
9.  - Removed Lines
10. -    $query = "SELECT * FROM movieListing WHERE id = $id";
11. -
12. -    $result = mysqli_query($dbc, $query)
13. + Added Lines
14. +    $query = "SELECT * FROM movieListing WHERE id = ?";
15. +
16. +    $result = parameterizedQuery($dbc, $query, 'i', $id)
17.    Unchanged Lines
18.              or trigger_error('Error querying database movieListing', E_USER_ERROR);
19.
20.      if (mysqli_num_rows($result) == 1)
21.      {
22.          ...
23.      }
```

Then, add a table row for number available with the table data set to $row['number_of_copies']
- $row['number_reserved'] just below the row for "Genre" as in Listing 25.21.

## Listing 25.21.

```
1.    Unchanged Lines
2.      ...
3.      <table class="table table-striped">
4.        <tbody>
5.          <tr>
6.            <th scope="row">Rating</th>
7.            <td><?= $row['rating'] ?></td>
8.          </tr>
9.          ...
10.          <tr>
11.            <th scope="row">Genre</th>
12.            <td><?= $row['genre'] ?></td>
13.          </tr>
14. + Added Lines
15. +        <tr>
16. +          <th scope="row">Number of Copies</th>
17. +          <td><?= $row['number_of_copies'] - $row['number_reserved'] ?></td>
18. +        </tr>
19.    Unchanged Lines
20.        </tbody>
21.      </table>
```

Finally, just below the new table row for the number of copies, add a row for the number in inventory that displays if the user has administrative privileges. See Listing 25.22.

## Listing 25.22.

```
1.   Unchanged Lines
2.     <table class="table table-striped">
3.       <tbody>
4.         <tr>
5.           <th scope="row">Rating</th>
6.           <td><?= $row['rating'] ?></td>
7.         </tr>
8.         ...
9.         <tr>
10.          <th scope="row">Genre</th>
11.          <td><?= $row['genre'] ?></td>
12.        </tr>
13.        <tr>
14.          <th scope="row">Number of Copies</th>
15.          <td><?= $row['number_of_copies'] - $row['number_reserved'] ?></td>
16.        </tr>
17. + Added Lines
18. +      <?php
19. +            if (isset($_SESSION['user_access_privileges'])
20. +                && $_SESSION['user_access_privileges'] == 'admin'):
21. +      ?>
22. +        <tr>
23. +          <th scope="row">Number in Inventory</th>
24. +          <td><?= $row['number_of_copies'] ?></td>
25. +        </tr>
26. +      <?php
27. +            endif;
28. +      ?>
29.   Unchanged Lines
30.        </tbody>
31.      </table>
```

# Persisting Movie Reservations for Users

Now that we can track the number of movies available and reserved, we have to add a table to the Movie database that tracks all movies reserved by a user. Therefore, we need a table that represents a many-to-many[1] relationship between users and movies, otherwise known as a "join" table.

A join table involves common fields, typically the ID fields, from two or more tables. These fields are set as foreign keys to the selected rows in the table they represent. In this case, we want to relate the user table to the movieListing table, and we want this relationship to represent a reservation. Foreign keys are usually named using the table field name concatenated with the table's primary key name. Therefore, if we create a table named reservation with the usual primary key set to id, it has the following foreign keys:

| Field Name | Purpose |
|---|---|
| id | Primary Key |
| user_id | Foreign Key |
| movieListing_id | Foreign Key |

In Adminer (Figure 25.9) create a table called reservation in the Movie database with the following attributes:

| Column Name | Type | Length | Auto Increment |
|---|---|---|---|
| id | int | 11 | Yes |
| user_id | int | 11 | No |
| movieListing_id | int | 11 | No |

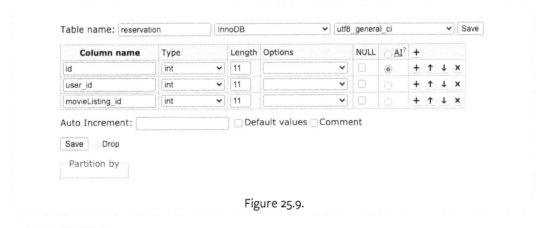

Figure 25.9.

---

[1]    many-to-many: https://phpa.me/sql-many-to-many

# Checking Movies Reserved by Users

We're going to need to know if a user has a movie reserved and the number of movies a user has reserved. Since we make these queries often, it makes sense to create functions in the queryutils.php script.

## Create IsMovieReservedByUser() Function

Let's create a function called isMovieReservedByUser(). It needs two parameters: $movie_id and $user_id. Open the queryutils.php script and add the header and function shown in Listing 25.23. This function queries the reservation table of the Movie database for a row containing the given movieListing_id and the given user_id. If a row is found in the database, the function returns true otherwise false.

## Listing 25.23.

```
1.  /**
2.   * Purpose:      Determines if a movie is currently reserved by a user
3.   *
4.   * Description: Given a movie id and a user id, queries to see if this user has
5.   *              this movie reserved. If so, true is returned, otherwise false.
5.   * @param        $movie_id
7.   * @param        $user_id
8.   * @return bool True if this movie is reserved by this user, otherwise false.
9.   */
10. function isMovieReservedByUser($movie_id, $user_id)
11. {
12.     require_once('dbconnection.php');
13.
14.     $ret_val = false;  // Assume failure
15.
16.     $dbc = mysqli_connect(DB_HOST, DB_USER, DB_PASSWORD, DB_NAME)
17.             or trigger_error(
18.                 'Error connecting to MySQL server for' . DB_NAME,
19.                 E_USER_ERROR
20.             );
21.
22.     $query = "SELECT id FROM reservation
23.             WHERE movieListing_id = ? AND user_id = ?";
24.
25.     $result = parameterizedQuery($dbc, $query, 'ii', $movie_id, $user_id)
26.             or trigger_error('Error querying database movieListing',
27.                             E_USER_ERROR);
28.
29.     if (mysqli_num_rows($result) == 1)
30.     {
31.         $ret_val = true;
31.     }
32.
33.     return $ret_val;
34. }
```

## Create NumberOfMoviesReservedByUser() Function

Let's create a function called numberOfMoviesReservedByUser(). It requires one parameter: $user_id. Add the header and function in Listing 25.24. This function queries the reservation table of the Movie database for all the rows containing the given user_id. In line 20, we use MySQL's COUNT() function to total the number of matching rows. This number returned indicates the number of movies this user has reserved.

### Listing 25.24.

```
1. /**
2. * Purpose:      Determines the number of movies reserved by a user
3. *
4. * Description: Given a user id, a query is made for the number of movies
5. *              reserved by this user. This number is returned.
6. *
7. * @param       $user_id
8. * @return int  The number of movies reserved by this user.
9. */
10. function numberOfMoviesReservedByUser($user_id)
11. {
12.     require_once('dbconnection.php');
13.
14.     $dbc = mysqli_connect(DB_HOST, DB_USER, DB_PASSWORD, DB_NAME)
15.             or trigger_error(
16.                 'Error connecting to MySQL server for' . DB_NAME,
17.                 E_USER_ERROR
18.             );
19.
20.     $query = "SELECT COUNT(id) FROM reservation WHERE user_id = ?";
21.
22.     $result = parameterizedQuery($dbc, $query, 'i', $user_id)
23.             or trigger_error('Error querying database movieListing',
24.                             E_USER_ERROR);
25.
26.     $retval = 0;
27.
28.     if (mysqli_num_rows($result) == 1)
29.     {
30.         $row = mysqli_fetch_row($result);
31.         $retval = $row['total'];
32.     }
33.
34.     return $retval;
35. }
```

## Modify Homepage Based On Access Privileges

We need to modify the homepage to show various information based on who is logged in. There are three different contexts for viewing information on the homepage:

1. When no one is logged in.
2. When a user is logged in with "admin" privileges.
3. When a user is logged in with "user" privileges.

When no one is logged in, we only want to display the movies as in Figure 25.10. When a user with admin privileges is logged in, we want the trashcan icon to be displayed for removing a movie (See Figure 25.11). Finally, when logged in with user privileges, the shopping cart icon can be displayed for adding the movie to a cart. The cart only shows if copies are available to reserve and the user has not already reserved it as in Figure 25.12.

Figure 25.10.

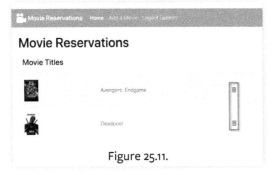

Figure 25.11.

Figure 25.12.

*The shopping cart icon is the Font Awesome fa-shopping-cart icon which is free to use.*

*The shopping cart link takes the user to a new page we create for reserving that movie.*

## Remove "Add a Movie" from Home Page

We already have the functionality to add a new movie from the navbar when a user with administrative privileges is logged in. Open the index.php script and let's remove the link to add a new movie from the homepage, just below the <h1><?= $page_title ?></h1> line. Open the index.php script and make the modifications in Listing 25.25.

### Listing 25.25.

```
1.    Unchanged Lines
2.      <body>
3.      <?php
4.        require_once('navmenu.php');
5.      ?>
6.        <div class="card">
7.          <div class="card-body">
8.            <h1><?= $page_title ?></h1>
9.  - Removed Line
10. -         <p class='nav-link'>If you have a movie you would like to include,
11. -                       feel free to <a href='addmovie.php'> add one</a></p>
12.   Unchanged Lines
13.         <?php
14.           require_once('dbconnection.php');
```

## Modify Movie Listing Query

Since we only want to show a link to reserve a movie if the movie is reservable, we need to modify the movie listing query to include the number_of_copies and number_reserved fields. Right below connection to the database, make the modifications from Listing 25.26.

### Listing 25.26.

```
1.    Unchanged Lines
2.      ...
3.      $dbc = mysqli_connect(DB_HOST, DB_USER, DB_PASSWORD, DB_NAME)
4.            or trigger_error(
5.                  'Error connecting to MySQL server for' . DB_NAME,
6.                  E_USER_ERROR
7.            );
8.
9.  - Removed Line
10. -   $query = "SELECT id, title, image_file FROM movieListing ORDER BY title";
11. + Added Line
12. +   $query = "SELECT id, title, image_file, number_of_copies, number_reserved
13. +           FROM movieListing ORDER BY title";
14.   Unchanged Lines
15.     $result = mysqli_query($dbc, $query)
16.                 or trigger_error('Error querying database movieListing', E_USER_ERROR);
```

## Show Icons Based On User Logged In

Currently, we always show the trashcan icon for each movie row as in Listing 25.27.

### Listing 25.27.

```
1.  <table class="table table-striped table-hover">
2.    <thead>
3.      <tr>
4.        <th scope="col"><h4>Movie Titles</h4></th>
5.        <th scope="col"></th>
6.        <th scope="col"></th>
7.      </tr>
8.    </thead>
9.    <tbody>
10. <?php
11.     while ($row = mysqli_fetch_assoc($result))
12.     {
13.         // ...
14.
15.         echo "<tr><td><img src='''" . $movie_image_file . "' class='img-thumbnail'"
16.             . "style='max-height: 75px;' alt='Movie image'></td>"
17.             . "<td class='align-middle'><a class='nav-link' href='moviedetails.php?id="
18.             . $row['id'] . "'>" . $row['title'] ."</a></td>"
19.             . "<td class='align-middle'><a class='nav-link' href='removemovie.php?id_to_delete="
20.             . $row['id'] ."'><i class='fas fa-trash-alt'></i></a></td></tr>";
21.     }
22. ?>
23.   </tbody>
24. </table>
```

We need to modify the logic based on who's logged in (if anyone). If someone with user privileges is logged in, we want to display a shopping cart link for this movie if it can be reserved. If someone with admin privileges is logged in, we want to show a trashcan link for removing the movie. If no one is logged in, we won't display any link. Listing 25.28 outlines what the logic should look like.

## Listing 25.28.

```
1.  while($row = mysqli_fetch_assoc($result))
2.  {
3.      // ...
4.      $movie_title_row = ... // Movie row info of first two columns (image and title)
5.
6.      IF user is logged in
7.
8.          IF logged in user has admin privileges
9.
10.             $movie_title_row .= ... // Add trashcan link to remove movie for third coloum
11.
12.         ELSE IF logged in user has user priviliges AND this movie can be reserved AND this user
13.                 doesn't already have this movie reserved
14.
15.             movie_title_row .= ... // Add shopping cart link to reserve movie for third column
16.
17.     ELSE user is not logged in
18.
19.         $movie_title_row .= ... // Add empty info for third column
20.
21.     ENDIF
22.
23.     echo $movie_title_row
24. }
```

*This example uses pseudo-code to focus on the logic.*

Make the code modifications in Listing 25.29 to implement this logic.

## Listing 25.29.

```
1.  Unchanged Lines
2.      while($row = mysqli_fetch_assoc($result))
3.      {
4.          $movie_image_file = $row['image_file'];
5.
6.          if (empty($movie_image_file))
7.          {
8.              $movie_image_file = ML_UPLOAD_PATH . ML_DEFAULT_MOVIE_FILE_NAME;
9.          }
10.
```

```
11. - Removed Lines
12. -    echo "<tr><td><img src=" . $movie_image_file . " class='img-thumbnail'"
13. -        . "style='max-height: 75px;' alt='Movie image'></td>"
14. -        . "<td class='align-middle'><a class='nav-link' href='moviedetails.php?id="
15. -        . $row['id'] . "'>" . $row['title'] ."</a></td>"
16. -        . "<td class='align-middle'><a class='nav-link' href='removemovie.php?id_to_delete="
17. -        . $row['id'] ."'><i class='fas fa-trash-alt'></i></a></td></tr>";
18. + Added Lines
19. +        $movie_title_row = "<tr><td><img src=" . $movie_image_file . " class='img-thumbnail'"
20. +            . "style='max-height: 75px;' alt='Movie image'></td>"
21. +            . "<td class='align-middle'><a class='nav-link' href='moviedetails.php?id="
22. +            . $row['id'] . "'>" . $row['title'] ."</a></td>"
23. +
24. +        if (isset($_SESSION['user_access_privileges']))
25. +        {
26. +            if ($_SESSION['user_access_privileges'] == 'admin')
27. +            {
28. +                $movie_title_row .= "<td class='align-middle'><a class='nav-link' '"
29. +                    . 'href='removemovie.php?id_to_delete="
30. +                    . $row['id'] ."'><i class='fas fa-trash-alt'></i></a></td></tr>";
31. +            }
32. +            else if ($_SESSION['user_access_privileges'] == 'user'
33. +                && ($row['number_of_copies'] > $row['number_reserved'])
34. +                && !isMovieReservedByUser($row['id'], $_SESSION['user_id']))
35. +            {
36. +                $movie_title_row .= "<td class='align-middle'><a class='nav-link' "
37. +                    . "href='reservemovie.php?id_to_reserve="
38. +                    . $row['id'] ."'><i class='fas fa-shopping-cart'></i></a></td></tr>";
39. +            }
40. +            else // We shouldn't ever get here, but it's a good practice
41. +            {
42. +                $movie_title_row .= "<td class='align-middle'></td>";
43. +            }
44. +        }
45. +        else
46. +        {
47. +            $movie_title_row .= "<td class='align-middle'></td>";
48. +        }
49. +
50. +        $movie_title_row .= "</tr>";
51. +
52. +        echo $movie_title_row;
53.   Unchanged Lines
54.      }
```

Note that in the `elseif()` condition:

```
else if ($_SESSION['user_access_privileges'] == 'user'
        && ($row['number_of_copies'] > $row['number_reserved'])
        && !isMovieReservedByUser($row['id'], $_SESSION['user_id']))
```

We have three conditions to satisfy before displaying the shopping cart link to reserve a movie:

- Does the logged-in user have user privileges?
- Are the number of copies for this movie currently more than the number currently reserved?
- And, has the user already reserved this movie (which we check with our `isMovieReservedByUser()` function)?

Also, note that the link refers to the script `reservemovie.php` we will create below.

Since we are calling the function `isMovieReservedByUser()`, which resides in the `queryutils.php` script, let's add an include for it right below our `dbconnection.php` and `movielistingfileconstants.php` includes. Refer to Listing 25.30.

```
<div class="card">
  <div class="card-body">
    <h1><?= $page_title ?></h1>
    <?php
        require_once('dbconnection.php');
        require_once('movielistingfileconstants.php');
        require_once('queryutils.php');
```

# Refactoring to Remove Duplicate Inclusions

Did you notice? Every script in our application that includes `queryytils.php` also includes `navmenu.php`. This script is a good place to remove duplicate inclusions and have `navmenu.php` include `queryutils.php`. Removing duplicate code improves maintainability. It would be tedious and error-prone to update all occurrences of the code in the future. Search for all `require_once('queryutils.php');` statements in the application and remove them. There should be an inclusion in these files:

- `addmovie.php`
- `editmovie.php`
- `index.php`
- `login.php`
- `moviedetails.php`
- `removemovie.php`
- `signup.php`

Open the navmenu.php script and include queryutils.php right below the first condition that calls session_start() if it has not already been started (Listing 25.30).

## Listing 25.30.

```
1.    Unchanged Lines
2.      <?php
3.          $page_title = isset($page_title) ? $page_title : "";
4.
5.          if (session_status() == PHP_SESSION_NONE)
6.          {
7.              session_start();
8.          }
9.
10. + Added Line
11. +          require_once('queryutils.php');
12.    Unchanged Lines
13.
14.      ?>
15.      <nav ...>
```

Also, notice that we have multiple inclusions of the Font Awesome style sheet in multiple scripts that already include navmenu.php. In addition to navmenu.php, there should be an inclusion in these files:

- login.php
- removemovie.php
- reservemovie.php
- unauthorizedaccess.php

Look for this line:

```
<link rel="stylesheet" href="https://use.fontawesome.com/...">
```

Remove it from all of the above scripts and add this link right before the opening <nav...> link as in Listing 25.31.

### Listing 25.31.

```
1.    Unchanged Lines
2.      <?php
3.          $page_title = isset($page_title) ? $page_title : "";
4.
5.          if (session_status() == PHP_SESSION_NONE)
6.          {
7.              session_start();
8.          }
9.
10.         require_once('queryutils.php');
11.     ?>
12.  + Added Lines
13.  +    <link rel="stylesheet" href="https://use.fontawesome.com/releases/v5.8.1/css/all.css"
14.  +         integrity="sha384-50oBUHEmvpQ+1lW4y57PTFmhCaXp0ML5d60M1M7uH2+nqUivzIebhndOJK28anvf"
15.  +         crossorigin="anonymous">
16.     Unchanged Lines
17.       <nav ...>
18.       ...
```

# Script for Reserving Movies

Browsing and reserving movies should be similar to shopping for items in an online store. When a user finds an item, in our case a movie they like, they should be able to add it to a shopping cart by clicking on the shopping cart icon for a movie they're interested in. See Figure 25.13.

We want them to see a page like Figure 25.14 allowing them to add it to their cart.

First open pagetitles.php and add the following MR_RESERVE_MOVIE_PAGE definition right after the MR_REMOVE_MOVIE_PAGE definition:

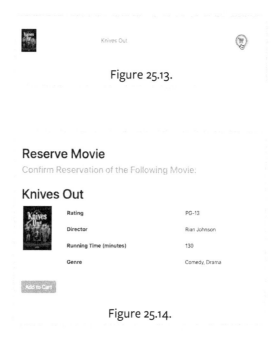

Figure 25.13.

Figure 25.14.

```
Unchanged Lines
  <?php
      // Page Titles
      define('MR_HOME_PAGE', 'Movie Reservations');
      ...
      define('MR_REMOVE_MOVIE_PAGE', 'Movie Reservations - Remove Movie');
+ Added Line
+     define('MR_RESERVE_MOVIE_PAGE', 'Movie Reservations - Reserve Movie');
```

The reservation page is a standard Bootstrap page showing the movie details with a button for adding the movie to a shopping cart. There are two ways to get to this script. The first is through an HTTP GET from the homepage that includes the movie ID as a query parameter. The second is through an HTTP POST that includes the movie ID as a hidden form parameter when someone adds the movie to their cart on the same page.

Create a new script called reservemovie.php and add the code in Listing 25.32.

## Listing 25.32.

```
1.  <!DOCTYPE html>
2.  <?php
3.    require_once('pagetitles.php');
4.    $page_title = MR_RESERVE_MOVIE_PAGE;
5.  ?>
6.  <html>
7.    <head>
8.      <title><?= $page_title ?></title>
9.      <link rel="stylesheet"
10.          href="https://stackpath.bootstrapcdn.com/bootstrap/4.2.1/css/bootstrap.min.css"
11.          integrity="sha384-GJzZqFGwb1QTTN6wy59ffF1BuGJpLSa9DkKMp0DgiMDm4iYMj70gZWKYbI706tWS"
12.          crossorigin="anonymous">
13.    </head>
14.    <body>
15.    <?php
16.      require_once('navmenu.php');
17.    ?>
18.      <div class="card">
19.        <div class="card-body">
20.          <h1>Reserve Movie</h1>
21.          <?php
22.              require_once('dbconnection.php');
23.              require_once('movieimagefileutil.php');
24.
25.              $dbc = mysqli_connect(DB_HOST, DB_USER, DB_PASSWORD, DB_NAME)
26.                  or trigger_error(
27.                      'Error connecting to MySQL server for' . DB_NAME,
28.                      E_USER_ERROR
29.                  );
```

```
30.
31.              if (isset($_POST['add_to_cart']) && isset($_POST['id'])):
32.
33.                  // ...
34.
35.              elseif (isset($_GET['id_to_reserve'])):
36.                  // ...
37.              else: // Unintended page link - No movie to reserve, redirect to index
38.
39.                  header("Location: " . dirname($_SERVER['PHP_SELF']));
40.                  exit();
41.
42.              endif;
43.          ?>
44.      </div>
45.    </div>
46.  <script src="https://code.jquery.com/jquery-3.3.1.slim.min.js"
47.          integrity="sha384-q8i/X+965Dz00rT7abK41JStQIAqVgRVzpbzo5smXKp4YfRvH+8abtTE1Pi6jizo"
48.          crossorigin="anonymous"></script>
49.  <script src="https://cdnjs.cloudflare.com/ajax/libs/popper.js/1.14.6/umd/popper.min.js"
50.          integrity="sha384-wHAiFfRlMFy6i5SRaxvfOCifBUQy1xHdJ/yoi7FRNXMRBu5WHdZYu1hA6ZOblgut"
51.          crossorigin="anonymous"></script>
52.  <script src="https://stackpath.bootstrapcdn.com/bootstrap/4.2.1/js/bootstrap.min.js"
53.          integrity="sha384-B0UglyR+jN6CkvvICOB2joaf5I4l3gm9GU6Hc1og6Ls7i6U/mkkaduKaBhlAXv9k"
54.          crossorigin="anonymous"></script>
55.  </body>
56. </html>
```

This code is a boilerplate script that should look familiar to you. Lines 3, 4, and 8 set and display the page title. Line 16 includes and displays the navbar. Line 20 displays "Reserve Movie" in an <h1> element set. Lines 22–29 include dbconnection.php, movieimagefileutil.php, and connect to the Movie database.

Line 31 (if (isset($_POST['add_to_cart']) && isset($_POST['id'])):) is the condition to check whether the user pressed the "Add to Cart" button. The name attribute for this button is named add_to_cart. We add code within this condition that adds this movie to the user's cart to be reserved.

Line 35 (elseif (isset($_GET['id_to_reserve'])):) is the condition where the user navigated from the homepage by selecting the shopping cart icon for this movie. This condition is where we display the movie details and the "Add to Cart" form button. Remember, use GET for read-only operations.

Line 37 (`else: // Unintended page link - No movie to reserve, redirect to index`) is a 'catch-all' condition that covers someone typing in the name of the script in the URL field of their browser. If this occurs, line 39 redirects the user back to the homepage.

The rest of the code is the standard Bootstrap boilerplate script inclusions.

### Show Details and Form for Adding to Cart

When the user first navigates to this page as a result of selecting the shopping cart icon for this movie, code will execute in this condition:

```
elseif (isset($_GET['id_to_reserve'])):
    // ...
```

Here we display the movie details and a form button for adding the movie to our cart. The code for the movie details will be identical to the code in `removemovie.php`, except we don't have to list the number of copies, and we only have one button.

Add the code in Listing 25.33 to the `elseif (isset($_GET['id_to_reserve'])):` condition:

### Listing 25.33.

```
1.      elseif (isset($_GET['id_to_reserve'])):
2.  ?>
3.              <h3 class="text-success">Confirm Reservation of the Following Movie:</h3><br/>
4.  <?php
5.          $id = $_GET['id_to_reserve'];
6.
7.          $query = "SELECT * FROM movieListing WHERE id = ?";
8.
9.          $result = parameterizedQuery($dbc, $query, 'i', $id);
10.
11.         if(mysqli_errno($dbc))
12.         {
13.             trigger_error('Error querying database movieListing', E_USER_ERROR);
14.         }
15.
16.         if (mysqli_num_rows($result) == 1)
17.         {
18.             $row = mysqli_fetch_assoc($result);
19.
20.             $movie_image_file = $row['image_file'];
21.
```

```
22.            if (empty($movie_image_file))
23.            {
24.                $movie_image_file = ML_UPLOAD_PATH . ML_DEFAULT_MOVIE_FILE_NAME;
25.            }
26.    ?>
27.    <h1><?= $row['title'] ?></h1>
28.    <div class="row">
29.      <div class="col-2">
30.        <img src="<?= $movie_image_file ?>" class="img-thumbnail"
31.            style="max-height: 200px;" alt="Movie image">
32.      </div>
33.      <div class="col">
34.        <table class="table table-striped">
35.          <tbody>
36.            <tr>
37.              <th scope="row">Rating</th>
38.              <td><?= $row['rating'] ?></td>
39.            </tr>
40.            <tr>
41.              <th scope="row">Director</th>
42.              <td><?= $row['director']? ></td>
43.            </tr>
44.            <tr>
45.              <th scope="row">Running Time (minutes)</th>
46.              <td><?= $row['running_time_in_minutes'] ?></td>
47.            </tr>
48.            <tr>
49.              <th scope="row">Genre</th>
50.              <td><?= $row['genre'] ?></td>
51.            </tr>
52.          </tbody>
53.        </table>
54.      </div>
55.    </div>
56.    <p>
57.    <form method="POST" action="<?= $_SERVER['PHP_SELF'] ?>">
58.      <button class="btn btn-success" type="submit" name="add_to_cart">Add to Cart</button>
59.      <input type="hidden" name="id" value="<?= $id ?>">
60.    </form>
61.    <?php
62.        }
63.        else
64.        {
65.        ?>
66.    <h3>No Movie Details :-(</h3>
67.        <?php
68.        }
69.
70.    else: // Unintended page link - No movie to reserve, redirect back to index
```

This code should be familiar to you by now. We use our parameterized query function to look up and display the movie details based on the movie ID parameter we receive or show an error message if no match is found.

> *Since we see some duplication of code in multiple pages, it would be an excellent exercise to refactor this out soon by modularizing. I leave that to you as an exercise.*

### Adding a Movie to the Cart

Once the user clicks the "Add to Cart" button (Figure 25.15), the HTML POST routes back to the same page since the form's action attribute is set to `<?= $_SERVER['PHP_SELF'] ?>`. Since the form's input element's name attribute is set to add_to_cart, the code will execute in this condition:

Figure 25.15.

```
if (isset($_POST['add_to_cart']) && isset($_POST['id'])):
```

Here is where we:

1. check to see if the movie is still reservable
2. reserve the movie if it is still reservable
3. update number_reserved in the movieListing table (if reserved).
4. Add the movie to the user's shopping cart.
5. Redirect back to the Home page.

Add the code in Listing 25.34 to the `if (isset($_POST['add_to_cart']) && isset($_POST['id'])):` condition, and I will walk through it below.

### Listing 25.34.

```php
1.  <?php
2.  if (isset($_POST['add_to_cart']) && isset($_POST['id'])):
3.
4.      $movie_id = $_POST['id'];
5.
6.      // Query if movie is still reservable
7.      $query = "SELECT id FROM movieListing
8.              WHERE id = ? AND number_of_copies - number_reserved > 0";
9.      $result = parameterizedQuery($dbc, $query, 'i', $movie_id);
10.
```

```
11.      if(mysqli_errno($dbc))
12.      {
13.          trigger_error('Error querying database movieListing', E_USER_ERROR);
14.      }
15.
16.      // Reserve movie if it's reservable, update the number of reserved copies
17.      //  in movieListing for reserved movies, and add it to the cart
18.      if (mysqli_num_rows($result) == 1 && isset($_SESSION['user_id']))
19.      {
20.          $user_id = $_SESSION['user_id'];
21.          $query = "INSERT INTO reservation (user_id, movieListing_id) VALUES (?, ?)";
22.          $result = parameterizedQuery($dbc, $query, 'ii', $user_id, $movie_id);
23.
24.          if (mysqli_errno($dbc))
25.          {
26.              trigger_error('Error querying database movieListing.reservation', E_USER_ERROR);
27.          }
28.
29.          $query = "UPDATE movieListing SET number_reserved = number_reserved + 1 WHERE id = ?";
30.          $result = parameterizedQuery($dbc, $query, 'i', $movie_id);
31.
32.          if (mysqli_errno($dbc))
33.          {
34.              trigger_error('Error querying database movieListing.reservation', E_USER_ERROR);
35.          }
36.
37.          if (isset($_SESSION['cart']))
38.          {
39.              array_push($_SESSION['cart'], $movie_id);
40.          }
41.          else
42.          {
43.              $_SESSION['cart'] = [$movie_id];
44.          }
45.      }
46.
47.      header("Location: " . dirname($_SERVER['PHP_SELF']));
48.      exit;
49.
50.  elseif (isset($_GET['id_to_reserve'])):
```

Lines 7–9 queries the database for the id in the movieListing database and returns a row if there are enough reservable copies (number_of_copies - number_reserved).

Line 18 checks the condition that we have a row for this query, indicating it is reservable. To do so, we should get information about the movie from the database and have a logged-in user.

```
if (mysqli_num_rows($result) == 1 && isset($_SESSION['user_id']))
```

Lines 20–44 execute if the movie is reservable.

Lines 21–27 insert the reservation into the reservation storing the movie and user ID.

Lines 29–35 update the number of reserved movies by 1 for the movie.

Lines 37–44 check for the existence of a shopping cart. This cart is an array held in the session variable: $_SESSION['cart']. If the cart exists, the movie ID is added or pushed onto the end of the array. Otherwise, we create the cart with the movie ID as the first element.

Line 47 routes to the home page and executes regardless if the movie is added to the cart or not.

## Race Conditions

*Since this movie reservation application is multi-user, and multiple users can be competing for a limited number of movies simultaneously, this presents a problem known as a "Race Condition". The best and most straightforward way to explain this is to think of it like multiple people are using an airline reservation system taking the same flight from Madison, Wisconsin, to Richmond, Virginia. Let's say ten people are trying to reserve this flight at the same time, and two people are about to pick seat 15A because we all know sitting closer to the front and having a window seat is the best! An airline seat, like a copy of a movie in our reservation system, is a resource. Any application that doles out limited resources needs to account for this situation. In the case of being the unlucky person who picked seat 15A second, you should be presented with a message that says, "We're sorry, that seat is no longer available." Then, you need to pick another seat. In the case of our movie reservation application, I did not add any code that would put up a modal dialog indicating the movie is no longer available because someone else had reserved it. But I should have! Again, I leave this as an exercise for you to do, which you should, especially if you were to deploy an application where you would need to handle race conditions.*

## Complete Code Listing

Listing 25.35 is the complete listing for the reservemovie.php page:

## Listing 25.35.

```
1.  <!DOCTYPE html>
2.  <?php
3.    require_once('pagetitles.php');
4.    $page_title = MR_RESERVE_MOVIE_PAGE;
5.  ?>
6.  <html>
7.    <head>
8.      <title><?= $page_title ?></title>
9.      <link rel="stylesheet"
10.           href="https://stackpath.bootstrapcdn.com/bootstrap/4.2.1/css/bootstrap.min.css"
11.           integrity="sha384-GJzZqFGwb1QTTN6wy59ffF1BuGJpLSa9DkKMp0DgiMDm4iYMj70gZWKYbI706tWS"
12.           crossorigin="anonymous">
13.    </head>
14.    <body>
15.    <?php
16.      require_once('navmenu.php');
17.    ?>
18.      <div class="card">
19.        <div class="card-body">
20.          <h1>Reserve Movie</h1>
21.          <?php
22.              require_once('dbconnection.php');
23.              require_once('movieimagefileutil.php');
24.
25.              $dbc = mysqli_connect(DB_HOST, DB_USER, DB_PASSWORD, DB_NAME)
26.                  or trigger_error(
27.                      'Error connecting to MySQL server for' . DB_NAME,
28.                      E_USER_ERROR
29.                  );
30.
31.              if (isset($_POST['add_to_cart']) && isset($_POST['id'])):
32.
33.                  $movie_id = $_POST['id'];
34.
35.                  // Query if movie is still reservable
36.                  $query = "SELECT id FROM movieListing
37.                          WHERE id = ? AND number_of_copies - number_reserved > 0";
38.
39.                  $result = parameterizedQuery($dbc, $query, 'i', $movie_id);
40.
41.                  if (mysqli_errno($dbc))
42.                  {
43.                      trigger_error('Error querying database movieListing', E_USER_ERROR);
44.                  }
```

```
45.
46.              // Reserve movie if it's reservable, update the number of reserved copies
47.              // in movieListing for reserved movies, and add it to the cart
48.              if (mysqli_num_rows($result) == 1 && isset($_SESSION['user_id']))
49.              {
50.                  $user_id = $_SESSION['user_id'];
51.
52.                  $query = "INSERT INTO reservation (user_id, movieListing_id) VALUES (?, ?)";
53.                  $result = parameterizedQuery($dbc, $query, 'ii', $user_id, $movie_id);
54.
55.                  if (mysqli_errno($dbc))
56.                  {
57.                      trigger_error('Error querying database movieListing.reservation', E_USER_ERROR);
58.                  }
59.
60.                  $query = "UPDATE movieListing SET number_reserved = number_reserved + 1 WHERE id = ?";
61.                  $result = parameterizedQuery($dbc, $query, 'i', $movie_id);
62.
63.                  if (mysqli_errno($dbc))
64.                  {
65.                      trigger_error('Error querying database movieListing.reservation', E_USER_ERROR);
66.                  }
67.
68.                  if (isset($_SESSION['cart']))
69.                  {
70.                      array_push($_SESSION['cart'], $movie_id);
71.                  }
72.                  else
73.                  {
74.                      $_SESSION['cart'] = [$movie_id];
75.                  }
76.              }
77.
78.              header("Location: " . dirname($_SERVER['PHP_SELF']));
79.              exit;
80.
81.          elseif (isset($_GET['id_to_reserve'])):
82.      ?>
83.              <h3 class="text-success">Confirm Reservation of the Following Movie:</h3><br/>
84.      <?php
85.              $id = $_GET['id_to_reserve'];
86.
87.              $query = "SELECT * FROM movieListing WHERE id = ?";
88.              $result = parameterizedQuery($dbc, $query, 'i', $id);
89.
90.              if (mysqli_errno($dbc))
91.              {
92.                  trigger_error('Error querying database movieListing', E_USER_ERROR);
93.              }
94.
```

```
95.              if (mysqli_num_rows($result) == 1)
96.              {
97.                  $row = mysqli_fetch_assoc($result);
98.
99.                  $movie_image_file = $row['image_file'];
100.
101.                 if (empty($movie_image_file))
102.                 {
103.                     $movie_image_file = ML_UPLOAD_PATH . ML_DEFAULT_MOVIE_FILE_NAME;
104.                 }
105.          ?>
106.          <h1><?= $row['title'] ?></h1>
107.          <div class="row">
108.            <div class="col-2">
109.              <img src="<?= $movie_image_file ?>" class="img-thumbnail"
110.                  style="max-height: 200px;" alt="Movie image">
111.            </div>
112.            <div class="col">
113.              <table class="table table-striped">
114.                <tbody>
115.                  <tr>
116.                    <th scope="row">Rating</th>
117.                    <td><?= $row['rating'] ?></td>
118.                  </tr>
119.                  <tr>
120.                    <th scope="row">Director</th>
121.                    <td><?= $row['director'] ?></td>
122.                  </tr>
123.                  <tr>
124.                    <th scope="row">Running Time (minutes)</th>
125.                    <td><?= $row['running_time_in_minutes'] ?></td>
126.                  </tr>
127.                  <tr>
128.                    <th scope="row">Genre</th>
129.                    <td><?= $row['genre'] ?></td>
130.                  </tr>
131.                </tbody>
132.              </table>
133.            </div>
134.          </div>
135.          <p>
136.          <form method="POST" action="<?=$_SERVER['PHP_SELF'];?>">
137.            <button class="btn btn-success" type="submit" name="add_to_cart">Add to Cart</button>
138.            <input type="hidden" name="id" value="<?= $id ?>">
139.          </form>
140.          <?php
141.              }
143.              else
144.              {
144.                  ?>
```

```
145.                <h3>No Movie Details :-(</h3>
146.                    <?php
147.                    }
148.
149.            else: // Unintended page link - No movie to reseve, redirect back to index
150.
151.                header("Location: " . dirname($_SERVER['PHP_SELF']));
152.                exit();
153.            endif;
154.        ?>
155.        </div>
156.    </div>
157.    <script src="https://code.jquery.com/jquery-3.3.1.slim.min.js"
158.            integrity="sha384-q8i/X+965Dz00rT7abK41JStQIAqVgRVzpbzo5smXKp4YfRvH+8abtTE1Pi6jizo"
159.            crossorigin="anonymous"></script>
160.    <script src="https://cdnjs.cloudflare.com/ajax/libs/popper.js/1.14.6/umd/popper.min.js"
161.            integrity="sha384-wHAiFfRlMFy6i5SRaxvfOCifBUQy1xHdJ/yoi7FRNXMRBu5WHdZYu1hA6ZOblgut"
162.            crossorigin="anonymous"></script>
163.    <script src="https://stackpath.bootstrapcdn.com/bootstrap/4.2.1/js/bootstrap.min.js"
164.            integrity="sha384-B0UglyR+jN6CkvvICOB2joaf5I4l3gm9GU6Hc1og6Ls7i6U/mkkaduKaBhlAXv9k"
165.            crossorigin="anonymous"></script>
166.    </body>
167. </html>
```

# Adding Cart to Navigation Menu

Now that we can reserve movies and put them into a shopping cart, let's add a shopping cart icon in the upper right-hand corner of the navigation menu (Figure 25.16). We can also add a numerical representation of how many items are in the cart when a user adds a movie to their cart, as shown in Figure 25.17.

When the user selects this shopping cart icon, the application navigates to a shoppingcart.php script we create in the following section. But first, let's add the code to navmenu.php for our shopping cart.

We want the shopping cart icon to show if a user with user privileges is logged in and to indicate the number of items next to the icon if there is more than one item in the cart. We also want this icon to be a right-side menu item in the navbar to separate it from the other navigation links.

Figure 25.16.　　　　　　　　　　　　　　　Figure 25.17.

First open pagetitles.php and add the following MR_SHOPPING_CART_MOVIE_PAGE definition right after the MR_RESERVE_MOVIE_PAGE definition:

```
Unchanged Lines
  <?php
      // Page Titles
      define('MR_HOME_PAGE', 'Movie Reservations');
      ...
      define('MR_RESERVE_MOVIE_PAGE', 'Reserve Movie - Remove Movie');
+ Added Line
+     define('MR_SHOPPING_CART_MOVIE_PAGE', 'Movie Reservations - Shopping Cart');
```

Next, open up the navmenu.php script. Before closing the </nav> element, add the code in Listing 25.36, and I'll explain it below.

### Listing 25.36.

```
1.      </div>
2.    </div>
3.    <?php if (isset($_SESSION['user_access_privileges'])
4.            && $_SESSION['user_access_privileges'] == 'user'): ?>
5.    <div class="collapse navbar-collapse" id="navbarNavAltMarkup">
6.      <div class="nav navbar-nav ml-auto">
7.        <a class="nav-item nav-link<?= $page_title == MR_SHOPPING_CART_MOVIE_PAGE ? ' active' : '' ?>"
8.          href='shoppingcart.php'><i class='fas fa-shopping-cart'></i>
9.          <span class="badge badge-light">
10.            <?= isset($_SESSION['cart']) ? count($_SESSION['cart']) : '' ?>
11.          </span>
12.        </a>
13.      </div>
14.    </div>
15.    <?php endif; ?>
16. </nav>
```

Line 3 is the condition for checking if a user is logged in and has user access privileges.

Line 5 creates a new navbar group to the right of the existing navbar.

Line 6 sets up any nav items in this group to be right-justified.

Lines 7–12 show the shopping cart icon with a link to shoppingcart.php. Also, notice the ternary operation that adds a badge with the number of items in the cart if $_SESSION['cart'] exists. It is set to a span to the right of the shopping cart icon.

## Add a Script for a Shopping Cart

Now that we can put movies into a shopping cart, we need to create a web page that allows us to manage our cart. We need to be able to remove items from our cart and reserve all the movies in our cart.

Let's say we have added the outlined movies to our cart as seen on the homepage shown in Figure 25.18.

When we select the shopping cart icon in the upper right of the navbar as in Figure 25.19, a user should go to a shoppingcart.php page that looks like Figure 25.20.

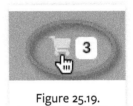

Figure 25.19.

Figure 25.18.

Figure 25.20.

Notice each movie can be deleted from the cart, so let's say we want to delete a movie as in Figure 25.21. That movie is removed from the cart and the reservation table. We're left with these movies (Figure 25.22) that we can reserve by pressing the "Reserve Movies" button.

> *Again, notice that the number of movies in our cart updates.*

When the user selects the "Reserve Movies" button, the user's cart is emptied. Then, the application displays the home page (Figure 25.23). You can see that the shopping cart is empty, and a new icon is displayed representing a movie projector (Figure 25.24). We will add this later when we update the navigation bar, and it will link to a page that will allow us to return movies that we've reserved.

> *There is a design flaw related to the fact that movies are reserved as soon as you add them into the cart. At the end of this chapter, I explain the flaws of this application and potential design solutions to consider.*

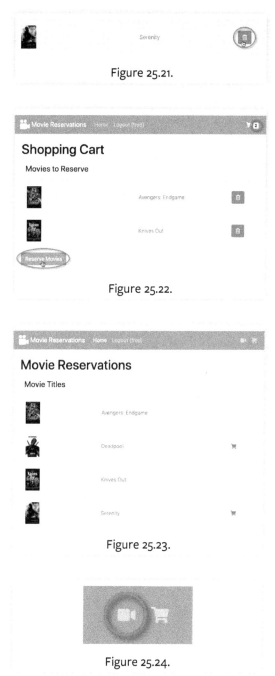

Figure 25.21.

Figure 25.22.

Figure 25.23.

Figure 25.24.

## Create Shopping Cart Page

First open pagetitles.php and add the following MR_SHOPPING_CART_MOVIE_PAGE definition right after the MR_RESERVE_MOVIE_PAGE definition:

```
Unchanged Lines
    <?php
        // Page Titles
        define('MR_HOME_PAGE', 'Movie Reservations');
        ...
        define('MR_RESERVE_MOVIE_PAGE', 'Movie Reservations - Reserve Movie');
+ Added Line
+       define('MR_SHOPPING_CART_MOVIE_PAGE', 'Movie Reservations - Shopping Cart');
```

The shopping cart page is a standard Bootstrap page. Create a new script called shoppingcart. php and add the code in Listing 25.37.

## Listing 25.37.

```
1.  <!DOCTYPE html>
2.  <?php
3.    require_once('pagetitles.php');
4.    $page_title = MR_SHOPPING_CART_MOVIE_PAGE;
5.  ?>
6.  <html>
7.    <head>
8.      <title><?= $page_title ?></title>
9.      <link rel="stylesheet"
10.          href="https://stackpath.bootstrapcdn.com/bootstrap/4.2.1/css/bootstrap.min.css"
11.          integrity="sha384-GJzZqFGwb1QTTN6wy59ffF1BuGJpLSa9DkKMp0DgiMDm4iYMj70gZWKYbI706tWS"
12.          crossorigin="anonymous">
13.    </head>
14.    <body>
15.  <?php
16.    require_once('navmenu.php');
17.  ?>
18.    <div class="card">
19.      <div class="card-body">
20.        <h1>Shopping Cart</h1>
21.        <?php
22.          require_once('dbconnection.php');
23.          require_once('movielistingfileconstants.php');
24.
25.          // Only display this page if the user is logged in
26.          if (!isset($_SESSION['user_id'])) :
27.
28.              header("Location: " . dirname($_SERVER['PHP_SELF']));
29.              exit;
```

```
30.
31.            elseif (isset($_POST_['id_to_delete'])):
32.
33.                // ...
34.
35.            elseif (isset($_POST['reserve_movies'])):
36.
37.                // ...
38.
39.            elseif (isset($_SESSION['cart']) && count($_SESSION['cart']) > 0):
40.
41.                // ...
42.
43.            else:
44.                ?>
45.                <hr/>
46.                <h3>No Movies in your cart :-(</h3>
47.            <?php
48.            endif;
49.          ?>
50.        </div>
51.    </div>
52.    <script src="https://code.jquery.com/jquery-3.3.1.slim.min.js"
53.            integrity="sha384-q8i/X+965Dz00rT7abK41JStQIAqVgRVzpbzo5smXKp4YfRvH+8abtTE1Pi6jizo"
54.            crossorigin="anonymous"></script>
55.    <script src="https://cdnjs.cloudflare.com/ajax/libs/popper.js/1.14.6/umd/popper.min.js"
56.            integrity="sha384-wHAiFfRlMFy6i5SRaxvfOCifBUQy1xHdJ/yoi7FRNXMRBu5WHdZYu1hA6ZOblgut"
57.            crossorigin="anonymous"></script>
58.    <script src="https://stackpath.bootstrapcdn.com/bootstrap/4.2.1/js/bootstrap.min.js"
59.            integrity="sha384-B0UglyR+jN6CkvvICOB2joaf5I4l3gm9GU6Hc1og6Ls7i6U/mkkaduKaBhlAXv9k"
60.            crossorigin="anonymous"></script>
61.    </body>
62. </html>
```

Again, this is a boilerplate script that should look familiar to you. Lines 3, 4, and 8 set and display the page title. Line 16 includes and displays the navbar. Line 20 displays "Shopping Cart" in an <h1> element set. Lines 22-23 include dbconnection.php, movielistingfileconstants.php.

Line 26 (if (!isset($_SESSION['user_id'])):) is the condition to check whether the user is not logged in. If the user is not logged in, line 26 redirects them to the home page.

Line 31 (elseif (isset($_POST['id_to_delete'])):) is the condition where the user selected a movie in the shopping cart to delete. This condition is where we remove the selected movie from the shopping cart and reservation table.

Line 35 (elseif (isset($_POST['reserve_movies'])):) is the condition to check if the user reserved the movies in their cart. This condition is where we delete the shopping cart and redirect the user back to the home page.

Line 39 (elseif (isset($_SESSION['cart']) && count($_SESSION['cart']) > 0):) is the condition to check that the user's shopping cart has movies in it. This condition is where we display a list of the movies in the user's cart with the ability to delete each movie. Displayed will also be a form with a button for reserving the movies in the cart.

Line 43 (else:) is a 'catch-all' condition indicating there are no movies in the user's cart, so line 43 will display there are no movies in the cart.

The rest of the code is the standard Bootstrap boilerplate script inclusions.

## Add Form for Reserving Movies

Let's add the following code for the shopping cart and the form for reserving the movies into the condition (elseif (isset($_SESSION['cart']) && count($_SESSION['cart']) > 0):). I will explain the code in Listing 25.38 below.

### Listing 25.38.

```
1.   elseif (isset($_SESSION['cart']) && count($_SESSION['cart']) > 0):
2.
3.       $dbc = mysqli_connect(DB_HOST, DB_USER, DB_PASSWORD, DB_NAME)
4.           or trigger_error(
5.               'Error connecting to MySQL server for' . DB_NAME,
6.               E_USER_ERROR
7.           );
8.
9.       $user_id = $_SESSION['user_id'];
10.
11.      $query = "SELECT movieListing.id, movieListing.title, movieListing.image_file
12.          FROM movieListing
13.              INNER JOIN reservation ON movieListing.id = reservation.movieListing_id
14.              WHERE reservation.user_id = ?";
15.
16.      $result = parameterizedQuery($dbc, $query, 'i', $user_id);
17.
18.      if(mysqli_errno($dbc))
19.      {
20.          trigger_error('Error querying database movieListing', E_USER_ERROR);
21.      }
22.
23.      if (mysqli_num_rows($result) > 0):
24.  ?>
```

```php
25.    <table class="table table-striped table-hover">
26.      <thead>
27.        <tr>
28.          <th scope="col"><h4>Movies to Reserve</h4></th>
29.          <th scope="col"></th>
30.          <th scope="col"></th>
31.        </tr>
32.      </thead>
33.      <tbody>
34.        <?php
35.
36.            while ($row = mysqli_fetch_assoc($result))
37.            {
38.                // Only display what's in the shopping cart
39.                if (array_search($row['id'], $_SESSION['cart']) !== false)
40.                {
41.                    $movie_image_file = $row['image_file'];
42.
43.                    if (empty($movie_image_file))
44.                    {
45.                        $movie_image_file = ML_UPLOAD_PATH . ML_DEFAULT_MOVIE_FILE_NAME;
46.                    }
47.
48.                    $movie_title_row = "<tr><td><img src=" . $movie_image_file . " class='img-thumbnail'"
49.                        . "style='max-height: 75px;' alt='Movie image'></td>"
50.                        . "<td class='align-middle'><a class='nav-link' href='moviedetails.php?id="
51.                        . $row['id'] . "'>" . $row['title'] ."</a></td>";
52.
53.                    $movie_title_row .= "<td class='align-middle'><form method='POST' action="
54.                        . $_SERVER['PHP_SELF'] . "'><button class='btn btn-danger' type='submit' "
55.                        . "name='id_to_delete' value='" . $row['id'] . "'>"
56.                        . "<i class='far fa-trash-alt'></i></button></form></td>";
57.
58.                    $movie_title_row .= "</tr>";
59.
60.                    echo $movie_title_row;
61.                }
62.            }
63.        ?>
64.      </tbody>
65.    </table>
66.    <form method="POST" action="<?= $_SERVER['PHP_SELF'] ?>">
67.      <button class="btn btn-success" type="submit" name="reserve_movies">Reserve Movies</button>
68.    </form>
69.    <?php
70.        else:
71.    ?>
72.    <h3>No Movies in your cart :-(</h3>
73. <?php
74.        endif;
75.    else:
```

After connecting to the `movieListing` database in line 3, we create an `INNER JOIN` query of the `movieListing` and `reservation` tables on lines 11–14 that returns the `id`, `title`, and `image_file` for each movie the user has reserved.

Assuming the query returns at least one movie (line 23), lines 25–65 display a table containing all the movies in the user's cart. Because the query returns all the movies from the `reservation` table, we need to keep only the ones in the cart. This distinction is important because the user might already have movies on reserve, which we display elsewhere.

Let's take a closer look at lines 36–62. Line 36 iterates through each reservation for the user. However, line 39 (`if (array_search($row['id'], $_SESSION['cart']) !== false)`) only allows the display of reservation rows that are also contained in the user's shopping cart, which are handled by lines 41–60.

On lines 48–51, we display the image and the title of the movie that links back to the `moviedetails.php` script with the movie ID as a query parameter:

```
$movie_title_row = "<tr><td><img src=" . $movie_image_file . " class='img-thumbnail'"
    . "style='max-height: 75px;' alt='Movie image'></td>"
    . "<td class='align-middle'><a class='nav-link' href='moviedetails.php?id="
    . $row['id'] . "'>" . $row['title'] ."</a></td>";
```

Notice on line 53 that the delete button in a form added to `$movie_title_row` links back to this page with a value of `id_to_delete` set to the movie ID:

```
$movie_title_row .= "<td class='align-middle'><form method='POST' action="
    . $_SERVER['PHP_SELF'] . "><button class='btn btn-danger' type='submit' "
    . "name='id_to_delete' value='" . $row['id'] . "'>"
    . "<i class='far fa-trash-alt'></i></button></form></td>";
```

Also, note that I'm using the Font Awesome icon for the trash can with a red background as in Figure 25.25.

Figure 25.25.

Lines 66–68 display a form with a "Reserve Movies" button with the `name` attribute set to `reserve_movies`.

Line 70 is the condition where the query returned no reservations, so line 72 displays that there are no movies in the cart.

## Removing a Movie from Cart

If a user changes their mind and doesn't want a movie, we need to remove it from their shopping cart and the reservation table. Add the code in Listing 25.39 into the condition (elseif (isset($_POST['id_to_delete'])):). I explain the code afterward.

### Listing 25.39.

```php
1. elseif (isset($_POST['id_to_delete'])):
2.
3.     $movie_to_delete = $_POST['id_to_delete'];
4.
5.     $dbc = mysqli_connect(DB_HOST, DB_USER, DB_PASSWORD, DB_NAME)
6.             or trigger_error(
7.                 'Error connecting to MySQL server for' . DB_NAME,
8.                 E_USER_ERROR
9.             );
10.
11.    $user_id = $_SESSION['user_id'];
12.
13.    $query = "DELETE FROM reservation
14.            WHERE user_id = ? AND movieListing_id = ?";
15.    $result = parameterizedQuery($dbc, $query, 'ii', $user_id, $movie_to_delete);
16.
17.    if (mysqli_errno($dbc))
18.    {
19.        trigger_error('Error querying database movieListing', E_USER_ERROR);
20.    }
21.
22.    $query = "UPDATE movieListing SET number_reserved = number_reserved - 1
23.            WHERE id = ?";
24.    $result = parameterizedQuery($dbc, $query, 'i', $movie_to_delete);
25.
26.    if (mysqli_errno($dbc))
27.    {
28.        trigger_error('Error querying database movieListing', E_USER_ERROR);
29.    }
30.
31.    if (($key = array_search($movie_to_delete, $_SESSION['cart'])) !== false)
32.    {
33.        unset($_SESSION['cart'][$key]);
34.    }
35.
36.    header("Location: " . $_SERVER['PHP_SELF']);
37.    exit;
38.
39. elseif (isset($_POST['reserve_movies'])):
```

After connecting to the movieListing database in line 5, we create a query to delete the reservation for this movie in lines 13-14 and perform the query in line 15.

In line 22, we create a query to decrement the number of reserved movies for this title and perform the query in line 24.

In line 31, we search for the key associated with the movie ID we want to delete, and in line 33, remove it from the user's cart.

Finally, line 36 redirects the browser to this shopping cart page. When that page loads, the updated shopping cart contents are refreshed in the table.

### Add Code for Reserving Movies in Cart

When the user reserves the movies in their cart, execution resumes in the (elseif (isset($_POST['reserve_movies'])):) condition. Because we've already added their movies to the reservation table, here we delete the shopping cart session variable, in effect emptying it, and redirect the user back to the home page.

Add the code from Listing 25.40 to this condition.

### Listing 25.40.

```
1. elseif (isset($_POST['reserve_movies'])):
2.
3.     // Delete the shopping cart (it's already in the reservation table),
4.     // and route back to the Home page
5.     unset($_SESSION['cart']);
6.
7.     header("Location: " . dirname($_SERVER['PHP_SELF']));
8.     exit;
9.
10. elseif (isset($_SESSION['cart']) && count($_SESSION['cart']) > 0):
```

## Complete Code Listing

Listing 25.41 is the complete listing for the shoppingcart.php page.

### Listing 25.41.

```
1.  <!DOCTYPE html>
2.  <?php
3.    require_once('pagetitles.php');
4.    $page_title = MR_SHOPPING_CART_MOVIE_PAGE;
5.  ?>
6.  <html>
7.    <head>
8.      <title><?= $page_title ?></title>
9.      <link rel="stylesheet"
10.           href="https://stackpath.bootstrapcdn.com/bootstrap/4.2.1/css/bootstrap.min.css"
11.           integrity="sha384-GJzZqFGwb1QTTN6wy59ffF1BuGJpLSa9DkKMp0DgiMDm4iYMj70gZWKYbI706tWS"
12.           crossorigin="anonymous">
13.    </head>
14.    <body>
15.  <?php
16.    require_once('navmenu.php');
17.  ?>
18.    <div class="card">
19.      <div class="card-body">
20.        <h1>Shopping Cart</h1>
21.        <?php
22.          require_once('dbconnection.php');
23.          require_once('movielistingfileconstants.php');
24.
25.          // Only display this page if the user is logged in
26.          if (!isset($_SESSION['user_id'])):
27.
28.              header("Location: " . dirname($_SERVER['PHP_SELF']));
29.              exit;
30.          elseif (isset($_POST['id_to_delete'])):
31.
32.              $movie_to_delete = $_POST['id_to_delete'];
33.
34.              $dbc = mysqli_connect(DB_HOST, DB_USER, DB_PASSWORD, DB_NAME)
35.                  or trigger_error(
36.                      'Error connecting to MySQL server for' . DB_NAME,
37.                      E_USER_ERROR
38.                  );
39.
40.              $user_id = $_SESSION['user_id'];
41.
42.              $query = "DELETE FROM reservation WHERE user_id = ? AND movieListing_id = ?";
43.              $result = parameterizedQuery($dbc, $query, 'ii', $user_id, $movie_to_delete);
44.
```

```php
45.             if (mysqli_errno($dbc))
46.             {
47.                 trigger_error('Error querying database movieListing', E_USER_ERROR);
48.             }
49.
50.             $query = "UPDATE movieListing SET number_reserved = number_reserved - 1 WHERE id = ?";
51.             $result = parameterizedQuery($dbc, $query, 'i', $movie_to_delete);
52.
53.             if (mysqli_errno($dbc))
54.             {
55.                 trigger_error('Error querying database movieListing', E_USER_ERROR);
56.             }
57.
58.             if (($key = array_search($movie_to_delete, $_SESSION['cart'])) !== false)
59.             {
60.                 unset($_SESSION['cart'][$key]);
61.             }
62.
63.             header("Location: " . $_SERVER['PHP_SELF']);
64.             exit;
65.
66.         elseif (isset($_POST['reserve_movies'])):
67.
68.             // Delete the shopping cart (it's already in the reservation table),
69.             // and route back to the Home page
70.             unset($_SESSION['cart']);
71.
72.             header("Location: " . dirname($_SERVER['PHP_SELF']));
73.             exit;
74.
75.         elseif (isset($_SESSION['cart']) && count($_SESSION['cart']) > 0):
76.
77.             $dbc = mysqli_connect(DB_HOST, DB_USER, DB_PASSWORD, DB_NAME)
78.                     or trigger_error(
79.                         'Error connecting to MySQL server for' . DB_NAME,
80.                         E_USER_ERROR
81.                     );
82.
83.             $user_id = $_SESSION['user_id'];
84.
85.             $query = "SELECT movieListing.id, movieListing.title, movieListing.image_file
86.                     FROM movieListing
87.                         INNER JOIN reservation ON movieListing.id = reservation.movieListing_id
88.                     WHERE reservation.user_id = ?";
89.             $result = parameterizedQuery($dbc, $query, 'i', $user_id);
90.
91.             if (mysqli_errno($dbc))
92.             {
93.                 trigger_error('Error querying database movieListing', E_USER_ERROR);
94.             }
```

```php
95.
96.                    if (mysqli_num_rows($result) > 0):
97.              ?>
98.              <table class="table table-striped table-hover">
99.                <thead>
100.                  <tr>
101.                    <th scope="col"><h4>Movies to Reserve</h4></th>
102.                    <th scope="col"></th>
103.                    <th scope="col"></th>
104.                  </tr>
105.                </thead>
106.                <tbody>
107.                  <?php
108.
109.                    while ($row = mysqli_fetch_assoc($result))
110.                    {
111.                        // Only display what's in the shopping cart
112.                        if (array_search($row['id'], $_SESSION['cart']) !== false)
113.                        {
114.                            $movie_image_file = $row['image_file'];
115.
116.                            if (empty($movie_image_file))
117.                            {
118.                                $movie_image_file = ML_UPLOAD_PATH . ML_DEFAULT_MOVIE_FILE_NAME;
119.                            }
120.
121.                            $movie_title_row = "<tr><td><img src=" . $movie_image_file . " class='img-thumbnail'"
122.                                . "style='max-height: 75px;' alt='Movie image'></td>"
123.                                . "<td class='align-middle'><a class='nav-link' href='moviedetails.php?id="
124.                                . $row['id'] . "'>" . $row['title'] ."</a></td>";
125.
126.                            $movie_title_row .= "<td class='align-middle'><form method='POST' action="
127.                                . $_SERVER['PHP_SELF'] . "><button class='btn btn-danger' type='submit' "
128.                                . "name='id_to_delete' value='" . $row['id'] . "'>"
129.                                . "<i class='far fa-trash-alt'></i></button></form></td>";
130.
131.                            $movie_title_row .= "</tr>";
132.
133.                            echo $movie_title_row;
134.                        }
135.                    }
136.                  ?>
137.                </tbody>
138.              </table>
139.              <form method="POST" action="<?= $_SERVER['PHP_SELF'] ?>">
140.                <button class="btn btn-success" type="submit" name="reserve_movies">Reserve Movies</button>
141.              </form>
142.              <?php
143.                  else:
144.              ?>
```

```
145.                <h3>No Movies in your cart :-(</h3>
146.            <?php
147.                endif;
148.            else:
149.                ?>
150.                <hr/>
151.                <h3>No Movies in your cart :-(</h3>
152.            <?php
153.                endif;
154.            ?>
155.        </div>
156.    </div>
157.    <script src="https://code.jquery.com/jquery-3.3.1.slim.min.js"
158.            integrity="sha384-q8i/X+965Dz00rT7abK41JStQIAqVgRVzpbzo5smXKp4YfRvH+8abtTE1Pi6jizo"
159.            crossorigin="anonymous"></script>
160.    <script src="https://cdnjs.cloudflare.com/ajax/libs/popper.js/1.14.6/umd/popper.min.js"
161.            integrity="sha384-wHAiFfRlMFy6i5SRaxvfOCifBUQy1xHdJ/yoi7FRNXMRBu5WHdZYu1hA6ZObLgut"
162.            crossorigin="anonymous"></script>
163.    <script src="https://stackpath.bootstrapcdn.com/bootstrap/4.2.1/js/bootstrap.min.js"
164.            integrity="sha384-B0UglyR+jN6CkvvICOB2joaf5I4l3gm9GU6Hc1og6Ls7i6U/mkkaduKaBhlAXv9k"
165.            crossorigin="anonymous"></script>
166.    </body>
167. </html>
```

# Navigating to Reserved Movies

We need to allow users to return reserved movies. Therefore we create another script and a projector icon link in the navbar to navigate to that page as shown in Figure 25.26.

Figure 25.26.

However, we only want to show this link if the user has movie reservations that are not already in their cart (i.e., movies they've already reserved). To do this, we need to create a function in queryutils.php that returns the number of reserved movies not in the user's cart. Open queryutils.php and let's create a function called numberOfMoviesReservedNotInCart(). It requires no parameters. Add the header and function shown in Listing 25.42.

## Listing 25.42.

```php
1.  <?php
2.  /**
3.   * Purpose:      Finds the number of movies reserved by current user not in cart
4.   *
5.   * Description: Based on the $_SESSION['user_id'] and the $_SESSION['cart']
6.   *              movie ids, query for the movies reserved by the user and compare
7.   *              to the movies in the cart. The number of movies reserved not in
8.   *              the cart are returned. NOTE, if $_SESSION['user_id'] is not set,
9.   *              0 is returned and if $_SESSION['cart'] is not set, the number
10.  *              of reservations for the user is returned (asumming
11.  *              $_SESSION['user_id'] is set).
12.  *
13.  * @return int  The number of movies reserved by the user not in the cart,
14.  *              or 0 if $_SESSION['user_id'] is not set.
15.  */
16.  function numberOfMoviesReservedNotInCart()
17.  {
18.      $number_of_movies_reserved = 0;
19.      $number_of_movies_reserved_in_cart = 0;
20.
21.      if (session_status() == PHP_SESSION_NONE)
22.      {
23.          session_start();
24.      }
25.
26.      if (!isset($_SESSION['user_id']))
27.      {
28.          return 0;
29.      }
30.
31.      require_once('dbconnection.php');
32.
33.      $dbc = mysqli_connect(DB_HOST, DB_USER, DB_PASSWORD, DB_NAME)
34.          or trigger_error(
35.              'Error connecting to MySQL server for' . DB_NAME,
36.              E_USER_ERROR
37.          );
38.
39.      $user_id = $_SESSION['user_id'];
40.
41.      $query = "SELECT movieListing_id FROM reservation WHERE user_id = ?";
42.      $result = parameterizedQuery($dbc, $query, 'i', $user_id)
43.          or trigger_error('Error querying database movieListing',
44.              E_USER_ERROR);
45.
```

```
46.    $number_of_movies_reserved = mysqli_num_rows($result);
47.
48.    if (!isset($_SESSION['cart']))
49.    {
50.        return $number_of_movies_reserved;
51.    }
52.
53.    $movies_in_cart = $_SESSION['cart'];
54.
55.    while ($row = mysqli_fetch_assoc($result))
56.    {
57.        // Accumulate count of reserved movies in cart
58.        if (array_search($row['movieListing_id'], $movies_in_cart) !== false)
59.        {
60.            $number_of_movies_reserved_in_cart++;
61.        }
62.    }
63.
64.    return $number_of_movies_reserved - $number_of_movies_reserved_in_cart;
65. }
```

This function queries the reservation table of the Movie database for all the rows containing the given user_id. In line 46, we get the total number of matching rows. Lines 55–62 accumulate the number of movies in the user's cart that do not match any of the movies the user currently has in the reservation table. This number is returned.

Now open pagetitles.php and add the following MR_RESERVED_MOVIES_PAGE definition right after the MR_SHOPPING_CART_MOVIE_PAGE definition:

```
Unchanged Lines
  <?php
      // Page Titles
      define('MR_HOME_PAGE', 'Movie Reservations');
      ...
      define('MR_SHOPPING_CART_MOVIE_PAGE', 'Movie Reservations - Shopping Cart');
+ Added Line
+     define('MR_RESERVED_MOVIES_PAGE', 'Movie Reservations - Reserved Movies');
```

Next, open up the navmenu.php script. Right before the <a class="nav-item nav-link<?= $page_title == MR_SHOPPING_CART_MOVIE_PAGE ...</a> element, and after the <div class="nav navbar-nav ml-auto">, add the code in Listing 25.43.

## Listing 25.43.

```
1.    Unchanged Lines
2.        <div class="collapse navbar-collapse" id="navbarNavAltMarkup">
3.          <div class="nav navbar-nav ml-auto">
4.  + Added Line
5.  +        <?php if (numberOfMoviesReservedNotInCart() > 0): ?>
6.  +          <a class="nav-item nav-link<?= $page_title == MR_RESERVED_MOVIES_PAGE ? ' active' : '' ?>"
7.  +              href='reservedmovies.php'><i class="fas fa-video"></i></a>
8.  +        <?php endif; ?>
9.    Unchanged Lines
10.          <a class="nav-item nav-link<?= $page_title == MR_SHOPPING_CART_MOVIE_PAGE ? ' active' : '' ?>"
11.             href='shoppingcart.php'><i class='fas fa-shopping-cart'></i> <span class="badge badge-light">
12.             <?= isset($_SESSION['cart']) ? count($_SESSION['cart']) : '' ?></span></a>
13.        </div>
14.      </div>
```

The first condition (`<?php if (numberOfMoviesReservedNotInCart() > 0): ?>`), only allows the code inside this condition to execute if there are reservations the user made that are not currently in their cart.

The (`<a class="nav-item nav-link<?= $page_title == MR_RESERVED_MOVIES_PAGE ...</a>`), is the standard ternary operation that shows the projector icon link either active or not depending on whether the reservedmovies.php script is being displayed or not.

> *The projector icon is the Font Awesome "fa-video" icon which is free to use.*

# Showing and Returning Reserved Movies

When the user clicks on the projector icon, their browser takes them to a reservedmovies.php page (we create here). We want this page to show a listing of the movies, a link to the movie details, a button for each movie to return it, and a form button to return all the movies. See Figure 25.27.

This way, movies can either be returned one at a time using the individual movie's return button as in Figure 25.28 or all of them can

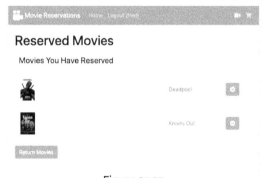

Figure 25.27.

be returned by pressing the **Return Movies** button on the form as shown in Figure 25.29

Figure 25.28.

Figure 25.29.

## Create Boilerplate Reserved Movies Page and Logic

The reserved movies page is a standard Bootstrap page. Create a new script called reservedmovies.php and the code shown in Listing 25.44.

### Listing 25.44.

```php
1.  <!DOCTYPE html>
2.  <?php
3.    require_once('pagetitles.php');
4.    $page_title = MR_RESERVED_MOVIES_PAGE;
5.  ?>
6.  <html>
7.    <head>
8.      <title><?= $page_title ?></title>
9.      <link rel="stylesheet"
10.         href="https://stackpath.bootstrapcdn.com/bootstrap/4.2.1/css/bootstrap.min.css"
11.         integrity="sha384-GJzZqFGwb1QTTN6wy59ffF1BuGJpLSa9DkKMp0DgiMDm4iYMj70gZWKYbI706tWS"
12.         crossorigin="anonymous">
13.    </head>
14.    <body>
15.    <?php
16.      require_once('navmenu.php');
17.    ?>
18.      <div class="card">
19.        <div class="card-body">
20.          <h1>Reserved Movies</h1>
21.          <?php
22.            require_once('dbconnection.php');
23.            require_once('movielistingfileconstants.php');
24.
25.            // Only display this page if the user is logged in
26.            if (!isset($_SESSION['user_id'])) :
27.
28.                header("Location: " . dirname($_SERVER['PHP_SELF']));
29.                exit;
30.
31.            elseif (isset($_POST['id_to_check_in'])):
32.
33.                // ...
34.
```

```
35.              elseif (isset($_POST['check_in_movies'])):
36.
37.                  // ...
38.
39.              else:
40.
41.                  // ...
42.
43.              endif;
44.          ?>
45.      </div>
46.  </div>
47.  <script src="https://code.jquery.com/jquery-3.3.1.slim.min.js"
48.          integrity="sha384-q8i/X+965Dz00rT7abK41JStQIAqVgRVzpbzo5smXKp4YfRvH+8abtTE1Pi6jizo"
49.          crossorigin="anonymous"></script>
50.  <script src="https://cdnjs.cloudflare.com/ajax/libs/popper.js/1.14.6/umd/popper.min.js"
51.          integrity="sha384-wHAiFfRlMFy6i5SRaxvfOCifBUQy1xHdJ/yoi7FRNXMRBu5WHdZYu1hA6ZOblgut"
52.          crossorigin="anonymous"></script>
53.  <script src="https://stackpath.bootstrapcdn.com/bootstrap/4.2.1/js/bootstrap.min.js"
54.          integrity="sha384-B0UglyR+jN6CkvvICOB2joaf5I4l3gm9GU6Hc1og6Ls7i6U/mkkaduKaBhlAXv9k"
55.          crossorigin="anonymous"></script>
56.  </body>
57. </html>
```

Again, this is a boilerplate script that should look familiar to you. Lines 3, 4, and 8 set and display the page title. Line 16 includes and displays the navbar. Line 20 displays "Reserved Movies" in an <h1> element set. Lines 22-23 include dbconnection.php, movielistingfileconstants.php, queryutils.php.

Line 26 (if (!isset($_SESSION['user_id'])):) is the condition to check whether the user is not logged in. If the user is not logged in, line 28 redirects the user back to the home page.

Line 31 (elseif (isset($_POST['id_to_check_in'])):) is the condition where the user selected a movie in the reserved movie list to return. This condition is where we remove the selected movie from the reservation table and update the number of copies reserved for this movie.

Line 35 (elseif (isset($_POST['check_in_movies'])):) is the condition to check if the user selected the **Return Movies** to return all the movies they have reserved. This condition is where we update the number of copies for all movies being returned and remove all the user's movie reservations from the reservation table, then redirect them back to the home page.

Line 39 (else:) is a 'catch-all' condition. This condition displays a list of the movies the user has reserved along with a button for returning each movie. We also show a form with a button for returning all the reserved movies.

The rest of the code is the standard Bootstrap boilerplate script inclusions.

## Listing Reserved Movies

Let's add the code in Listing 25.45 for listing all the movies the user has reserved and the form for returning the movies into the catch-all condition (else:). I will explain the code below:

### Listing 25.45.

```
1.    else:
2.
3.        $dbc = mysqli_connect(DB_HOST, DB_USER, DB_PASSWORD, DB_NAME)
4.            or trigger_error(
5.               'Error connecting to MySQL server for' . DB_NAME,
6.               E_USER_ERROR
7.            );
8.
9.        $user_id = $_SESSION['user_id'];
10.
11.       $query = "SELECT movieListing.id, movieListing.title, movieListing.image_file
12.              FROM movieListing
13.                INNER JOIN reservation ON movieListing.id = reservation.movieListing_id
14.              WHERE reservation.user_id = ?";
15.
16.       $result = parameterizedQuery($dbc, $query, 'i', $user_id)
17.              or trigger_error(
18.           'Error querying database tables movieListing and reservation',
19.           E_USER_ERROR);
20.
21.       if (mysqli_num_rows($result) > 0):
22.   ?>
23.   <table class="table table-striped table-hover">
24.     <thead>
25.       <tr>
26.         <th scope="col"><h4>Movies You Have Reserved</h4></th>
27.         <th scope="col"></th>
28.         <th scope="col"></th>
29.       </tr>
30.     </thead>
31.     <tbody>
```

```php
32.          <?php
33.              while ($row = mysqli_fetch_assoc($result))
34.              {
35.                  // Only display what's NOT in the shopping cart
36.                  if (empty($_SESSION['cart'])
37.                      || array_search($row['id'], $_SESSION['cart']) === false)
38.                  {
39.                      $movie_image_file = $row['image_file'];
40.
41.                      if (empty($movie_image_file))
42.                      {
43.                          $movie_image_file = ML_UPLOAD_PATH . ML_DEFAULT_MOVIE_FILE_NAME;
44.                      }
45.
46.                      $movie_title_row = "<tr><td><img src=" . $movie_image_file
47.                          . " class='img-thumbnail' style='max-height: 75px;'"
48.                          . " alt='Movie image'></td>"
49.                          . "<td class='align-middle'><a class='nav-link' "
50.                          . " href='moviedetails.php?id="
51.                          . $row['id'] . "'>" . $row['title'] ."</a></td>";
52.
53.                      $movie_title_row .= "<td class='align-middle'><form method='POST' "
54.                          . "action=" . $_SERVER['PHP_SELF'] . ">"
55.                          . "<button class='btn btn-success' type='submit' "
56.                          . "name='id_to_check_in' value='" . $row['id'] . "'>"
57.                          . "<i class='fas fa-check-circle'></i></button></form></td>";
58.
59.                      $movie_title_row .= "</tr>";
60.
61.                      echo $movie_title_row;
62.                  }
63.              }
64.          ?>
65.          </tbody>
66.      </table>
67.      <form method="POST" action="<?= $_SERVER['PHP_SELF'] ?>">
68.        <button class="btn btn-success" type="submit"
69.              name="check_in_movies">Return Movies</button>
70.      </form>
71.      <?php
72.          else:
73.      ?>
74.      <h3>No Movies Reserved :-(</h3>
75. <?php
76.          endif;
77.      endif;
```

After connecting to the movieListing database in line 3, identical to what we did with the shopping cart, we create an INNER JOIN query of the movieListing and reservation tables on lines 11–14 that returns all the movies the user has reserved containing the id, title, and image_file for each movie.

Assuming the query returns at least one movie (line 21), lines 23–66 display a table containing all the movies the user has reserved (which does not include what the user currently has in their cart).

Let's take a closer look at lines 33–63. Line 33 iterates through each reservation for the user. However, lines 36–37 only allow the display of reservation rows that are not in the user's shopping cart, handled by lines 39–61.

On line 46, we display the image and the title of the movie that links back to the moviedetails.php script with the movie ID as a query parameter:

```
$movie_title_row = "<tr><td><img src=" . $movie_image_file
    . " class='img-thumbnail' style='max-height: 75px;'"
    . " alt='Movie image'></td>"
    . "<td class='align-middle'><a class='nav-link' "
    . " href='moviedetails.php?id="
    . $row['id'] . "'>" . $row['title'] ."</a></td>";
```

Notice on line 53 the checked circle button in a form added to $movie_title_row that links back to this page with a value of id_to_check set to the movie ID:

```
$movie_title_row .= "<td class='align-middle'><form method='POST' "
    . "action=" . $_SERVER['PHP_SELF'] . ">"
    . "<button class='btn btn-success' type='submit' "
    . "name='id_to_check_in' value='" . $row['id'] . "'>"
    . "<i class='fas fa-check-circle'></i></button></form></td>";
```

Note that I'm using the Font Awesome icon for the checked circle with a green background. See Figure 25.30.

Lines 67–70 display a form with a "Return Movies" button with the name attribute set to check_in_movies.

Line 72 is the condition where no reservations were returned from the query, so line 74 displays there are no movies reserved.

Figure 25.30.

## Add Code for Returning a Movie and Removing from reservation Table

When the user selects a movie to return, we need to remove the movie from the reservation table. Add the code in Listing 25.46 into the condition (elseif (isset($_POST['id_to_check_in'])):).

### Listing 25.46.

```
1. elseif (isset($_POST['id_to_check_in'])):
2.
3.    $movie_to_check_in = $_GET['id_to_check_in'];
4.
5.    $dbc = mysqli_connect(DB_HOST, DB_USER, DB_PASSWORD, DB_NAME)
6.            or trigger_error(
7.                'Error connecting to MySQL server for' . DB_NAME,
8.                E_USER_ERROR
9.            );
10.
11.   $user_id = $_SESSION['user_id'];
12.
13.   $query = "DELETE FROM reservation WHERE user_id = ? AND movieListing_id = ?";
14.
15.   parameterizedQuery($dbc, $query, 'ii', $user_id, $movie_to_check_in);
16.
17.   if (mysqli_errno($dbc))
18.   {
19.      trigger_error('Error querying database movieListing', E_USER_ERROR);
20.   }
21.
22.   $query = "UPDATE movieListing SET number_reserved = number_reserved - 1
23.            WHERE id = ?";
24.
25.   parameterizedQuery($dbc, $query, 'i', $movie_to_check_in);
26.
27.   if (mysqli_errno($dbc))
28.   {
29.      trigger_error('Error querying database movieListing', E_USER_ERROR);
30.   }
31.
32.   header("Location: " . $_SERVER['PHP_SELF']);
33.   exit;
34.
35. elseif (isset($_POST['check_in_movies'])):
```

After connecting to the movieListing database in line 5, we create a query to delete the reservation for this movie in line 13 and perform the query in line 15.

In lines 22-23, we create a query to decrement the number of reserved movies for this title and perform the query in line 25.

Finally, line 32 redirects to this shopping cart page, so the updated shopping cart contents are displayed in the table.

### Add Code for Returning All Movies

When the user returns the movies, execution will resume in the (elseif (isset($_POST['check_in_movies'])):) condition. This clause is where we update the number of copies reserved for each movie, remove all the movies the user has reserved from the reservation table, and redirect the user to the home page.

Add the code in Listing 25.47 to this condition.

### Listing 25.47.

```
1. elseif (isset($_POST['check_in_movies'])):
2.
3.     // Remove all reservations and update number of reserved copies
4.     // in movieListing for returned movies
5.     $dbc = mysqli_connect(DB_HOST, DB_USER, DB_PASSWORD, DB_NAME)
6.           or trigger_error(
7.               'Error connecting to MySQL server for' . DB_NAME,
8.                E_USER_ERROR
9.           );
10.
11.    $user_id = $_SESSION['user_id'];
12.
13.    $query = "SELECT movieListing_id FROM reservation WHERE user_id = ?";
14.
15.    $result = parameterizedQuery($dbc, $query, 'i', $user_id)
16.           or trigger_error('Error querying database table reservation', E_USER_ERROR);
17.
18.    // Decrement number of reserved in movieListing
19.    while ($row = mysqli_fetch_assoc($result))
20.    {
21.       $movie_to_check_in = $row['movieListing_id'];
22.
23.       $query = "UPDATE movieListing
24.               SET number_reserved = number_reserved - 1 WHERE id = ?";
25.
26.       parameterizedQuery($dbc, $query, 'i', $movie_to_check_in);
27.
```

```
28.        if (mysqli_errno($dbc))
29.        {
30.            trigger_error('Error querying database table movieListing', E_USER_ERROR);
31.        }
32.    }
33.
34.    // Delete all reservations for this user
35.    $query = "DELETE FROM reservation WHERE user_id = ?";
36.
37.    parameterizedQuery($dbc, $query, 'i', $user_id);
38.
39.    if (mysqli_errno($dbc))
40.    {
41.        trigger_error('Error querying database table reservation', E_USER_ERROR);
42.    }
43.
44.    header("Location: " . dirname($_SERVER['PHP_SELF']));
45.    exit;
46.
47. else:
```

After connecting to the movieListing database in line 5, we create a query for all reservations for this user in line 13 and perform the query in line 15.

Lines 19–32 iterates through IDs from the reservation and decrements the number of copies reserved by 1 for each movie.

Line 35 is the query for deleting all the reservations for this user and is executed in line 37.

Finally, line 44 redirects the user to the home page.

## Complete Code Listing

Listing 25.48 is the complete listing for the reservedmovies.php page.

### Listing 25.48.

```php
1.  <!DOCTYPE html>
2.  <?php
3.    require_once('pagetitles.php');
4.    $page_title = MR_RESERVED_MOVIES_PAGE;
5.  ?>
6.  <html>
7.    <head>
8.      <title><?= $page_title ?></title>
9.      <link rel="stylesheet"
10.          href="https://stackpath.bootstrapcdn.com/bootstrap/4.2.1/css/bootstrap.min.css"
11.          integrity="sha384-GJzZqFGwb1QTTN6wy59ffF1BuGJpLSa9DkKMp0DgiMDm4iYMj70gZwKYbI706tW5"
12.          crossorigin="anonymous">
13.    </head>
14.    <body>
15.  <?php
16.    require_once('navmenu.php');
17.  ?>
18.      <div class="card">
19.        <div class="card-body">
20.          <h1>Reserved Movies</h1>
21.          <?php
22.              require_once('dbconnection.php');
23.              require_once('movielistingfileconstants.php');
24.              require_once('queryutils.php');
25.
26.              // Only display this page if the user is logged in
27.              if (!isset($_SESSION['user_id'])) :
28.
29.                  header("Location: " . dirname($_SERVER['PHP_SELF']));
30.                  exit;
31.
32.              elseif (isset($_POST['id_to_check_in'])):
33.
34.                  $movie_to_check_in = $_POST['id_to_check_in'];
35.
36.                  $dbc = mysqli_connect(DB_HOST, DB_USER, DB_PASSWORD, DB_NAME)
37.                      or trigger_error(
38.                          'Error connecting to MySQL server for' . DB_NAME, E_USER_ERROR
39.                      );
40.
41.                  $user_id = $_SESSION['user_id'];
```

```
42.
43.                  $query = "DELETE FROM reservation WHERE user_id = ? AND movieListing_id = ?";
44.
45.                  parameterizedQuery($dbc, $query, 'ii', $user_id, $movie_to_check_in);
46.
47.                  if (mysqli_errno($dbc))
48.                  {
49.                      trigger_error('Error querying database movieListing', E_USER_ERROR);
50.                  }
51.
52.                  $query = "UPDATE movieListing SET number_reserved = number_reserved - 1 WHERE id = ?";
53.
54.                  parameterizedQuery($dbc, $query, 'i', $movie_to_check_in);
55.
56.                  if (mysqli_errno($dbc))
57.                  {
58.                      trigger_error('Error querying database movieListing', E_USER_ERROR);
59.                  }
60.
61.                  header("Location: " . $_SERVER['PHP_SELF']);
62.                  exit;
63.
64.          elseif (isset($_POST['check_in_movies'])):
65.
66.                  // Remove all reservations and update number of reserved copies
67.                  // in movieListing for returned movies
68.                  $dbc = mysqli_connect(DB_HOST, DB_USER, DB_PASSWORD, DB_NAME)
69.                          or trigger_error(
70.                              'Error connecting to MySQL server for' . DB_NAME, E_USER_ERROR
71.                          );
72.
73.                  $user_id = $_SESSION['user_id'];
74.
75.                  $query = "SELECT movieListing_id FROM reservation WHERE user_id = ?";
76.
77.                  $result = parameterizedQuery($dbc, $query, 'i', $user_id)
78.                          or trigger_error('Error querying database table reservation', E_USER_ERROR);
79.
80.                  // Decrement number of reserved in movieListing
81.                  while ($row = mysqli_fetch_assoc($result))
82.                  {
83.                      $movie_to_check_in = $row['movieListing_id'];
84.
85.                      $query = "UPDATE movieListing SET number_reserved = number_reserved - 1 WHERE id = ?";
86.
87.                      parameterizedQuery($dbc, $query, 'i', $movie_to_check_in);
88.
```

```
89.                 if (mysqli_errno($dbc))
90.                 {
91.                     trigger_error('Error querying database table movieListing', E_USER_ERROR);
92.                 }
93.             }
94.
95.             // Delete all reservations for this user
96.             $query = "DELETE FROM reservation WHERE user_id = ?";
97.
98.             parameterizedQuery($dbc, $query, 'i', $user_id);
99.
100.             if (mysqli_errno($dbc))
101.             {
102.                 trigger_error('Error querying database table reservation', E_USER_ERROR);
103.             }
104.
105.             header("Location: " . dirname($_SERVER['PHP_SELF']));
106.             exit;
107.
108.         else:
109.
110.             $dbc = mysqli_connect(DB_HOST, DB_USER, DB_PASSWORD, DB_NAME)
111.                     or trigger_error(
112.                         'Error connecting to MySQL server for' . DB_NAME,
113.                         E_USER_ERROR
114.                     );
115.
116.             $user_id = $_SESSION['user_id'];
117.
118.             $query = "SELECT movieListing.id, movieListing.title, movieListing.image_file
119.                     FROM movieListing
120.                         INNER JOIN reservation ON movieListing.id = reservation.movieListing_id
121.                     WHERE reservation.user_id = ?";
122.
123.             $result = parameterizedQuery($dbc, $query, 'i', $user_id)
124.                     or trigger_error(
125.                 'Error querying database tables movieListing and reservation', _USER_ERROR);
126.
127.             if (mysqli_num_rows($result) > 0):
128.         ?>
129.         <table class="table table-striped table-hover">
130.           <thead>
131.             <tr>
132.               <th scope="col"><h4>Movies You Have Reserved</h4></th>
133.               <th scope="col"></th>
134.               <th scope="col"></th>
135.             </tr>
```

```php
136.            </thead>
137.            <tbody>
138.            <?php
139.              while($row = mysqli_fetch_assoc($result))
140.              {
141.                // Only display what's NOT in the shopping cart
142.                if (empty($_SESSION['cart'])
143.                    || array_search($row['id'], $_SESSION['cart']) === false)
144.                {
145.                  $movie_image_file = $row['image_file'];
146.
147.                  if (empty($movie_image_file))
148.                  {
149.                    $movie_image_file = ML_UPLOAD_PATH . ML_DEFAULT_MOVIE_FILE_NAME;
150.                  }
151.
152.                  $movie_title_row = "<tr><td><img src=" . $movie_image_file
153.                    . " class='img-thumbnail' style='max-height: 75px;'"
154.                    . " alt='Movie image'></td>"
155.                    . "<td class='align-middle'><a class='nav-link' "
156.                    . " href='moviedetails.php?id="
157.                    . $row['id'] . "'>" . $row['title'] ."</a></td>";
158.
159.                  $movie_title_row .= "<td class='align-middle'><form method='POST' "
160.                    . "action=" . $_SERVER['PHP_SELF'] . ">"
161.                    . "<button class='btn btn-success' type='submit' "
162.                    . "name='id_to_check_in' value='" . $row['id'] . "'>"
163.                    . "<i class='fas fa-check-circle'></i></button></form></td>";
164.
165.                  $movie_title_row .= "</tr>";
166.
167.                  echo $movie_title_row;
168.                }
169.              }
170.            ?>
171.            </tbody>
172.          </table>
173.          <form method="POST" action="<?= $_SERVER['PHP_SELF'] ?>">
174.            <button class="btn btn-success" type="submit"
175.                name="check_in_movies">Return Movies</button>
176.          </form>
177.          <?php
178.            else:
179.          ?>
180.          <h3>No Movies Reserved :-(</h3>
181.      <?php
182.          endif;
```

```
183.             endif;
184.         ?>
185.     </div>
186.     </div>
187.     <script src="https://code.jquery.com/jquery-3.3.1.slim.min.js"
188.         integrity="sha384-q8i/X+965Dz00rT7abK41JStQIAqVgRVzpbzo5smXKp4YfRvH+8abtTE1Pi6jizo"
189.         crossorigin="anonymous"></script>
190.     <script src="https://cdnjs.cloudflare.com/ajax/libs/popper.js/1.14.6/umd/popper.min.js"
191.         integrity="sha384-wHAiFfRlMFy6i5SRaxvfOCifBUQy1xHdJ/yoi7FRNXMRBu5WHdZYu1hA6ZOblgut"
192.         crossorigin="anonymous"></script>
193.     <script src="https://stackpath.bootstrapcdn.com/bootstrap/4.2.1/js/bootstrap.min.js"
194.         integrity="sha384-B0UglyR+jN6CkvvICOB2joaf5I4l3gm9GU6Hc1og6Ls7i.6U/mkkaduKaBhlAXv9k"
195.         crossorigin="anonymous"></script>
196.     </body>
197. </html>
```

# Features to Add

This code by no means is a complete and polished application. While working code is essential, there are always ways to improve it or adapt it to new uses. Several features could and should be added to improve the user experience and add robustness to the application. I've listed a few here below.

### Add Pagination of Movie Titles

As the movie reservation library grows, it would be good to add pagination to the application instead of listing all the movies in the database. Pagination would improve response time and reduce the amount of vertical scrolling needed to display the results on each page.

### Add a Search and Filter Movies Feature

Along with pagination, adding a search feature to limit results would add to the user experience. This feature can be a title search or maybe a director search. Along with this, adding the ability to filter movies of various ratings would be helpful too.

### Add Details to Movie Records

We can track more information about each movie than we do now. We can add fields for a release date, producer, actors, and more. You could even link to reviews or sites about the movie.

## Track Date of Reservation

Currently, the database does not track when a user checked out a movie or provide a due date for returning them. Adding these would allow administrators to ensure someone doesn't keep a movie copy out indefinitely.

## Add Reservation Management Features for Administrator

Many of the features that we developed for the Movie Reservation app focused on the user. To streamline site administration, it would be nice to have the following administrative features:

1. A table showing reserved movies
   - Clicking on a movie brings up a page listing each user that has each movie checked out
   - Clicking on a user links to the page listing only the movies that the user has reserved
2. A table listing users that have one or more movies reserved
   - Clicking on a user brings up a page listing the movies they have checked out
3. Ability to manage lost movies

# Flaws in This Application

There is quite a bit of duplicate code in some of these pages, especially the boilerplate Bootstrap links. You should move this duplicate code into its own header page to be included by all other scripts that need it.

There a several design issues with this application as well.

One problem is if a user has movies in their cart and they log out, the movies are reserved without the user actively reserving them. Putting a movie in the shopping cart actually reserves the movie in the reservation table. A better design for managing movies in a cart would have a database table that maintains movies that are currently in all users' shopping carts at any one time (i.e., multiple users are logged in adding movies to their carts). Then, we only create the reservation once they decided to reserve the movies in their cart. This change adds complexity but is a more robust solution by keeping shopping cart items out of the reservation table. Another potential solution is to remove all the reservations when users log out before reserving the movies in their shopping cart. It would also be a good idea to pop up a modal dialog letting the user know of the situation and allow them to either reserve the movies or continue to log out. The shopping table maintaining users' shopping carts is a better idea because it will enable users to keep things in their cart between logins. However, now we would have to manage the problem of a user keeping a movie in their cart, preventing other users from reserving it.

These are fun design and usability problems to consider with many different, acceptable solutions and trade-offs.

## Exercises

1. Add the reservation features, including a database table, changes to the add/edit pages, and allow users to reserve movies that have copies available for check out.
2. Add admin-only features for showing who's reserved movies.

# Chapter

# 26

# Introduction to Object-Oriented Programming in PHP

*"In the one and only true way. The object-oriented version of 'Spaghetti code' is, of course, 'Lasagna code'. (Too many layers)."*

–Roberto Waltman.

Object-Oriented Programming (OOP) is a programming paradigm that allows for a more modular way to develop programs. Many modern programming languages have OOP features, and PHP is no exception. There are many conceptual components to OOP. At its most basic level, it allows for combining what a program knows (its data) and what a program does (its functionality) into modular components. This approach is different from basic procedural-based programming, where you have many functions separated from the data that they typically work on. This chapter gives a brief overview of object-oriented programming using PHP.

Since this book covers web development using PHP, I cover the more common uses of OOP supported by the language. If you want to learn more about the principles and design practices of OOP, I would recommend David Kung's book: *Object-Oriented Software Engineering: An Agile Unified Methodology*[1] published by McGraw-Hill Education.

I briefly cover the following topics:

- Classes
- Properties
- Encapsulation using access modifiers
- Accessor Methods (Getters/Setters)
- The $this variable
- General Purpose Methods
- Instantiating and using a class
- Validating input to a Setter Method
- Inheritance
- Overriding Methods
- Constructors
- PHP Database Objects (PDO)

## Classes

Classes organize code into modular components. It is typical to put a single class into its own file. In PHP, you define a class using the class keyword:

```php
<?php
    class Radio
    {

    }
```

---

[1]  *Object-Oriented Software Engineering: An Agile Unified Methodology*: http://phpa.me/mhws-oop-engineering

In this example, we would probably want to name this file `Radio.php`.

Class names follow the same rules as variable names. However, unlike variable names, class names are not case-sensitive. In practice, the coding standard for naming classes is to start the first word with an upper-case letter and to start every word in the class name with an upper-case letter (i.e., `CustomerAccount`). This convention is known as "StudlyCaps."

One thing to keep in mind about classes is that they are like blueprints or recipes for PHP objects. We explore this later when discussing the difference between an instance of a class—known as an object—and the class definition itself.

## Properties

Of course, we need to add data to our classes. In some programming languages, these are called instance or class member variables. In PHP, we call them "properties."

Using our `Radio` example, here are a few properties:

```php
<?php
   class Radio
   {
      private $powered;   // true or false
      private $volume;    // 0 - 10
      private $channel;   // 535kHz - 1700kHz, 87.5MHz - 108MHz
   }
```

### On Class Design

*As I mentioned previously, at the most basic level, a class should define what a program knows (its data) and what a program does (its functionality). Ideally, in object design, you want to think of your class as a single thing. In this case, we are modeling the concept of a radio in software. Before writing any code, think about how one would interact with our radio. Since this is a simple example, we need our radio to know (i.e., hold data for) whether it is on or off, its volume, and what channel or frequency it is set to. Likewise, we also need functionality to turn on and off the radio, set its volume, and change its channel or frequency. The properties and methods your class needs should be informed by your software requirements. We will fill this in when we talk about methods.*

## Encapsulation Using Access Modifiers

So, what's the meaning of putting private before our properties?

The keyword private is what's known as an access modifier. PHP calls this "visibility"[2] and uses it to restrict access to properties and methods. There are three levels of access to properties and methods: private, protected, and public.

- private means only the code within the class can access a property or call a method.
- protected means only the code within this class or subclasses of it can gain access to the property or method.
- public means everyone can gain access to the property or method.

In object-oriented programming, it is a best practice to restrict access to your properties by making them private. Then, add public methods that grant read or write access to these properties. This is the principle of encapsulation and is one of the main pillars of OOP.

## Accessor Methods

To add functionality to our class, we create a method. A method is a fancy OOP term we use that means the same thing as a function, except that we are embedding our methods inside our class. The OOP idea behind methods is that they manipulate or get the data in our class.

If we want to manipulate the data in our Radio class, we need methods to set the data like channel or volume. Likewise, if we're going to retrieve data from our class, we need methods that get this data. We typically call these accessor methods getters and setters.

The convention used for creating getters and setters is to put either the word get or set in front of our property and capitalize the first letter of each word in the property (e.g., "camel case" style). We usually make the getters public, and we often make the setters public (see below).

> *Mutability and immutability in class design*
>
> *Although this is a more advanced topic, you should think about how code interacts with objects created from your classes during the object's life. You have the freedom to design a class that allows users of these objects to manipulate data within the object throughout the life of the object or only upon the creation of the object. This concept is known as*

---

[2] "visibility": https://www.php.net/language.oop5.visibility

*the "mutability" of your object. If you create ANY setters in your class with* public *access, your object is known to be mutable (i.e., changeable). Conversely, if you create ALL the setters in your class with* private—*or possibly* protected—*access, your object is known to be immutable (i.e., unchangeable). You might be asking, how do you even set the properties of an object if it is immutable? Immutable objects must have their properties set upon construction. Further on, I'll show you how to create a constructor. Immutable objects tend to be preferred because they've been shown to be less error-prone.*

So, to create getters for our Radio class we need the following methods:

- getPowered()
- getVolume()
- getChannel()

Listing 26.1 shows what they should look like.

## Listing 26.1.

```php
1.  <?php
2.     class Radio
3.     {
4.        private $powered;    // true or false
5.        private $volume;     // 0 - 10
6.        private $channel;    // 535kHz - 1700kHz, 87.5MHz - 108MHz
7.
8.        // Getters
9.        public function getPowered()
10.       {
11.          return $this->powered;
12.       }
13.
14.       public function getVolume()
15.       {
16.          return $this->volume;
17.       }
18.
19.       public function getChannel()
20.       {
21.          return $this->channel;
22.       }
23.    }
```

Note the getters have public access so users of our class can retrieve the state of the properties. Now let's take a look at the setters (Listing 26.2). Note the setters have public access,
which means objects created from this class will be mutable.

Listing 26.2.

```php
1. <?php
2.   class Radio
3.   {
4.       private $powered;   // true or false
5.       private $volume;    // 0 - 10
6.       private $channel;   // 535kHz - 1700kHz, 87.5MHz - 108MHz
7.
8.       // ...
9.
10.      // Setters
11.      public function setPowered($powered)
12.      {
13.          $this->powered = $powered;
14.      }
15.
16.      public function setVolume($volume)
17.      {
18.          $this->volume = $volume;
19.      }
20.
21.      public function setChannel($channel)
22.      {
23.          $this->channel = $channel;
24.      }
25.  }
```

# The $this Variable

In the above getters and setters, we made a reference to the $this variable:

```php
return $this->volume;
// ...
$this->volume = $volume;
```

The $this variable is a built-in variable available to all classes. It refers to the current object
of the class, or *this* specific instance of this class. To use a class, it has to be "instantiated."
The $this variable refers to just this particular instance of the class. -> is the object operator
and allows you to reference the properties or methods of a class by value. PHP requires
using $this-> to access these properties or methods, unlike other languages like Java.

## Why Don't Other Languages Require the $this Keyword?

Welp, that's a good question, and it's something PHP gets right. Other programming languages such as Java, C#, and C++ also use the this keyword to refer to class instance variables. However, it is not required to use this in these other languages. It is meant as a convenience to leave it out. I feel it is a mistake not to require the use of the this keyword. Consider the example written in Java from Listing 26.3.

### Listing 26.3.

```
 1. class Radio
 2. {
 3.    private int _volume; // 0 - 10
 4.    ...
 5.    public void setVolume(int volume)
 6.    {
 7.        _volume = volume;
 8.    }
 9.    ...
10. }
```

Without requiring the use of the this keyword, we have to make up a scheme for how we differentiate instance variables from our local variables. Prefixing instance variable names with an underscore (_) is one of the typical ways I've seen this done.

The problem with leaving out the this keyword is two-fold. First, we require a future developer maintaining this code to know the style of creating instance variables is to precede them with an underscore. Second, it's hard at first glance to understand that the variables with underscores are instance variables. All developers have to remember not to name local variables starting with an underscore. Contrast the previous example with the same Java code rewritten to use the this keyword in Listing 26.4.

### Listing 26.4.

```
 1. class Radio
 2. {
 3.    private int volume; // 0 - 10
 4.    // ...
 5.    public void setVolume(int volume)
 6.    {
 7.        this.volume = volume;
 8.    }
 9.    // ...
10. }
```

The above example is unambiguous and leaves no doubt as to the intent of the code. It does not rely on unenforceable naming schemes for instance variables, all to get around not having to use the this keyword. You should always use the this keyword when directly referencing an instance variable in any programming language. Thank goodness PHP makes this a requirement!

## General Purpose Methods

In addition to getters and setters, your class can include utility methods to perform various tasks. For example, many radios have a scan button to look for the next channel with a strong signal. These methods don't have to change your object state (i.e., modify properties) but they may calculate or perform some operation based on your properties as in Listing 26.5.

Listing 26.5.

```
 1. class Radio
 2. {
 3.     public function scanChannels()
 4.     {
 5.         // find the next channel with a strong signal
 6.     }
 7.
 8.     public function getCurrentSong()
 9.     {
10.         // reads live metadata from current channel about current song
11.         // being played and returns song title, etc...
12.     }
13. }
```

## Instantiating and Using a Class

Instantiating classes as objects and creating multiple instances of that class demonstrates another powerful concept of OOP. In the same way, you can have multiple variables that are strings, integers, etc., a class is another more complex data type that you can use in this way.

To use our class, we first need to include it in a PHP script:

```
require_once('Radio.php');
```

To instantiate or create a new instance of our class we have to use the new keyword:

```
require_once('Radio.php');

$car_radio = new Radio();
```

$car_radio is now referencing a new instance which is an object of the Radio class. Note the () following the class name Radio is the *default constructor* (more on this to follow). As I mentioned earlier, we can create multiple instances from our single Radio class:

```php
require_once('Radio.php');

$car_radio = new Radio();
$boat_radio = new Radio();
```

It is best to think of a class as a recipe for making something like cookies and a class's object to fulfill that recipe (i.e., a batch of chocolate chip cookies—yum!) Next, we can use our object:

```php
$car_radio->setVolume(4);

echo 'My car radio\'s volume is set to: ' . $car_radio->getVolume() . '.';
```

Notice again that we use the object operator (->) to reference the setVolume() method. We can reference any property or method that has public visibility. OOP is a deep topic. Check out what the PHP Manual has to say regarding classes and objects[3].

## Complete Listing for Radio.php` (v1)

### Listing 26.6.

```php
 1. <?php
 2.    class Radio
 3.    {
 4.        private $powered;   // true or false
 5.        private $volume;    // 0 - 10
 6.        private $channel;   // 535kHz - 1700kHz, 87.5MHz - 108MHz
 7.
 8.        // Getters
 9.        public function getPowered()
10.        {
11.            return $this->powered;
12.        }
13.
14.        public function getVolume()
15.        {
16.            return $this->volume;
17.        }
```

---

[3]  classes and objects: https://php.net/language.oop5

```
18.
19.        public function getChannel()
20.        {
21.            return $this->channel;
22.        }
23.
24.        // Setters
25.        public function setPowered($powered)
26.        {
27.            $this->powered = $powered;
28.        }
29.
30.        public function setVolume($volume)
31.        {
32.            $this->volume = $volume;
33.        }
34.
35.        public function setChannel($channel)
36.        {
37.            $this->channel = $channel;
38.        }
39.    }
```

## Complete Listing for UseRadio.php (v1)

### Listing 26.7.

```
 1. <?php
 2.    require_once('Radio.php');
 3.
 4.    $car_radio = new Radio();
 5.    $boat_radio = new Radio();
 6.
 7.    $car_radio->setPowered(true);
 8.    $car_radio->setVolume(4);
 9.    $car_radio->setChannel(88.6);
10.
11.    $boat_radio->setPowered(true);
12.    $boat_radio->setVolume(7);
13.    $boat_radio->setChannel(1640);
14.
15.    echo 'My car radio is ';
16.
17.    if ($car_radio->getPowered())
18.    {
19.        echo 'turned on';
20.    }
```

```
21.    else
22.    {
23.        echo 'turned off';
24.    }
25.
26.    echo ' with the volume set to ' . $car_radio->getVolume() . ', ';
27.    echo ' and the channel set to ' . $car_radio->getChannel() . '.<br /><br />';
28.    echo 'My boat radio is ';
29.
30.    if ($boat_radio->getPowered())
31.    {
32.        echo 'turned on';
33.    }
34.    else
35.    {
36.        echo 'turned off';
37.    }
38.
39.    echo ' with the volume set to ' . $boat_radio->getVolume() . ', ';
40.    echo ' and the channel set to ' . $boat_radio->getChannel() . '.';
```

# Validating Input to a Setter Method

Frequently, we need to constrain the input to our methods. For example, in our Radio class, volume settings will have an upper and lower limit. Many entertainment centers have a volume setting between 0 and 10. Let's add some class constants[4] for these to our Radio class:

```
<?php
   class Radio
   {
      const MIN_VOLUME = 0;
      const MAX_VOLUME = 10;

      // ...
   }
```

In our setVolume() method, we get access to these *class* constants by using self::. self represents the class's self, and the :: is called the scope resolution operator[5]. It is needed when referencing constants inside the class. You also use the :: when referencing external variables, but you use the name of the class instead. For example, we can update setVolume() to ensure a user can't set it outside of the allowable range as in Listing 26.8.

---

[4]  class constants: *https://php.net/language.oop5.constants*
[5]  scope resolution operator: *https://php.net/language.oop5.paamayim-nekudotayim*

## Listing 26.8.

```php
1.  <?php
2.     class Radio
3.     {
4.         const MIN_VOLUME = 0;
5.         const MAX_VOLUME = 10;
6.         // ...
7.
8.         public function setVolume($volume)
9.         {
10.            if ($volume < self::MIN_VOLUME)
11.            {
12.                $volume = self::MIN_VOLUME;
13.            }
14.            else if ($volume > self::MAX_VOLUME)
15.            {
16.                $volume = self::MAX_VOLUME;
17.            }
18.
19.            $this->volume = $volume;
20.        }
21.
22.        // ...
23.    }
```

## Complete Listing for Radio.php (v2)

Listing 26.9 the complete listing for our Radio class which enforces frequency limits when they are set.

## Listing 26.9.

```php
1.  <?php
2.     class Radio
3.     {
4.         const   MIN_VOLUME = 0;
5.         const   MAX_VOLUME = 10;
6.
7.         const   MIN_AM_FREQ = 535;
8.         const   MAX_AM_FREQ = 1700;
9.
10.        const   MIN_FM_FREQ = 87.5;
11.        const   MAX_FM_FREQ = 108;
12.
13.        private $powered;    // true or false
14.        private $volume;     // 0 - 10
15.        private $channel;    // 535kHz - 1700kHz, 87.5MHz - 108MHz
16.
17.        // Getters
```

```
18.         public function getPowered()
19.         {
20.             return $this->powered;
21.         }
22.
23.         public function getVolume()
24.         {
25.             return $this->volume;
26.         }
27.
28.         public function getChannel()
29.         {
30.             return $this->channel;
31.         }
32.
33.         // Setters
34.         public function setPowered($powered)
35.         {
36.             $this->powered = $powered;
37.         }
38.
39.         public function setVolume($volume)
40.         {
41.             if ($volume < self::MIN_VOLUME)
42.             {
43.                 $volume = self::MIN_VOLUME;
44.             }
45.             else if ($volume > self::MAX_VOLUME)
46.             {
47.                 $volume = self::MAX_VOLUME;
48.             }
49.
50.             $this->volume = $volume;
51.         }
52.
53.         public function setChannel($channel)
54.         {
55.             if ($channel < self::MIN_FM_FREQ)
56.             {
57.                 $channel = self::MIN_FM_FREQ;
58.             }
59.             else if ($channel > self::MAX_FM_FREQ && $channel < self::MIN_AM_FREQ
60.                     && $channel < (self::MIN_AM_FREQ - self::MAX_FM_FREQ))
61.             {
62.                 $channel = self::MAX_FM_FREQ;
63.             }
64.             else if ($channel > self::MAX_FM_FREQ && $channel < self::MIN_AM_FREQ
65.                     && $channel >= (self::MIN_AM_FREQ - self::MAX_FM_FREQ))
66.             {
67.                 $channel = self::MIN_AM_FREQ;
68.             }
69.             else if ($channel > self::MAX_AM_FREQ)
70.             {
71.                 $channel = self::MAX_AM_FREQ;
72.             }
```

```
73.
74.                $this->channel = $channel;
75.        }
76.    }
```

## Complete Listing for UseRadio.php (v2)

## Listing 26.10.

```
1. <?php
2.     require_once('Radio.php');
3.
4.     $car_radio = new Radio();
5.     $boat_radio = new Radio();
6.
7.     $car_radio->setPowered(true);
8.     $car_radio->setVolume(4);
9.     $car_radio->setChannel(88.6);
10.
11.    $boat_radio->setPowered(true);
12.    $boat_radio->setVolume(11);
13.    $boat_radio->setChannel(430);
14.
15.    echo 'My car radio is ';
16.
17.    if ($car_radio->getPowered())
18.    {
19.        echo 'turned on';
20.    }
21.    else
22.    {
23.        echo 'turned off';
24.    }
25.
26.    echo ' with the volume set to ' . $car_radio->getVolume() . ', ';
27.    echo ' and the channel set to ' . $car_radio->getChannel() . '.<br /><br />';
28.    echo 'My boat radio is ';
29.
30.    if ($boat_radio->getPowered())
31.    {
32.        echo 'turned on';
33.    }
34.    else
35.    {
36.        echo 'turned off';
37.    }
38.
39.    echo ' with the volume set to ' . $boat_radio->getVolume() . ', ';
40.    echo ' and the channel set to ' . $boat_radio->getChannel() . '.';
```

Figure 26.1 Here's the output from running version 2:

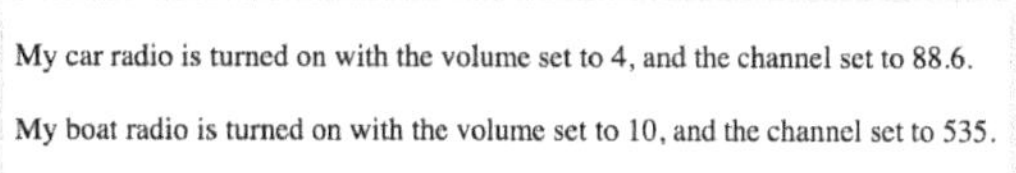

My car radio is turned on with the volume set to 4, and the channel set to 88.6.

My boat radio is turned on with the volume set to 10, and the channel set to 535.

Figure 26.1.

# Inheritance

In OOP, "inheritance"[6] extends the behavior of one class (called the base or parent class) and reuses it as the basis of another class (called the sub or child class). Doing so allows for efficient reuse of code from a base class and is considered another central pillar of OOP. Another way to take advantage of inheritance is to design your base classes with the thought of more generalization and the sub-classes with more specificity.

This is best illustrated through an example. Let's say we want to represent the idea of a pet. Our Pet class might look like Listing 26.11.

Listing 26.11.

```php
1.  <?php
2.      class Pet
3.      {
4.          protected $name;
5.
6.          // Getters / Setters
7.          public function getName()
8.          {
9.              return $this->name;
10.         }
11.
12.         public function setName($name)
13.         {
14.             $this->name = $name;
15.         }
16.
17.         // Do some exercise!
18.         public function exercise()
19.         {
20.             echo 'Exercising my pet ' . $this->name . '.<br />';
21.         }
22.     }
```

*Use* protected (*not* private) *to make parent properties available to your sub-classes.*

---

[6]  *"inheritance":* https://php.net/language.oop5.inheritance

The Pet class will serve as our base class. If we want to create a more specific class with all the knowledge and methodology of a Pet, we need to create a sub-class. We do that by defining our subclass and extending the base-class using the keyword extends:

```php
<?php
    require_once('Pet.php');
    class Dog extends Pet
    {
        ...
    }
```

Since we are extending the Pet class, don't forget to include it before declaring our sub-class. Now let's add more specific functionality (Listing 26.12) to our sub-class.

## Listing 26.12.

```php
1. <?php
2.     require_once('Pet.php');
3.     class Dog extends Pet
4.     {
5.         public function bark()
6.         {
7.             echo $this->name . ' is barking.<br />';
8.         }
9.     }
```

In Listing 26.13, let's create another sub-class.

## Listing 26.13.

```php
1. <?php
2.     require_once('Pet.php');
3.     class Cat extends Pet
4.     {
5.         public function meow()
6.         {
7.             echo 'My cat ' . $this->name . ' is meowing.<br />';
8.         }
9.     }
```

Listing 26.14 shows how we can use these classes. You can see the output in Figure 26.2.

### Listing 26.14.

```
1.  <?php
2.      require_once('Pet.php');
3.      require_once('Dog.php');
4.      require_once('Cat.php');
5.
6.      // Create a pet, dog, and cat
7.      $my_pet = new Pet();
8.      $my_dog = new Dog();
9.      $my_cat = new Cat();
10.
11.     // Set Pet's name and exercise
12.     $my_pet->setName("Gerald");
13.     $my_pet->exercise();
14.
15.     echo '**********<br />';
16.
17.     // Set Dog's name, exercise, and bark
18.     $my_dog->setName('Sparky');
19.     $my_dog->exercise();
20.     $my_dog->bark();
21.
22.     echo '**********<br />';
23.
24.     // Set Cat's name, exercise, and meow
25.     $my_cat->setName('Boo');
26.     $my_cat->exercise();
27.     $my_cat->meow();
```

Exercising my pet Gerald.
\*\*\*\*\*\*\*\*\*\*

Exercising my pet Sparky.
Sparky is barking.
\*\*\*\*\*\*\*\*\*\*

Exercising my pet Boo.
My cat Boo is meowing.

Figure 26.2.

*You'll notice that I include a reference to the* Pet *class even though* Dog *and* Cat *also include the* Pet *class. It is a best practice, as long as I am instantiating an object of a base class to include the base class, even though an instantiated sub-class inherits the base class as well. The reason is, I would minimize any breaking changes if the inheritance structure were to be redesigned. Remember to use* require_once *so you don't get a fatal error when including a class that already exists.*

## Overriding Methods

With inheritance, I can create more specific data and methods based on the details in my sub-class. However, I don't like that my dog and cat are portrayed as exercising the same way. It would be handy to customize or "override" the different ways my dog and cat exercise.

Another central pillar of OOP is the ability to override the behavior of methods based on the specificity of the subclass. In fact, with the ability to override methods, we don't have to keep track of which specific method to use. We can rely on each subclass taking care of its unique details for how something is done. It is done automatically for us based on the sub-class type. This behavior is called "polymorphism" (meaning many forms), another main pillar of OOP.

We override the behavior of a base class's method by redefining it in the sub-class. The rule is: the method in the subclass must have the exact same signature as the method in the base class.

Listing 26.15 is our Dog class with the exercise() method overridden:

### Listing 26.15.

```php
1.  <?php
2.      require_once('Pet.php');
3.
4.      class Dog extends Pet
5.      {
6.          public function bark()
7.          {
8.              echo $this->name . ' is barking.<br />';
9.          }
10.
11.         // Do some dog exercise!
12.         public function exercise()
13.         {
14.             echo 'Walking my dog ' . $this->name . '.<br />';
15.         }
16.     }
```

Our Cat class is in Listing 26.16 with the exercise() method overridden:

## Listing 26.16.

```php
1.  <?php
2.      require_once('Pet.php');
3.      class Cat extends Pet
4.      {
5.          public function meow()
6.          {
7.              echo 'My cat ' . $this->name . ' is meowing.<br />';
8.          }
9.
10.         // Do some cat exercise!
11.         public function exercise()
12.         {
13.             echo 'My cat ' . $this->name . ' is chasing mice!<br />';
14.         }
15.     }
```

A powerful feature of OOP is we don't have to make any changes to code that uses the Pet, Dog, and Cat class since we call the methods the same way. Just rerun it and notice the change in the output in Figure 26.3.

Exercising my pet Gerald.
**********
Walking my dog Sparky.
Sparky is barking.
**********
My cat Boo is chasing mice!
My cat Boo is meowing.

Figure 26.3.

# Constructors

Constructors are used in object-oriented languages to initialize an object from a class as part of instantiation. So far, when we've instantiated an object, we have done so using an empty set of parenthesis following the name of the class using the new keyword:

```php
$myDog = new Dog();
```

This method of initialization is using the default constructor. If you do not define a constructor, PHP will try to initialize your object's properties.

A constructor is a function that runs during the initialization of your object. You want to define a constructor if you have some specific initialization you want to perform in your class.

We define a constructor using the PHP *Magic Method* __construct(). PHP has a number of "Magic Methods"[7] which are functions starting with a double-underscore (__). I will only talk about __construct() and __destruct() in this chapter.

---

[7] *"Magic Methods"*: https://php.net/language.oop5.magic

Let's take a look at an example where we create a constructor. Let's say we have a simple Student class where we want to store an id, name, and email, but we want our objects to be immutable (i.e., we want the data set for the life of the object, but not be modifiable). We'll start out defining the class and the properties:

```php
<?php
    class Student
    {
        private $id;
        private $name;
        private $email;
    }
```

Next, we need to define our constructor that takes $id, $name, and $email as parameters. We do that using the __construct() magic method in Listing 26.17.

## Listing 26.17.

```php
1. <?php
2.     class Student
3.     {
4.         private $id;
5.         private $name;
6.         private $email;
7.
8.         // Constructor
9.         public function __construct($id, $name, $email)
10.        {
11.            $this->id = $id;
12.            $this->name = $name;
13.            $this->email = $email;
14.        }
15.    }
```

Finally, we'll create getters*() (Listing 26.18) so users of our class can retrieve the values of the properties.

## Listing 26.18.

```php
1. <?php
2.     class Student
3.     {
4.         private $id;
5.         private $name;
6.         private $email;
7.
8.         // Constructor
```

```
9.          public function __construct($id, $name, $email)
10.         {
11.             $this->id = $id;
12.             $this->name = $name;
13.             $this->email = $email;
14.         }
15.
16.         // Getters
17.         public function getId()
18.         {
19.             return $this->id;
20.         }
21.
22.         public function getName()
23.         {
24.             return $this->name;
25.         }
26.
27.         public function getEmail()
28.         {
29.             return $this->email;
30.         }
31.     }
```

Listing 26.19 is a script that uses our class. Note that three arguments are passed to the constructor upon instantiation of the object. This produces the following output (Figure 26.4).

**Name:** Jane Doe
  **ID:**  7
**Email:** jane@madisoncollege.edu

Figure 26.4.

Listing 26.19.

```php
1.  <?php
2.      require_once('Student.php');
3.
4.      $jane = new Student(7, 'Jane Doe', 'jane@example.com');
5.  ?>
6.  <table>
7.    <tr>
8.      <th>Name:</th>
9.      <td><?= $jane->getName() ?></td>
10.   </tr>
11.   <tr>
12.     <th>ID:</th>
13.     <td><?= $jane->getId() ?></td>
14.   </tr>
15.   <tr>
16.     <th>Email:</th>
17.     <td><?= $jane->getEmail() ?></td>
18.   </tr>
19. </table>
```

## About Constructors

When working with constructors and destructors[8] in PHP, something to keep in mind is that they may function differently in other OOP languages. Take a look at this quote from the PHP manual regarding constructors to make sure you know how to design your classes to take advantage of construction in the way you intend:

> Parent constructors are not called implicitly if the child class defines a constructor. To run a parent constructor, you must call parent::__construct() within the child constructor. If the child does not define a constructor, then it may be inherited from the parent class and called just like a standard class method (if it was not declared as private)."

## Constructor Property Promotion in PHP 8

Although this book assumes PHP 7.x, as of the time of publishing for this book, PHP version 8 is out and offers several new features and enhancements. I'd like to introduce just one of them to you called constructor property promotion.

Constructor property promotion allows you to combine class properties, constructor definition, and variable assignments all in the __construct() parameter list. In a standard definition of class instance properties, construction, and assignment, you would use code like Listing 26.20.

### Listing 26.20.

```php
1. <?php
2.
3. class Student
4. {
5.     private $id;
6.     private $name;
7.     private $email;
8.
9.     // Constructor
10.    public function __construct(
11.        $id,
12.        $name,
13.        $email
14.    ) {
15.        $this->id = $id;
16.        $this->name = $name;
17.        $this->email = $email;
18.    }
19. }
```

[8] constructors and destructors: https://php.net/manual/en/language.oop5.decon

We saw this above. In constructor property promotion, we can rewrite the same code as in Listing 26.21 with fewer boilerplate lines of code.

### Listing 26.21.

```php
1. <?php
2. class Student
3. {
4.     // Constructor
5.     public function __construct(
6.             private $id,
7.             private $name,
8.             private $email)
9.     {
10.     }
11.     // ...
12. }
```

As long as there is an access modifier (private, protected, or public) preceding the variable in the constructor's parameter list, PHP will create the properties *under the hood*, and assign the values passed into the parameter list. You can still directly access the properties in the class using the this keyword.

Details are buried in the PHP manual section on constructors[9]. For in-depth information, you can refer to the Request for Comments (RFC) for constructor property promotion[10] that was approved for PHP 8 on the PHP manual Wiki if you'd like to know more.

## Creating Parameterized Queries Using OOP

Back in Chapter 23: Prepared Statements, I showed you how to create more secure parameterized database queries by using the procedural functions mysqli_prepare(), mysqli_stmt_bind_param(), mysqli_stmt_execute(), and mysqli_stmt_get_result(). However, there is an object-oriented way to parameterize your database queries with less code using PHP Data Objects[11] (PDO). I'll demonstrate how to use PDO by creating a simple database table and a class that manages our data in and out of the table to implement the PDO functionality.

---

[9]  constructors: *https://php.net/language.oop5.decon.constructor.promotion*
[10] constructor property promotion: *https://wiki.php.net/rfc/constructor_promotion*
[11] PHP Data Objects: *https://php.net/book.pdo*

PDO is the library of choice for interacting with databases, primarily because it works with many different database technologies. This library gives us a familiar API no matter where we store our data.

First, we need to create a database and a simple table we can work on. I'll make a simple database called Student and a table called student used to hold a student's first name, last name, and email address for this demonstration as shown in Figure 26.5

A common way to use PDO is to create a class known as a CRUD wrapper that manages all queries to a database table. CRUD stands for Create, Read, Update, and Delete, which are the common operations we perform on database tables. It is a good practice to name our classes using a "Studly Caps" interpolation of our database table and concatenate the word "Manager" onto the end of our class. In this case, we should name our class StudentManager since our table is called student.

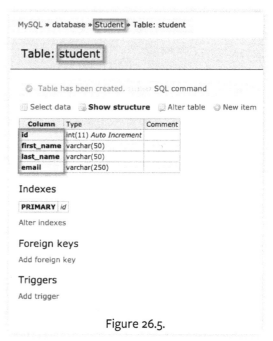

Figure 26.5.

## Using PDO to Create New Database Entries

Listing 26.22 is the class along with a create() method to insert rows into our student table.

### Listing 26.22.

```php
1.  <?php
2.
3.  class StudentManager
4.  {
5.      // Database connection constants
6.      private const DB_TECHNOLOGY = "mysql";
7.      private const DB_HOST = "localhost";
8.      private const DB_NAME = "Student";
9.      private const DB_USER = "testuser";
10.     private const DB_PASSWORD = "testuser";
11.
```

```
12.     // Results in DSN = "mysql:host=localhost;dbname=Student"
13.     private const DSN = self::DB_TECHNOLOGY
14.                       . ':host=' . self::DB_HOST
15.                       . ';dbname=' . self::DB_NAME;
16.
17.     public function create($first_name, $last_name, $email)
18.     {
19.        $db = new PDO(self::DSN, self::DB_USER, self::DB_PASSWORD);
20.
21.        // Insert  a new record
22.        $sql = "INSERT INTO student(`first_name`, `last_name`, `email`)
23.                    VALUES (:first_name, :last_name, :email)";
24.
25.        $db->setAttribute(PDO::ATTR_ERRMODE, PDO::ERRMODE_EXCEPTION);
26.
27.        try
28.        {
29.           $query = $db->prepare($sql);
30.           $query->bindParam(":first_name", $first_name, PDO::PARAM_STR);
31.           $query->bindParam(":last_name", $last_name, PDO::PARAM_STR);
32.           $query->bindParam(":email", $email, PDO::PARAM_STR);
33.           $query->execute();
34.        } catch (Exception $ex)
35.        {
36.           echo $ex->getMessage() . "<br/>";
37.        }
38.
39.        // Returns the primary key of this INSERT
40.        return $db->lastInsertId();
41.     }
42. }
```

The constructor for instantiating a new PDO object takes three parameters: a data source name, user name, and password, and when created, connects to the database. When connecting to a MySQL database, the data source name must look like this:

```
"mysql:host=localhost;dbname=Student"
```

The constants in lines 6–10 set the data source name, user name, and password input parameters to the PDO constructor.

Lines 17 is our create() method that takes the first and last name and the email address, which correspond to the three fields we want to insert into the student table.

To use PDO, we instantiate a new object on line 19, which creates the connection to our database.

We create our SQL statement on line 22 to insert the data into the student table. Notice that instead of using ? and relying on the order of them, we can create named parameters using an arbitrary name preceded by a colon (:):

```
$sql = "INSERT INTO student(`first_name`, `last_name`, `email`)
        VALUES (:first_name, :last_name, :email)";
```

Here we use :first_name, :last_name, and :email as our named parameters that we will bind the incoming parameters of $first_name, $last_name, and $email to.

Line 25 allows us to enable error reporting and exception handling by setting a couple of PDO class constant attributes. Doing so allows us to use Exceptions to handle database errors without the complexity of too much conditional logic.

```
$db->setAttribute(PDO::ATTR_ERRMODE, PDO::ERRMODE_EXCEPTION);
```

*I haven't covered exception handling, but a simple explanation is that it allows us to* try *executing some code that might cause some exceptional behavior (like not being able to query a database table successfully). If an exception occurs, we can* catch *it in an orderly fashion that hopefully allows our application to recover gracefully. If everything runs correctly in the* try *block, the* catch *block does not execute.*

The OOP way of preparing and binding our parameters is handled in these lines of the try block:

```
$query = $db->prepare($sql);
$query->bindParam(":first_name", $first_name, PDO::PARAM_STR);
$query->bindParam(":last_name", $last_name, PDO::PARAM_STR);
$query->bindParam(":email", $email, PDO::PARAM_STR);
```

First, we call the prepare() method of the PDO object passing in the SQL statement as an argument that returns a PDOStatement object we assign to a variable we'll call $query. This is the object we bind our parameters to. Notice the third parameter to the bindParam() method is a PDO class constant specifying the data type. Although this argument is optional, you should explicitly include it so that PDO escapes your data type correctly.

Then we execute the query with this call:

```
$query->execute();
```

If the SQL statement is malformed, an exception is thrown. Then, the error is echoed on line 36 with a call to the getMessage() method of the exception object passed into the catch block:

```
catch(Exception $ex)
{
    echo $ex->getMessage() . "<br/>";
}
```

If everything works as planned, we can return the primary key of the newly inserted row into the student table to the caller by calling the PDO object's lastInsertId() method:

```
return $db->lastInsertId(); // Returns the primary key of this INSERT
```

Listing 26.23 is an example of using this method by creating several entries using a pre-populated array of associative arrays.

Listing 26.23.

```
1.  <?php
2.  require_once('StudentManager.php');
3.
4.  // Manage some Simpsons
5.  $simpsons_manager = new StudentManager();
6.
7.  $simpsons = [];
8.
9.  $simpsons[] = [
10.     'first_name' => 'Bart',
11.     'last_name' => 'Simpson',
12.     'email' => 'kowabungadude@simpsons.com'
13. ];
14.
15. $simpsons[] = [
16.     'first_name' => 'Lisa',
17.     'last_name' => 'Simpson',
18.     'email' => 'lisa@simpsons.com'
19. ];
20.
21. $simpsons[] = [
22.     'first_name' => 'Marge',
23.     'last_name' => 'Simpson',
24.     'email' => 'marge@simpsons.com'
25. ];
26.
27. $simpsons[] = [
28.     'first_name' => 'Homer',
29.     'last_name' => 'Simpson',
30.     'email' => 'ilovedonuts@simpsons.com'
31. ];
32.
```

```
33. // Insert each Simpson into the students table
34. foreach ($simpsons as $simpson)
35. {
36.    echo "Creating a new entry for: "
37.       . $simpson['first_name'] . " " . $simpson['last_name']
38.       . " with email of: " . $simpson['email'] . "<br/>";
39.
40.    $id = $simpsons_manager->create(
41.       $simpson['first_name'], $simpson['last_name'], $simpson['email']
42.    );
43.
44.    echo $simpson['first_name'] . "'s id is: $id<br/><br/>";
45. }
```

This code produces the output in Figure 26.6. Figure 26.7 shows the entry in the student table.

Creating a new entry for: Bart Simpson with email of: kowabungadude@simpsons.com
Bart's id is: 1

Creating a new entry for: Lisa Simpson with email of: lisa@simpsons.com
Lisa's id is: 2

Creating a new entry for: Marge Simpson with email of: marge@simpsons.com
Marge's id is: 3

Creating a new entry for: Homer Simpson with email of: ilovedonuts@simpsons.com
Homer's id is: 4

Figure 26.6.

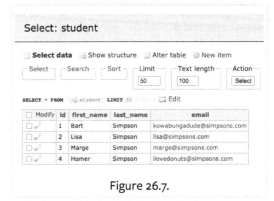

Figure 26.7.

## Reading Database Entries with PDO

When reading entries from a database table, we either want to read a single row or multiple rows. I'll demonstrate reading all rows and a single row using two different methods. First, let's create a readAll() method that returns all the rows in the student table. Listing 26.24 is the readAll() method:

### Listing 26.24.

```
1. public function readAll()
2. {
3.    $db = new PDO(self::DSN, self::DB_USER, self::DB_PASSWORD);
4.
5.    // Read all records
6.    $sql = "SELECT * FROM student";
7.
8.    try
9.    {
10.       $query = $db->prepare($sql);
11.       $query->execute();
```

```
12.
13.        // Gets a numeric array of the query results with each element
14.        // set to a Student object containing the row's fields
15.        $results = $query->fetchAll(PDO::FETCH_CLASS, "Student");
16.    }
17.    catch(Exception $ex)
18.    {
19.        echo "{$ex->getMessage()}<br/>";
20.    }
21.
22.    return $results;
23. }
```

There is no parameterization needed since we are not passing in any parameters to the readAll() method. This method is self-explanatory with the exception of line 15:

```
$results = $query->fetchAll(PDO::FETCH_CLASS, "Student");
```

The fetchAll() method has many options for how it can return results from a query, but my favorite option is the ability to return a row set with each row represented within an object. Notice the second parameter takes a string that you should set to the class name. This class name is used to instantiate an object for each row returned from the query. The one catch is that the class must have properties defined that exactly match the field names of the table.

Therefore, we also need to create a Student class that contains properties with all the fields in the student table and include them in our StudentManager class file. Listing 26.25 is the Student class.

## Listing 26.25.

```
1. <?php
2.
3. class Student
4. {
5.     private $id;
6.     private $first_name;
7.     private $last_name;
8.     private $email;
9.
10.    // Getters/Setters
11.    public function getId()
12.    {
13.        return $this->id;
14.    }
15.
```

```
16.    public function getFirstName()
17.    {
18.        return $this->first_name;
19.    }
20.
21.    public function getLastName()
22.    {
23.        return $this->last_name;
24.    }
25.
26.    public function getEmail()
27.    {
28.        return $this->email;
29.    }
30. }
```

Notice lines 5–8 contain properties with the exact names of the fields in the student table. This is a convenient feature within PHP and speeds up creating CRUD wrappers around database tables we can easily use in our applications.

The rest of the Student class contains the get methods for accessing all the properties. If we wanted, we could create set*() methods to update the database table when called. I'll leave that as an exercise for you.

Listing 26.26 is an example of how we can use our readAll() method, which produces the output shown in Figure 26.8. Now let's create a readById() method that takes the id of the row we want to read from the student table as a parameter.

First name: Bart
Last name: Simpson
Email: kowabungadude@simpsons.com

First name: Lisa
Last name: Simpson
Email: lisa@simpsons.com

First name: Marge
Last name: Simpson
Email: marge@simpsons.com

First name: Homer
Last name: Simpson
Email: ilovedonuts@simpsons.com

Figure 26.8.

## Listing 26.26.

```
1. <?php
2.
3. require_once('StudentManager.php');
4.
5. // Manage some Simpsons
6. $simpsons_manager = new StudentManager();
7.
8. $the_simpsons = $simpsons_manager->readAll();
9.
10. foreach ($the_simpsons as $simpson)
11. {
12.    echo "First name: " . $simpson->getFirstName() . "<br/>";
13.    echo "Last name: " . $simpson->getLastName() . "<br/>";
14.    echo "Email: " . $simpson->getEmail() . "<br/>";
15.    echo "<br/>";
16. }
```

Let's look at Listing 26.27 for reading a single row based on the ID.

## Listing 26.27.

```
1. public function readById($id)
2. {
3.     $db = new PDO(self::DSN, self::DB_USER, self::DB_PASSWORD);
4.
5.     // Read the record given by the id
6.     $sql = "SELECT * FROM student WHERE id=:id";
7.
8.     try
9.     {
10.        $query = $db->prepare($sql);
11.        $query->bindParam(":id", $id, PDO::PARAM_INT);
12.        $query->execute();
13.
14.        // Fetch result into instance of a Student object
15.        $result = $query->fetchObject("Student");
16.    }
17.    catch(Exception $ex)
18.    {
19.        echo "{$ex->getMessage()}<br/>";
20.    }
21.
22.    return $result;
23. }
```

Everything in this method should be straight forward except for line 15:

```
$result = $query->fetchObject("Student");
```

*Another way to specify our class is* Student::class—*without quotes. PHP uses the* ::class *constant to reference the fully-qualified name of a class which includes its namespace.*

```
$result = $query->fetchObject(Student::class);
```

In our readAll() method, we used the fetchAll() method which returned an array of Student objects. We could have done the same thing on line 15, but we would return a single object inside an array with one element. It's more convenient to return a single object since we know we're only looking for a single row. Therefore, we need to use the fetchObject() method, which takes a string with the name of the class we want to use that contains properties with all the fields in the student table, which in our case is Student.

If an ID that does not exist in the student table is passed in, readById() returns false.

Listing 26.28 is an example of how we can use our `readById()` method. It produces this output in Figure 26.9.

First name: Marge
Last name: Simpson
Email: marge@simpsons.com

Figure 26.9.

### Listing 26.28.

```
1. require_once('StudentManager.php');
2.
3. // Manage some Simpsons
4. $simpsons_manager = new StudentManager();
5.
6. $a_simpson = $simpsons_manager->readById(3);
7.
8. if ($a_simpson)
9. {
10.     echo "First name: " . $a_simpson->getFirstName() . "<br/>";
11.     echo "Last name: " . $a_simpson->getLastName() . "<br/>";
12.     echo "Email: " . $a_simpson->getEmail() . "<br/>";
13.     echo "<br/>";
14. }
```

## Updating Database Entries Using PDO

Now we'll create a method called `update()` that updates a row in the `student` table. See Listing 26.29.

### Listing 26.29.

```
1. public function update($id, $first_name, $last_name, $email)
2. {
3.     $db = new PDO(self::DSN, self::DB_USER, self::DB_PASSWORD);
4.
5.     // UPDATE a record with a given first name, last name, and email for a given id
6.     $sql = "UPDATE student SET `first_name`=:first_name, `last_name`=:last_name, "
7.         . "`email`=:email WHERE id=:id";
8.
9.     $db->setAttribute(PDO::ATTR_ERRMODE, PDO::ERRMODE_EXCEPTION);
10.
11.     try
12.     {
13.         $query = $db->prepare($sql);
14.         $query->bindParam(":id", $id, PDO::PARAM_INT);
15.         $query->bindParam(":first_name", $first_name, PDO::PARAM_STR);
16.         $query->bindParam(":last_name", $last_name, PDO::PARAM_STR);
17.         $query->bindParam(":email", $email, PDO::PARAM_STR);
18.         $query->execute();
19.         $rows_affected = $query->rowCount();
20.     }
```

```
21.    catch(Exception $ex)
22.    {
23.        echo $ex->getMessage() . "<br/>";
24.    }
25.
26.    return $rows_affected; // Returns the number or rows affected by the UPDATE
27. }
```

We obviously need to parameterize every incoming parameter which we do on lines 6,7, and 14–17. The only other line that needs explanation is line 19:

```
$rows_affected = $query->rowCount();
```

Since we are only updating a single row in the student table, rowCount() returns 1 if the row was successfully updated. If the ID is not found, 0 is returned. We return this value to the caller of update() so they know if the update was successful or not.

Listing 26.30 is an example of how we can use our update() method. Running it results in the output shown in Figure 26.10.

First name: Homer
Last name: Simpson
Email: ilikedonuts@simpsons.com

First name: Maggie
Last name: Simpson
Email: maggie@simpsons.com

Figure 26.10.

## Listing 26.30.

```
1. require_once('StudentManager.php');
2.
3. // Manage some Simpsons
4. $simpsons_manager = new StudentManager();
5.
6. $update_homer_to_maggie = $simpsons_manager->readById(4);
7.
8. if ($update_homer_to_maggie)
9. {
10.     echo "First name: " . $update_homer_to_maggie->getFirstName() . "<br/>";
11.     echo "Last name: " . $update_homer_to_maggie->getLastName() . "<br/>";
12.     echo "Email: " . $update_homer_to_maggie->getEmail() . "<br/>";
13.     echo "<br/>";
14. }
15.
16. if ($simpsons_manager->update(4,"Maggie", "Simpson", "maggie@simpsons.com") == 1)
17. {
18.     $update_homer_to_maggie = $simpsons_manager->readById(4);
19.
```

```
20.     if ($update_homer_to_maggie)
21.     {
22.         echo "First name: " . $update_homer_to_maggie->getFirstName() . "<br/>";
23.         echo "Last name: " . $update_homer_to_maggie->getLastName() . "<br/>";
24.         echo "Email: " . $update_homer_to_maggie->getEmail() . "<br/>";
25.         echo "<br/>";
26.     }
27. }
```

## Deleting Database Entries with PDO

Finally, let's look at what a delete() method should look like. See Listing 26.31.

### Listing 26.31.

```
1. public function delete($id)
2. {
3.     $db = new PDO(self::DSN, self::DB_USER, self::DB_PASSWORD);
4.
5.     // Delete a record
6.     $sql = "DELETE FROM student WHERE id=:id";
7.
8.     $db->setAttribute(PDO::ATTR_ERRMODE, PDO::ERRMODE_EXCEPTION);
9.
10.     try
11.     {
12.         $query = $db->prepare($sql);
13.         $query->bindParam(":id", $id, PDO::PARAM_INT);
14.         $query->execute();
15.         $rows_affected = $query->rowCount();
16.     }
17.     catch(Exception $ex)
18.     {
19.         echo $ex->getMessage() . "<br/>";
20.     }
21.
22.     return $rows_affected; // Returns the number of rows affected by the DELETE
23. }
```

Since we need to pass in the id as a parameter to delete(), we need to parameterize it as indicated on lines 6 and 13. As we did in the update() method, we will return the number of rows affected by the DELETE.

You can see an example of how we can use our `delete()` method in Listing 26.32. Calling this method generates the output in Figure 26.11.

Deleting Bart Simpson
Successfully deleted Bart Simpson

Figure 26.11.

## Listing 26.32.

```
1.  require_once('StudentManager.php');
2.
3.  // Manage some Simpsons
4.  $simpsons_manager = new StudentManager();
5.
6.  $bart = $simpsons_manager->readById(1);
7.
8.  if ($bart)
9.  {
10.     echo "Deleting " . $bart->getFirstName() . " " . $bart->getLastName() . "<br/>";
11.
12.     if ($simpsons_manager->delete($bart->getId()) == 1)
13.     {
14.         echo "Successfully deleted " . $bart->getFirstName() . " "
15.             . $bart->getLastName() . "<br/>";
16.     }
17. }
```

# Exercises

1.  Rewrite Bad Libs using Object-Oriented Programming

    1. Create a class called BadLibs and save it in a PHP script called MadLibs.php.

    2. Create properties for holding a noun, verb, adjective, adverb, and story

    3. Create getters and setters for ALL your properties

    4. Create a method for inserting the new properties into your mad libs database table

    5. Create a method for querying the stories that returns a result set sorted newest to oldest.

    6. Create a method that takes the results set (from the query) as an argument and returns the results in a formatted HTML table

    7. You may use your existing Bad Libs database or create a new one.

2. Use PDO to create a ToDo List application
   1. Create a database called ToDo.
   2. Create a table called todo with the following fields for id, description. Make the id the primary key, and the description should be a varchar[100].
   3. Use PDO to create a CRUD class for the todo table
   4. Create a ToDo list application with a form that allows a user to create, read all, read by id, update, and delete ToDo list items
   5. When the user reads all of the ToDo items, display the results in a table that includes the id.
   6. When the user updates a ToDo list item, return 1 indicating one row was affected and the update was successful, or 0 if it was unsuccessful.
   7. When the user deletes a ToDo list item, return 1 indicating a single row was affected and the update was successful, or 0 if it was unsuccessful.

# Index

## A

access
  credentials, 282
  modifiers, 452, 454, 473
  privileges, 324–25, 327, 353, 400–401, 403
adminer, 12–14, 98, 112, 136–37, 139, 155, 217, 325, 380, 397
algorithm, 304, 325
  password hashing, 304–5
algorithms, encryption, 306
apache, 9–10, 12, 219, 223, 302
  apt install, 9
  restart, 12
API, 30, 315, 474
  external, 88
  unsafe JavaScript, 315
application security risk (ASR), 302, 306, 315
array, 27–30, 43–52, 54, 69–70, 75, 77–78, 92, 119–20, 150–51, 161, 198, 203, 228, 348–49, 413–14, 425–27, 430–31, 481
  associative, 27–28, 45, 53–54, 77, 91, 94, 119, 477
  empty, 27, 44, 295
  functions, 46–47, 49, 51
  indexed, 44
  multidimensional, 52–53
  numeric, 44–45, 479
  short syntax, 28, 44–46
  superglobal, 161, 178, 180, 182, 184–85, 192, 202, 205, 271

attack, 306, 315–16, 319
  collision, 302
  directory path traversal, 319
  man-in-the-middle, 321
authentication, 277–80, 282–84, 352
  basic, 278–79
  headers, 281, 283, 352

## B

Bash, 98–101, 106
Bootstrap, 141–42, 149, 160, 164, 178, 183
  card, 159, 178
  Client-Side Validation, 164, 203, 291, 328, 343

## C

callables, 30, 69
Canonical, 6
CAPTCHAs, 326
characters
  special, 19, 24
  string escape, 35
class
  base, 465–68
  constants, 461, 481
  definitions, 29, 453
  design, 453–54
  instantiating, 458
  name, 24
  naming, 453
CLI (command-line interface), 13, 98, 106

code
  conditional, 127, 160
  legacy, 109
  procedural-based, 313
  vulnerable, 317
concatenate, 34, 36, 305, 474
condition, 55–64, 74, 184–86, 205–6, 208, 225–26, 230–31, 237, 330–31, 334–36, 344–47, 366, 371, 383–84, 387–89, 409–10, 423–24, 426–28, 437–38, 440–42
  catch-all, 410, 424, 438
  elseif, 225, 344
  ternary, 366, 372
conditional logic, 56, 59, 93, 288, 313, 330, 476
conditional statements, 59–62, 281
  compound, 62–64
constants, 25, 31, 85–86, 142, 223, 225, 229, 461, 475
  global, 85
  referencing, 461
constructors, 452, 455, 469–73, 475
  child, 472
  default, 459, 469
cookies, 184, 286–92, 295–300, 314, 459
  referencing, 296
  saved, 288, 290, 292
  values, 288
CrackStation, 303–4

# php[architect] Books

The php[architect] series of books cover topics relevant to modern PHP programming. We offer our books in both print and digital formats. Print copy price includes free shipping to the US. Books sold digitally are available to you DRM-free in PDF, ePub, or Mobi formats for viewing on any device that supports these.

To view the complete selection of books and order a copy of your own, please visit: http://phparch.com/books/.

- **Beyond Laravel**
  By Michael Akopov
  ISBN: 978-19401119

- **PHP Development with Windows Subsystem for Linux (WSL)**
  By Joe Ferguson
  ISBN: 978-1940111902

- **WordPress Development in Depth**
  By Peter MacIntyre, Savio Resende
  ISBN: 978-1940111834

- **The Grumpy Programmer's Guide to Testing PHP Applications (print edition)**
  By Chris Hartjes
  ISBN: 978-1940111797

- **The Fizz Buzz Fix: Secrets to Thinking Like an Experienced Software Developer**
  By Edward Barnard
  ISBN: 978-1940111759

- **The Dev Lead Trenches: Lessons for Managing Developers**
  By Chris Tankersley
  ISBN: 978-1940111711

- **Web Scraping with PHP, 2nd Edition**
  By Matthew Turland
  ISBN: 978-1940111674

- **Security Principles for PHP Applications**
  By Eric Mann
  ISBN: 978-1940111612

- **Docker for Developers, 2nd Edition**
  By Chris Tankersley
  ISBN: 978-1940111568 (Print edition)

- **What's Next? Professional Development Advice**
  Edited by Oscar Merida
  ISBN: 978-1940111513

## 26. INDEX

- **Functional Programing in PHP, 2nd Edition**
  By: Simon Holywell
  ISBN: 978-1940111469

- **Web Security 2016**
  Edited by Oscar Merida
  ISBN: 978-1940111414

- **Integrating Web Services with OAuth and PHP**
  By Matthew Frost
  ISBN: 978-1940111261

- **Zend Framework 1 to 2 Migration Guide**
  By Bart McLeod
  ISBN: 978-1940111216

- **XML Parsing with PHP**
  By John M. Stokes
  ISBN: 978-1940111162

- **Zend PHP 5 Certification Study Guide, Third Edition**
  By Davey Shafik with Ben Ramsey
  ISBN: 978-1940111100

- **Mastering the SPL Library**
  By Joshua Thijssen
  ISBN: 978-1940111001

# Feedback and Updates

Please let us know what you thought of this book! What did you enjoy? What was confusing or could have been improved? Did you find errata? Any feedback and thoughts you have regarding this book will help us improve a future edition.

## Contact the Author

Ken Marks is on twitter, @FlibertiGiblets, and can be reached via email at KennethEMarks@gmail.com. He's open to feedback about the material and hearing how this book has helped you learn web development.

## From the Publisher

To keep in touch and be notified about future editions to this book, visit http://phparch.com and sign up for our (low-volume) mailing list.

You can also follow us on twitter, @phparch, as well as on facebook at https://facebook.com/phparch/

Stefanie Leimeister

# IT Outsourcing Governance

Client Types and
Their Management Strategies

With a foreword by Prof. Dr. Helmut Krcmar

GABLER

RESEARCH

Bibliographic information published by the Deutsche Nationalbibliothek
The Deutsche Nationalbibliothek lists this publication in the Deutsche Nationalbibliografie;
detailed bibliographic data are available in the Internet at http://dnb.d-nb.de.


Dissertation Technische Universität München, 2009


1st Edition 2010

Editorial Office: Ute Wrasmann | Anita Wilke

Gabler Verlag is a brand of Springer Fachmedien.
Springer Fachmedien is part of Springer Science+Business Media.
www.gabler.de

Coverdesign: KünkelLopka Medienentwicklung, Heidelberg
Printed on acid-free paper
Printed in Germany

ISBN 978-3-8349-2275-5